PROUDLY WE CAN BE
AFRICANS

The John Hope Franklin Series in
African American History and Culture

WALDO E. MARTIN JR. AND PATRICIA SULLIVAN, EDITORS

PROUDLY WE CAN BE AFRICANS

BLACK AMERICANS AND AFRICA, 1935–1961

James H. Meriwether

The University of North Carolina Press
Chapel Hill and London

This book was set in Sabon and Charter Types
by Keystone Typesetting, Inc.
Book design by Jacquline Johnson

Publication of this work was aided by a generous grant from
the Z. Smith Reynolds Foundation.

The paper in this book meets the guidelines for permanence
and durability of the Committee on Production Guidelines for
Book Longevity of the Council on Library Resources.

Portions of Chapter 4 appeared previously in "African
Americans and the Mau Mau Rebellion: Militancy, Violence,
and the Struggle for Freedom," *Journal of American Ethnic
History* 17, no. 4 (Summer 1998): 63–86.

Library of Congress Cataloging-in-Publication Data
Meriwether, James Hunter, 1963–
Proudly we can be Africans : Black Americans and Africa,
1935–1961 / by James H. Meriwether.
p. cm. — (The John Hope Franklin series in African American
History and culture)
Includes bibliographical references (p.   ).
ISBN 0-8078-2669-3 (cloth: alk. paper)
ISBN 0-8078-4997-9 (pbk.: alk. paper)
1. African Americans — Relations with Africans. 2. African
Americans — Ethnic identity. 3. African Americans —
Intellectual life — 20th century. 4. United States — Relations —
Africa. 5. Africa — Relations — United States. 6. Africa —
Politics and government — 20th century. 7. Africa — Social
conditions — 20th century. 8. Blacks — Civil rights — Africa —
History — 20th century. 9. Civil rights movements — Africa —
History — 20th century. I. Title. II. Series.
E185.61 .M56 2002
305.896′073 — dc21   2001042533

cloth 06 05 04 03 02   5 4 3 2 1
paper 06 05   5 4 3 2

For my family, with love

CONTENTS

ACKNOWLEDGMENTS

This book sits astride many of the major issues and events of the twentieth century: race, civil rights, World War II, the Cold War, anticolonialism. In assessing the dynamic nature of Africa's role in African American lives during the mid-twentieth century, we gain new insights into these issues as well as an international perspective on African American, American, and African history. Yet in undertaking this project, I learned along the way that even as the historical profession speaks about the need to "internationalize" history and break down barriers that divide us into narrow fields, there remains a certain institutionalized discomfort in addressing work that does so. For those involved in transnational history, the effort to move outside the compartments and toward a richer international history can be difficult, yet the rewards are fulfilling.

The legion of wonderful people who helped along the way should share the rewards; hopefully my heartfelt thanks at the time and my continuing sincere appreciation offer some compensation. Still, the opportunity to give extra thanks to those who helped beyond all reasonable expectation is a particular pleasure. Robert Hill deserves most special mention for the power of his intellect and the graciousness with which he shared his ideas and time. This book is far better for the advice he gave and the pitfalls he helped me avoid. Just as importantly, James Campbell provided sage advice as I struggled to launch this project and then gave even more as I struggled to end it. Early in the going, Robert Dallek kept me cognizant of the larger picture while showing me what a scholar can achieve by wrestling with the sources for a vast topic with grace and balance. Bill Worger consistently prodded me to probe further, while Robert Harris provided excellent advice after reading an earlier, much muddier version. Thanks also to Joyce Appleby, who shared both her valuable intellect and her valuable driveway, and to Ben Keppel and Christoph Schulze, who furnished helpful references. Peggy Cordray should be praised by all those who venture further in this book for rescuing them from all too many unclear thoughts and turgid prose.

As an initially anonymous reader for the University of North Carolina

Press, Tim Borstelmann gave the manuscript a particularly thoughtful reading, for which I am most grateful. The editors of the John Hope Franklin Series in African American History and Culture, Waldo Martin and Patricia Sullivan, similarly gave the book thorough, helpful, and highly appreciated readings. For their efforts to accommodate someone who sometimes seemed to be all over the map while meeting academic and familial demands, my history department colleagues merit particular thanks. Finally, I cannot say enough about Bruce Schulman, who showed me that there are those who can do it all when it comes to being a scholar, teacher, and guide.

Archivists and librarians around the country have assisted generously with their time and knowledge. I want to thank especially Paul Andersen and Roberta Medford, both of whom went out of their way to assist this project. Others across the country also have been most helpful, particularly at the Beinecke Rare Book and Manuscript Library at Yale University, the Chicago Historical Society, the Library of Congress, the Martin Luther King Jr. Center for Nonviolent Social Change in Atlanta, the Martin Luther King Jr. Papers Project, the Moorland-Spingarn Research Center at Howard University, the Mugar Memorial Library at Boston University, the National Archives, the Oral History Collection at Columbia University, the Schomburg Center for Research in Black Culture, and the Young Research Library at the University of California, Los Angeles.

Thanks also to the J. William Fulbright Foreign Scholarship Board for granting me a Fulbright award to spend a year teaching and researching at the University of Zimbabwe, affording me the opportunity to finish this book during that time. I also owe thanks to the University Research Council and the Teaching and Learning Center of the California State University for grants along the way that helped make completion of this book possible. In the endeavor to publish this book, the people at the University of North Carolina Press, particularly Chuck Grench and Kathy Malin, have been wonderful. The care and attention they have given has been enormously valuable and much appreciated.

Finally, a last pause to extend my appreciation to friends and family who have helped ease the way. John Majewski has provided intellectual and personal support since day one. Peggy and Richard Cordray, Lisa Jacobson, Harry Litman, Lisa and Bob Novick, Jonathan and Laura Sassi, Cindy and Steve Snell, and Melinda and Jim Warren all provided valuable support along the way. My parents deserve special thanks, which is a small return on a particularly large debt, for they instilled in me the ethos needed to accomplish this work and taught me that even in this day when the market economy reigns supreme, the pursuit of deeper understanding offers a reward that cannot be priced. Lindsay and Christian consistently found creative ways to help me keep a sense of proportion and equipoise. Claire constantly managed to make even the dreariest days at the computer turn bright. Above all, Heather remains my polestar.

PROUDLY WE CAN BE
AFRICANS

INTRODUCTION

In the summer of 1935, as Italian dictator Benito Mussolini gathered his forces to invade Ethiopia, African Americans looked on in dismay, for Ethiopia and Liberia remained the last black-ruled nations in Africa. Yet the *Pittsburgh Courier*, one of the leading African American newspapers of the day, pondered the fate of Ethiopia and pronounced, "Much as we all sympathize with Ethiopia, it is evident that our burdens here are sufficiently heavy without assuming those of Negroes 7,000 miles away. It is noteworthy that, while our disabilities have been fairly well publicized throughout the world since Emancipation, no aid has ever come from our brethren across the seas. We have fought the battle alone and they will have to do likewise."[1]

Just over twenty years later, in early 1957, Ghana celebrated its independence, becoming the first African nation south of the Sahara to cast off colonial rule. This time the *Courier* offered a far different portrait of the meaning of African freedom struggles: "[As] Ghana enters the society of free nations today, the event has a particularly pertinent significance for American Negroes.... Are American Negroes an inferior people? Can they meet the full challenge of modern, Western civilization? We American Negroes look to Ghana to furnish the answers to these questions.... Ghana's contributions, as a free nation, to peace, to art, to industry, to government, will be regarded by American Negroes as symbols of their own worth and potential."[2]

The book that follows analyzes, over the course of a quarter century and a series of specific events, major shifts in the salience and significance of contemporary Africa in African American intellectual and political life. This complex and ever-changing relationship underwent critical changes during the pivotal years between 1935 and 1961 — from the anger and bitterness over Italy's invasion of Ethiopia in 1935–36 to the heady years of the early 1960s, when dozens of colonized African nations gained their independence. Responding to the development of independence in Africa, during this time African Americans embraced contemporary, as opposed to historic, Africa.

Previously, in the late nineteenth and early twentieth centuries, African American missionary advocates and emigrationists had spoken reverentially about Africa's glorious past, yet they typically had much less regard for

Africans of their own day. For them, what held meaning was the influence of black Americans on Africa, not the reverse. Nineteenth-century African Americans in fact helped establish a tradition of arrogating a primacy in transatlantic economic, political, and intellectual exchanges with Africa. Indeed, much attention has been paid to how African Americans aided Africa in the twentieth century, from missionaries' work to save pagan "savages" to W. E. B. Du Bois's leadership of pan-African efforts to unify and strengthen the black world. Just a few years ago the inaugural issue of a magazine billing itself as "The Forum of People of African Descent" hit the presses emblazoned with the headline, "Can African Americans Save Africa?"[3]

The focus on black America aiding and influencing Africa has obscured the profound transformations that African freedom struggles fostered in black America, and particularly in black Americans' relations with Africa. These freedom struggles drove and shaped discourse about Africa in mid-twentieth-century black America, so it was Africans themselves who compelled people in America to consider with fresh eyes their relationship to contemporary Africa. Black Americans did not just inspire and provide a model for Africans; they also watched and considered African political activities. The nonviolent, direct action tactics of the protesters in South Africa's 1952 Defiance Campaign, for instance, resonated in black America, as did the more militant approach of Mau Mau fighters in Kenya. Viewing these events, African Americans reflected on the possibilities for their own situation, with discussion about Africa refracting as well as reshaping debates within black America.

In the discourse about the relationship with Africa and Africans, black America contained a vast array of views. Some felt close affinity to Africa, viewing Africa as the motherland and considering Africans to be blood brothers, and some argued that experiences of oppression created binding links and group identity. Yet others felt no such ties and found instead that three centuries divided by the Atlantic had altered fundamentally, even severed, former relations. Between these points, the abundance of differing forms and degrees of interest in Africa ensured that there would be highly varied engagements with contemporary Africa, with African Americans regularly contesting their often conflicting attitudes.

These debates reflected any number of influences in black America, not least of which were ongoing tensions over how much to focus on and identify with an Africa that for so long had been stereotyped in disturbingly negative terms. Even as African Americans increasingly embraced contemporary Africa, there continued to be highly varied opinions as to how strongly ties should be pursued. Even deeply emotional and enthusiastic responses did not always result in practical action or investment. The liberal civil rights leadership in particular questioned how fully to pursue transatlantic links, regularly arguing that black America's energies and resources should concentrate on the daunting challenges of domestic issues. Yet others promoted a transatlantic frame of reference and stronger diasporic ties to Africa. Any number of times ordinary African Americans pushed their leaders to adopt stronger pro-African stances, and, as shall be seen, civil rights leaders often found themselves scrambling to catch up on African issues. Public letters to the black press and private missives to individual leaders reveal that many black Americans drew pride and inspiration from African struggles and pushed their leaders to act more aggressively in regard to African interests — as well as in the domestic struggle. We can gauge and learn from the character and levels of responses — the depth of verbal support, actual donations of money or time, the creation of support organizations — and should recognize that all of these complexities speak to the absolute need for disaggregating the relationship between African Americans and Africa.

As black Americans wrestled with the meaning and relevance of events in Africa, they also debated how best to translate their concerns into action in the international arena. These debates shed still more light on issues of significance within black America and on the constantly evolving relationship with Africa. At the same time, efforts to influence U.S. foreign policy toward Africa of course speak to the underexamined history of U.S. foreign relations with Africa. Recently there have been notable additions to the literature regarding this history; however, like Africa itself, this history remains remarkably marginalized. This is unfortunate, for the enormous significance of race and ethnicity in world politics during the twentieth century can be better understood by examining the African American transnational relationship with Africa and the complex interaction of the domestic race issue and international politics.

Black America's relationship with Africa existed not in a vacuum but in a world of rising fascism, world war, superpower rivalry, and an emerging Third World. International influences played a powerful role in shaping how African Americans responded to developments in Africa. Italy's invasion of Ethiopia stands as part of the long descent into World War II and the horrible slaughter of peoples based on doctrines of racial superiority, but it also marked the start of black America's transformed engagement with contemporary Africa. The war itself fundamentally altered the European powers' relations with colonial nations, helping lay the groundwork for a liberated Africa and a profoundly different African American relationship with Africa. In the postwar world, the rapid onset of the Cold War held tremendous consequences for the development of that relationship, with anticommunism stifling domestic dissent and transatlantic connections even as it opened the argument that equality at home would be the most powerful weapon in the fight against communism overseas. The rising Third World, with an emerging independent Africa as a large component, further influenced the terms of engagement. The United States could ill afford to alienate vast numbers of the world's population, and yet in the fight against communism Washington felt it imperative to support its European allies, who were the colonial powers in Africa. African Americans had to negotiate these complex global developments as part of their reshaping of the relationship with Africa. Two caveats should be noted at this point. First, that the Caribbean, with its large black population and immigrant peoples creating numerous ties to the United States, also held deep meaning in the context of an emerging Third World and a rising black Atlantic; still, the focus of this book is on African Americans' interaction specifically with Africa. Second, that while the vast cultural dimensions of this engagement deserve a book in their own right, here they only enter into the story and are not this book's central focus.

Ethiopia's defense of its national sovereignty in the mid-1930s energized African American internationalism and engagement with contemporary Africa, and in the following years African Americans became strongly anticolonial. Over time, debates raged about the extent and shape of the anticolonial engagement, but, broadly speaking, African Americans' anticolonialism shifted toward a focus more specifically on Africa. As a group, black Americans became more determined to influence international policies along particular, race-conscious lines. By the early 1960s, even as liberal civil rights leaders espoused an integrationist vision for America, they sought influence in racially defined terms. For example, these black American leaders did not seek to become the voice of expertise on affairs with Asia, an area that also experienced colonial rule and oppression; rather, they sought to position themselves as a guiding force in U.S. relations with Africa. African liberation struggles not only promoted greater international attention among black Americans, they guided African American interest in anticolonialism and foreign policy toward more African-centered lines.

Yet even as African Americans claimed this special role and relationship with Africa, they struggled to process the complexities of independent Africa, particularly the reality of internecine domestic conflicts within that continent's many new nations. Twentieth-century African Americans generally did not disaggregate areas of Africa in their transatlantic thinking. The "imagined" Africa was just that: Africa as a whole. This meant that African Americans responded to events ranging across the entire continent, and in interpreting these events they projected their meanings just as broadly. Yet, by the same measure, this approach to Africa generally resulted in minimal consideration of the vast ethnic and cultural differences at work on the continent.

A world of leftist revolutionaries, authoritarian strongmen, democratic hopefuls, military coups, and civil wars could not easily sustain imaginings of Africa as a more or less unified whole. One consequence, arrived at consciously or unconsciously, was African Americans' greater focus on countries embroiled in national liberation struggles, as opposed to countries that already had gained independence. Such a prioritization enabled African Americans to continue building transatlantic bridges while finessing direct engagement with the deep complications of independent Africa. Furthermore, focusing on an Africa still struggling for independence helped sustain a broader coalition of forces in black America as the U.S. civil rights movement fragmented in the 1960s. People who differed over the course of the struggle in the United States or over the source of woes in independent Africa could still rally together against the injustices in African nations that continued to face white minority rule. Yet of course this left unresolved the engagement with an entirely independent Africa, an issue that the dawn of black majority rule in South Africa brought into sharper relief.

In recent years historians have paid closer attention to the transnational dimensions of race and racial politics during the twentieth century. The field covers a vast amount of history, a crucial part of which includes African Americans and Africa. Research in this particular historical field sometimes has been explicitly comparative, while in other cases the work has reconstructed the transatlantic bridges across which people and ideas flowed.[4] Scholars also have been examining more closely the complex interactions between U.S. race relations, politics, and foreign affairs, and recently a number of notable works have appeared that specifically engage black American attitudes toward Africa, colonialism, the Cold War, and U.S. foreign policy during the mid-twentieth century.[5]

The following work complements and expands this growing body of literature by exploring the ways in which African Americans responded to pivotal developments in Africa during these years. Taking place during the confluence of the modern freedom struggles on both sides of the Atlantic, this interaction had a profound impact on black America, helping to recast the place of Africa in African American consciousness. By examining more fully black America's engagement with African freedom struggles and independence, we reshape and internationalize our understanding of the freedom struggle in America while gaining insight into the development of racial identity and political consciousness during these critical years of twentieth-century freedom movements. Historical accounts generally have understated the role that African liberation struggles played in promoting action by black Americans, perhaps in part due to the understandable desire to highlight African Americans' own efforts during the struggle. Unfortunately, the downplaying of the international forces that informed black America divorces our understanding of the black freedom struggle in America from the broader, worldwide context. The domestic civil rights movement in fact absorbed knowledge and lessons from African liberation struggles, which in turn helped shape ongoing interpretations of the domestic struggle. Hopefully, this book contributes to a greater balance in our understanding of the dialectic nature of the links.

Examining more fully the international character of black America's relationship with contemporary Africa also helps reshape our understanding of the forces informing that relationship. Historians have shown that throughout the course of American history there have been ties linking African Americans to Africa. Yet, just as plainly, the shape and meaning of these links have varied and been transformed over time. Indeed, periods of downturn and dissociation existed, as did surges in interest. Historically, the most common explanation of why African Americans' engagement with Africa waxes and wanes over time maintains that African Americans promote stronger ties with Africa when they feel more alienated in the United States; when their situation appears to be improving, it is argued, they feel less need to pursue links with Africa — that is, identifying with the ancestral homeland is viewed as a substitute for identifying with America. This explanation points to the fact that domestic social downswings and, to a lesser degree, economic downturns give rise to emigration sentiment. Thus, increased interest in emigration during the 1890s coincided with the rise of Jim Crow and "separate but equal" policies; emigration in the late 1910s and early 1920s coincided with the surge in racial violence highlighted by the "Red Summer" of 1919.[6] This "bad times" thesis, however, has trouble explaining why worsening economic times in the late 1920s and early 1930s did not result in more widespread interest in Africa at that time and, more significantly, why rising interest in Africa and emigrating waves of black Americans in the late 1950s and early 1960s coincided with early advances in the modern civil rights movement. Notwithstanding the enormous frustrations raised by white southerners' "Massive Resistance," rising interest in Africa among black Americans occurred contemporaneously with relatively greater social and economic advances in America. The growing interest in Africa among middle- and upper-class African Americans clearly suggests that interest in Africa was not merely a refuge from the problems in America.

An alternative explanation for the shifts in African American interest in Africa, then, has been that as blacks in America increase their confidence in their status as Americans, they feel greater comfort in looking to Africa as the fountainhead of the dignity and pride denied them in America. In this view, black integration occurring with an attendant rising interest in and attachment to Africa means that integration and rising cultural nationalism are not mutually exclusive developments. Yet this thesis faces the reverse challenge of how to explain increasing interest in Africa during periods of adversity.[7]

These two relatively blunt interpretive approaches contain important elements of analysis, yet essentially they remain domestically self-referential, thereby eliding the role of Africa and other international influences. Of the myriad complexities shaping the terms of the engagement, the critical importance of contemporary Africa itself all too often has been neglected. The era of African liberation struggles held profound meaning for renewing and reshaping African American ties with Africa. Starting with Haile Selassie's defense of the Ethiopian homeland in the 1930s and rising most emphatically with the successful independence movements of the 1950s, Africa itself compelled black America to look anew at contemporary Africa. In the continual process of reinventing and reinterpreting racial identities, developments in contemporary Africa reshaped African American views of Africans and promoted the positive inclusion of modern Africa in black American lives. It should be noted that during these years there would be no necessary connection between a burgeoning U.S. civil rights movement — with equal treatment and integration as its goal — and the building of diasporic identities across national boundaries. Changes obviously took time, too, for negative images and cultural memory maintained powerful holds on shaping feelings toward Africa long after new data about Africa came to the fore. However, by the late 1950s and early 1960s any number of African Americans reached out to draw lessons from and promote a stronger diasporic unity with contemporary Africa.

Of course, even then just how to shape the relationship with Africa would remain a salient issue for African Americans, and the discourse over the ever evolving relationship would serve as a continuing marker of issues and attitudes and identities in black America. African Americans are an enormously diverse group, and we should be careful not to flatten the intellectual terrain. The transformations analyzed in the following pages are subtle and uneven, often cases of shifting weight and emphasis rather than sharp change, and certainly never monolithic in nature. This book takes as a premise that accepting and analyzing the enormous wealth and creativity of the historical actors' views and lives is a greater service to them than depicting them as having an essentialized response to and interaction with Africa. Examining the varied and changing African American views in this transnational context ultimately broadens the understanding we have of the complexities of black America.

To access the dizzying array of opinions in black America, I have drawn upon a wide range of sources, which include the papers of leading civil rights organizations, prominent African Americans, and official government documents and records. Yet perhaps the most important and vibrant source for understanding black America's range of views in the mid-twentieth century is the black press. African American newspapers are familiar sources and yet curiously underutilized, especially in regard to Africa, where they played a crucial role in providing forums for debates about Africa's meaning and relevance. The pages of editorials, opinion pieces, and letters to the editors provide a fecund range of opinion. Indeed, letters to the editors have the particular advantage of offering access to an array of voices not usually registered in the ongoing discourse.

While African American newspapers always have struggled for survival, the 1930s, 1940s, and 1950s represented the height of their power and influence. In 1945 the weekly circulation of the black press passed the 1.8 million mark, and in 1954 it topped 2 million.[8] Moreover, the black press reached and influenced a proportion of the African American population far greater than its circulation figures alone would indicate. As Gunnar Myrdal noted in 1944 in *An American Dilemma*, newspapers passed from family to family and could be found in barbershops, churches, lodges, and pool parlors. Their contents passed by word of mouth among those who could not read. "The importance of the Negro press for the formation of Negro opinion, for the functioning of all other Negro institutions, for Negro leadership and concerted action generally, is enormous," wrote Myrdal. He even felt that the press might have been "the greatest single power of the Negro community." It seems more likely that black churches retained that position of primacy in black America, but the black press, by providing a broad forum for opinion and argument from all quarters of black America, eclipsed the churches in offering an arena for debate about Africa.[9]

The press served as a well-worn medium for disseminating ideas between African American elites and the broader community, with the newspapers' dependency on circulation revenues helping ensure that their content did not reflect only the views of the relatively elite publishers. In continually trying to capture readership, papers offered a mix of tabloid-press sensationalism, large quantities of human interest material, and lots of local news. They typically balanced this with sober editorial pages and prominent columnists.

The resultant mix was a powerful transmitter of the concerns and interests of black America. In 1943, W. E. B. Du Bois remarked, "Today it is probably true that there is scarcely a Negro in the United States who can read and write who does not read the Negro press. It has become a vital part of his life." "But," he added, "as I have said before, instead of guiding and ordering Negroes it is rather the expression and reflection of that life. . . . Probably by and large a wide reading of the Negro press would reflect a most accurate picture of present conditions among Negroes than any other source." Myrdal concurred with Du Bois, feeling that "by and large the Negro press provides the news and the opinions which its reading public wants" and noting that "this inference has the corollary conclusion that Negro opinion—at least among the more alert and articulate groups—can be ascertained and studied in the Negro press." When a 1943 nationwide survey asked the question, "Does the Negro press speak for most Negroes in your opinion?" 86 percent of black Americans responded "yes," while only 10 percent said "no."[10]

The leading African American newspapers, considering both circulation and influence, maintained remarkable stability in terms of ownership and editorship from 1935 to 1961. During this period each one remained under the control of a single person or family: the renowned *Chicago Defender*, initially led by founder Robert Abbott and then his son-in-law John Sengstacke; the increasingly popular *Pittsburgh Courier*, under the control of the Robert Vann family; the *New York Amsterdam News*, bought by C. B. Powell in 1935; and the *Baltimore Afro-American,* with its multiple editions sold throughout the Mid-Atlantic region all published under the direction of president Carl Murphy. Finally, the leading newspaper in the Deep South was the *Atlanta Daily World*, one of a handful of black newspapers ever to succeed as a daily, with C. A. Scott as general manager and editor.

While African American newspapers shared common ground on certain fundamental issues, such as making the promotion of equality and full citizenship for black Americans a top priority, the press nevertheless ranged across the spectrum on political and social issues. More socially and politically conservative newspapers, such as the *Daily World*, in many respects operated under the principles of Booker T. Washington, promoting a social philosophy of industriousness, thriftiness, strict morality, and adapting to existing conditions, and a political philosophy of voting Republican. "Gradualist" papers such as these believed in the primacy of economics and urged the value of hard work, practical education, and self-help. Advocating the view that one could rise within the system and break down barriers in the process, these papers tended to not take stands that could be perceived as inflammatory, for fear that such tactics harmed the cause. In international affairs, their coverage focused on displaying prominent patriotism and, particularly after World War II, staunch anticommunism. With their determinedly integrative stance, they typically displayed little interest in promoting racial nationalism, black history, or links with Africa. The more influential and widespread liberal activist newspapers — including the *Defender*, *Courier*, *Afro-American*, and *Amsterdam News* — more determinedly demanded specific political and social changes that would promote civil rights and equality. These papers often supported U.S. foreign policy but certainly did not mindlessly toe the official line, and they contended that one could be patriotic while maintaining active pressure for civil rights. They more commonly promoted racial pride, often through encouraging an awareness of black history, and accordingly generally displayed more interest in Africa. As might be expected, during the course of the quarter century covered in the following pages, the specific positions on domestic and international issues taken by these newspapers and others varied. The nuances speak to concerns within black America as well as to its evolving relationship with contemporary Africa.

Examining African Americans' discourse about Africa, then, ultimately not only deepens our understanding of this historic relationship but also opens a window onto black America as it transformed itself during the mid-twentieth century. Indeed, the African American engagement with Africa offers a powerful way to search into the issues and concerns of black America. In addressing the broad relationship, this book weaves together many ongoing issues: the role that Africa played in the black freedom struggle in America, the changing nature of African American identities and the influence Africa had on them, the reshaped and more widespread African American interest in Africa that emerged in these middle years of the twentieth century. The roots of each of these issues, as well as others addressed herein, can be traced to years well before the timeframe of this book; similarly, these issues continued to help shape the relationship long after. Still, this book concentrates on the roughly quarter century from 1935 to 1961 in which the relationship with contemporary Africa, as opposed to historical Africa, was redefined. The chapters are structured around African American responses to influential events in Africa. Undoubtedly one could include other African events that held import for African Americans during this quarter century, but the following chapters show how these specific events crystallized thought and debate over particular issues and caused fundamental shifts in the abiding relationship.

PROLOGUE

The Negroes in the United States and the other Americas have earned the right to
fight out their problems where they are, but they could easily furnish from time to
time technical experts, leaders of thought, and missionaries of culture for their
backward brethren in the new Africa.

W. E. B. Du Bois, Darkwater *(1920)*

Once I thought of you Africans as children, whom we educated Afro-Americans
would lead to liberty. I was wrong. We could not even lead ourselves, much less you.

W. E. B. Du Bois, 1960, Autobiography *(1968)*

For the nearly four centuries that blacks in America have engaged in an ever-changing relationship with Africa, African Americans' complex and layered attitudes toward Africa have reflected a range of domestic concerns and international influences. These varying forces have affected discrete parts of black America to differing degrees, so individual African Americans have experienced competing impulses toward Africa — ranging from ambivalence and disregard to solidarity and return — and have waged vigorous debates about them. These debates have taken place in specific political, intellectual, and institutional contexts that also have changed over time. Yet even as the discourse about Africa constantly evolved, the African American relationship with Africa during the late nineteenth and early twentieth centuries established patterns of thought and behavior that would carry over into the mid-twentieth century.

Missionaries, Emigrationists, Vindicationists, and Pan-Africanists

In postbellum America, the African American engagement with Africa often took place in the context of the "mission movement." Situated within the rise of a broad evangelical movement in American Protestantism, black and white church organizations underwrote the sponsorship of numerous missionaries to "Christianize and civilize" African peoples. Between 1877 and 1900, independent black churches alone sent at least seventy-six missionaries to Africa. Arrogating the duty to "uplift" and "redeem" Africa, African American churches supported the belief that blacks from America could return to Africa to spread Christianity and Western civilization.

The idea that African Americans should play a special role in "redeeming" Africa can be traced back at least into the late eighteenth century and the rise of the "Fortunate Fall" doctrine. While the idea had several variations, historian Wilson Moses broadly defines it as "the belief that slavery, although a terrible affliction on the African people, would become, through the workings of divine providence, a blessing in the fullness of time." Moses points out that in the early nineteenth century — most particularly in response to the 1817 founding of the American Colonization Society (ACS), whose members included a number of slaveholders with the goal of removing the "free African" population from the country — "most [black] writers became aware of the dangers of asserting that the enslavement of the Africans had been permitted by God as a means of bringing about African redemption." "But," he adds, "African Redemptionism did not die out as a result, nor did the religious arguments used to support African emigration movements."[1]

So, although an emphasis explicitly linking African redemption with the "Fortunate Fall" declined, the belief that blacks from the New World would play a vital role in Africa's uplift continued to infuse discourse through the nineteenth century. For years, two of the central figures shaping postbellum debate about Africa, Edward Blyden and Alexander Crummell, based their thinking and arguments about the African American relationship to Africa on the idea that the ancestral land had to be Christianized and "civilized." Blyden, born and raised in the Dutch West Indies, emigrated to Liberia in the 1850s after trying in vain to enter a seminary in the United States. In Liberia he became a Presbyterian minister and an agent for the ACS, while also actively involving himself in Liberian politics for the next thirty years. Blyden commonly spoke of the providential call to Christian African Americans to return to Africa as cultural, religious, and economic missionaries, even though by the end of his life he concluded that Africans themselves would play the leading role in redeeming the continent. Crummell, born free in New York in 1819, followed his religious calling by becoming an Episcopalian minister. After suffering innumerable indignities at the hands of white Americans in general and his fellow Episcopalians in particular, he accepted a fellowship to study at Cambridge. There he took a degree in 1853, after which he embarked as a missionary to Liberia. For the next twenty years he would be, in the words of Wilson Moses, "the African civilizationist and colonizationist par excellence." Although Crummell later in life shifted away from strongly advocating emigration, he nevertheless continued to support the need for black Americans to help redeem Africans from heathenism and barbarism.[2]

Black missionaries such as Blyden and Crummell undoubtedly believed in and found motivation from their gospel mission, yet they also knew that relieving Africa of its "pagan" status would redound favorably to blacks in America. Black evangelists would help elevate the status of Africa in the eyes of the West and, in a trickle-across effect, the status of all descendants of Africa. Black missionary advocates "conceived missions not only as a way to redeem Africa but as a way to enhance black status within America," writes historian James Campbell. "Lifting Africa from 'barbarism' to the light of 'civilization' promised to alleviate a major source of the stigma that attached to black people everywhere, while providing a compelling demonstration of African American progress and prowess." "Primitive" and "uncivilized" Africans compared to educated and refined black Americans helped show that a black person could "advance" and become as valued a citizen as the next person. Indeed, blacks from America helping to "uplift" Africans provided living proof of black American advancement, while the "improvement" of Africans showed the ability of all blacks to advance.[3]

Closely interwoven with missionary activity targeting Africa were debates over African American emigration to Africa. In antebellum America, colonization plans had caused raging debates over whether colonization schemes primarily aided efforts by whites to rid the country of free blacks or offered a genuine solution to race problems in America. The establishment of the ACS, followed shortly thereafter by its sending an initial ninety colonists in 1820 to Sherbro Island off the coast of what is now Liberia, sharpened debate over colonization efforts. Some black Americans, perhaps most prominently Daniel Coker, a founder of the African Methodist Episcopal (AME) church, supported and even participated in ACS efforts. Yet most black leaders overwhelmingly opposed colonization efforts. Colonizationism reeked too strongly of forced removal of free blacks, and on these terms most African Americans turned away from ACS endeavors. Yet given the intense discrimination against free blacks in America, interest in voluntary emigration continued. Schemes to emigrate to a wide variety of places—Canada, Mexico, Haiti, Africa—emerged in following decades. Africa tended to receive no more support than other destinations, which reflected at least in part ongoing fears by free blacks that identifying too strongly with Africa would undermine the quest for freedom and for full citizenship. Indeed, these concerns contributed to blacks' starting to advocate the previously derided term "Negro," instead of the more commonly used "African." Such concerns would continue to underlie the ongoing complex relationship with Africa.

When Liberia declared itself an independent republic in 1847, rending its longstanding tie to the ACS, the changed status prompted black Americans to take a fresh look at Liberia as a destination. In the following year, migration grew tenfold. Even more, Liberia became a reference point for African Americans to help prove the legitimacy of their claims to republican citizenship. With the nineteenth-century emphasis on nationhood, and the attendant idea that a nation served as a measure of a people, Liberia's status and course of development took on tremendous significance. Down through the rest of the century, and into the twentieth century, Liberia would continue as a key reference point for African Americans engaging Africa.[4]

After the Civil War, and particularly amidst the terror and poverty of the post-Reconstruction South, thousands of blacks demonstrated their desire to search elsewhere for a better life by supporting emigration schemes. While the "Exodusters" migration to Kansas offered the most graphic testimony of desires to find true freedom and independence, others sought a return to Africa, most commonly to Liberia. As leaders such as Blyden, Crummell, Martin Delany, Frederick Douglass, and Henry Highland Garnet debated whether black Americans should emigrate and, if so, where to, AME Bishop Henry McNeal Turner emerged as the most vocal post-Reconstruction back-to-Africa proponent. Turner had fervently supported and recruited for the Union cause during the Civil War and had been an official of the Freedman's Bureau after the war. When he won election to the Georgia state legislature in 1868, he never took his seat because the white-dominated chamber refused to seat blacks. Reconstruction's complete collapse in the following decade fully convinced Turner that whites unalterably opposed black equality in America and that freedom therefore would come only among other blacks in Africa.

Turner spoke of his belief in emigration, and also shared his archly hierarchical views, when he predicted in 1884 that "the better class of colored men of this country will go to Africa and build up a mighty nation, while the riffraff of our race will remain here." Turner was joined by other emigration advocates who believed they could raise a stronger contemporary Africa, one that would rid blacks of the stigma of a downtrodden Africa and would demand that people of African descent be treated with dignity and respect.[5] Turner in fact provided a telling combination of missionary and emigrationist thinking. While he spoke with pride about his African heritage and of his admiration for particular characteristics he saw in Africans, at the same time he clearly believed contemporary Africa had fallen and needed to be raised.

James Campbell notes, "[One] searches Turner's writing in vain for any suggestion that African culture was legitimate or worthy of preservation in its own right." To the contrary, Turner declared, "The heathen Africans, to my certain knowledge . . . eagerly yearn for that civilization which they believe will elevate them and make them a potential for good."[6]

Indeed, the idea of "civilization" itself divided black Americans from Africa. Few black Americans could divorce themselves from Western ideas of civilization. Accordingly, most found themselves viewing contemporary Africans as, on the whole, at least semibarbaric. A Whiggish sensibility, in which history was the march of humankind toward ever higher degrees of "civilization," permeated the thinking of turn-of-the-century Americans, be they black or white. The movement of the West out of its feudalistic past was viewed as the vanguard of a universal advance. "Democratic capitalism, civic equality, and enlightened Christianity compatible with modern science and technology," writes George Fredrickson, "were not regarded as 'Western' in any racial or ethnic sense but as universal, reflecting the God-given capacity and destiny of all the nations and races of the world."[7] Yet, of course, these were Western ideals, even as they were seen as the hallmarks of modern "civilization."

Given the broad faith in Western civilization, black American leaders in the late nineteenth century generally did not initially oppose colonialism in Africa. They believed in the "civilizing" mission of the Europeans, particularly when executed by the British. Blyden, Crummell, and Turner all condoned the expansion of European rule as an essential phase in civilizing the African continent. Writing in 1891 of the colonial endeavor, Crummell declared that he had "the largest expectations of good and beneficence from its operations . . . the most thorough conviction of its need, its wisdom, and its practicality." Crummell, with his particularly low regard for African culture and civilization, viewed the European drive to open up Africa as "the highest philanthropy or the most zealous religionism." Historian Kevin Gaines connects support for the imperialist "civilizing mission" with the domestic "racial uplift" strategy of the late nineteenth and early twentieth centuries. Supporting colonialism and portraying themselves as agents of civilization and progress served as a way for black elites to defend themselves against racial stereotypes, hopefully topple racial barriers, and regain citizenship rights.[8]

Americans and Europeans who had contact with Africa at the turn of the century typically painted an almost wholly derogatory portrait of Africans, and broader Western society largely accepted the denigrating views of contemporary Africans. In 1889, National Geographic Society president Gardiner Hubbard asserted in the inaugural issue of *National Geographic* that Africa had "never developed any high degree of civilization." Only when Western civilization contacted Africans did they make any progress; remove Western contact, and Africans "deteriorated back into barbarism," according to Hubbard. Since that issue, *National Geographic* has played a continuing role in introducing to Americans all that is exotic and different in the "other" world of Africa. Literature in general picked up similar themes, and someone like Edgar Rice Burroughs, creator of Tarzan, could never go to Africa yet be perfectly comfortable writing as if he knew it.[9]

Americans who traveled and worked in Africa reported their impressions of the peoples and the continent, and these firsthand descriptions profoundly influenced how Americans shaped their ideas about Africa. Travel accounts, argues scholar Michael McCarthy, in effect "form[ed] the cultural prism through which Africa was seen by the majority of Americans at home." Travelers' descriptions usually focused on the evocative landscape and the fierce game, creating a world sometimes romantic yet one always laced with mystery and danger. In fact, for those interested in commercial success, the more exotic the experience and description, the better. Teddy Roosevelt, amateur historian and former president, ably represented this tradition in his 1910 book *African Game Trails*. Accounts such as his would help establish the tradition of Americans having more interest in, knowledge of, and eventually concern for African wildlife than for African peoples. At the same time, the portrayals of Africans in these accounts shaped American readers' perceptions of contemporary Africans. Roosevelt from the outset made clear to his readers his opinions about the inhabitants of East Africa: "The dark-skinned races that live in the land vary widely. Some are warlike, cattle-owning nomads; some till the soil and live in thatched huts shaped like beehives; some are fisherfolk; some are ape-like naked savages, who dwell in the woods and prey on creatures not much wilder or lower than themselves." Roosevelt reinforced his blatantly racist views throughout his book, sharing impressions such as "the low culture of many of the savage tribes, especially of the hunting tribes, substantially reproduces the conditions of life in Europe as it was led by our ancestors ages before the dawn of anything that could be called civilization."[10]

Travelers' accounts created a framework for Americans to order their views of the continent, in which the historical process of settling America was imposed on understanding Africa. Africans were likened to Indians, Europeans to the pioneers. Africa, an undeveloped, hostile, primitive land, needed to be tamed and developed. Upon his return in 1906 from the brutally pacified Anglo-Egyptian Sudan, Herbert Bridgman waxed proud before the National Geographic Society about Britain's colonizing efforts: "Great Britain, applying the same principles which have made her the great colonial power of the world, goes on developing the industrial and commercial resources of the countries which have fallen under her influence, establishing law and order, schools . . . and pouring in upon places which for centuries have been shrouded in darkness the light of modern civilization."[11]

Black Americans' limited knowledge of Africa, then, generally came filtered through a distorted lens. Europeans of course maintained a vested interest in portraying Africans as primitive heathens: it helped justify their colonial rule. White Americans readily accepted and promoted similar views of Africans. Some, imbued with Western standards of culture and civilization, simply saw Africans as intellectual and cultural primitives; others used the images to help justify, via association, the second-class status they imposed on African Americans.

At the same time, black American missionaries themselves contributed to spreading denigrating images of Africa. Missionary reports served as a prime source for black Americans to learn about Africa. Although perhaps more sympathetic to Africans than were their white counterparts, black missionaries still had to legitimize the importance of their work. Missionaries needed to offer grandiose views of their work in the vineyards of Africa to keep donations flowing from churches in America. "Missionary paternalism" often portrayed Africans as heathen savages and/or primitive children in need of Christianity and civilization. According to AME mission secretary H. B. Parks, Africans groped "beneath a black cloud of heathen darkness." The 1880 constitution of the black Baptist Foreign Mission Convention of the U.S.A. declared, "The benighted condition of more than three hundred million souls in Africa, now held in chains of the grossest idolatry, cannibalism, domestic slavery, and every species of superstition, claim our most profound attention and help."[12] Thus, black Americans not only imbibed but also at times perpetuated the very images that they sought to overcome. "I was given the missionary's concept, and the picture we got of African people was of ugly, unkempt, naked savages who had to be civilized," recollected one young churchgoer. "We had to take them Christianity and the Bible."[13]

Broader popular culture reinforced the idea that benighted contemporary Africa needed salvation. As movies came into prominence, they offered visual images to reinforce ideas of African "primitiveness." Countless Americans received their first, and often only, visual impressions of Africa from Tarzan movies, the first of which came out in 1918. "I hardly ever went [to movies] but every once in awhile I did see savages," remembered one black American who grew up in the first part of the century. "There was something painful, sort of embarrassing about it. I suppose it was because that savage was black like me and was making a fool of himself in front of the whole white world which laughed at him and exploited him. I wanted not to be identified with that!" Blatantly caricatured pictures of cannibals running around half naked with spears and cooking missionaries in pots, recalled other African Americans, provided little more than feelings of embarrassment and even shame.[14]

With negative stereotypes of Africans permeating the broader culture, not surprisingly such images reached into the nation's classrooms. Educational experiences taught children from an early age about the "primitiveness" of Africans, with textbooks for schoolchildren buttressing ideas of African inferiority. Geography textbooks, for instance, exposed young students to the "five races of mankind." Invariably a noble-looking person represented Europeans, while the other caricatures varied in their personification of ideal humanity. The African always ranked low, looking crude and fierce.[15] "First I'll tell you what [the African] was when I was a child going to primary school," reflected P. L. Prattis, editor of the *Courier*, in a 1961 speech. "He was a fierce savage who ate his brothers and sisters. I grew up afraid of this African and I flinched every time they turned to the page in the geography book where his naked head and torso were shown. This I was made to understand was my background." Many African Americans had early memories and ideas about Africa and their ancestry, indeed about themselves, shaped by the depictions of Africans found in their textbooks. "[T]hose pictures of the races of man . . . with a handsome guy to represent the whites, an Indian with a feathered cap, a Chinese and an East Indian, and then a black, kinky-haired specimen—that was me, a savage, a cannibal, he was just the tail end of the human race, he was at the bottom. . . . That picture in the book was the picture of where and what I came from. I carried the idea along with me for years."[16]

The power of language further fed blatant stereotypes. Mysterious "primitive tribes" inhabited the "Dark Continent." Historically, Western society has used the appellation "tribes" to signify relatively less "civilized" cultures. In post-Biblical Europe, for instance, the only "tribes" have been the barbaric Germanic tribes who pillaged and ravaged and carved up the Roman Empire, after which the "Dark Ages" occurred. In nineteenth-century America, hardy "pioneers" vanquished the "Indian tribes" and tamed the West. In late twentieth-century Europe, Balkan "ethnic groups" undertook the undoubtedly terrible but antiseptically labeled "ethnic cleansing," while in Africa, Hutu "tribesmen" savagely "slaughtered" and "massacred."[17]

Even for black Americans, the term "African" developed pejorative connotations. Associating someone with being an African degraded him or her, and this drew meaning from the broad image of Africa within the community at large. "To call a kid an African was an insult," recalled Lorraine Hansberry, author of *A Raisin in the Sun*, about her elementary school days. "It was calling him savage, uncivilized, naked, something to laugh at. A naked black savage with a spear and war paint. It was equivalent to ugliness. Everything distasteful and painful was associated with Africa."[18]

Facing the overwhelmingly negative images of and ideas about Africa and recognizing that when white Americans engaged these images they never clearly distinguished blacks in America from those in Africa, some early-twentieth-century African American intellectuals promoted another approach to Africa: to redeem the continent's history and, thereby, the ancestry of persons of African descent everywhere. People such as W. E. B. Du Bois, Carter Woodson, and Joel Rogers actively sought to resurrect the past greatness of Africa and Africans. These men helped form the "vindicationist" school, determined to reclaim for Africa its proper heritage as a continent of great peoples with noble pasts and mighty contributions to human progress. To this end, Woodson founded the Association for the Study of Negro Life and History, while Rogers contributed the regular "Your History" feature in the *Courier* and published books on the great people and deeds of the African past. Du Bois framed his book *The World and Africa*, along with numerous other writings, as "not so much a history of the Negroid peoples as a statement of their integral role in human history from prehistoric to modern times."[19] The vindicationists believed that they should promote the race and be advocates for Africa, not merely scholars striving for an idealistic ethical objectivity. As Manning Marable points out, when Du Bois's pioneering thesis on the suppression of the African slave trade was critiqued as occasionally characterizing the work of "the advocate rather than the historian," for Du Bois that was the point: "scholarship served to advance racial interests." While the vindicationists' more intellectually oriented endeavor necessarily involved limited numbers of persons, this movement sought to redeem Africa and African Americans on the broadest level.[20]

Yet the vindicationists' approach remained grounded in the African past. They emphasized African achievements in history; they made little of the African present. Black Americans interested in Africa in the late nineteenth and early twentieth centuries may have felt strongly about the glorious African past, but they almost uniformly felt that contemporary Africa offered little of value and needed to be raised. They believed it would be blacks in the diaspora who would pilot Africans toward a new day in the sun. Indeed, up through the present day the idea of African Americans having a role in "redeeming" Africa—be it in a religious, intellectual, or now, more commonly, an economic way—has continued to weave through the African American relationship with Africa.

The belief that blacks in the New World would lead Africans also appeared in early pan-Africanism, which crystallized as a movement in the early twentieth century. To a striking degree, nineteenth-century missionary, emigration, and "pan-Negro" thought had had intertwining strands, with Blyden, Crummell, and Turner illustrative of people who engaged all three through their far-ranging careers and writings. Just as striking, the movements all arrogated the idea that they could build and lead a better Africa. At the century's turn, while missionaries sought to uplift Africans and emigrationists hoped they could build a strong nation within Africa, pan-Africanists offered from outside Africa a more secular leadership and path to racial unity and strength. Pan-Africanism, advocates anticipated, would bring together blacks in the New World and Africa, with those in the diaspora leading Africans toward building a stronger black nationality.[21]

Formal Pan-African conferences began in 1900, with a meeting in London carried out under the leadership of the Trinidadian lawyer Henry Sylvester Williams and the African Methodist Episcopal Zion bishop Alexander Walters. The conference took a moderate stance, calling for the just and humane treatment of people of African descent throughout the world while forgoing any demand for the end of European rule in Africa. Upon the death of Williams in 1911, Du Bois took the lead in promoting a liberal, reformist pan-Africanism, most visibly through a series of Pan-African Congresses.

Du Bois, by that time already a towering figure in black America, would play a vital role in the international movement for black solidarity for more than another half century. Born in Massachusetts in 1868, by the time he had assumed (in both senses of the word) leadership of the pan-African movement, Du Bois had had time to formulate his early views about race and its centrality in shaping human civilization. In doing so, he accepted the common turn-of-the-century idea that particular races had unique characteristics, and in his view all black people carried with them what he called an essential racial "genius." Du Bois firmly believed that all races could attain the highest stages of human progress, and that to do so blacks needed to work together and use, not abandon, their unique qualities and gifts. "For the development of Negro genius, of Negro literature and art, of Negro spirit, only Negroes bounded and welded together, Negroes inspired by one vast ideal, can work out in its fullness the great message we have for humanity," wrote Du Bois. Even as blacks appropriated some of the ideas and talents from other races, assimilation into white society was not the answer to advancement. Addressing the "two-ness" of blacks in America, Du Bois spelled out that birth, citizenship, political ideals, language, and religion created black Americans' "Americanism," but from that point on, as he put it, "we are Negroes."[22]

For Du Bois, "the advance guard of the Negro people — the eight million people of Negro blood in the United States of America," needed to realize that their destiny was not absorption by white Americans "if they are to take their just place in the vanguard of pan-Negroism."[23] With his extraordinary outpouring and range of writings during a span of over seventy years, Du Bois's thinking over time shifted, evolved, and even contradicted itself. Yet it is clear that in the early twentieth century Du Bois held hierarchical ideas about African Americans' assuming the lead in the relationship and guiding contemporary Africans. In 1920, contemplating the creation of a large African state south of the Sahara and north of South Africa, Du Bois accepted that international control and oversight would be needed at first, for "no one would expect this new state to be independent and self-governing from the start." Independence, however, would be expected as "the only possible end of the experiment." In the evolution of this state, Du Bois envisioned black Americans commanding a crucial role in raising Africa's civilization and leading it to that independence.[24]

Du Bois's Pan-African Congresses, then, were both powerful expressions of diasporic unity as well as statements of diasporic leadership. The first Pan-African Congress led by Du Bois came in the wake of World War I, convening in 1919 in Paris as the Versailles Peace Conference deliberated. In speaking out on behalf of the interests of Africans in the former German colonies, congress delegates stressed objectives such as "political rights for the civilized" and "development of autonomous governments along the lines of native customs with the object of inaugurating gradually an Africa for the Africans." At no point did the delegates demand the right for Africans to exercise immediate self-determination.[25] Liberal reformist pan-Africanists believed Africans would be raised, and they envisioned their ultimate objective as a liberated Africa. They did not, however, demand immediate freedom. Subsequent conferences in 1921, 1923, and 1927 continued this relatively moderate approach, with none of them calling for the complete independence of African colonies.[26]

As Du Bois promoted Pan-African Congresses, in the late 1910s and 1920s Marcus Garvey broadened and energized black American interest in Africa with his own populist pan-Africanism. Having established the Universal Negro Improvement Association and African Communities League (UNIA) in Jamaica in 1914, Garvey had sought a meeting with Booker T. Washington to receive advice on setting up his own institute modeled along the lines of Tuskegee. But by the time Garvey arrived in New York in 1916, Washington had died and Garvey's ambitions had broadened. He decided to shift his base of operations to New York, opening up the first U.S. branch of the UNIA there in 1917. From this modest beginning exploded the remarkable growth of the UNIA and Garveyism.

Blending themes of racial solidarity and self-help with an emphasis on pride in one's African heritage, Garvey rallied hundreds of thousands of African Americans to the cause of African redemption. Garvey injected the issue of Africa into black America's intellectual and political life on a mass scale, forcing African Americans to examine their relationship to Africa. The discourse revolved most critically around the old issue of emigration, so that African Americans debated anew their situation in America in the crucible of their relationship to Africa. In the often vitriolic debate Garvey himself did not always follow the same line, shifting positions as to whether blacks should continue to fight for their rights in America with the hope that African liberation and uplift would help guarantee the protection of black people in America, or whether it would be necessary for blacks in the New World to go "back to Africa" for true freedom. The scale of emigration, let alone the ultimate destiny of blacks in America, of course changed dramatically depending on this answer.

As part of the engagement with Africa, Garvey consistently invoked pride in Africa and its glorious past. He made historic Africa resonate in black America, prompting a widespread upsurge of interest in African heritage. Yet in drawing on Africa, the symbolism of a glorious past worked better than the reality of a colonized present. Indeed, Garvey did much less to reshape the relationship with contemporary Africa. In Garvey's formulation, Africa remained a place that first had to be redeemed in order for it then to have a profound influence on African American lives. Garvey carried on in the tradition of drawing upon African history, not contemporary Africa, for stoking pride in the race.

Garvey sought to further transatlantic links between blacks in the Americas and those in Africa, but he certainly did not view Africans as equals. Garvey combined appeals to race pride with calls for the diaspora to help raise and develop Africa into a great empire, and illustrated his own small regard for contemporary Africans in the constitution of the UNIA: two of the eleven stated UNIA objectives and aims were "to assist in civilizing the backward tribes of Africa" and "to promote a conscientious Spiritual worship among the native tribes of Africa." In the assessment of pan-Africanist scholar St. Clair Drake, while the glories of ancient Egypt and Ethiopia assumed great symbolic import for the UNIA movement, "Garvey exhibited very little appreciation for contemporary African cultures." Early-twentieth-century pan-Africanist approaches linked African Americans with Africa, yet at the same time did so in the hierarchical manner that so characterized the nineteenth-century relationship with Africa.[27]

On the Eve of War

In the late nineteenth and early twentieth centuries, then, even those most engaged with defining the African American relationship with Africa — the religious community, emigrationists, concerned intellectuals, pan-Africanists — all felt that they needed to uplift and direct Africans. Furthermore, although there was some organized interest in Africa, links to Africa and Africans generally depended on individuals rather than on organizations. Undoubtedly at times events in Africa resonated in broader black America's consciousness — as, for instance, when the horrific treatment of Africans by King Leopold's minions in the Belgian Congo outraged African Americans at the turn of the century. Yet, all in all, most black Americans felt at minimum an ambivalence about, and many dissociated themselves from, contemporary Africa.

By the late 1920s, even the long-standing interest in and discourse about Liberia had taken a tragic downturn. Given the Americo-Liberian leadership of that country, hopes had been invested that Liberia might exemplify the black right to republican citizenship and independence. Yet Liberia had struggled, particularly economically. In the early 1900s, enormous financial problems had prompted a commission from the United States to investigate Liberia's political and economic conditions. Financial reorganization and loans, obtained at the cost of increased United States and European control over Liberian affairs, failed to provide financial stability. In the 1920s, faced with economic problems and enormous pressures from the United States, Liberia agreed to a 1 million–acre concession for the Firestone Tire and Rubber Company. As part of the agreement, the Liberian government agreed to supply 50,000 laborers per year under a "contract system." In return, the country received a $5 million loan at 7 percent interest from a subsidiary of the Firestone Company.[28]

Soon after, questions over the sovereignty of Liberia took an even more ominous turn, with the exposure of the forced labor systems at work in the country. The forced labor at the Firestone plantation combined with the worldwide depression to drive down the price of rubber, from over $1.40 per pound in 1925 to less than $.16 per pound in 1930. More notoriously, news of the capturing and sending of young male laborers to work cocoa fields in Fernando Po led in 1929 to the League of Nations' establishing the International Commission of Inquiry into the Existence of Slavery and Forced Labor in the Republic of Liberia. The commission's damaging report, along with exposés such as George Schuyler's *Slaves Today: A Story of Liberia* (1931), forced the resignations of Liberia's president Charles King and vice president Allen Yancey. As embarrassing revelations of corruption, racist treatment of indigenous people, and slave labor cascaded into the public eye, black Americans could hardly hold up Liberia as a source of pride and evidence of black national capability.[29]

It should not be surprising, then, that any number of black Americans, bombarded with negative images of Africa, turned away and girded themselves to fighting their own fight for freedom and equality in America. In struggling to overcome racist theories that labeled them as inferior and accorded them second-class status in society, many black Americans found little incentive to associate themselves with the overwhelmingly negative and uncivilized images of Africa. Consciously or not, many felt that Africa held no meaning for or bearing upon their own existence. And so some black Americans, particularly members of the middle class and elites who believed themselves to be on a plane separate from and higher than that of Africans, built their identities apart from any sense of connection to their African heritage. An easier and seemingly more logical path to first-class citizenship seemed to be constructing an identity that would reinforce black Americans' full inclusion in American society.[30]

Tensions over whether to concentrate solely on the domestic struggle or to view it as part of a larger worldwide struggle for freedom and equality continually underscored debate about Africa, with many arguing that black Americans should focus their efforts on improving things where they lived and gaining equal treatment in America. Du Bois found himself frustrated by what he termed "race provincialism" among black Americans. Strongly supportive of transatlantic links, Du Bois lashed out at the problem he defined as "the idea that the race problem in America is a segregated case, standing by itself, and to be settled by itself[,] . . . [t]hat it not only has no real connection with other race and color problems, but any fancied connection or possible connection must be vigorously fought against." Du Bois felt deeply concerned that misinformation and misunderstanding undermined the relationship, prompting black Americans "in their attempt to settle the Negro problem to mention Africa and think of Africa and study Africa just as little as possible." While "race provincials" viewed the struggle for full citizenship as a purely domestic affair, Du Bois in contrast believed it impossible to settle

America's race problem in isolation: "I do not believe that the descendants of Africans are going to be received as American citizens so long as the peoples of Africa are kept by white civilization in semi-slavery, serfdom and economic exploitation." He argued that attacking racial prejudice should be done not by giving up local fights, or by Africans and African Americans trying to solve the other's problems, but by forging a common cause.[31]

Du Bois illustrates how some black Americans would struggle to reconcile their interest in Africa with their desire for equal citizenship in America. The decision would not necessarily be a case of simply choosing to follow either a universalistic integrationism with a sole focus on America or a racialistic pan-Africanism with a complete turning to Africa. Black Americans often fought to reconcile the two paths, in an effort to find a harmony in which they were seen as and treated as equal human beings while also carving out a place as a special, unique people. George Fredrickson speaks to this when discussing "nationalistic integrationism" in his comparison of liberation ideologies in the United States and South Africa. A critical issue for black Americans would be how contemporary Africa and all the different meanings it held fit into the picture, amidst all the other issues roiling their place in America.[32]

Yet in the early 1930s, African Americans continued to have little foundation for reconceptualizing their relationship with contemporary Africa. Indeed, as had been true throughout the first part of the century, several prominent factors continued to shape the African American relationship with contemporary Africa: negative, racist imagery of Africa; an attendant ambivalence about the continent and its peoples; a general view of African Americans' domestic struggles as being separate from rather than a part of a worldwide struggle for freedom and equality; and a frustrating inability to influence U.S. foreign policy toward Africa. Visible threads of connection to Africa clearly existed, seen particularly in continuing missionary interest, back-to-Africa movements, and pan-African efforts. However, these issues hardly dominated African American thinking. Further, those African Americans animated by diasporic sensibilities felt they first had to work hard, through their variety of ways, to "redeem" the African continent and its inhabitants. They typically predicated their beliefs on the idea of African Americans' having a special calling to "raise" or "uplift" Africa, and they exhibited little respect for contemporary Africans and African cultures. Even progressive internationalists like Ralph Bunche and Paul Robeson harbored such patronizing sentiments. Bunche, on the way to establishing himself as a leading radical intellectual at Howard University, struggled to balance his Western sensibilities with a desire to reshape views of Africa. In his 1933 dissertation, he wrote: "The African is no longer to be considered a Barbarian, nor even a child, but only an adult retarded in the terms of Western Civilization. This Western Civilization surrounds him in his daily life, and he consumes it greedily." The following year, Robeson—the brilliant singer, actor, athlete, and scholar, whose interest in Africa had been growing for a number of years—wrote, "[T]he lead in culture is with the American Negro, the direct descendent of African ancestors . . . if the real great man of the Negro race will be born, he will spring from North America."[33]

Ultimately, the powerful force of the modern African freedom struggles would be what compelled African Americans to rethink their beliefs about Africa, about their primacy in diaspora relations, and about the role of contemporary Africa in their lives. Even as Du Bois bemoaned a lack of black internationalism, events in Africa pushed black Americans to consider Africa anew in their racial consciousness. In particular, the passion surrounding Italy's assault on independent Ethiopia generated tremendous activity on the part of black America. As the crisis atmosphere mounted in the days preceding Italy's invasion, Floyd Calvin, a regular columnist for the *Courier*, shared his conviction that "for the first time in the history of America, the Negro citizen has a burning interest in the international policy of his country." Efforts to influence policy toward Africa and to protect the black nationality in Africa, efforts that typically had been confined to small numbers of African American elites and missionaries, now became the concern of an enlarged "African lobby" among black Americans. Yet the Italo-Ethiopian crisis prompted far more than just foreign affairs concern, for it also ignited black America's more engaged interest in and reshaping of the relationship with contemporary Africa.[34]

1

ETHIOPIA
The Italo-Ethiopian War and Reconceptualizing
Contemporary Africa, 1935–1936

*The most notable reaction of this Italo-Ethiopian conflict is the crystallization of
interests of the black people of the world. The violation of Ethiopia's sovereignty
provided the much needed platform of racial solidarity on which all may stand.*

*Having seen Africa through the prism of its white detractors, Negroes had come
to regard it with disdain and disaffection, evincing little or no concern in its people,
its history past or future. Today, however, he has an absorbing interest in both
Africa and the Africans; he is beginning to be proud of the history of his ancestral
land as the film of prejudice is gradually removed from his field of vision.*

Metz Lochard, Chicago Defender *(4 January 1936)*

In the years before Italy's invasion of Ethiopia, few black Americans
felt they could learn or gain much from contemporary Africans. Even Liberia, with charges of slavery and corruption, had become a tarnished emblem. But in black American reactions to Ethiopia's efforts during the war,
one sees growing linkages being created with modern Africa. The war nurtured a rising consciousness of contemporary Africa and an increasing trend
of engaging Africa's present. Ethiopia's plight stirred a concern with Africa
that cut across social, economic, and political lines. To Garvey and Du Bois,
to poor sharecroppers in the South and tenement dwellers in Harlem, the
threat to Ethiopia registered. Particularly when compared to African American responses during other crises in the preceding half century, black America's response to Italy's assault was one of broad and deep outrage. As journalist and author Roi Ottley reflected a few years later, "I know of no other
event in recent times that has stirred the rank-and-file of Negroes more than
the Italo-Ethiopian War."[1]
During this crisis, black Americans reexamined their relations with the

ancestral continent and expanded their conceptions of ethnicity. Widespread volunteering to fight for Ethiopia, the nationwide springing to life of Ethiopian aid organizations, and lobbying efforts on behalf of the Ethiopians all indicate a wellspring of pan-African commitment in black America, as well as a growth in tapping such commitments. African Americans—expanding their interest in international affairs beyond the traditional leading concerns of Liberia, Haiti, and the Virgin Islands—became the single most important pressure group in the United States pushing the government to act against Italy's transgressions. In the words of historian John Hope Franklin, with the Italian invasion "[a]lmost overnight even the most provincial among Negro Americans became international-minded."[2] Realizing the vulnerability of this bastion of black independence, African Americans used the means at their disposal, such as lobbying the U.S. government and the League of Nations, to help protect Ethiopia. While their success may have been limited, the efforts marked an increase in broader efforts to influence American foreign policy, particularly toward Africa.

Heightened awareness of Africa helped create conditions in which there germinated a willingness to respect Africans, to draw lessons from Africans, and to associate with things African. Yet while the war fostered a new relationship with contemporary Africa, responses differed, too, for black America contained a vast array of views about Africa and one's relationship with it. Not all black Americans believed the invasion of Ethiopia to be of direct importance, and many argued against being diverted from the domestic struggle. Examining the complex, at times even whipsawing, African American reactions to Italy's invasion provides insight into the role Africa played in black Americans' lives at the time, as well as to how much change there would be during the following quarter century.

The Italian Invasion

In the early 1930s, the fascist dictator Benito Mussolini conjured up a number of reasons to invade Ethiopia. Certainly his desire to recreate the glories of the Roman past led him to seek lands to conquer and incorporate into an Italian Empire. He also sought to reverse the particularly bitter recollection of Italy's stinging defeat at the hands of the Ethiopians in 1896. At that time, Ethiopian Emperor Menelik II had repulsed the Italian imperialists at Adowa, inflicting severe losses and securing Ethiopia's independence. Mussolini in fact used the memory of the battle of Adowa as a rallying point for a fresh attempt at conquering Ethiopia. A handful of imaginary slights, a border controversy, and shopworn appeals to Ethiopia's need for "civilizing forces" furnished Mussolini the basis for invasion. In early October of 1935, Italian troops poured across Ethiopia's borders.

Desiring to avoid war and knowing he was at a military disadvantage, Ethiopia's emperor Haile Selassie turned to the League of Nations and its doctrine of collective security. But the League's limited response actually became a factor that hindered Ethiopia. The seemingly noble policy of refusing to sell arms to warring nations resulted in an underequipped Ethiopia suffering far more than the Italian war machine. Additional sanctions imposed by the League on Italy were mainly cosmetic, largely because they did not include an oil embargo. Oil was the one import Italy needed to keep its mechanized troops on the move.

Nevertheless, the experts of the day felt that the Italians had assumed a daunting task. They considered the climate and terrain of Ethiopia a match for the invading army. Italy's few, slow gains in the first weeks inspired joy and confidence among Ethiopia's supporters, and prompted Mussolini to switch commanders. But the happiness of Ethiopia's champions proved short-lived, as after the turn of the year Italian forces picked up steam in their drive toward Addis Ababa. The engineering corps made roads out of barren land, enabling Italy's mechanized power to push through toward the capital. Ultimately, the combination of a virtually unopposed Italian air force, superior weaponry, and Italy's use of poison gas enabled Italy to advance steadily.

Selassie also faced internal difficulties. Because Selassie had not claimed the throne without some degree of controversy and because he had to contend with traditions of ethnic loyalties, he could not claim unquestioned command of all Ethiopians.[3] The need for coalition building forced him to suffer the headstrong ways of some leaders of Ethiopian troops. Despite Selassie and his closest military advisers advocating a guerrilla campaign, certain commanders refused to abandon the tradition of meeting the enemy out in the open, face to face, man to man. Such military decisions left Ethiopian forces more vulnerable than necessary to the invading Italians.

African American Links with Ethiopia

As Italy had readied itself to invade Ethiopia, certain domestic factors in black America had helped prime African Americans to take a deep interest in the threat to this black sovereignty. The emergence of the "New Negro" in the 1920s had led to an increased assertiveness in displaying African American feelings and attitudes, and pent-up anger had been fed by continued racial oppression as well as by economic hardships that the Great Depression exacerbated in the early 1930s. In March 1935, Harlem erupted in riots. The

Scottsboro and Angelo Herndon cases continued to drag on, acting as steady symbols of injustice under white supremacy. Responses to the looming crisis in Ethiopia, then, were grounded at least in part in frustrations and concerns within black America.[4]

For black America, Ethiopia stood as a lonely symbol of black achievement, resistance, freedom, power, and ultimately the last, best hope of African independence. The smashing victory at Adowa, which had secured Ethiopia's independence while the rest of Africa fell under the rule of European powers, had forced the Western world to accord Ethiopia the status and privileges of an independent country. Indeed, the nation's 7,000-year tradition of independence held special symbolism for all those interested in black pride and freedom.

A number of specific links to Ethiopia further heightened concern for that land. Contacts with the kingdom had been fostered by Ethiopian diplomatic and educational missions sent to America in 1919, 1927, and 1930, and in return approximately one hundred black Americans emigrated to Ethiopia in the early 1930s. These missions raised the level of knowledge and awareness of Ethiopia in the United States and had, in the words of historian Joseph Harris, the "effect of reinforcing African American identification with Ethiopia and Africa." Further, as the woes of Liberia aired out in public in the late 1920s and early 1930s, the pomp and ceremony of Haile Selassie's coronation as Ethiopian emperor offered a far more pleasing symbol to African Americans.[5]

Religious connections to Ethiopia also permeated much of black America. With the term "Ethiopia" used as a generic reference for Africa in the King James translation of the Bible, the African American Christian community invested Ethiopia in its modern state with great import. Selassie reputedly traced his lineage to a liaison between King Solomon and the Queen of Sheba, and then obviously further back through those parties. The Ark of the Covenant reportedly resided in Ethiopia.[6] Most importantly, Psalm 68, a psalm of David that centers on God punishing the wicked while the righteous rejoice and sing praises, reads in part: "Princes shall come out of Egypt; Ethiopia shall soon stretch forth her hands unto God." According to Albert Raboteau, this passage stands as "without doubt the most quoted verse in black religious history." That the verse's precise meaning is obscure extends its explanatory range, but interpretations of the passage generally take it to represent God's promise to deliver the entire African race from oppression and to redeem Africa. African Americans seemed destined to be, then, part of God's chosen people. As one reader expressed to the *Afro-American*, school teachers and leaders should be teaching the glorious history of Ethiopia because this "will be a great factor in reviving the crushed souls of our race everywhere and in re-establishing such racial solidarity that when 'Ethiopia stretches forth her hand' we will be included."[7]

The religious connection could act as a double-edged sword, however. For those who had ultimate faith in God's plan, there really existed no need to help Ethiopia, for He would look after that country and its people. The previous defeat of the Italians at Adowa helped convince religiously devout persons that the Ethiopians again would hurl back the Italians and possibly trigger a worldwide redemption of blacks from white oppression. Francis Baker of Roxbury, Massachusetts, wrote that she had no fear because she knew God would ensure that the Ethiopians would win. Even when the Italians entered Addis Ababa, the editor of the religion section in the *Daily World* wrote that while the Ethiopians may not have a victory yet, one must look further over the hill. God had not let down Selassie; He might in due course allow the European nations to fight among themselves, and then their colonial possessions would be impossible to hold.[8]

Religious connections nevertheless spurred most African Americans to develop a deeper interest in the situation. Churches and church organizations offered both prayers and money for the Ethiopian cause. As the crisis heated up, churches set aside Sunday, 18 August 1935, as a Day of Prayer for Ethiopia. The Mt. Olive Methodist Church of Memphis held an all-night prayer vigil for Ethiopia. Ministers preached sermons on the situation. Reverend Father T. J. H. Alcantara of St. Ambrose's Church in New York entitled one Sunday sermon, "Choose ye now whether ye shall be actors or spectators in this Italo-Ethiopian drama." Church organizations condemned the Italian aggressions against Ethiopia and called upon the U.S. government to intervene to prevent war. Churches raised funds for the cause, and organizations established to help Ethiopia, such as the Committee on Ethiopia, had clergymen among their leading members.[9]

Religiosity even infused secular writings on the war. As war clouds darkened, under the banner headline "Troops Mass For War" the *Defender* offered a boldfaced note: "For an almost exact prediction of the present crisis in Africa and in the whole world today, we ask our readers to read the eleventh chapter of Daniel in the Bible. Here the prediction is made with most startling exactness, even to foretelling intervention of Eastern powers on behalf of Ethiopia."[10] The *Daily World* called Ethiopia the cradle of Christianity, observed that people had every reason to believe that Christ was a black man, and speculated that maybe God planned now to bring a new day for all people in the very cradle of Christian civilization. An *Afro-American* lead article noted that the Ethiopians had driven the Italians back seventy miles as they carried the Ark of the Covenant into battle. Perhaps the most evocative example of religion infusing the outlook on Ethiopia came from Miss B. B. Susaye of Chicago, who asked, "Who can tell but that Joe Louis and Haile Selassie and Jesus Christ aren't the same man? . . . I just believe He is on his return in this twentieth century in the form of these other heroes."[11]

Religiously inclined or not, African Americans routinely invoked a blood relationship between themselves and the Ethiopians as Italian saber rattling grew more menacing throughout 1935. African Americans increasingly articulated an expanded view of their conceptions of ethnicity and clearly included modern Ethiopians within their definitions of race. In fact, many promoted the idea of close kinship as they referred to Ethiopia as the "motherland" or the "fatherland." Bethune Robinson of Asheville, North Carolina, wrote to the *Courier* offering a prayer to Ethiopia, "my motherland," in which she characterized America as her "foster country." Alexander Keys urged African Americans not to be jovial on Halloween "while our black brothers and sisters of our Fatherland are being slaughtered by Italians and lynched by the American white man."[12] These letters show an obvious interest in Ethiopia, even as they also suggest that African Americans often did not distinguish areas of Africa in their thinking. The symbolism of the Ethiopian nationhood and the imagining of the African connection overrode any strict genealogical tracing. "I am deeply concerned in Ethiopia's well-being and why not?" wrote Cable Lockey of Lockland, Ohio, to the *Defender*. "Am I not one of the sons of African descent? My very soul is grieved for blood is thicker than water. . . . Listen if you please to the cry of our brothers, or are we not the same blood; Isn't it true that Italy is fighting us?"[13]

Feeling a close bond, any number of black Americans wrote about Ethiopia as though it were their own country. As one "Constant Reader" from Shreveport lamented, "We haven't sent nearly the money to our country as the Italians have." To help offset this deficit, Harry Rooks of Omaha suggested that the National Association for the Advancement of Colored People (NAACP) and various lodges raise at least a dollar per person "to help finance our Emperor to fight this war." Mrs. Wimley Thompson from Gallup, New Mexico, declared, "I'd like to go to Ethiopia and fight Italy. Why? Aren't these Ethiopians the same type of people who were stolen and made slaves, are they not the same people who suffered for our freedom? . . . Let every heart within a black man's body be with Ethiopia, the country which is ours."[14]

The issue of whether Ethiopians and African Americans had a blood relationship escalated into a full-fledged controversy, in which letters to the editor, columnists, and editorials all took to task people who theorized that Ethiopians actually were not African. Those who discounted Ethiopians as Africans, generally whites, argued that Ethiopians were of Arabic stock, with any African features coming from some minor miscegenation. This thinking received much more emphasis after the Italian defeat at Adowa, as white supremacists did not want an example of a European defeat at the hands of Africans blemishing their theories.[15] The *Afro-American*, on the other hand, stressed that Ethiopians had at minimum a heavy mixture of African blood and often seemed fully African. It concluded: "Maybe Dr. Osgood [a white 'expert' castigated in the editorial] can explain why one drop of colored blood in America makes a person colored (Virginia law), but in Africa natives with black faces, curly hair, flat noses, generous lips, and three-fourths African blood aren't African at all." Pride, interest, and hopes were invested in this independent black country. Du Bois straightforwardly sought to finalize the issue: "They are as Negroid as American Negroes. If there is a black race, they belong to it."[16]

Occasionally voices in black America questioned whether Selassie and the Ethiopian elite themselves felt ties to black Americans, but one sees little evidence during the wartime months that black Americans felt Selassie refuted an association with them. Much of any existing tension seems to have stemmed from Americans' use of the word "Negro," which Ethiopians viewed as a derogatory term imposed by whites. However, Ethiopian rejection of the term "Negro" did not imply a rejection of African Americans.[17] Selassie and his representatives sent out appeals for support to black Americans, met with black American delegations, and even encouraged black Americans with skills to emigrate to the country.[18] Black Americans, in turn, instead of seeing Africa as a place to "uplift," expressed rising pride and interest in contemporary Africa.

As the Italian threat charged interest in Africa, Ethiopia represented for many the hopes of an entire continent, its people, and its diaspora. Ethiopia even seemingly offered to play a potentially critical future role for black America. Just how it might do so remained open to debate, with letters to the African American press offering numerous scenarios. Perhaps at some unspecified time in the future an independent Ethiopia would act as a mediator on behalf of African Americans. Perhaps, if Jim Crowism grew increasingly worse, Ethiopia could be a sanctuary. Perhaps African Americans might be able to migrate to Ethiopia and establish themselves.[19]

The outpouring of letters to black newspapers, civil rights organizations, groups established to aid Ethiopia, and the State Department indicate clearly that blacks from throughout America felt racial connections and solidarity with the Ethiopians. In the final analysis, whether one believed that Ethiopia was the fountainhead of the diaspora, or believed that through Ethiopia God would call all blacks, or believed that as Africa's one true black-ruled country Ethiopia could be a safe haven for black people everywhere, such feelings caused an upswelling of concern about Ethiopia's fate. Further, in this crisis, modern Africa for the first sustained time became a source of pride and racial hope, rather than a place to uplift and redeem.

International Lobbying Efforts

African Americans, seeing the threat to Ethiopia as another step in the steady advancement of white supremacy throughout the world, initiated concerted efforts to influence international actors. Like white supremacy in America, Italian imperialism in Ethiopia had to be stopped. African Americans thus embarked on their broadest efforts to date to lobby worldwide policymaking organs. Indeed, blacks became the most important pressure group in America acting on behalf of Ethiopia. Yet they faced tremendous odds in prompting any U.S. government action to help rein in Mussolini. Further, they faced tensions over how extensively to pursue these efforts.

In taking action, African Americans struggled to overcome their traditional lack of influence in foreign affairs. Foreign policymaking, much more than its domestic counterpart, has tended to be concentrated in the hands of a small elite, and through this period few African Americans could be found in positions of power. In addition, lack of political power due to disfranchisement, gerrymandering, and minimal economic clout greatly hindered any ability to apply pressure on other institutions involved in foreign policy, such as Congress. Given the array of pressing issues facing black America, African American leaders generally chose to focus lobbying efforts on immediate domestic concerns and built no strong frameworks for lobbying on foreign policy. Such constraints hampered African American efforts to influence African policy, making it even easier for the foreign policy establishment in Washington to rank the concerns of black Americans dismally low on their scale of priorities.[20]

The low priority given to black American concerns coincided with pervasive disinterest toward Africa among the makers of foreign policy. During and after the late-nineteenth-century scramble for Africa, the U.S. government generally had followed the lead of European colonial powers regarding African affairs. Other than connections with Liberia, the United States had no territorial stake in the continent. Trade and investment were miniscule, especially after South Africa was subtracted from the totals. Few American nationals lived in Africa. Altogether, especially given their racial views, which showed little concern for the fate of black Africans, U.S. officials took little interest in Africa.[21]

There existed little basis to hope for official U.S. intervention in the Ethiopian crisis, and from the start the State Department made every effort to avoid any entanglement. In the aftermath of the border dispute at the Wal Wal oasis, which initiated the crisis in December of 1934, Wallace Murray, chief of the Division of Near Eastern Affairs, under which the State Department subsumed Africa at the time, warned that at some point Ethiopia might invoke the Kellogg-Briand Pact, whose signatories had pledged not to go to war with each other. If this occurred, Murray advised leaving the issue to the League of Nations and making "every effort to avoid having the matter dumped in our lap on the score that we were the original initiators of the Pact." The next day Secretary of State Cordell Hull cabled instructions to the American chargé d'affaires in Ethiopia, W. Perry George: "You should keep the Department fully informed of developments and scrupulously refrain from taking any action which would encourage the Ethiopian government to request the mediation of the United States."[22]

The American domestic mood increased the obstacles. Black Americans faced the prospect of prodding to action a nation in which determinedly pacifist, isolationist, and neutralist elements held tremendous influence. Fears that Mussolini's actions were a prelude to another world war contributed to passage of the Neutrality Acts of 1935 and 1936. Roosevelt himself may have wanted embargoes imposed in order to keep Mussolini at bay, but he recognized that sentiment in America prevented him from working actively to halt Italian aggression.[23] Thus, personal pleas like the one Cornelius Williams of Newark penned to Roosevelt fell on deaf ears. Williams lamented the law that prevented 12 million blacks from going to Ethiopia to help, and he decried the State Department refusal to press the Kellogg-Briand Pact: "I again beg that you do not allow yourself to be guilty of hiding behind a smokescreen, but give this twelve million American citizens a chance to help their brothers across the seas by the way of supplying arms and munitions, because you have already said that they cannot go in person. Please give Ethiopia a fair chance for her life by not putting or causing any embargo on arms and munitions. I ask this in the name of God."[24]

African Americans also found little support among the powers in the League of Nations. In March 1935, France and Britain suffered the shock of Hitler's open repudiation of the Versailles Treaty's disarmament clauses when he revealed the existence of a German air force and plans to build an army of a half-million. Fearful of the growing German threat, the two powers did not want to alienate Italy, and their concerns ensured that the League would not take forceful action against Mussolini.

No effective Western entity, then, welcomed efforts on behalf of Ethiopia, yet African Americans still tried. Starting in February of 1935, NAACP secretary Walter White corresponded extensively with Professor Manley Hudson, member of the NAACP board of directors and law professor at Harvard, about drafting protests against Italy's "attitude" and sending them to various officials. In March the NAACP called upon Secretary of State Hull to ensure that the United States would do everything possible to support the remaining independent states in Africa. A follow-up letter asked Hull to tell Italy that America "does not look with favor" upon her attempt to plunder Ethiopia and to remind Italy and Ethiopia of their commitments under the Kellogg-Briand Pact.[25] The NAACP's 1935 annual conference, held in late June, adopted a resolution unequivocally condemning Italian aggression in Ethiopia and vigorously urging the president and the State Department to voice publicly their disapproval of the Italian government's actions. It also urged the U.S. government to put itself squarely on record against encroachment. In line with these resolutions, on 3 July 1935 the NAACP sent telegrams to Roosevelt and Hull.[26]

Yet the State Department simultaneously was doing all it could to avoid taking any role in the dispute. George, the chargé in Ethiopia, informed Washington that on 4 July Selassie had summoned him to the palace and mentioned that even as he pursued League procedures he wanted to examine means of securing Italy's observance of the Kellogg-Briand Pact. The State Department counseled George to deliver a note telling Selassie that the United States felt the proper course to follow lay in Geneva.[27]

As tensions heightened, the NAACP considered sending a delegation to see Roosevelt and Hull in order to urge the government to denounce Italian aggression in Ethiopia, impose an arms embargo against both belligerents (under the mistaken presumption that it would hurt Italy more), and impose a ban on all government or private loans to Italy. In Walter White's thinking, whether or not Roosevelt and Hull did anything did not matter as much as the possible affect the delegation could have in helping crystallize public opinion against Italy. For this reason, he hoped to get Joe Louis to head the delegation. NAACP leaders recognized that Roosevelt could do far more with the weight of public opinion behind him, and the board of directors authorized a committee consisting of Walter White, Manley Hudson, and Lewis Gannett to explore possible courses of action.[28]

In trying to arrange the most powerful delegation possible, White solicited opinions on his proposed list: R. R. Moton, Frederick Douglass Patterson, John Hope, Mordecai Johnson, James Weldon Johnson, Mary McLeod Bethune, Carl Murphy, Robert L. Vann, Robert S. Abbott, P. B. Young, Congressman Arthur Mitchell, W. E. B. Du Bois, Carter Woodson, Rayford Logan, and representatives of various social, religious, and fraternal organizations. Charles Houston wanted organizations emphasized over individuals, arguing that institutions would lend more weight. Roy Wilkins advocated including more women. Yet other voices questioned the efficacy of arranging a delegation. Rayford Logan felt that preventing Italy from receiving any loans could have more practical effect. Lewis Gannett, member of the three-man steering committee, declared himself "almost opposed" to sending any delegation, as he felt the U.S. government should not be used as an international Don Quixote. As the summer progressed, the delegation floundered, with the NAACP unable to garner the commitments needed to make the delegation practicable.[29]

Further hampering NAACP efforts was the clash of personalities at work. This factor, one that would be repeated in following years and would tug at any development of pan-African solidarity, reared its head when White contacted Du Bois about being in the delegation. Du Bois, in the midst of his 1935 split from the NAACP, replied that he was about to leave on vacation and his time in the fall was fully occupied.[30]

The NAACP then joined others, such as the *Amsterdam News*, in urging the State Department to constrain Italy by insisting that Rome pay its debts to the United States. African Americans prodded the State Department to keep Italy in line by using the Johnson Act of 1934, which barred loans to any country that was in default on World War I debts. They faintly hoped that if the U.S. government forced Italy to repay its loans, Italy would then have no money to wage war on Ethiopia. White telegrammed the State Department to inquire whether Italy was in default under terms of the Johnson Act; it in fact was, but the State Department did not act. Yet these African American voices contributed to Secretary of State Hull's warning to the Italian ambassador that during the past months Hull had been urged to demand, aggressively if necessary, payment by the Italian government of loans made during and after World War I, so that Italy could not spend money conquering Ethiopia. Hull, however, never carried the threat further. Throughout the war, U.S. officials refused to use the economic levers at their disposal to pressure the Italians.[31]

African Americans, recognizing that the U.S. government was disinclined to act on behalf of Ethiopia, looked to other avenues for lobbying. Two Ethiopian aid organizations, the Provisional Committee for the Defense of Ethiopia and the Committee on Ethiopia, worked in conjunction with the American League Against War and Fascism to send the educator and historian Dr. Willis N. Huggins to Geneva to lobby the League of Nations. Huggins carried a petition urging the League to restrain Italy, to assure Ethiopia of the League's support, and to send a neutral commission to report on boundary disputes. The NAACP also contacted the League of Nations on several occasions, urging action to stop Italian aggression.[32]

The NAACP attempted a different gambit, too, trying to shame the Soviet Union into supporting Ethiopia by calling on Moscow to "put up or shut up" when it came to denouncing imperialism and speaking out against Italian aggression. With at least one powerful nation on her side, perhaps Ethiopia could resist the invasion. The Soviets, however, maintained more interested in promoting the "Popular Front" against Nazi Germany than in pursuing a forceful anti-imperialist line.[33]

By mid-July the Roosevelt administration had received plain warning that Italy intended to attack yet continued to temporize, despite the lobbying efforts of black Americans. In the critical weeks before Italy's invasion, the State Department actively worked to avoid any involvement. On 12 September, Hull instructed the chargé in Ethiopia to tell Selassie's government to await the outcome of the League of Nations' efforts before suggesting that some other peace machinery "be projected into the situation." The Roosevelt administration argued that any effort it made to mediate "might interfere with the efforts of the League." Hull reiterated this stance on 27 September, days before the start of the war.[34]

After hostilities began, the State Department cynically altered the explanation for not invoking the Kellogg-Briand Pact. Having pressed Selassie to delay any invocation of the pact, Hull now argued that the most opportune time to invoke the pact had passed — that a collective invocation of the pact or a conference on the subject should have been done before the outbreak of hostilities. He further noted that the pact contained no provision for signatories to act when a country broke its commitment. Just in case he had not covered all angles, Hull reiterated that any action using the pact as a basis might "seriously interfere with the League's program."[35]

African Americans thus had little chance of convincing the Roosevelt administration to act once the war itself started. Washington's response to the clear evidence of Italian atrocities, including the bombing of hospitals, made this even more apparent. After the Italians bombed a Seventh Day Adventist hospital in January 1936, the State Department responded to demands that it protest by claiming that as the hospital had no U.S. government authorization and as the organization operating it was not clearly and wholly American, there was "neither necessity nor any clear basis for protest." That same month the State Department received clear evidence of the Italians using mustard gas, but again it used legalistic footwork to avoid taking any action. In short, the Roosevelt administration left Ethiopia alone to face its fate.[36]

Shaping Diasporic Ties during the Crisis

As Italy massed its invasion forces, black Americans faced the central and ongoing issue of whether they should focus more or less exclusively on the fight against white supremacy in the United States or try to link their efforts with a more worldwide struggle. This debate played out in the pages of the black press. The *Courier*, for example, in mid-July 1935 editorialized that black America needed to keep money and resources at home; accordingly, the Ethiopians would have to go it alone. The paper condemned the "rash" of proposals to aid Ethiopia as mostly without merit and designed to line the pockets of the promoters; found resolutions and petitions "valuable solely as a method of blowing off steam"; and argued that because of the scarcity of food and clothing in Ethiopia, "Sending an Aframerican Expeditionary Force to Ethiopia, assuming the money for passage and equipment could be secured from a people who give but $50,000 yearly to fight for their citizenship rights, would prove almost as embarrassing as the Italian army to Selassie." Dismissing these methods of aid left the *Courier* to weigh the option of African Americans sending money directly. "Aframerica has a war on its own hands . . . a war against discrimination, segregation, disfranchisement, illiteracy, ignorance, shiftlessness, peonage, ruthless exploitation, bad housing, and bad health. It needs every dollar it can spare in this war right here." The *Courier* offered comparisons to show that people needed bread at home more than guns abroad: the cost of a machine gun would provide a black college student tuition for a year; the price of a bomb could win a court school segregation case or snatch a person from the shadow of the electric chair. The *Courier* offered militancy, but militancy trained on the home front. As the coup de grâce, the *Courier* concluded, "Much as we all sympathize with Ethiopia, it is evident that our burdens here are sufficiently heavy without assuming those of Negroes 7,000 miles away. It is noteworthy that, while our disabilities have been fairly well publicized throughout the world since Emancipation, no aid has ever come from our brethren across the seas. We have fought the battle alone and they will have to do likewise."[37]

The *Defender* similarly argued that people should worry about correcting domestic problems before worrying excessively about the situation in Ethiopia, let alone all of Africa. While moral support of Ethiopia was understandable, neither money nor manpower should be offered. African Americans might pray for Ethiopia, write letters of protest to the Italian embassy, even boycott Italian products, but black America's problems were not in Ethiopia. While troubled by the threat of the further spread of white supremacy, the *Defender* stood firm in maintaining focus on resolving racial discrimination in America. The *Defender* felt so strongly about this that in late July it offered a rare front-page editorial, "Why Go to Ethiopia?" This editorial questioned why young men and women would violate U.S. law by enlisting in a foreign military to fight a country with whom America was not at war, risk sickness and death, leave family and friends, "and go to a country in which you have neither friend, nor kin, nor common tongue": "You are wroth at Italy and at Mussolini — and you want to travel to far off Africa to repel an invasion of a country about which you know nothing and actually care less." The editorial offered explicit direction: "Go to Ethiopia? Why not fight at home? Is there not enough here to fight for? Why don't you fight lynchings, peonage, bastardy, discrimination, segregation? Why don't you fight for jobs to which you are entitled? Why don't you fight for your own independence? . . . if you have money to spend . . . if you have the desire to fight . . . why not dedicate both to the task of making America safe for Americans?" The editorial finally concluded, "Yes, you MUST think of Ethiopia. You MUST be world minded. You MUST realize that you have kinship with all peoples of the world — but above all, you MUST FIGHT to correct evils at home. Think this over, young men and women of America!" In short, the *Defender* told black Americans to think about international problems but not to act on those thoughts.[38]

These papers, reflecting the view that Du Bois condemned as "race provincial," clearly dissociated the situation in Africa from that in America. How to achieve equality in America always had been problematic for African Americans, and solidarity with contemporary Africa was not a leading method of choice. Most black Americans did not believe that their problems would be solved by international racial approaches. The domestic struggle trumped any international concerns; ties of condition or race did not bind.

Black Americans, still conditioned to see their relationship to Africa as one of helping to raise Africans out of paganism and savagery and to view themselves as more or less alone in the struggle against white supremacy, understandably could feel that events in Ethiopia distracted from the very real problems they faced. Indeed, the long-standing negative images of contemporary Africa still influenced African Americans to the point that they themselves commonly expressed their views by using images that white Westerners perpetuated about Africa. "Yes, sir, Ethiopia is weak and backward, perhaps, and despised by Italy . . ." prayed a deacon in the Abyssinian Baptist Church. "Those helpless tribes in Africa need aid and we Americans should do all that is possible," added a reader of the *Afro-American*. Ralph Matthews, a columnist for the *Afro-American*, in fact had to use his forum to castigate those in the theaters who laughed when they saw barefoot Ethiopians in the newsreels.[39]

Matthews notwithstanding, newspapers themselves continued as prime disseminators of such imagery. Although most papers believed in promoting pride in the African past, their views of the modern era remained predicated on the negative imagery of colonialist and missionary accounts, textbooks, and movies. The *Afro-American* included in its articles such morsels as Selassie having armed "an Ethiopian tribe that lives on raw rhinoceros meat"; reported that "wild tribesmen beg their chiefs for a chance to get to the front"; and recounted how "field hospitals are enough to inspire dread even among civilized persons." The rest of the press slipped into similar vocabulary and imagery. The *Courier* printed photos with captions about the "semi-barbaric" army of Selassie; the *Amsterdam News* referred to "savage chieftains"; the *Daily World* discussed how "the whir of big planes, the induction of poison gas and high pressure modern warfare startled and put to wonderment the unfortunate natives whose quiet had never been so disturbed." The cartoonists who sent their characters to Ethiopia had them encounter exotic animals, pygmies, and beautiful, scantily clad women. The papers at various moments promoted images of the Ethiopians as innocent savages deserving paternal protection or barbaric savages worthy of curiosity — even as these papers preached pride in black history.[40]

Pride in Africa's past had its proponents, but pride in the present remained much rarer. The idea of "civilization" continued to be a key stumbling block. Western ideas of civilization still established the lens through which African Americans viewed Africa, and accordingly most still saw modern Africans as, on the whole, semibarbaric. In fact, during the war the *Defender* even berated Ethiopians for not having adopted "white civilization": "[Ethiopia's] love of the shadow, her infatuation with and for useless rituals, her urge for pomp and ceremony, robbed her of that intensity of purpose which would have made for the development of the treasures which abound in her land. This flagrant disregard of the white man's definition of civilization makes her today the victim of her own short-sightedness."[41] One could take pride in the glories of an idealized past, but identifying with a contemporary group of people who allegedly lived on raw rhinoceros meat was harder. Many were not convinced that advocating solidarity with African peoples was the way to advance those in the diaspora.

So, even as interest in Ethiopia heightened, resonating through the community was the argument that African Americans needed to focus primarily on America and its problems. "It would be better if persons sponsoring the Ethiopian movement would organize to improve conditions in America," wrote Carrie Wilkins Elliott of Washington, D.C. She pointed out that money raised could help the NAACP and asked rhetorically if Ethiopians would fight lynchers in America. Harry Douglass of Jackson, Mississippi, declared that he was going nowhere, explaining, "For me, this is home. I am duty bound to stay here and protect the sacrifices my slave ancestors have made."[42]

People who argued that African Americans should remain focused on the situation in America undoubtedly felt events in Ethiopia were regrettable but believed involvement in them would have little bearing on what was happening in America. Philadelphian William Bishop voiced his view this way: "Instead of wanting to die for Africa, let us fight right here in America, and if necessary die for better conditions here." Frank St. Clair of Chicago observed that Ethiopians held no parades for black Americans, and asked, "When are we going to learn to fight our own battles here at home?" "Let us not be so anxious to claim relationship with the Ethiopians," warned Thomas Smith from Bethlehem, Pennsylvania, saying, "We are Americans and we have our own battles to fight." Summed up Rev. Taschereau Arnold: "While we may sympathize with our darker brother in Africa, we must not neglect our own blood in America . . . our more immediate problem concerns itself with the future welfare of the American Negro."[43]

Some black Americans worried, too, that white Americans would misinterpret support for Ethiopia. The old concern about "proving" one's loyalty as a way to "merit" full citizenship compelled the *Daily World* to be reassuring about black American loyalty: "While the Negro's sympathy may go out for Ethiopia as his traditional fatherland, there will never be an absence of genuine Americanism in his fabric. . . . His loyalty has always been unquestioned, and wherever his face was shown, beamed a spirit of true devotion."[44] The *Daily World* saw no need for black Americans to associate with Africa. In fact, the paper's overall position reflected the line of thinking that considered the war relatively unimportant and completely unrelated to the issue of rights in America. When it came time for the venerable tradition of "top ten" lists for the outgoing year, Lucius Jones, soon to become managing editor for the paper, ranked in order his top stories of 1935: Joe Louis, the changing of the administration at Tuskegee Institute, the death of the actor Richard Harrison, the Supreme Court sending the Scottsboro verdict back for retrial because African Americans had been excluded from the jury, and Jesse Owens. The Italo-Ethiopian "controversy" followed, in sixth place.[45]

Yet those who did not view the Ethiopian crisis in terms of pan-African solidarity faced a rising tide of racial interest in the Ethiopian crisis. Outpourings of black pride and race consciousness animated discourse about the war, with many black Americans demanding that stronger positions be taken in defense of Ethiopia. Historian William R. Scott has identified parts of black America that vigorously pursued support of Ethiopia: social-gospel clerics, such as the Reverend Adam Clayton Powell Jr.; avowed nationalists who often were ex-Garveyites, such as Captain A. L. King, president of the New York UNIA Central Division; leftist and nationalist scholars, such as Willis Huggins; political ideologues, such as communist leader James Ford; and certain newspapermen, such as Joel Rogers. These figures maintained close ties to poorer, less-educated African Americans, for whom the Ethiopian cause held particular meaning. Garvey's black nationalism had appealed to these people, and his regular use of the term "Ethiopia" to encompass all of Africa led many of his followers to identify with the name. Religious connections to Ethiopia also coursed strongly through this part of black America. Indeed, religion and nationalism combined to make the threat to Ethiopia register widely among working-class black Americans.[46]

By the time of the Ethiopian crisis, many of these black Americans felt frustrated by moderate leadership, and the rank and file pushed the leadership to adopt more vigorous stances. In the wake of Italy's invasion, one frustrated patron of the NAACP queried why the leaders "remain idle and let the golden opportunity pass to regain our Black Kingdom. . . . I ask you in the name of God, why can't we fight and win one war for ourselves? Think of the wars we have won for the white race."[47] Broader African American responses to the war dramatically cast into an international context the idea that one could promote black pride and black interests while still advocating a universalist cosmopolitanism that transcended racial categories. Many black leaders would wrestle with how they engaged and balanced these strands of thinking in upcoming years.[48]

Black Americans turned their attention to Ethiopia on a sustained level unmatched by that accorded any previous event in Africa. The eruption of war and its effect on African Americans prompted the *Courier* columnist Floyd Calvin to write that "the fever of 'race consciousness' spread like an epidemic" after the Italian invasion.[49] In the weeks following its cautionary editorial about focusing at home, the *Courier* received numerous letters taking umbrage with its position. Even more letters came repeating themes of racial solidarity and the desire to do something for Ethiopia. The *Defender* also found itself facing irate readers. Letters responded to the editorial "Why Go to Ethiopia?" with support for Ethiopia, offering sentiments of racial solidarity and a willingness to sacrifice blood and treasure. The letters pouring in crossed gender lines: women offered nursing skills, money, and prayers; men offered their fighting abilities—several declared they had fought in the Great War—as well as money and prayers.[50]

With many in broader black America reexamining their relationship with Africa, those in leadership roles had to hurry and shift positions in order not to be left behind. With its tradition of militancy and interest in the African past and with readers' correspondence encouraging it to rethink its stance, the *Courier* quickly shifted from urging caution and a focus on America to offering a more pan-African view. The new position: that as the last truly independent black-ruled nation in Africa, Ethiopia should be supported by those in the diaspora, who should send both material and manpower for the Ethiopians. After this adjustment, circulation rose dramatically, passing the 100,000 mark by mid-September. When the *Courier* sent Joel Rogers to Ethiopia as a war correspondent, circulation shot up by 25,000. When Rogers received an exclusive interview with Selassie, the issue sold an additional 25,000 copies. The *Defender* for its part started a feature on the proper pronunciation of Ethiopian words, which began, "Since interest in the Italo-Ethiopian feud has developed to a fever heat among our readers, ..." By the end of the year, the *Defender* had decided the most important event of 1935 was the Italian invasion of Ethiopia.[51]

The world of political cartoons picked up the mood. One cartoonist penned a drawing of an interested line of men gathered under the sign "Ethiopian Volunteers Register Here, P.A.R.A. [Pan-African Reconstruction Association]." The other half of the drawing had a sign that read, "Bulletin—2 Lynched in Mississippi; Florida Mob Hangs Victim," under which no one stood. Another cartoonist drew "A Light in the East!" with a clenched black fist over a mountain and the words "manhood, liberty, freedom, courage, equality" emanating from the rising light behind the mountain. In the foreground people of color, en masse, gazed at the scene.[52]

Answering the Call of Ethiopia

African Americans who promoted a pan-African solidarity with contemporary Africa projected themselves into the fight against European aggression in Africa. Increasing racial consciousness and solidarity reverberated in the calls to fight shoulder to shoulder with the Ethiopians. "I feel that it is my duty to answer the call of Ethiopia and shall endeavor to fulfill any job or position given to me, and give all that is in me to help the cause of the black race," wrote George Wood from Detroit. Similar statements coursed through the letters to the African American press. "I feel confident that thousands of Afro-Americans would gladly go to war and shed blood in defense of Ethiopia," declared Frank Ferrell, "for the call of 'blood to blood' has been made and the black man of America stands ready to answer that call." George Terry from Masontown, Pennsylvania, offered his services, proclaiming his willingness to "go and fight to the last to assist our people in this battle. The time has come for us to join together and do whatsoever duty calls for us to do." By claiming the solidarity of black people across the span of thousands of miles, these African Americans animated strands of thinking seen in earlier black nationalist and pan-African thought: the emphasis on unity, the desire for a strong black nationality, the promotion of black pride, the aim of ending white supremacy.[53]

Letters about volunteering for Ethiopia poured into the *Courier* from at least thirty-eight of the forty-eight states. In response, the *Courier* cabled Selassie about the possibility of African Americans enlisting on behalf of Ethiopia, reporting to its readers, "When Italy does declare war, it is just possible that thousands of black Americans, veterans of the World War, and sympathizers in the impending conflict will be wearing the khaki of Abyssinia. Last week, the *Courier*, realizing the intense interest Colored America is taking in the Ethiopian-Italian conflict, cabled Emperor Selassie to ascertain Ethiopia's attitude in connection with volunteering for service." But the legal obstacle to African Americans serving in Ethiopia — U.S. law prohibiting enlistment in a foreign nation's military to fight a country with which America was not at war — meant that any citizen accepting a commission to serve in Ethiopia's military could be fined up to $2,000 and imprisoned up to three years. Nevertheless, the *Courier*, on behalf of "the thousands of American Negroes, from every section of the country, who have not only volunteered to go to Ethiopia in case of war, but are willing to start an Ethiopian Defense Fund here," offered the hope that a special dispensation would be made.[54]

In linking arms with Ethiopia, African Americans also found a new role, recast from the old providential design theories that had them proving their capabilities while uplifting and redeeming Africans. Now African Americans would show their abilities while *working together* with Africans. Mobilizing a legion for Ethiopia would provide "an excellent chance for us to show whether we have guts in our abdomen or sawdust," wrote one reader of the *Afro-American*. Caldwell Jones of Los Angeles offered another approach, namely designating church collections on certain Sundays to go to Ethiopia in order to "raise $1,000,000 and attract the attention of the world."[55]

African Americans, with connections felt and hopes invested, rallied to support Ethiopia. People by the thousands turned out to hear speakers on the subject. On 3 August, 20,000–25,000 persons attended a demonstration in Harlem against Italian aggression. In late September, just before the war commenced, 8,000–10,000 people gathered in Madison Square Garden to listen to Du Bois, A. L. King, and Walter White discuss the situation. When Willis Huggins returned from his trip to the League of Nations in Geneva, 2,000 people turned out at the Rockland Palace in Harlem to hear him speak.[56]

News coverage heated emotions over the situation. Immediately after the war's outbreak, the *Courier* printed the banner front-page headline: "Babies, Women Slaughtered as Italy's 'War of Conquest' Rages in Ethiopia." Joel Rogers's dispatches provided readers with an African American perspective, even as they resorted to boosterism and sensationalism that at times echoed World War I propaganda.[57] Papers painted Selassie and the war on an epic scale. In October the *Defender* provided a large color photo of Selassie — billed as suitable for framing — under which the caption read, "The fate of civilization will be determined by his success or failure in defending his sovereignty against unprovoked aggression." Huggins declared that Selassie "is the greatest black man in the modern world, surpassing Toussaint L'Ouverture as the 'First of the Blacks.'"[58]

African Americans could hardly miss all the references to the Ethiopian situation. Cartoonists sent their characters off to Ethiopia, where they experienced wild adventures and fought dastardly Italians. Serialized fiction stories used Ethiopian motifs as central aspects of their plots. Papers printed poems from readers who praised the Ethiopians. Langston Hughes's "Ballad to Ethiopia" found its way into several publications. The *Afro-American* even centered its Christmas card for 1935 on Ethiopia, depicting an Ethiopian family holding weapons along with a poem lamenting that Christ could not be reborn in contemporary, bloody Ethiopia.[59]

The black press maintained a remarkably optimistic view on the situation up until the bitter end. In January, readers of the *Courier* learned that: "Its airplanes shot down like buzzards, its tanks trapped by ingenious Ethiopians, its officers picked off by lynx-eyed sharpshooters, its massed soldiery the victims of nerves and tropical diseases, Fascism admits it has bit off more than it can chew." The Italians accordingly had turned to bombing the sick and wounded, and soon they would turn to "the use of more horrible tactics, perhaps disease germs, poison gases, liquid fire, and death rays." Even as late as 4 April 1936, when Italian troops stood poised to capture Addis Ababa, the same readers learned that "Italy's campaign in Ethiopia is history's greatest military flop." That same day the *Amsterdam News* similarly scoffed at Mussolini's "exaggerated claims" that actually fooled some into believing he was successfully conquering Ethiopia.[60]

Such coverage and commentary helped lead to enormous, even unrealistic, hopes and expectations in black America. The Pan-African Reconstruction Association launched a drive for $10,000,000 and 20 million members. Wilbur Douglaston of Brooklyn felt sure that the Vatican would be leading prayers after Selassie and the Ethiopians wiped out the Italian armies and started to march on Rome.[61]

African Americans hoped that at minimum Selassie would decisively repulse the Italian invasion, mirroring Emperor Menelik's 1896 defeat of the Italians at Adowa. Selassie even vied for the hearts of African Americans with Joe Louis, who through the time of the crisis battered his way to the top of the heavyweight ranks. The intense pride and joy in Louis sweeping through black America welled from a deep desire for an internationally recognized hero who African Americans could call their own, and for a time Selassie's stature rose close to that of Louis.[62]

Victory by the Ethiopians would present to the world solid evidence refuting those who believed blacks somehow inferior. Further, it could even reverse the flow of white supremacy. "I pray for Ethiopia to win," wrote William Johnson of Jacksonville, "for in such a victory I see the dawn of a new day for the black race."[63] Indeed, success in Ethiopia might even spark a global challenge to white supremacy. "The stage is now set for what may turn out to be the most devastating of all world conflicts," according to the *Defender*. "Despite the pleas of the great powers who see the handwriting on the walls — the uprising of black people everywhere to throw off the yoke of white domination — Mussolini has kept true to his course. . . . If he [Selassie] is successful, then the salvation of the black man in the world scheme of things is assured." When hostilities broke out, Walter White felt that, "Italy, brazenly, has set fire under the powder keg of white arrogance and greed which seems destined to become an act of suicide for the so-called white world." People of color would "rise up against white people everywhere, especially Africa and the Far East," believed E. A. Abbott of Mobile.[64]

Given the potentially enormous stakes involved, and given their understanding of the world political economy and of geopolitical realities, African Americans speculated early on that Britain and France would conspire to use the League of Nations for their own ends. In this case, that meant abandoning Selassie and preventing effective action by the League against Italian aggression. Even before the war began, the *Crisis* surveyed the field and declared that the world's nations had left Selassie to fend for himself. The European powers, it argued, would not even let the Ethiopians buy the munitions they needed, for fear that the defeat of Mussolini would cause his dictatorship to collapse and bring chaos to Europe.[65]

After the war commenced, African Americans clearly articulated their beliefs that a conspiracy lurked among Europeans to ensure that the Italians would not lose. One path of analysis maintained that while Britain and France actually wanted no expansionism from Mussolini, they certainly did not want their colonial subjects to have the slightest hint of Africans successfully standing up to Europeans. The League's lack of action led the *Defender* to conclude that powers in the world body were "endeavoring to work out a plan to rescue Italy, which faces defeat in Ethiopia. . . . The League of Nations is well aware of the fact that there are millions of darker people who must not be allowed to become aware of the fact that they are being controlled by a handful of white men for economic and commercial advantages." A second line of analysis argued that fears in London and Paris of an ascendant Hitler meant that officials there primarily desired the cementing of Mussolini into an alliance opposing Hitler. If all this meant allowing Mussolini to grab Ethiopia, so be it. As the League continued to enact nothing other than ineffectual, token sanctions, the *Courier* pointedly asked whether Italy, Britain, and France had an agreement to ensure that Italy would not be defeated. Understandings of such geopolitical machinations directly contributed to readers praising the *Courier* for sending Joel Rogers as a war correspondent, as they believed that now the true story would be told. Perhaps a reader of the *Amsterdam News*, Paul Socker, best summed up the feelings of many African Americans when he wrote after the fall of Addis Ababa that the only salvation for people of color is "our ganging up — just as all the white countries have done to hasten the subjugation of Ethiopia."[66]

The race consciousness and solidarity evoked by Socker emerged in numerous forms through black America, providing evidence of the closeness many felt with Ethiopia's cause. North and south, people issued calls to patronize black-owned businesses and boycott products imported from Italy and stores owned by Italian Americans. Tensions between African Americans and Italian Americans caused police to double their numbers in Harlem. Despite the police presence, the two sides still clashed in the streets of New York, and when Mussolini's forces rolled across Ethiopia's border in October 1935, police had to add 1,000 extra officers and 300 detectives in Harlem and Brooklyn to quell disturbances. According to the *Amsterdam News*, few could have "foresee[n] a rising and militant spirit of race consciousness among colored peoples on four continents."[67]

Grassroots organizations, legitimate and otherwise, sprouted quickly to aid Ethiopia. The Friends of Ethiopia of Ansonville, North Carolina, for example, sent $1.25 to the Ethiopian consul in New York, while the Ethiopian Aiding Club of East Chicago sent $13.00.[68] The mushrooming number of aid organizations created genuine concerns over the legitimacy of these groups' efforts. In one of his first actions, John Shaw, named in July 1935 as Ethiopian Consul General in New York City, publicly called for suspending money- and volunteer-raising activities until organizations could be vetted. Shaw was not alone in wanting to end operations that lined the pockets of the organizers and in cautioning those impassioned by Ethiopia's plight to be careful with where they sent money. The *Afro-American*, for example, warned of scam operations, while Walter White advised associates that he knew of two reputable organizations for getting money to Ethiopian medical relief: American Aid for Ethiopia and Friends of Ethiopia. The U.S. Attorney General's office and the State Department investigated the actions of some aid organizations; no prosecutions took place, however, even though investigators collected evidence of illegitimate activities.[69]

Reputable churches and organizations existed, of course, and donations could be made safely to them. Continuing their longstanding multifaceted role in the African American community, churches helped raise funds, perhaps most prominently during the speaking tour through the northern United States by Lij Tasfaye Zaphiro, a secretary to the Ethiopian legation in London. Zaphiro launched his campaign on Christmas Eve at the Abyssinian Baptist Church in New York City, the church of the Adam Clayton Powells, and 3,000 to 4,000 people attended. His tour then continued on to several major cities, where he usually spoke and raised money at churches.[70]

The main organizations specifically created to aid Ethiopia were centered primarily in New York City: the Provisional Committee for the Defense of Ethiopia, the Committee for Ethiopia, the Friends of Ethiopia, the American Committee on the Ethiopian Crisis/American Aid for Ethiopia, the Medical Committee for the Defense of Ethiopia, and the United Aid for Ethiopia alliance. Other previously established groups, such as the Pan-African Reconstruction Association, turned their interests almost completely onto the Ethiopian crisis. Outside of New York, the most important organization was the Washington, D.C.–based Ethiopian Research Council. Black Americans established and operated all these organizations except for the Committee for Ethiopia and the American Committee on the Ethiopian Crisis/American Aid for Ethiopia, which were interracial organizations dominated by white philanthropists, religious leaders, and journalists.[71]

Over the course of the war these groups and others formed various formal and informal alliances as they sought to subscribe volunteers as well as solicit money and supplies. When it became clear that the U.S. government would actively discourage sending volunteers, that Ethiopia needed money and munitions more than manpower, and that the estimated cost to send a volunteer to Ethiopia had reached a prohibitive $350 per person, these organizations then concentrated mainly on raising money and medical supplies. The varying degrees of success that their efforts achieved speak to the complex and evolving relationship of the day.[72]

The War's End and the Evolving Relationship

In early 1936, Italian troops moved slowly but steadily toward Addis Ababa. Italian victories in a series of battles allowed strategic heights and passes to be captured, all but clearing the way to Addis Ababa. Selassie tried to rally a defense of the capital until the rains fell and bogged down the Italians, but his scattered and demoralized forces mounted little opposition. By late April only a matter of days remained before the Italians would enter the city, leaving Selassie with two options: retreat into the rugged mountains of western Ethiopia, establish his government there, and wage guerrilla warfare; or, escape to the French colony of Djibouti, and from there go into exile in Europe, with the faint hope of either rallying the League's help or someday returning under favorable circumstances. Selassie listened to the pleadings of his family and influential advisers and chose to establish a government in exile. In early May, a few days after Selassie's departure, Italian forces captured Addis Ababa.

The war had reverberated throughout black America, as the outpouring of letters and emotions plainly show; at the same time, we should recognize that the story underneath these real and important responses is fraught with complexities. Black Americans, wrestling with the evolving relationship with contemporary Africa, were not all of the same mind. Black Americans had offered strong displays of pan-African solidarity as they volunteered, raised funds, and lobbied on behalf of Ethiopia during the war. Yet assessing the extent and character of the links also reveals notable limits on these activities.

Selassie and his government officials had issued numerous appeals for material donations, specifically for medical supplies and money for armaments; yet, good intentions ran higher than actual support. Emotionally and vocally, African Americans generously supported Ethiopia, but actual material backing, especially in the midst of the Great Depression, was more than most would deliver. Calls for every African American to donate one dollar, in order to raise approximately $12 million, garnered choruses of support but made little substantive progress. When Zaphiro spoke to the 4,000 people at the Abyssinian Baptist Church, the collection for the Ethiopian cause totaled just $300. Frustration over the fundraising effort had become apparent even before the war ended. In March 1936 the *Courier* excoriated African Americans for not donating more money. The paper's political cartoonist penned "The Phantom Ship," in which the apparition of a ship labeled "Afro-American Aid to Ethiopia" hovered near a pier. Selassie waited there, saying, "I don't understand. They talked so much of sending aid." The *Amsterdam News* lent support to the sentiment, declaring, "Negroes who say that they revere and love Ethiopia for her valiant stand against the Roman robbers ought to do something about it." The *Courier* continued to criticize African American support, chastising the community for preferring to "invest its money in numbers slips, bridge trophies, and railroad fare to conferences and conventions." It even claimed that black America produced "not enough funds to purchase a bombing plane, although Negroes here were more vociferous than any in the world." The *Courier* did not note the irony that just a year earlier it had advised against sending money because the cost of a machine gun could provide a black student college tuition.[73]

In April 1936, desiring to improve fundraising efforts, the *Courier* even had written to John Shaw about establishing its own fundraising arm. The money would be sent to Ethiopia along with an "Ethiopian Roll of Honor" listing the names of all contributors. This would serve as "tangible evidence of the American Negro's kinship with Ethiopia." Shaw acknowledged with gratitude the newspaper's efforts. Unfortunately, the Italians captured Addis Ababa as the campaign began, forcing the *Courier* to declare that it would hold donations in a trust until Selassie or his authorized representative called for the funds; if the *Courier* found that it was impossible for the money to aid Ethiopia, it would return the money to contributors. Over the course of the next few months the *Courier* periodically updated the Roll of Honor until the campaign slowly faded away.[74]

Furthermore, given that the expense of bringing ordinary volunteers across the Atlantic far outstripped any resulting benefit, Ethiopia had wanted specialized personnel such as aviators and medical doctors. John Shaw claimed that more than 2,000 persons inquired about going to Ethiopia as physicians and nurses, yet no medical personnel ventured abroad.[75] The African American presence in Ethiopia ultimately devolved to two aviators. The first, Col. John "The Brown Condor" Robinson of Chicago, lent valuable service to Selassie. The second, Harlem-based Hubert "The Black Eagle" Julian, provided nothing more than problems.[76]

As Ethiopia's fortunes waned, most African Americans slipped back into worrying about life in America. After Addis Ababa fell and Selassie went into exile, news coverage of Ethiopia and Africa fell precipitously. Interest surged briefly when Selassie went before the League of Nations, where he berated member nations for abandoning Ethiopia and tried to secure support for a free and independent Ethiopia, but interest soon subsided again. Lynching, poll taxes, white primaries, and segregation all needed to be fought. Daily life had to be lived. After Selassie spoke before the League, the front page of the *Amsterdam News* typified the changed response to Ethiopia. An article reprised the essence of Selassie's eloquent words, highlighting the fact that this was the first time a head of state had personally addressed the League. The issue's banner headline, however, was, "Louis And Marva Deny Love Row Caused K.O. By German."[77]

In the final count, the Medical Committee for the Defense of Ethiopia raised several thousand dollars, shipped a fifty-bed hospital unit, and sent medical supplies; American Aid for Ethiopia sent a ton of medical supplies, an ambulance truck, and $2,000; United Aid for Ethiopia sent $2,000 worth of medical supplies. The "Ethiopian Role of Honor" raised several hundred dollars. These were significant numbers in the middle of the Great Depression, but by way of comparison, Italian Americans in the New York City area raised $500,000 for the Italian Red Cross by the end of 1935. In the end, the American Red Cross raised more funds for Ethiopia than any other organization.[78]

Several factors constricted the actual supply of personnel and material. Legal concerns about black Americans enlisting for Ethiopia plainly worked against the sending of personnel. Also, mired in the midst of the Great Depression, no group was in a worse position to support a cause, either abroad or at home. Donating a dollar to an Ethiopian fundraising campaign often constituted a deep personal sacrifice. And for many black Americans the issue of where one's limited funds should go, to the war in Ethiopia or the struggle in America, was a dilemma not easily resolved.

In a world of limited resources, concerns over the efficacy of focusing efforts on the situation in Ethiopia dampened support. While virtually all black Americans opposed the Italian aggression, one could justifiably question whether it was best to help the black struggle in America by sending money to Ethiopia. Despite all the interest in Ethiopia's fate, that nation existed thousands of miles away from the very real discrimination African Americans felt in their daily lives. Organizations closer to home, be it the NAACP or the Urban League or any number of other groups, needed support too. In every newspaper, editorials advocated donations to underfunded domestic causes, so at every turn someone or something needed money. In such circumstances diverting resources became hard, even for those who believed that Ethiopia deserved help. Walter White, for instance, in declining a request by the International Press Service director to contribute money for sending an African American war correspondent to Ethiopia explained: "While the

NAACP would like very much to see a colored correspondent in Ethiopia, for the prestige it would give the race, it is faced by so many tasks at home which call for all the funds it can raise that the NAACP regrets its inability to assist in the raising of this fund to send a correspondent to Africa."[79]

Established civil rights and social welfare groups, including the NAACP and the Urban League, in fact provided significantly less material support for the Ethiopian cause than did the organizations that sprouted in direct response to the crisis. Once the actual fighting began, the NAACP largely discontinued its efforts to aid Ethiopia.[80] Concerned primarily with the rights and welfare of black Americans, these organizations did not create structures within their institutions for questions concerning Africa. They instead handled African issues on an ad hoc basis, with the result being, as future years would bear out, a limited capacity for wielding influence on issues relating to Africa.

Solidarity with Africa in fact seemed to some to go against the integrationist ideals for which they fought in America. The *Defender*, for instance, believed in the importance of promoting black pride but saw black solidarity across borders as much more problematic. During the Ethiopian crisis, black nationalist beliefs and universalistic integrationism generally remained separate currents, with the latter a far more predominant ideal. On the other hand, the Ethiopian crisis and the subsequent quarter century of African struggles for independence would play a critical role in fostering "nationalistic integrationism."

While support for Ethiopia did not lead to universal feelings of solidarity, at the same time the outpouring of sentiment during the war clearly reveals an increased consciousness of contemporary Africa and an increasing respect for Africans of the day. Organizing, volunteering, fundraising, and lobbying efforts on behalf of Ethiopians all indicate a reservoir of as well as a growth in pan-African commitment in black America. Despite Italy's success in capturing Addis Ababa and forcing Haile Selassie into exile, the Ethiopian resistance offered a deep source of pride for black Americans.

During the Ethiopian crisis, one sees the stirring of a new commitment to contemporary Africa, with African Americans more involved in African affairs outside Liberia than ever before. Spurring African American interest in international affairs, the war marked an important step in generating broader participation and efforts in foreign policy lobbying vis-à-vis Africa.[81] Even after Addis Ababa fell, black Americans continued to try to influence events on the international stage. With Selassie in exile in England, another diplomatic initiative crossed the Atlantic. In the summer of 1936, three African Americans traveled to see Selassie: Dr. Philip Savory, treasurer of United Aid for Ethiopia and co-owner of various businesses, including the

Amsterdam News; Reverend William Imes, pastor of New York City's St. James Presbyterian Church and member of the board of United Aid for Ethiopia; and Cyril Phillips, an activist for Ethiopia also involved in United Aid for Ethiopia. They planned to encourage Selassie to tour the United States and to find out the best ways for African Americans to help continue the war effort.

Not until the delegation reached England did the State Department catch wind of the mission. At that point, Washington worked to discourage Selassie or even an appointed representative from coming to America to spearhead fundraising efforts. The State Department used the pretext that the upcoming presidential elections made a visit by Selassie unadvisable, as he would receive "scant attention" and not achieve the desired results. H. Murray Jacoby, the U.S. special ambassador to Selassie's coronation in 1930, was briefed to impress upon Selassie "the futility of making a visit to the United States at this time." When it appeared that Selassie might send as his representative the Ethiopian ambassador to Britain, Azaj Martin, the State Department informed Martin that his visit would contradict the spirit of U.S. neutrality laws and that public knowledge of the government's feelings about a fundraising visit by him surely would affect Martin's enterprise adversely. The State Department also worked on the western side of the Atlantic to deter a visit by Selassie. People interested in inviting the emperor were called in and pressed to end their endeavors. Undeterred, the African American delegation continued working to facilitate the sending of an Ethiopian representative. In the end, Dr. Malaku Bayen — a cousin and adviser to the emperor, graduate of Howard University's Medical School, and husband of an African American — came to America as "His Majesty's Special Envoy for the Western Hemisphere."[82]

During the course of the war and its aftermath, then, African Americans had sought to influence national and international policymakers in numerous ways. Telegrams to President Roosevelt, Secretary of State Hull, Soviet Foreign Minister Litvinov, and the League of Nations, delegations sent to Geneva and Washington, and mass rallies all contributed to the effort to convince Washington and others to support Ethiopia. The fact that African Americans worked against a tide of neutralism, fears of entanglement in the affairs of the League, and a racism that left policymakers little concerned with the fate of Africans meant these efforts yielded few specific successes. However, the intensity of black reaction "helped considerably in arousing a general American sympathy for Ethiopia."[83]

Most critically, the war marked the point at which, on a broad basis, African Americans projected themselves into the affairs of contemporary Africa while taking pride in that relationship. The invasion of Ethiopia nurtured the engagement of Africa's present and its relationship to black Americans. Developing a wider pan-African perspective, broader black America increasingly associated with things African and connected African Americans with contemporary Africa. Indeed, the threat to Ethiopia offered a wonderful rallying point around which black pride and unity could be promoted. The *Courier* had responded to the more racially minded and pan-African-oriented parts of black America when it reshaped its stance to one urging physical support for Ethiopia. Similarly, the *Amsterdam News* explicitly linked the fates of African Americans and Ethiopians when it launched the new year of 1936: "Negroes in America, whose heritage and destiny is interminably linked with those of the heroic Ethiopian people, should be shocked — shocked to action. That action should assume immediate form and bring Selassie a flood of contributions to provide new Red Cross units, hospitals and medical supplies." African Americans did not want the final chunk of clearly independent Africa to be rolled up under white colonialism, for no one relished the thought of more subjugation at the hands of whites.[84]

The view that black America and contemporary Africa had ties, ones that made Ethiopian independence of deep concern, continued after the war ended, when there came numerous expressions about how this sordid episode should cause the diaspora to close ranks. Charles Mitchell, a former U.S. diplomat in Liberia, declared after the fall of Addis Ababa, "This latest outrage on Ethiopia should certainly pull the Negroes of the world together for the common welfare." The *Amsterdam News* concluded its lament on the fascist victory by announcing, "All Negro nations may perish within our generation, yet we should learn one lesson from the tragedy of Ethiopia: RACIAL UNITY!"[85]

The basis for interest in contemporary Africa was shifting away from one of "uplift" to one of a mutuality of interests, completely dissipating any turn-of-the-century notion that European colonialism benefited Africa. The war in fact prompted African Americans to read and learn more about Africa, and thereby understand more fully that in the past images of Africans often had been distorted.[86] This understanding, in turn, would help reshape their future relationship with Africa. Whereas before the war most African Americans felt they had little to learn from contemporary Africans, after the Ethiopian crisis African Americans increasingly started taking direct lessons from modern Africa. This appreciation ranged from the need to stand together with more unity to finding virtue in being black — lessons intended for and promoting of a racially conscious people. The *Courier*, for instance, found two important lessons: one, that if Ethiopians, a people divided by three major religions, could unite, then African Americans should be able to unite more easily; two, that the Ethiopians' courage in fighting in the face of such huge odds should inspire African Americans. As one *Courier* editorial put it, "Would that the Negroes in America were willing to sacrifice as much for their manhood rights." The *Amsterdam News* aimed a lesson ostensibly at children, but clearly intended it for their elders too: "[Y]ou, as a child, can make up your mind from the example of the Ethiopians that it is possible for you to do as much as any white person, even though you may not get the credit. In other words, children, you must grow up to be proud of yourself and your race." And finally, the *Defender* made clear its pride in Selassie and Ethiopians, declaring: "The Ethiopian has never tried to be white. Unlike the American black people he finds virtue in being black. Think about him, read about him, and your thought will be lifted to appreciate his value of manhood."[87]

Drawing lessons from the contemporary African experience constituted a new chapter in the African American relationship with Africa. Even during the heyday of Garvey, African Americans did not so much learn from contemporary Africans as view the continent as a place where they would arrogate a primary role in uplifting and building a powerful black nationality. The next quarter century crystallized the growing willingness to absorb lessons from modern Africa and to use contemporary Africa as a source of solidarity, courage, and black pride — vital components in the reconceptualized role of Africa in the lives of black Americans.

2

IN WORLD WAR AND COLD WAR
Configuring Anticolonialism and
Internationalism, 1941–1950

World War II has given to the Negro a sense of kinship with other colored — and also oppressed — peoples of the world . . . he senses that the struggle of the Negro in the United States is part and parcel of the struggle against imperialism and exploitation in India, China, Burma, Africa, the Philippines, Malaya, the West Indies, and South America.

Walter White, A Rising Wind *(1945)*

While Negroes in Dixie were struggling to do something about conditions here and now, Mr. [Paul] Robeson was lavishing his attention on an outfit called the Council on African Affairs. While his people in Mineral Wells, Tex., and Bessemer, Ala., and Waycross, Ga., were battling as best they knew how and yelling for help, Mr. Robeson was writing and talking about Africa, singing Russian work songs, and dispensing the comfort-to-be when and if the Soviet cabal replaced the Talmadge-Rankin cabal.

The Crisis *(May 1949)*

Italy's victory in 1936 resulted in five years of fascist rule in Ethiopia, as well as the moral bankruptcy of the League of Nations. To the distress of African Americans, fascism seemed on the rise around the globe: Italy, then Germany, followed by Spain. So as the world moved from the specific fascist invasion of Ethiopia into a general world war, African Americans' particular concerns about Ethiopia expanded to a broad antifascism as well as a strong anticolonialism. During World War II, African Americans often connected the fight for equality in America to the struggle for independence by people of color throughout the world.

The broad anticolonialism of the war years carried into the immediate postwar years. The war shattered myths of white invincibility, partly because of the capitulation of the colonial powers of Belgium, France, and Holland to the Germans, and partly from early Japanese victories against Britain, France, and the United States. Colonial powers clearly had been weakened while nationalism in the Third World grew stronger; the tide seemed to be turning against the rule of the colonizers. As the victorious Allies established a successor to the failed League of Nations, black Americans lobbied for the U.S. government to affirm the equality of all races and to work for international trusteeships and rapid decolonization.

The rhetoric and changes of the war and immediate postwar years helped promote an expanded internationalist perspective among African Americans. Colonial struggles that moved toward success, in places such as India, particularly impressed them.[1] They believed racial changes would occur globally and willingly identified with liberation struggles in Asia and Africa. Leaders of the major African American rights organizations expressed solidarity with the struggles of colonial peoples around the world.[2]

Yet in a dual shift during the late 1940s and early 1950s, this growing internationalist perspective reverted to a domestic focus, while specific links between the black freedom struggle in America and the rising Third World nationalism largely slipped away into a more vaguely constructed and pursued anticolonialism. Although most African Americans remained in support of decolonization, the view that this was intimately linked to their own fight for freedom and equality faded. African Americans, emphasizing universalist ideas about the essential equality of all humans, tended to downplay racial connections with Africa. African American anticolonialism became packaged as part of an integrationist agenda that affirmed human equality and minimized racial differences. At the same time, in the ongoing debate over where to train attention and resources, perceived racial progress in America seemed to indicate that focusing domestically and working with the Truman administration and white America would yield long-hoped-for results. Perhaps most importantly, international forces worked to fray African American linkages with Africa. The Cold War created a pressure to support Truman's foreign policy, along with a felt need to conform and show patriotic colors. Black Americans, like most groups in the country, sought to emphasize their "Americanness" during the early Cold War years.

As African American leaders generally emphasized anticommunism over anticolonialism, they reconfigured and largely decoupled African American connections to the worldwide struggle for freedom and equality. Civil rights leaders found they could use the issue of anticommunism as a lever to press for rights in America or to argue against colonialism in Africa, yet these arguments typically were disconnected from each other. And as support for Africa devolved into merely another anticommunist issue, transatlantic links frayed further: Africa as a tool provided little basis for race consciousness. It is no coincidence that a low point of African American relations with Africa occurred at the height of Cold War tensions during the late 1940s and early 1950s. By the end of the 1940s, beyond a broad concern about colonialism, few strong ties existed between black America and contemporary Africa. Other than the radical left, African Americans showed little concrete interest in helping emerging African liberation struggles. It would take the force of African struggles achieving success, along with the demise of McCarthyism and advances in the black freedom struggle in America, for African Americans once again to reshape their views.

World War II, African Americans, and Africa

Turning from the Italian assault on Ethiopia to a world sweeping toward war, African Americans remained much more internationally aware than they had been before the Ethiopian war. Anticolonial sentiment continued to infuse the community, and specific links with contemporary Africa continued to be laid. In January of 1937, Paul Robeson and Max Yergan spearheaded the establishment of the International Committee on African Affairs (ICAA). Robeson by then was a world-renowned performer, while Yergan was a religious and social worker who had been in South Africa from 1920 to 1936 as a representative of the YMCA. Five years after its founding the ICAA renamed itself the Council on African Affairs (CAA) and became one of the most important voices for Africa in the United States during the next decade. Robeson credited increased African American solidarity with other people of color to the fascist invasion of Ethiopia, remarking that since then, "the parallel between his [the African American's] own interests and those of oppressed peoples abroad has been impressed upon him daily as he struggles against the forces which bar him full citizenship, from full participation in American life." As the 1930s continued, increased internationalism also manifested itself in African American enlistment in the Abraham Lincoln Brigade fighting in the Spanish Civil War. The fascist invasion of Ethiopia, the Spanish Civil War, and then World War II itself channeled African American internationalism toward a broad antifascism and anticolonialism.[3]

World War II had, as many scholars make clear, a tremendous influence in shaping African American lives and their struggle against discrimination and segregation. Yet this impact cut both ways when it came to their relationship with Africa. On the home front, numerous changes in African American life coalesced during the war. The decline in southern agriculture combined with wartime labor shortages in defense industries to prompt the migration of thousands upon thousands more black Americans to northern urban centers. Greater employment expanded the still tiny black middle-class, and in urban areas the black vote aided the growth of black political power. From the March on Washington Movement to the NAACP's legal strategies, African Americans struggled in numerous ways throughout the war to end job discrimination, lynching, unequal provision of public services, the poll tax, white primaries, the mistreatment of blacks by police, and segregation in the military.[4]

The rhetoric of fighting the war to restore freedom and destroy racism heightened black pressure for changes at home and forced white Americans to examine their own racial policies. Because the Nazis based their doctrines on the supposed superiority of the Aryan race, the fight against Nazism also became a fight against ideas of racial superiority. The scientific racism of the late nineteenth and early twentieth centuries lost respectability while the gap between America's declared principles about democracy and Americans' practice of them became more fully exposed. As white Americans learned about the wholesale atrocities inflicted by those operating with theories of racial superiority, the issue of race was raised, in the words of scholar Paul Lauren, "in a way that nothing in history ever had done before." As the world moved into the postwar years, the mounting evidence of Nazism's horrors would prod further reflection on the meaning of racial equality and the consequences of extreme racial prejudice. The war, then, helped create conditions favorable to the reception of Gunnar Myrdal's *An American Dilemma*, which in turn helped establish a liberal orthodoxy around the ideas of integration, equal opportunity, social engineering to repair the damage of racial discrimination, and educational campaigns to reduce race prejudice.[5]

Internationally, the war also spurred further interest in world affairs. Journalist Roi Ottley prefaced his 1943 book on black America by declaring that African Americans "are feeling a great resurgence of racial kinship to other colored peoples of the world." The militancy of black protest opinion during World War II helped lead to a stronger anticolonialism, and this anticolonialism then became a way to affirm and broaden the antiracist struggle.[6]

Anticolonial thinking permeated the African American leadership, which generally adopted an international orientation toward the race problem. A. Philip Randolph, for example, announced in 1944 that his March on Washington Movement demanded a free Africa, Asia, and America, and intended to link "the interest of the Negro people in America to the interest of Negroes all over the world."[7] In April of the same year, the Council on African Affairs sponsored a conference, "Africa — New Perspectives," that brought together representatives of the black American community interested in Africa and African nations. The conference arose out of a dialogue between the CAA's officers and the Division of African Affairs in the State Department, which stated that it would welcome an expression of views about U.S. relations with Africa. At the conference, over one hundred people called on the U.S. government to support progress for Africans and other colonial peoples consistent with the Atlantic Charter.[8]

By 1944 the CAA had become an important voice in the African American engagement with Africa. Initially organized by men who held internationalist perspectives and felt strong antipathy toward fascism and colonialism, the CAA had been energized by the addition of Alphaeus Hunton Jr. to its executive council in 1943. Born in Atlanta in 1903, Hunton had parents who had inculcated in him from an early age an internationalist vision. His father, William Alphaeus Hunton Sr., had traveled internationally as the YMCA's first paid black secretary, while his mother, Addie Hunton, had traveled abroad during her career as an activist for black rights and women's rights. His parents had helped instill in him a specific interest in Africa, too, which perhaps is most tellingly exemplified by his mother's service as a principal organizer for the 1927 Pan-African Congress in New York City. In the 1930s Alphaeus taught English at Howard University while completing his doctorate in English at New York University. During this period he increasingly involved himself in politics, joining the National Negro Congress in 1936 and serving on its national executive board. Sometime during this period he joined the Communist Party, remaining a member for the rest of his life. In 1943 he came on board as the CAA's educational director and editor of its journal *New Africa*.[9] Robeson, Yergan, and Hunton would be the CAA's leading figures at the height of the council's influence from 1943 to 1947, yet other notable African American members in that period included Charlotta Bass, Mary McLeod Bethune, W. E. B. Du Bois, E. Franklin Frazier, Alain Locke, Rayford Logan, Adam Clayton Powell Jr., and Channing Tobias.[10]

The CAA's primary leaders situated their interest in Africa within a leftist internationalism. Historian Penny Von Eschen clearly establishes links among diaspora intellectuals for an anticolonialism that believed "the bonds black Americans shared with colonized people were rooted not in a common culture but in a shared history of the racism spawned by slavery, colonialism, and imperialism." Yet even as CAA leaders placed the anticolonial struggle in the context of a broad history and the worldwide political economy, at the same time they specifically promoted strong connections with Africa and concerns for its problems. The CAA and its more prominent proponents, particularly Robeson, illustrate that radical internationalism could be blended with a black nationalism, with its emphasis on racial consciousness and unity.[11]

When the CAA clarified its immediate objectives in 1943 — disseminating accurate information concerning Africa and its peoples, giving concrete help to the struggle of the African masses, influencing the adoption of government policies designed to promote African advancement and freedom and to preserve international peace — these objectives coincided with broader black American concerns and international approaches of the day. The CAA pursued an anticolonialism that emphasized Africa, and with this blending it maintained an important substream within the broadly anticolonial perspective felt by African Americans. African Americans supported improving social and economic conditions in Africa and advancing the political liberation of African nations.[12]

Still, most African Americans grounded their anticolonial interest in the desire to fight white supremacy and doctrines endorsing racial superiority rather than in a material analysis of the world's political economy. Most black Americans felt chary of leftist, specifically communist, elements. This did not arise just in the post–World War II years, when associating with communism opened oneself and one's organization to persecution. By the time World War II ended, the relationship between African Americans and the Communist Party already had an involved, complicated history. Communists had held a special appeal for blacks, due not least to their advocacy of and willingness to fight for the end of discrimination. Any number of black Americans, from cultural and literary figures to activists in the labor movement, maintained membership in, close association with, or loose alliances with the Communist Party during the 1930s and into the 1940s. Indeed, early southern civil rights organizers working in concert with the left, and often as members of the Communist Party, played crucial roles in advancing the struggle for civil rights during the Popular Front era. Yet of course the Communist Party never held broad support among African Americans, even at the height of its popularity during the 1930s. Internal beliefs and dynamics in black America, including disagreement with the atheism of communism and the experience of Communist Party policy shifts on racial questions, and not merely fears of reprisals influenced the relationship. Such factors must be taken into account when considering the complicated nature of the African American relationship with the left, and the reluctance by most to ally with leftists throughout this era.[13]

At the same time, in the mid-1940s black nationalism and pan-Africanism did not drive African American anticolonialism. Garveyism had ceased to be a major force in black American life, the Pan-African Congresses of Du Bois had petered out in the 1920s, and the options of returning to Africa or creating a separate black nation in America hardly entered widespread discourse. The Ethiopian crisis had sharpened African American sensibilities about white supremacy in Africa and had promoted broad anticolonialism, but it had not specifically reignited a continuing black nationalism. While "[t]he black quest for full citizenship in matters affecting the foreign interests of the United States is often viewed as linked to traditional pan-Africanist or black nationalist concerns," writes Brenda Plummer, during the 1940s "these enthusiasms were at a low ebb."[14]

Colonialism everywhere, not simply in Africa, incurred the ill will of African Americans. Liberal activist African American leaders exhibited interest in the oppression of all peoples, a perspective consistent with their hopes for a colorblind world. This mirrored domestic trends in black America where, steering between radical leftists and racialist nationalists, integrationist ideals and demands for inclusion in America's democracy held the most prominence. Broad anticolonialism generally animated perspectives even as colonialism in Africa generated a particular concern in some.

This broad anticolonial position animated African American actions during the ongoing series of conferences that took place as the world transitioned from the war into the postwar world. The NAACP, frustrated that the 1944 Dumbarton Oaks conference had deliberately sidetracked the issue of colonies while hammering out the framework for the UN charter, started developing its own plans for a conference on the colonial issue. Du Bois, who in 1944 returned to the NAACP as director of special research, spearheaded the effort to hold the conference as he prodded the NAACP to take a more prominent role in colonial issues.[15]

Early in 1945 the NAACP allocated money to organize a conference, and in March, Du Bois and Roy Wilkins of the NAACP, Hunton of the CAA, Lawrence Reddick of the Schomburg Collection, and historian Rayford Logan met to organize the colonial conference. Due to constrictions placed by the Office of Defense Transportation, they could invite only a small number of people, so they targeted people from various colonies and experts on colonial affairs. Despite these limitations, they created what historian Gerald Horne argues "may have been the most significant meeting of its type held in North America before or since."[16]

On 6 April 1945, forty-nine people registered for the colonial conference, representing the far-flung lands of Barbados, British Guiana, Burma, the Gold Coast, India, Indonesia, Jamaica, Nigeria, Puerto Rico, and Uganda. The conference clearly sought to oppose colonialism on a broad basis, far beyond the shores of Africa. People in attendance included Kumar Goshal of India, Mung Saw Tun of Burma, Akiki Nyabongo of Uganda, and Kwame Nkrumah of the Gold Coast. The conference drew up a statement to be presented at the formative UN Conference on International Organization in San Francisco, scheduled to begin a few weeks later. The delegates emphasized that colonialism must be ended, that there should be an international body to oversee the transition from colonial status to such autonomy as colonial peoples themselves desired, that colonial peoples should have representation on this body, and that the international body being created should have as its prime objective the economic and social condition of the colonial peoples.[17]

In a related development, the CAA circulated a petition that took very similar positions. Sent to Roosevelt and Secretary of State Edward Stettinius, the petition urged that the UN organization proposed at Dumbarton Oaks should make "adequate provision for the progressive advancement of the people of Africa so that they may play their full part in a system of world-wide democracy and prosperity." This should be done, in part, by providing "the maximum opportunity for Africans to manage their own affairs within the framework of international cooperation," with the view that self-determination and self-government should be achieved "within a specified time limit." The CAA and NAACP at this time, then, stood close together in how they viewed anticolonial processes and objectives.[18]

The worldwide representation at the NAACP's colonial conference and the nature of the resolutions reflected the broadly internationalist, anticolonialist thinking in black America as the war came to an end. This thinking also clearly appeared in the efforts by the NAACP delegation that attended the organizing conference of the UN. Angered by the Dumbarton Oaks Conference's omission of all reference to the postwar future of 750 million persons of color living under colonial rule, by the fact that those who crafted the agenda of the San Francisco conference apparently did not even contemplate any discussion of the topic, and by Washington's refusal to designate an official or semiofficial spokesman on colonial questions at San Francisco, the NAACP vigorously protested. It made clear that the treaty's provisions for improving the status and welfare of colonial peoples and establishing programs for their eventual independence would condition to a great extent black American attitudes toward the peace treaty draft. Walter White, before departing for San Francisco, wired Roosevelt expressing concern over the government's failure to express a position on colonial issues. White insisted that full discussion of colonial trusteeship and dependent peoples be placed on the San Francisco agenda. He then embarked as the NAACP consultant to the American delegation to the conference, with Du Bois and Mary McLeod Bethune designated as his assistants. As he boarded the train to San Francisco, White issued a statement: "We are particularly concerned with what is done about colonial empires and the well-being of colonial peoples around the world. Most of these colonial peoples are colored. What happens to even the most exploited of these has direct bearing on the future of Negroes in the United States."[19]

The NAACP delegation focused on achieving two primary goals: first, a strong declaration of human rights that would convey the equality of all races and peoples; and second, a forceful anticolonial section in the UN charter that would create an international body to oversee colonies and push them speedily toward self-governance and independence. While in San Francisco, White and Du Bois worked tirelessly for these objectives, although not always in concert, due to their icy personal relations. They presented proposals, lobbied the American delegation, consulted foreign delegations, sent telegrams, and tried to build a groundswell of opinion that would push higher on the agenda human rights, equality of peoples, and the ultimate abolition of colonialism. NAACP branches were asked to apply further pressure by telegramming Stettinius, who chaired the American delegation, urging the delegation to press for these objectives.[20]

White felt certain that this pressure helped prod the American delegation toward stronger support of human rights. He and Du Bois remained concerned, however, that gains on human rights could be offset by the "domestic jurisdiction" clause that prohibited the UN from interfering in matters deemed completely internal to a country. They perceptively recognized that this "dangerous and unfortunate" clause, as Du Bois termed it, would be used by countries to fend off UN action, and they worried that colonial powers would claim colonial issues as strictly internal. South Africa, for one, would use this clause ad infinitum in its efforts to prevent UN action on apartheid. Further, the NAACP delegation remained bitterly disappointed with the American stand on colonialism. The San Francisco conference produced no specific timetables or procedures for the independence of colonial peoples, causing the NAACP to continue registering its displeasure in the conference's aftermath. The *Crisis* called the United States refusal to affirm even the principle that dependent peoples have the right to look forward to independence a "bald compromise of basic American principle."[21]

While the NAACP delegation failed to achieve all its lofty aims, the scope of its objectives bears noting. They encompassed the entire world; they were not specifically grounded in the situation in Africa. After the war, broad anticolonialism continued to be at work in concern over the Dutch rule in Indonesia and the British in India, as well as the disposition of the Italian colonies in Africa and the South African mandate in South West Africa (Namibia).

The broad anticolonialism also influenced responses to Du Bois's efforts to convene a Pan-African Congress in 1945. This was to be the Fifth Pan-African Congress, and the first one held since 1927. Du Bois had long wanted to hold another Congress, and he began to promote the idea again after returning to the NAACP. Du Bois advocated a date six months after the defeat of Germany, at a location preferably in Africa. In early 1945 he learned of efforts among African and Caribbean pan-Africanists living in Britain, headed by George Padmore, to organize a Congress. Padmore himself had a long odyssey as an anticolonial activist. During his career he would shift from being a member of the Communist Party and a prominent expert on race and imperialism in the Communist International to being a staunchly anticommunist and pro-pan-African advocate who would advise Kwame Nkrumah's government in newly independent Ghana. By the mid-1940s Padmore had split with the Communist Party and was in London promoting pan-Africanism. Padmore and his colleagues favored a meeting in Paris in September, so that delegates to the second Congress of the World Federation of Trade Unions could also attend the Pan-African Congress, and Du Bois eventually accepted the idea.[22]

Du Bois pressed the NAACP to commit to a conference, generating a report covering both the history of the Pan-African Congresses as well as the more recent efforts by Padmore and others to launch another meeting. Having done so, Du Bois then revealed both his real personal concerns about losing the mantle of diasporic leadership as well as the continuing view that black Americans held about their place in the diaspora. He urged the NAACP to take charge of future preparations, for, he argued, "If we do not lead the way, there is nothing to hinder them from forming a Pan-African movement of their own without the participation and guidance of American Negroes."[23]

Du Bois's desire to stage a Pan-African Congress did receive backing from the NAACP. In fact, in April 1945 the board of directors endorsed the idea of NAACP sponsorship for a Pan-African Congress in Paris in September. A committee of NAACP board members then explored further the idea of hosting a congress. The committee configuration changed over the following months, finally including Louis Wright as chairman, Ralph Bunche, Elmer Carter, Russell Davenport, William Hastie, Rayford Logan, Arthur Spingarn, Channing Tobias, Roy Wilkins, Walter White, and Du Bois.[24] The committee met on 12 July and immediately fell out over numerous issues, not the least of which was simply naming the conference. Du Bois and Tobias favored retaining the name Pan-African Congress, with its links to past efforts; Logan and Wilkins wanted to change the name so it would not be confused with the Pan-African movement. Logan suggested as an alternative the Dependent People's Conference. Concerns over how much money could be and should be spent, the details of the program, and whether or not delegates could make it back to America given the transportation demands of demobilizing troops sparked further debate. Unable to resolve all the questions, the committee created a subcommittee comprised of Bunche, Du Bois, Hastie, and Tobias.[25]

At this point, plans for active NAACP involvement clearly carried the day, with Walter White writing to Mary White Ovington on 19 July that, chiefly due to weariness with his hectic travel schedule, he felt "a little reluctant to see the committee designate me to attend along with Dr. Du Bois, but I suppose I shall have to go." But in the following month, differences of opinion over the proposed congress continued to wrack the committee and the subcommittee. Du Bois favored a geographically and racially pan-African emphasis; Hastie and Bunche maintained strong reservations about this approach. A frustrated Du Bois described Hastie as questioning whether the NAACP should even support a Pan-African Congress and Bunche as doubting the advisability of a pan-African movement at all.[26]

These men wrestled over whether pan-Africanism should be seen as a pan-black or a pan-human movement. Taken as a pan-black movement, it meant that Africans throughout the continent and the diaspora shared a common destiny through sharing a common race, whether that race was conceived in terms of physical characteristics or sociohistorical experiences. Taken as pan-humanism, it meant that all those degraded and dispossessed shared a broad kinship, thereby including but extending beyond people of African descent. For those engaged in trying to get America to look beyond the construct of race, inherent questions and problems riddled accepting pan-Africanism as a pan-black movement. Those who saw class, rather than race, as the determinative force in world history found the pan-black construct similarly problematic. Even so, most pan-Africanists, Du Bois included, viewed pan-Africanism as a pan-black movement, a perspective that did not rest comfortably on liberal activists and staunch integrationists in the NAACP.[27]

In essence, a majority of NAACP leaders supported holding a congress as a dramatic expression of unity by people of color against colonialism and white supremacy, but balked at sponsoring a conference limited to the diaspora. Their broad anticolonialism hinged not upon racial pan-Africanism but on opposition to the oppression of white supremacy, which included in its scope Asia as well as Africa. White, reflecting this, stated his strong support for a conference on colonial and racial problems but, like Hastie and Bunche, opposed calling it a Pan-African Congress. Instead, he advocated a "World Races Congress" or a "Conference on Colonial Problems."[28]

Not surprisingly, given its internal dissension over the very nature of the proposed Congress, the NAACP quietly backed off as Padmore and his associates pressed forward with their arrangements.[29] When the Committee on the Pan-African Congress met again in early September, it simply recommended that the NAACP send Du Bois as a representative to the proposed Congress. With NAACP support and despite logistical nightmares getting there, Du Bois made it to the conference, which finally ended up in Manchester, England, due to transportation and lodging difficulties. The committee also recommended that the NAACP cooperate with a Pan-African Congress in the Spring of 1946, but the congress never came about, and the NAACP leadership made no effort to sponsor it.[30]

Clearly the broad anticolonialist feeling of the day among the civil rights leadership did not translate into any strong, organized pan-African impulse. "The N.A.A.C.P. has taken no stand nor laid down any program with regard to Africa," lamented Du Bois toward the end of 1946. "I have repeatedly urged this since my return from the Pan-African Congress. Individually I have done what I could but I have neither the help, funds, nor authority to accomplish much."[31]

Notably, the CAA did not participate at all in the Manchester Pan-African Congress, although the event was seemingly in line with the aims of the organization. The CAA's failure to send even a single delegate was due in no small measure to the politics of the organization itself. The communist element detested Padmore for leaving and condemning the Communist Party and so refused to involve itself with any project associated with him. Padmore returned the feeling, all of which speaks to the difficulty of creating a unified anticolonial front and the reality that differences between nationalists and communists could not always be papered over. The weakness of the radical black left was revealed, then, within a few months in 1945. The CAA as an organization had little significant presence at either the UN conference in San Francisco or the Pan-African Congress in Manchester, meaning that even at the height of its influence it was not a party to the major mid-1940s conferences affecting colonized people in general, and Africans in particular. The CAA would be an important voice in black American internationalism and anticolonialism during the 1940s and into the early 1950s, but at the same time leftist ties, competition from and conflict with the NAACP and other organizations, and a limited membership weighed against the CAA's ability to mobilize resources and wield widespread influence.[32]

Post–World War II America and Anticolonialism

Coming out of World War II, America's historical and ideological commitment to anticolonialism might have combined with its superpower status to place it in a position of authority in world decolonization. The American Revolution indeed had established the first successful modern revolt against a colonial power. In the twentieth century, Wilsonian internationalism touted national self-determination, albeit not directed toward non-European peoples. And throughout World War II, the rhetoric of the Roosevelt administration placed the United States on the side of anticolonialism and freedom for all peoples. In his annual message to Congress in January 1941, Roosevelt enunciated his four freedoms, declaring: "Freedom means the supremacy of human rights everywhere. Our support goes to those who struggle to gain those rights or keep them." A more elaborate expression of these ideals came in August 1941, when Roosevelt and Churchill met off the coast of Newfoundland to draw up a joint declaration of war aims. The Atlantic Charter outlined eight propositions with principles that included sovereign rights and self-government for all peoples, as well as a postwar peace assuring safety to all nations and freedom from fear and want for all men. The colonial peoples of the world interpreted the principles contained within these documents to mean that democratic freedoms would come for them, too.[33]

Behind this rhetoric lay pragmatic concerns. Colonies, as sources of friction between European powers, provided potential flash points in the world system. Eliminating colonies therefore should reduce the possibility of war. Economic concerns also inspired anticolonial rhetoric. Since the late nineteenth century the United States had pursued the Open Door Policy, and colonies were not open for trade. Fears of an economic depression following the war, such as the one that occurred after the First World War, and beliefs that restrictive trade practices had helped spiral the world into depression in the 1930s reinforced views that world trade, especially in a world that the United States expected to dominate, would be better off without colonies.[34]

On the other hand, a tradition of ambivalence marked U.S. attitudes about revolutions. American policymakers always had been wary about social and political upheavals, especially those arising from the left. The waves of revolutions from the late eighteenth to early twentieth centuries reinforced beliefs that a "good" revolution needed to be conducted with a minimum of disorder, led by respectable citizens, harnessed to moderate political goals, and culminate in a balanced constitution safeguarding human and property rights. Absent these conditions, U.S. policymakers reacted to changes with attitudes ranging from disappointment to open hostility.[35]

In the fifty years preceding the end of World War II, the United States generally acted as a decidedly conservative power when it came to colonies and revolutions. The United States itself added overseas colonies as a direct result of the Spanish-American War of 1898. During his term in office Woodrow Wilson sent troops into Mexico and Russia in attempts to guide the revolutions and keep them in "safe" bounds. Throughout the first half of the century, as well as the second half, American troops intervened in the Caribbean basin in order to impose U.S. prerogatives. During World War II itself, even as the Roosevelt administration spoke in anticolonial terms and held a position of strength in the Western alliance, it refused to forcefully push European allies to divest themselves of their colonies. The highest priority for U.S. policymakers during the war was defeating Nazi Germany and its Axis allies. Anticolonial objectives paled in the light of this task.[36]

As the world emerged from World War II, tensions in the relationship between the United States and the Soviet Union took on a greater prominence. Differences over Germany, Eastern Europe, Iran, the control of atomic weapons, and access to markets led President Harry Truman to believe the United States needed to follow a "get tough with Russia" policy. The Soviet Union and communism replaced Nazi Germany in U.S. officials' minds as the greatest threat to Western democratic ideals. Domestic politics, namely fears that Republicans would outflank him on the communism issue, reinforced Truman's shift away from Roosevelt's wartime policy of trying to work with the Soviets. By the end of 1946, a more hardline U.S. policy was in place. When Britain informed the United States in February of 1947 that she could no longer provide economic and military aid either to civil-war-torn Greece or to Turkey, the Truman administration decided to make a dramatic call for support for a global battle against communism.

Truman designed his speech before Congress on 12 March 1947 to "scare hell out of the American people" in an effort to rally them against the "communist menace." Less than two weeks after the Truman Doctrine speech, the president gave impetus to the domestic counterpart of the anticommunist crusade by announcing the establishment of a loyalty program designed to root out all communist security risks from government ranks.[37]

Actions such as these effectively rallied people to support anticommunism, but at tremendous costs. Domestically, the loyalty program legitimized anticommunism as a national ideology, creating an environment in which the loosely worded directives behind the loyalty program allowed for the abrogation of civil liberties at home: those accused of "disloyalty" did not even have to be told the precise charges against them nor the identities of those providing evidence. Further, the ill-defined concept of "disloyalty" left a person susceptible to prosecution simply based on thoughts or beliefs. Internationally, the distinction between threats genuinely posed by communists and crises stemming from other causes, such as nationalistic desires for self-determination, fell victim to anticommunist zeal.[38]

Fears of communist advances led U.S. officials to actively support their Western allies — the countries that also were the colonial powers in Africa. By 1947, communist parties in Italy and France were threatening to take power through democratic elections. Leftist movements in Asia also were gaining strength, most spectacularly in China. A world in flux seemingly offered numerous opportunities for communist intrigue and advance. Shoring up the Western allies in the face of the perceived communist threat became the top priority. Shortly after the Truman Doctrine speech, Secretary of State George Marshall pledged the United States to making substantial contributions to the rebuilding of Europe. Within a year the Marshall Plan started pumping billions of dollars, as well as machinery, material, and experts, into Western European governments and economies.

The Marshall Plan strengthened the devastated economies of Western Europe and reduced the possibility that turmoil and privations would turn the people toward communism. It also meant that the European allies had more resources available to keep their colonial empires. U.S. officials accepted European arguments that aid for the development of their overseas territories was indispensable to their own recoveries. American aid was seen as a temporary measure, while Western European trade and investment expansion in the Third World would sustain long-term recovery. U.S. dollars would flow to Third World countries through American procurement of raw materials, Western Europe would earn those dollars through investments and exports, and eventually European economies would recover to the point at which they would no longer be dependent on U.S. grants and loans. After the United States and its Western European allies established NATO in 1949, American funds made available through NATO would further support Europeans in their efforts to maintain control over their colonies. Convinced that recovering European economies relied on resources extracted from their colonies as well as on American dollars, European efforts to maintain colonial control met with little resistance from U.S. officials.[39]

The U.S. military establishment's desire for strategic islands in the Pacific also placed the United States in an awkward position when it came to any demands that the European allies relinquish their empires. Given Soviet encroachment on the Kurile Islands, military arguments for U.S. control of islands in the Pacific became all the more powerful and made it all the more difficult for Washington to press its European allies to divest themselves of their colonies.[40]

Thus, as Washington's interest in Africa quickly subsided after the war, U.S. officials returned to their tradition of favoring the interests of European colonial powers over those of Africans, and U.S. diplomats tended to approach most issues pertaining to the continent through the Europeans.[41] This traditional modus operandi combined with the host of other pressing problems around the globe, the absence of any pressing crisis on the African continent, and the lack of a strong domestic constituency for Africa to revert the world's second largest continent to its traditionally low priority in Washington. Outside of the mineral-rich and strategically located Union of South Africa, Africa south of the Sahara held virtually no interest for Washington. What interest existed usually focused on the strategic value of the area, not the people. The minerals in the soil of the Congo or South Africa meant more than the people residing on top of them. As late as 1958 the State Department would maintain more diplomats in West Germany than in all of Africa.

As the United States slowly carved out policies toward Africa, concerns about communism and strategic minerals consistently outweighed principles such as self-determination and majority rule. Faced with what they perceived as a choice between continued colonialism under the control of European allies or newly independent nations potentially ripe for communist penetration, U.S. officials clearly preferred the first alternative. Indeed, the western sensibilities of U.S. officials predisposed them to believe that colonial peoples actually were better off under the guidance of Westerners. Few would warrant that Africans or Asians were ready for self-government. Phrases such as "at a rate commensurate with their capacities" and "at the maximum practicable rate" and calls for no "premature independence" peppered State Department policy papers and speeches.[42] In essence, policymakers determined that no independence should come until the West could be confident that, upon independence, a former colony would be inoculated against communism and safely pro-Western. In an address delivered in June 1951 to the Institute on Contemporary Africa at Northwestern University, George McGhee, then assistant secretary of state for Near Eastern, South Asian, and African affairs, declared, "Immediate independence is, however, not the cure for all colonial problems. The United States government has always maintained that premature independence for primitive, uneducated peoples can do them more harm than good and subject them to exploitation by indigenous leaders, unrestrained by the civil standards that come with widespread education, that can be just as ruthless as that of aliens. Also, giving full independence to peoples unprepared to meet aggression or subversion can endanger not only the peoples themselves but the security of the free world."[43]

Postwar Black American Internationalism: The Former Italian Colonies

Black Americans, then, faced a situation in which strong anticommunism and support for European allies topped the postwar foreign policy agenda. In light of this, African American leaders could have chosen to continue voicing strong anticolonial rhetoric and forging ties with emerging liberation movements in Africa as well as Asia. Some, such as Du Bois, Robeson, and other members of the CAA, strove to do so. Alternatively, they could have adopted staunch anticommunism and generally supported Truman's foreign policy agenda, choosing to work within the dominant national atmosphere to attain objectives. As the Cold War heightened, the civil rights leadership and mainstream press chose this latter course. In doing so, the NAACP and other leading black organizations did not simply abandon their anticolonial efforts to support Truman's foreign policy. Their broad anticolonialism undoubtedly was affected, even blunted, but certainly was not ended. The left's role in speaking out against colonialism remained vibrant and should not be ignored; at the same time, the record shows that the left should not be seen as the only voice speaking against colonialism. The work of Brenda Plummer on African American involvement in foreign affairs during this era makes clear not only that African Americans had an abiding interest in global issues but also that African American opinion on foreign affairs never has been univocal. The complexity speaks to a need to "nuance discussions of Afro-American engagement with global issues."[44]

That African Americans maintained a vigorous anticolonialism in the immediate postwar years can be seen in their efforts regarding the post–World War II disposition of Italy's former colonies. The issue of these colonial areas was thornier for the Western powers than it had been after World War I. The decreasing legitimacy of theories behind racial superiority and colonialism, along with vocal criticism by formerly colonized areas such as the Philippines, made adopting the post–World War I model of other colonial powers assuming mandates over the colonies of vanquished nations more problematic. Increasing Cold War tensions, which affected the world powers' views on all issues, further complicated the search for a resolution. In the protracted negotiations, African Americans saw a way to establish a precedent of former colonies gaining independence, and thus they saw the question of the Italian colonies as wrapped up in larger issues of decolonization.

Meeting in London in September 1945, the Four Powers' foreign ministers discussed the issue of the former Italian colonies of Eritrea, Italian Somaliland (Somalia), and Libya as part of the problem of preparing a peace treaty for Italy.[45] U.S. secretary of state James Byrnes proposed placing the former Italian colonies under a UN trusteeship with an administrator subject to the Trusteeship Council. Ralph Bunche drafted this plan using Article 81 of the UN Charter, which permits the UN itself to be an administering authority over a trust territory. Under this proposal, Libya and Eritrea were to be granted independence at the end of ten years, while Somaliland's trusteeship would be of an indefinite duration. Each of the other major powers gave a cool response. The proposal negated Soviet demands, raised at Yalta and Potsdam, for control in the former Italian colonies, for the Soviets especially wanted a place on the Mediterranean by controlling part of Libya. France worried about the destabilizing effect that eventual independence for Libya would have on its own African colonies. France and Britain both worried about the feasibility of a collective trusteeship. The problem remained unresolved and threatened to forestall an Italian peace treaty. The foreign ministers decided to defer a decision, agreeing that if the issue could not be resolved within a year of the peace treaty's enactment it would be referred to the UN General Assembly.[46]

The Italian Peace Treaty went into effect on 15 September 1947, tripping the one-year clock for resolving the issue before referring it to the UN — all in all an unlikely prospect given the intensifying Cold War. In 1947, the Italian Communist Party was surging to the point where it carried the potential of sharing or even taking power through the ballot box. Italian national sentiment wanted the reinstatement of her former colonies, and Moscow now accepted Italian trusteeship as a way to make Italian voters more receptive to the Communist Party platform. Washington, for its part, sought to minimize communist involvement in the postwar administration of any territories throughout the world. The prospect of either a communist-led Italy governing the territories or an international trusteeship arrangement in which the Soviets played a prominent role held less and less appeal. The Joint Chiefs of Staff argued against allowing the Soviets any foothold in Libya, emphasizing that in the event war erupted any Soviet presence in North Africa would jeopardize the airspace needed for a strategic bombing offensive against the Soviet homeland. Just as worrisome, a Soviet presence could influence ripening Libyan nationalist sentiment. Yet the United States could not forge a consensus among the Western allies, for fundamental disagreement over Italy's role prevented a unified position. London and Washington hesitated at returning the areas to Italian authority and thought a British trusteeship more desirable; Paris preferred Italian trusteeship as a way to ensure that her own colonies developed no ideas about changing their status. When Italy's Christian Democrats soundly defeated the Italian Communists in the April 1948 elections, positions once again shifted. The United States moved toward accepting a governing role by Italy, while the Soviets shifted to supporting a collective trusteeship. With no agreement in place, in mid-September the issue became part of the UN deliberations at the 1948 General Assembly meetings in Paris.[47]

Before the General Assembly meetings, an alliance of twenty-two African American organizations — including the NAACP, the Brotherhood of Sleeping Car Porters, the National Council of Negro Women, the National Baptist Convention, the Negro Newspapers Publishers Association, and Alpha Phi Alpha — coalesced to be better heard on the issue. In early September they wired to the Four Powers their support for holding a plebiscite among the peoples of the former Italian territories, one conducted under the auspices of the General Assembly and in accordance with the UN Charter principles of self-determination. Under this proposal, an international administration under UN trusteeship would govern the areas until the plebiscite could be held.[48]

This support of international trusteeship, as opposed to full and immediate independence, had a long-established pedigree in African American thinking. It linked back to nineteenth-century views on Africans needing to be "uplifted" to the standards of western civilization. It certainly held specific connections to the earlier pan-African efforts of Du Bois. In Du Bois's memorandum for the 1919 Pan-African Congress in Paris he had stressed objectives such as "development of autonomous governments along the lines of native customs with the object of inaugurating gradually an Africa for the Africans." Resolutions from the congress cautiously declared that Africans "should have the right to participate in the government as fast as their development permits." The following Pan-African Congresses in 1921, 1923, and 1927 also did not call for the complete independence of African colonies. Similarly, African American lobbying at San Francisco in 1945 had supported shifting colonies from the rule of individual nations to the governance of an international trusteeship. Any number of leading African Americans opposed colonialism while still believing Africans were not ready for complete independence, and they therefore supported an internationally run mandate system.[49]

Yet at the 1945 Manchester Pan-African Congress fundamental shifts in the pan-African movement took place, with Africans taking a leading role and African Americans in particular having a far reduced role. When Du Bois had launched his effort in 1944 to organize a Pan-African Congress, he declared, "The object shall be for consultation and information so as to set before the world the needs of African Negroes and their descendants overseas. No political changes in the relation between colonies and mother countries will necessarily be contemplated in cases where it is evident that no freedom of development is possible under present circumstances."[50] Du Bois soon found that he dominated neither the organizing nor the agenda of the 1945 meeting and that the conference pushed forward in a far more militant tone. No longer did a cautious reformist agenda hold sway; the idea that African independence was not something to be argued for but a right that should be handed over forthwith took hold. The conference rejected the "trusteeship" line.

Du Bois, through his attendance at the conference and his general contacts, personally came to understand the shift underway, yet most African Americans had no clear conception that the leadership and agenda dominating the pan-African movement had moved overseas. International trusteeship still seemed to offer a compromise, a halfway step on the road to ending colonialism, and offered a wedge that would lever more and more independence. Black American individuals and organizations continued to voice support for at least an intermediate stage of a UN-sponsored international trusteeship.

Thus, when the NAACP sent Walter White to represent the organization at Paris in September 1948, he focused his efforts on establishing a powerful UN Trusteeship Council as well as marshaling forces to support a strong UN Declaration of Human Rights with substantive implementation measures. His specific efforts included getting the former Italian colonies and South West Africa placed under direct UN trusteeship. White reasoned that putting these territories under direct UN control could help speed the general decolonization process by removing areas from the direct control — and thus the vested interests — of individual countries. Establishing the precedent with the former Italian colonies would enable the formula then to be extended to other parts of the world.[51]

White's broad anticolonial view and his deliberate use of the threat of communism were hallmarks of the evolving anticolonialism of the liberal civil rights leadership. At a meeting hosted by the U.S. delegation in Paris, White pointed out that "if the UN returned her former African colonies to Italy and let the Union of South Africa get away with her bluff of resigning from the UN unless she is permitted to annex Southwest Africa[,] it would mean the deathknell of hope to hundreds of millions of people in Africa and Asia and inevitable revolt[,] which the Russians would use." A motion passed to appoint a committee to draft a strong memorandum to the U.S. delegation insisting on a more courageous course. White served as chairman and organized a "confidential statement" by consultants from various American nongovernmental organizations regarding U.S. positions on colonial issues. The statement encouraged officials to act on the positive principle of proving that the United States supported building a more lasting and equitable society than any totalitarian regime, as opposed to the negative policy of merely stopping the Soviets. The statement argued that under a UN trusteeship no country, including the Soviet Union, could obtain an advantage in these areas, and it advocated a return to the Byrnes proposal of 1945. Finally, the signatory organizations offered their support in providing mass backing for an enlightened and courageous position on colonialism.[52]

The CAA, operating in a parallel universe, similarly advocated a quick solution to the issue, one that gave paramount consideration to the needs and aspirations of the African peoples. It likewise urged international trusteeships with definite timetables for independence for Libya and Somaliland, and as well the return of Eritrea to Ethiopia. The CAA drafted a petition and urged its supporters to send letters endorsing it to the U.S. mission to the UN and to the State Department. Despite the similarities in their positions on this issue, the CAA and NAACP did not operate in coordination, but stood on different sides of an increasingly widening Cold War chasm.[53]

Because the many national delegations in Paris had little time to prepare themselves on the Italian colonies issue, the General Assembly deferred any resolution to the meeting in New York in the spring of 1949. In the interim, both the NAACP and the CAA continued their efforts. The NAACP again rallied organizations to fight against the restoration of Eritrea, Libya, and Somalia to Italy in any form and for an international trusteeship arrangement for these nations. The NAACP sponsored a meeting on 8 April to which sixteen national organizations, ranging from the National Council of Negro Women to the National Negro Insurance Association, sent representatives. There they highlighted what seemed clear to them: that the United States was caving in to Italian designs in Africa and to Dutch desires in Indonesia in order to encourage those two nations' participation in NATO, the treaty for which was being signed that month. Conference delegates sent a statement in protest to President Truman, the State Department, and the U.S. delegation to the UN. The NAACP also encouraged its branches to seek congressional support for a plan endorsing UN trusteeship for the African colonies and independence for Indonesia. "This is a vital issue," wrote Roy Wilkins, "in that the disposition of these lands may chart the trend of colonialism."[54] The CAA also exposed the geopolitical machinations at work, pulling no punches in stating that the current American position "represents an attempt toward promoting the war plans embodied in the North Atlantic Pact" by reinforcing Africa's colonial subjugation by America's North Atlantic allies. The CAA now emphasized more strongly the need for immediate independence, calling upon the American people to support Libyan independence, a free Somaliland, and a unification of Eritrea with Ethiopia. If immediate independence were not to come, then a joint trusteeship with a guarantee of independence within five years would have to do.[55]

Other avenues for lobbying also were followed. The NAACP worked with representatives from the former Italian colonies, particularly the Somali Youth League, in order to enable their voices to be heard. The NAACP furnished stenographic and mimeographic services, shepherded the Somali representatives to various countries' delegations in an effort to sway their votes, arranged press conferences, and solicited press coverage for their cause. In return, the spokesman for the Somali Youth League delegation expressed "deepest gratitude for the kind and invaluable assistance received from the NAACP, without which the delegation would have faced insurmountable difficulties."[56] And African Americans lobbied on an individual level as well. A. Philip Randolph personally appealed to Secretary of State Dean Acheson to withdraw support for any plan that returned former colonies to Italy, citing Italy's oppression and exploitation of her colonies and her invasion and devastation of Ethiopia. Walter White sent letters with clippings from his newspaper column on the issue to every member of Congress, as well as to radio commentators and journalists.[57]

However, the U.S. representative to the UN, Warren Austin, responded to these extensive efforts by indicating to White that the United States would not support an international trusteeship arrangement for two reasons: the danger of Soviet obstructionism in multiple administration of these colonies and the expense involved in setting up a whole new body of administrators. Even though U.S. officials garnished their opposition with other reasons, it was clear to African Americans that they were up against the anti-Soviet imperatives of the Truman administration.[58]

With the General Assembly unable to agree upon a plan, it once again put over the problem for further consideration, this time until September 1949. The NAACP continued its efforts to produce a UN trusteeship arrangement with a specified timetable for independence. With Walter White on leave for a year, Roy Wilkins contacted Truman, Acheson, UN Secretary General Trygve Lie, and all the delegations to the UN in an effort to sway opinions. Slight shifts of positions and attitudes, due at least in part to African American pressure, enabled the removal of some of the provisions most favorable to Italy. In November 1949 a resolution finally passed the General Assembly. While not encompassing everything for which the NAACP and CAA had fought, it was at least a partial victory. Britain and France would have a brief interim administration of Libya, with independence for the country mandated by 1 January 1952; a UN trusteeship over Somalia would be administered by Italy, in conjunction with a UN Advisory Council, with independence guaranteed at the end of ten years; and the Eritrean question would be discussed further. The Ethiopian claims to Eritrea and the desire of the Eritreans for independence not only were intractable questions that bedeviled the world community at the time; they also portended the difficulties African Americans would have when it came to deciding who to support when Africans themselves made claims against each other.[59]

The U.S. civil rights leadership thus maintained an active interest in the fight against colonialism in the immediate postwar years. Concerted actions, special conferences, international lobbying — all constituted part of the effort to establish clear mechanisms for ending colonial rule. The resolution of the former Italian colonies issue came to symbolize a potential path for breaking down colonial rule: the establishment of UN trusteeships with definite timetables for independence. Yet even as African Americans spoke out on behalf of colonial peoples, escalating tensions between the United States and the Soviets, in conjunction with domestic gains by black Americans, were working to disengage many black Americans from postwar solidarity with Africans and their struggles against white supremacy.

African American Internationalism in the Early Cold War

While it is clear that after World War II African American civil rights leaders initially maintained strong criticism of policies and actions that supported colonialism, by the end of the decade just as plainly their anticolonial rhetoric had become less vigorous. In following a path of working within the anticommunist framework, liberal civil rights organizations such as the NAACP still voiced their anticolonialism, but they more often did so in broad terms with less concrete supporting efforts.[60] On the other hand, as the liberal civil rights leadership moved to generally support the Truman administration's foreign policy priorities and agenda, the CAA moved to articulate a more radical leftist anticolonial critique.

In 1948, ruptures in both the CAA and the NAACP showed the parting of the ways between the liberal civil rights leaders and the radical left. First, in early 1948 the CAA broke apart on the shoals of the communist issue. The emerging Cold War repression of the left, and the attendant fears by many of associating with the left, had started to undermine the organization the previous year. While the CAA had sent $505 for "African Relief" in 1945 and

$3,600 in 1946, in 1947 it had sent nothing and ended the year more than $8,000 in debt.[61] In November 1947, U.S. Attorney General Tom Clark listed the CAA as a subversive organization. In the wake of this action, director Max Yergan claimed he wanted to shield the CAA by moving it into an avowedly nonpartisan position. In truth, Yergan, in the process of personally veering sharply to the right on his way to becoming a hard-line anticommunist, wanted to take the CAA along similar lines. Robeson, viewing this as a sellout to reactionary forces, led the fight to keep the CAA on a leftist course. A nasty struggle ensued from February to October 1948, during which time the CAA largely ceased its operations. It did not publish its newsletter *New Africa* and could not devote much attention to Africa. Views of what occurred and what it meant varied widely. Alphaeus Hunton, as educational director and then secretary, described the rift as stemming from one man, Yergan, attempting to defy the will of the majority of the organization. William Jay Schieffelin, vice chairman before he resigned, saw Robeson and Hunton as out-and-out communists with a minority of support, who won out after a series of devious maneuvers. In the end, Yergan and his allies were vanquished, and the CAA rested firmly in the hands of Robeson, Hunton, and now Du Bois.[62]

The internecine bloodletting undoubtedly weakened the organization. Membership never had been very large in numbers in any event. In March 1948, as the rift began, sixty-nine people constituted the CAA. During the power struggle, membership declined further, with several charter members and influential figures, such as Channing Tobias and Adam Clayton Powell Jr., resigning.[63] Further weakening the organization was the fact that many African Americans either had not fully engaged the left, or had done so and found fault with it. While a number of leading and influential African Americans either were communists or allied with the left, such as Du Bois and Robeson, by and large black Americans maintained a distance from the left. Indeed, given a choice in the 1948 presidential election between the Progressive Party, a left-wing party that opposed the escalating Cold War and strongly supported domestic civil rights, and the Democratic Party, with a platform that was strongly anticommunist and considerably weaker on civil rights, a large majority of African Americans supported Truman. Of course, for many African Americans it may have been a pragmatic choice to vote Truman in that tight election, for Henry Wallace had no chance for victory and Thomas Dewey and the Republicans offered even less on civil rights, but still they made that decision.[64]

That being said, as the CAA resumed efforts on behalf of Africa after the internal resolution of its course and directorship, it suffered most grievously from the government's repression of the organization and its directors. Robeson, as a hugely popular singer and actor, suffered a much more public fall from grace than did Du Bois. Robeson had campaigned vigorously for the Progressive Party during the 1948 presidential race, serving as one of five cochairmen of a national Wallace for President committee. Robeson also had publicly and forcefully testified before the Senate Judiciary Committee against the Mundt-Nixon bill, which would require all communist and "communist-front" organizations to register. The bill's provisions eventually would be incorporated into the notorious 1950 McCarran Act. Robeson's high profile made him a prime target in the inflamed, red-baiting atmosphere of the late 1940s. In April 1949 Robeson went to Paris to attend the Congress of the World Partisans of Peace. Two thousand delegates from fifty nations attended. Du Bois headed the American delegation, while Robeson was a featured speaker. Robeson ended his remarks by declaring that the wealth of America had been built on the backs of black and white workers and vowed, "We are resolved to share it equally among our children. And we shall not put up with any hysterical raving that urges us to make war on anyone. Our will to fight for peace is strong. We shall not make war on anyone. We shall not make war on the Soviet Union." An Associated Press (AP) dispatch, purporting to "quote" from the speech, reported that Robeson had compared the U.S. government to that of Hitler and the Nazis and that Robeson had ended by declaring, "It is unthinkable that American Negroes would go to war on behalf of those who have oppressed us for generations against a country [the Soviet Union] which in one generation has raised our people to the full dignity of mankind."[65]

Reprinted throughout the United States, this AP accounting became the basis for the ensuing national furor. In the words of Robeson's biographer Martin Duberman, "the white press rushed to inveigh against him as a traitor; the black leadership hurried to deny that he spoke for anyone but himself; agencies of the U.S. government excitedly exchanged memos speculating about possible grounds for asserting that he had forfeited his citizenship." The House Un-American Activities Committee (HUAC) summoned leading black figures to hearings on the loyalty of black Americans. In a sign of the now complete and bitter divide between liberals and the left, the *Crisis* printed an editorial titled "Robeson Speaks for Robeson," which attacked Robeson's credibility as a black American leader, questioned his motives, and reminded readers that black Americans always had fought for America. Only five years before, the NAACP had honored Robeson with its highest award, the Spingarn Medal.[66]

A few weeks later, riots broke out when Robeson tried to give a concert in

Peekskill, New York. The following month riots occurred again, leading to a grand jury investigation. Shortly thereafter the State Department voided Robeson's passport and then diligently prevented him from traveling outside the country until 1958.[67] The *Courier* supported the government's action, reasoning that when fighting the greatest propaganda war in history against the greatest lie factory ever conceived, America should not permit its own citizens to "travel around the world and malign it with falsehoods and even more vicious half-truths." In November 1951, the *Crisis* ran an article that labeled Robeson "Moscow's No. 1 Negro" and a "Kremlin Stooge." It quoted a Walter White article from *Ebony* that called Robeson "a bewildered man who is more to be pitied than damned."[68]

Du Bois suffered similar treatment, culminating in the Justice Department's indictment of him as an "unregistered foreign agent" in early 1951. Other leftist organizations with an interest in Africa and colonialism, such as the Civil Rights Congress, also faced intense pressure from the U.S. government. With communists allegedly working from within and without to destroy "the American Way," movements that challenged the status quo — in the workplace, in politics, on civil rights — faced the real threat of opponents smearing them as being communist-inspired.[69]

During World War II, liberal civil rights leaders and leftist internationalists had followed a course of antifascism and anticolonialism. Both strongly opposed the racism intrinsic to fascism and colonialism. During the war the NAACP at times worked with or donated money to CAA-sponsored drives, even as a wariness about the leftist nature of the CAA marked NAACP responses. But as the Cold War gathered intensity, liberal organizations and the mainstream press skirted ties to anything hinting of socialism and communism. In the intensely anticommunist atmosphere of post–World War II America, black American leaders sought to protect the civil rights struggle from any lethal linkage with communism or Moscow. Civil rights leaders worked within the prevailing atmosphere and severed connections with leftist groups or individuals. The protection of the domestic civil rights campaign circumscribed unyielding support for civil liberties or for Africa.[70]

Many black Americans felt compelled to emphasize more than ever their loyalty to America. Black America historically had portrayed itself as being "100% loyal" and used this to argue for equal citizenship. Such arguments usually emphasized black participation in every war in which the United States had ever fought and the absence of divided loyalties that might, for example, afflict Italian Americans or German Americans. In honor of Flag Day in 1948, the *Daily World* proclaimed, "We have no other flag; we have no other anthem; for we are Americans, citizens of the great Republic of the

United States." Highlighting 100% loyalty, however, generally meant minimizing connections to Africa. In the climate of Cold War America, to speak of Africa threatened to undercut professions of loyalty to America.[71]

In this atmosphere, on 7 September 1948, Du Bois sent a memorandum to Walter White and the NAACP Board of Directors in which he denounced Truman's foreign policy as "reactionary, war-mongering colonial imperialism." Du Bois cited as evidence the Truman administration's prevention of discussion about African American civil rights before the UN, support for colonial powers in the Trusteeship Council, and opposition to the best interests of India, the only country defending the interests of Africa before the General Assembly. Du Bois accused the NAACP of supporting Truman's foreign policy to the detriment of the struggle of people of color throughout the world. He called for the organization to issue a clear statement of foreign policy, one that would be independent of Truman's.[72]

Du Bois's tense relationship with Walter White and with other powerful members of the NAACP already had worsened noticeably in the preceding months. Disagreement and animosity had built primarily over Du Bois's work for the Wallace campaign and his role in continuing to press the issue of United States racism at the UN. While the NAACP initially had supported petitioning the UN, Du Bois's *An Appeal to the World* had angered many influential people, both conservative and liberal. Eleanor Roosevelt, in her capacity as a member of the UN Economic and Social Council as well as a member of the NAACP board, provided a telling case. She viewed the petition as an embarrassment that only would help the Soviets in the emerging Cold War, and she therefore worked hard to prevent the petition from making any progress. Work by Du Bois on behalf of Wallace and the Progressive Party further embittered liberals such as Roosevelt toward Du Bois. When the many percolating tensions came to a boil over Du Bois's memo and a *New York Times* article two days later that publicly detailed some of the internal divisions, the NAACP board moved at its meeting on 12 September to oust Du Bois.[73]

Du Bois's accusations, followed by his sacking from the organization that he had helped found, highlighted the fact that while African Americans may not have agreed with the Truman administration on many issues, leading voices generally, and the NAACP particularly, chose to work within the predominant anticommunist framework. NAACP criticism of Truman's foreign policy had quieted over the previous year. Historian James Roark writes that in the latter part of 1947 "critical comments about American foreign policy fell off sharply . . . the NAACP did not abandon the Third World, but concern lagged and its expression often took on a ritualistic quality."[74] From 1948 onward, the *Crisis* regularly warned black Americans to remain on guard against communists seeking "to worm their way into Negro organizations." At its 1950 annual convention the NAACP passed an anticommunist resolution by a vote of 309 to 57. It instructed the board of directors to eradicate communist infiltration by any necessary action, including suspending, reorganizing, lifting the charter, or expelling any chapter that fell under communist control. Subsequent conventions overwhelmingly reaffirmed this resolution.[75]

The decision by most black leaders to confirm their Americanness and to ally themselves with Truman's foreign policy received reinforcement from economic and social advances in America during the war and immediate postwar years. African Americans came out of World War II in a stronger position than they had entered it. Nonwhite income had been only 41 percent of white income in 1939, but had risen to 54 percent by 1947. While still terribly imbalanced, such advances created the expectation for further progress in the postwar period, and the anticipation that by focusing efforts at home long-sought breakthroughs would result. Du Bois himself, no pie-eyed observer of race relations in America, in July 1948 solicited two magazines about writing an article on the improved state of racial affairs. Du Bois asserted that "There can be no question but that the relations between American Negroes and the balance of the population in the United States have improved during the last generation."[76]

While President Truman had no long history of support for civil rights, during the immediate postwar years he became, however gingerly, more determined and outspoken in backing civil rights. In 1946 he responded to brutal attacks on African Americans by appointing a Committee on Civil Rights to investigate the problem. On 29 October 1947, the committee released its report, *To Secure These Rights*, in which it advocated vigorous federal action to secure the rights of all Americans.

Also in 1947 Truman became the first U.S. president to address the NAACP's annual convention, giving a speech that the *Crisis* termed "the most comprehensive and forthright statement on the rights of minorities in a democracy, and on the duty of the government to secure and safeguard them that has ever been made by a President of the United States." On 2 February 1948 Truman sent a message to Congress asking for a broad range of actions on civil rights. Recommendations included establishing a permanent Commission on Civil Rights, a Joint Congressional Committee on Civil Rights, and a Civil Rights Division in the Justice Department; strengthening existing civil rights statutes; providing federal protection against lynching; protecting more adequately the right to vote; and prohibiting discrimination in interstate transportation facilities. Many of these recommendations carried tremendous actual and symbolic weight with African Americans, who had long pursued such objectives. And while these measures did not all materialize, the fact that some movement seemed to be taking place held import.[77]

At its national convention in July 1948 the Democratic Party adopted the strongest civil rights plank in its history. Later that month Truman issued an executive order banning racial discrimination in the hiring of federal employees, then days later signed Executive Order 9981, which in time would desegregate the military. Truman knew he needed at least to appear to promote civil rights for African Americans in order to boost his standing among people of color and negate Wallace's challenge for the black vote during the 1948 campaign. Politically motivated or not, his actions built the impression that the executive branch might aid the freedom struggle.[78]

Truman designed such actions not only to secure African American support for his reelection but also to blunt the Soviets' exploitation of American racial problems. In the post–World War II era, race relations became a global issue, forcing U.S. leaders to confront the issue in the light of world scrutiny. As Secretary of State George C. Marshall wrote in July 1947, the foreign policy of a nation that does not want to rely upon possible military aggression depends "on the moral influence which that nation exerts throughout the world," adding, "The moral influence of the United States is weakened to the extent that the civil rights proclaimed by our Constitution are not fully confirmed in actual practice." Truman could not fail to recognize the detrimental impact that American race relations had on the global fight for the "hearts and minds" of the Third World. Lynchings, for example, provided powerful ammunition for communists. "U.S. government officials realized that their ability to sell democracy to the Third World was seriously hampered by continuing racial injustice at home," writes scholar Mary Dudziak. "Accordingly, efforts to promote civil rights within the United States were consistent with, and important to, the more central U.S. mission of fighting world communism."[79]

Not surprisingly then, in his message to Congress asking for action on civil rights Truman invoked the international situation. He declared that the peoples of the world faced the choice of freedom or enslavement and voiced this appeal: "If we wish to inspire the peoples of the world whose freedom is in jeopardy, if we wish to restore hope to those who have already lost their civil liberties, if we wish to fulfill the promise that is ours, we must correct the remaining imperfections in our practice of democracy." State Department officials recognized that "no American problem receives more widespread attention, especially in dependent areas, than our treatment of racial minorities, particularly the Negro." One remedy the State Department considered, accordingly, was assigning more African Americans as Foreign Service officers in Africa, and it solicited the NAACP for names of qualified applicants. In Africa, it noted, black officials might help "offset the widespread and growing African criticism of racial practices in the United States."[80]

Concern that American race relations undermined U.S. efforts throughout the colonial world continued to play a salient role in American politics during ensuing years. Harvard Sitkoff notes that "[r]arely in the first two decades after the Second World War did a plea for civil rights before the Supreme Court, on the floor of Congress, or emanating from the White House, fail to emphasize the point that white racism adversely affected our relations with the rest of the world."[81] Perhaps the most prominent manifestation occurred in the *Brown v. Board of Education* case. The amicus curiae brief filed by the Justice Department in December 1952 invoked global concerns when it declared: "The existence of discrimination against minority groups in the United States has an adverse effect upon our relations with other countries. Racial discrimination furnishes grist for the Communist propaganda mills, and it raises doubts even among friendly nations as to the intensity of our devotion to the democratic faith." In deliberations over the case, Justice Stanley Reed, persuaded to concur at the last moment, was pressed to consider the effects of segregation on America's position in international affairs.[82]

Shameful American race relations causing foreign policy problems abroad offered civil rights leaders an opportunity that they might exploit. Testifying before Congress in 1948, A. Philip Randolph declared that racial segregation "is the greatest single propaganda and political weapon in the hands of Russia and international communism today." Black Americans could and did argue regularly that improvements in race relations in America would improve the nation's image and advance the fight against communism throughout the world. Anticommunism in fact seemed to offer leverage in promoting equal treatment and standing for African Americans. NAACP lawyers mirrored some of the Justice Department's arguments when they stated in their own brief on reargument for *Brown* that the "[s]urvival of our country in the present international situation is inevitably tied to resolution of this domestic issue." Equality at home, they urged, could be the strongest weapon in the fight against communism overseas.[83]

With some economic and social advances being made during and after the war, with the Truman administration offering some rhetoric and action in support of civil rights and desegregation, and with the anticommunist struggle available as a tool to promote further civil rights advances, most African

American leaders slipped into supporting Truman, adopting the anticommunist agenda, and focusing on promoting domestic gains for black Americans. Improvement did not seem to be hitched to the worldwide struggle, especially the struggle in Africa, from whence there were few signs of success. Civil rights at home stood as a greater priority than foreign policy, especially as civil rights was the raison d'être for organizations like the NAACP.

This inward turn was criticized at the time by contemporaries such as Du Bois and Robeson, and more recently by some historians.[84] The path chosen by the liberal civil rights leadership meant that generally they did not vigorously protest the U.S. government's role in suppressing struggles for independence from Western domination and that they were not closely linked to worldwide freedom movements. Yet while these historical judgments have force, it is perhaps easier to judge the pitfalls of the path taken by the civil right leadership in hindsight. At the time, especially given the politically repressive climate, the shift toward anticommunist-based arguments seemed a viable, even fruitful choice. In contrast, criticism of U.S. foreign policy, especially when this criticism would have been condemned as echoing the communist line, held the real prospect of damaging efforts for civil rights reform.[85]

African American Internationalism at Midcentury

By the decade's end, the Cold War had reached full-blown proportions. In September 1949 the Soviets exploded their first atomic weapon. In October 1949 Mao established the People's Republic of China. In January 1950 a jury convicted Alger Hiss of perjury. In February 1950 Joseph McCarthy made his initial public accusations about communists working in the State Department.

Black America did not unconditionally support U.S. foreign policy; criticism of various aspects of U.S. policy continued, even by those working within the Cold War parameters. But the impact of the Cold War on African Americans became unmistakable. In 1948 the five national African American newspapers devoted four times more space to world communism than to European colonialism.[86] The *Courier* commended NAACP leaders for screening out communists and fellow-travelers. The *Afro-American* advised against signing a peace initiative circulated by Du Bois and others in many black churches. The initiative asked two questions: "Do you favor outlawing the hydrogen, atomic, and bacteriological bombs?" and "Do you favor a meeting between the United States and Soviets so that they can negotiate their differences and strengthen world peace?" The *Afro-American* counseled that the

United States had already proceeded more than halfway to meet with the Soviets and concluded, "Without our atomic and hydrogen bombs the Russians will march through Alaska and Canada and Chicago and Detroit and straight to Washington where peace will be dictated."[87]

Broad anticolonial rhetoric remained but with little indication that black Americans were part of a worldwide coalition of oppressed peoples or that progress in decolonization would aid the struggle for freedom and equality in America. The reasoning in support of decolonization now typically came couched in anticommunist terms: decolonization prevented areas from ripening for communist penetration; supporting colonial independence enabled Western policymakers to show the world's population that the Western powers believed in democracy and independence; decolonization produced free and equal peoples who would be partners instead of disgruntled subjects in the struggle against communism.[88] When Walter White returned from an international tour in late 1949, he felt convinced that "the fate of the entire world is inextricably interwoven with the issues of colonialism and race." If America moved to counteract Russia's wooing of the world's people, communism could be stopped; however, he said he "shudder[ed] to think of what may happen if we don't wake up on time." White still felt strongly that colonialism must end but now argued from an exclusively anticommunist slant.[89]

Arguments for racial advances in America likewise commonly bore a Cold War stamp: discrimination must be ended to undermine the communists' ability to exploit the treatment of black Americans for propaganda purposes; segregation must be ended and full citizenship extended to black Americans to win the battle for Third World hearts and minds. In a representative blending of these arguments, the *Courier* praised Truman for proclaiming a worldwide campaign to combat Soviet lies and efforts to crush the democratic way of life, then declared that some Soviet truths needed to be combated, too — namely, those about discrimination against black Americans. The editorial suggested a series of actions for Truman to take, concluding, "Such forthright steps would not win the propaganda war and stop Soviet lying, but they would make the Kremlin's propaganda job far more difficult." The *Daily World* played the communist card when it urged equality in the military, arguing, "America stands in a unique position in the community of nations. Small nations, wavering between our way of life and that of communism, are influenced greatly by the way our minorities are treated." In condemning both the Republicans and the Democrats for failing to pass legislation for a permanent Fair Employment Practices Commission (FEPC), the *Afro-American* concluded that this failure showed the world the white supremacist character of the United States. The result of continuing such failures, argued the *Afro-American*, would be that "when the showdown comes, not only will we be up against Russia, but up against China, Asia, Africa and South America."[90]

Anticommunism worked as a common denominator in these arguments for supporting worldwide advances in freedom and equality; beyond that, however, viewing the domestic struggle as part of a broader fight for freedom and equality became marginalized. Concerns about colonialism remained but did not necessarily generate links among freedom struggles. After Roy Wilkins attended a State Department conference about U.S. foreign policy in May 1951, he offered Walter White only a single recommendation: that the NAACP do whatever it could to get a qualified black American on the staff of the Public Affairs Division of the State Department in order to improve the quality of the coverage of the race situation in America in its war against Soviet propaganda.[91]

For a period immediately after World War II, African Americans spoke from a position of solidarity with the exploited peoples of the world. Their voices, however, were soon lost in the Western world's anticommunist chorus. African Americans still expressed concern about colonialism in Africa, but nascent connections with contemporary Africa, established during the Italo-Ethiopian War, had been stretched by subsequent events to become part of a broad anticolonialism and antifascism, and then snapped by the Cold War.[92]

It would take the force of liberation struggles in Africa to replenish arguments that African Americans were part of a larger struggle and to reinvigorate black American ties to contemporary Africa. Integrationism and universalism would remain; at the same time, these would coexist with more racially nationalistic views. In the 1950s a dual process would be at work — the growth of renewed pride in contemporary Africa and the rise of an anticolonialism rebuilt with a focus on Africa. And as this occurred, some situated this process in a continuing yet reshaped integrationism, while others built a more particularist, black nationalist view with it.

3

SOUTH AFRICA

Apartheid and Nonviolent Resistance, 1948–1953

On Sunday, April 6, thousands of South Africans launched a nation-wide campaign against Prime Minister Daneil F. Malan's [sic] race laws in South Africa. This is the most significant news that has come out of South Africa in years. . . .

[A passive resistance movement] might even work in the United States and this possibility indeed intrigues me. Just suppose that one bright Monday morning every Negro in the United States woke up and decided not to act like a Negro. Suppose that every colored person conducted himself that day just as if he were white: went into every restaurant, hotel, barber shop and applied for any job where there was a vacancy. . . .

What is happening in South Africa today and what will continue to happen there may prove a lesson to dark people throughout the world.

Horace Cayton, Pittsburgh Courier *(19 April 1952)*

In the midst of the escalating early Cold War, on the southernmost extremes of Africa there occurred an election that would propel South Africa into the forefront of the world's engagement with issues of race. Daniel Malan and his Nationalist Party, stumping on a platform of "apartheid" and continuing white domination, swept to power in South Africa's 1948 general election. Malan's victory highlighted the reality that while most of the world was moving away from policies of racial discrimination and segregation, white South Africans were tightening their grip.

Yet while black Americans denounced the Rankins and Talmadges and Dixiecrats of the South, they had little to say about Malan's election. As the South African Parliament enacted apartheid legislation, black Americans remained largely silent. The intensifying Cold War, combined with domestic priorities, a universalistic integrationism, and the traditional ambivalence about associating with Africa, all worked against African Americans' responding forcefully. But as people of color in South Africa mounted their resistance to Malan's imposition of apartheid, most dramatically through the 1952–53 Campaign of Defiance of Unjust Laws, black Americans joined their voices in protest. Although at the time there were limits to this shift, as increasing numbers of African Americans trained their eyes on events in Africa, reactions to this nonviolent resistance campaign portended important changes in the relationship with Africa.

The Defiance Campaign initiated a new chapter in black America's engagement with African resistance to white supremacy. African freedom struggles became sources of inspiration to African Americans, helping to reverse negative images of Africa, establish an "African lobby" in the civil rights community, and reconfigure the role of contemporary Africa in the lives of black Americans. The Defiance Campaign in particular pushed African Americans to rethink their own struggle for freedom as it offered a striking model of nonviolent resistance and mass action against white supremacy. The five-year period from the election of Malan as prime minister of South Africa in May 1948 to the end of the Defiance Campaign in the Spring of 1953 illustrates both the disconnection during the early Cold War as well as African freedom struggles driving a resurgent interest in Africa in the early 1950s.

Malan's Election and African American Responses

In the first half of 1948, Czechoslovakia fell to a communist coup, the Soviets blockaded Berlin, the British and French became further embroiled in Malaya and Indochina, and the U.S. Congress approved the Marshall Plan. Amidst this Cold War maelstrom, South African prime minister Jan Smuts faced reelection.

After more than four decades in politics, Smuts enjoyed the role of international elder statesmen. That he presided over a country well known for its oppression of Africans seemed to mean little to the powers of the West, especially in light of the strong support Smuts delivered to the Allies during World War II and the early Cold War. At the United Nations' San Francisco convention in April 1945, Smuts in fact chaired the commission in charge of drafting the constitution of the General Assembly. He became the principal author of the preamble to the UN Charter, despite his domestic record of repression.

Ironically, while he cemented his role as elder statesmen on the world stage, Smuts lost his grip on power at home. As he dallied in international politics, his white opponents at home hammered out a reactionary message of racial dominance and segregation. Appealing to Afrikaner nationalism and to fear ignited by accelerating African urbanization, Malan forged a winning combination in South African politics. In May 1948 the white voters of South Africa gave the Nationalist Party under Malan a slim victory over Smuts and his ruling United Party. Aided by electoral rules that advantaged rural areas (dominated by Afrikaner farmers) over urban areas (dominated by wealthier English-speakers), Malan and his Nationalist Party successors would consolidate their electoral majority in subsequent elections, remaining in power for nearly a half century.

The message of Malan and the Nationalists actually differed little from historical practices in South Africa. The Nationalists intended to further the longstanding norms of white supremacy and racial segregation by solidifying their legal basis and execution. They preached the merit of apartheid—the separation of the races in South Africa. The Nationalists claimed that apartheid enabled "separate development," allowing the races to keep and promote their unique lifestyles and customs. In reality, of course, apartheid allowed whites to take away more rights from nonwhites and further entrench a white supremacist state in South Africa.

Smuts had not been expected to lose, with victory coming somewhat unexpectedly even to the Nationalists, so the fact that African Americans had little comment prior to the election is not that surprising. Yet even after the rabid white supremacist's victory, black America remained largely silent. During the weeks following Malan's election only a smattering of articles appeared in the African American press. The number and depth of the articles are indicative of the relative disconnection of the day. The *Afro-American*, for instance, published only two international news items on the day it announced the election results: a small article discussed Malan's election, while a larger story came headlined, "Polygamy in Africa, Ancestor Worship in China on Way Out." The *Afro-American*, the *Crisis*, and the *Defender* did provide brief editorial comments. The *Defender* called upon the U.S. government to throw its moral, economic, political, and military weight against what it termed the Nationalist Party's version of Nazi fascism. The *Crisis*, in its sole reference to South Africa during that entire year, predicted that Malan would be a greater evil than Smuts, a position the *Afro-American* echoed. Neither journal connected South Africa to the lives of black Americans or pushed the U.S. government to take concrete action. Still, readers of the above organs fared better than purchasers of the *Daily World*, which provided absolutely no coverage of the South African elections. Even the CAA, torn by its internal upheavals, remained silent, suffering, in Robeson's words, a "total failure" in addressing events in Africa.[1] Thus, black America heard and said little about Malan's victory. Instead, the Cold War and domestic affairs dominated discussion. The *Courier* informed its readers in the week following the election that the preceding week's most important news was the announcement of the establishment of a technical school in Harlem.[2]

1950 Apartheid Legislation and African American Responses

In the first half of 1950 Malan hammered through Parliament several legislative pieces that were central to imposing apartheid. The Population Registration Act provided for classifying the entire population of South Africa in racial categories. The Group Areas Act set up the machinery to demarcate separate residential and business areas for the different racial groups. In theory, any racial group could be moved from an area it occupied and placed in another area reserved for it. In practice, this came to mean removing so-called "black spots" in an effort to create purely white areas. The Suppression of Communism Act gave the government sweeping powers to suppress dissent. The act defined communism in an extraordinarily loose manner, including any doctrine "which aims at bringing about any political, industrial, social, or economic change within the Union by the promotion of disturbance or disorder, by unlawful acts or omissions or by the threat of such acts or omissions." This allowed the government to equate resistance to apartheid as communism. In turn, the government could impose severe sanctions. Any organization defined as communist could be banned and its members removed from public office, placed under house arrest, restricted in their movements, and/or prohibited from attending public or social gatherings.[3]

The onset of apartheid galvanized opposition inside South Africa, with the African National Congress (ANC) standing at the forefront. Adopting its Programme of Action in 1949, the ANC moved from moderation to militancy and stood committed to mass action and the tactics of boycotts, strikes, and civil disobedience. Along with Indian, Coloured, and white communist groups, the ANC worked to coordinate a one-day national work stoppage as a protest against the government's reactionary policies. Communist elements advocated May Day, the international workers' day, as the day to stay away. African nationalist elements opposed adopting this date, fearing its close connection with communism. Nonetheless, a number of African workers heeded the May Day appeal, with tragic consequences. The government declared the stay-away illegal and warned that it would break up any public meeting of more than a dozen people. Although the leaders of all major black organizations publicly urged people not to disobey the ban on demonstrations, gatherings formed in various locations. Confrontations with the police ensued, and resulted in at least eighteen Africans killed and thirty injured.[4]

In the weeks following the May Day violence, plans formalized for a nationwide stay-at-home. ANC president-general James S. Moroka announced that 26 June 1950 would be a "National Day of Protest and Mourning." The stay-at-home achieved mixed results, with parts of the country largely shut down while other areas went unaffected. Still, this date would be chosen two years later to launch the Defiance Campaign in order to commemorate "the greatest demonstration of fraternal solidarity and unity of purpose on the part of all sections of the non-European people in the national protest against unjust laws."[5]

As the ANC led opposition to apartheid, black Americans trained their eyes on domestic civil rights. As the ANC girded for protests, liberal black American leaders generally accepted the U.S. foreign policy priority of fighting against communism, not colonialism. Cold War considerations coursed strongly throughout black America. In warning that the Soviets were gearing to arm Asians and Africans, Willard Townsend, president of the United Transport Service Employees of America (UTSEA) and executive board member of the Congress of Industrial Organizations (CIO), summed up some of the contradictions at work during this era. In Townsend's words, the communist threat put every black American "in a very interesting role": "He is part and parcel of this culture. He has enjoyed the high standards of living which America provides . . . and therefore he must, while engaged in his own struggle for equality of opportunity in all fields, help those who oppose him to preserve this great nation of ours."[6]

When African Americans did speak out against white supremacy in South Africa, they typically voiced their opposition in terms of anticommunism, warning that color barriers would play into communist designs. The *Defender* offered a common response when it denounced Malan's apartheid policy as aiding the communist world movement, arguing, "Unless America steps in to champion the cause of the oppressed natives, Africans will be lured into the Communist camp. We can save Africa from the communists by demanding a new deal for the natives and stop giving aid and comfort to the Union of South Africa and the white supremacists."[7]

A second predominant theme also emerged when African Americans engaged South Africa. Highlighting the evils and inhumanity of white supremacy, African Americans commonly compared Malan and apartheid to Hitler and Nazism. "The *Amsterdam News* is positive that South African racism must be stopped without further delay, hypocrisy, or evasion," editorialized the paper. "Like Hitlerism, the racial policies of the South African

Boers are a threat to the peace, security and progress of a democratic society." In more hyperbolic imagery the *Afro-American* opined, "Nothing in all of Hitler's treatment of the Jews or Russia's slave camps in Siberia has equaled the cruelty with which the Boers have oppressed the native Africans and appropriated their land and wealth."[8]

This comparison offered an easily identifiable analogy by which Americans could understand the horrors of the apartheid system. Malan, like Hitler, was a deformed human being; apartheid, like Nazism, was a deviant and bestial system. The reasoning functioned to give instant credibility to the struggle against white supremacy. It also offered encouragement, suggesting that in order to achieve success the struggle simply needed to rectify a warped system. This thinking reflected the prevailing civil rights mindset of the day, which held that if laws could be changed and enforced, then equality and full citizenship surely would follow. Such reasoning, however, divorced apartheid from the context of South Africa's history, removing the situation from the political and economic realities of African life. White rule in South Africa, and colonialism in general, were rooted in oppressive economic and political systems, not simply aberrant behavior. And, as black Americans found in the 1950s and 1960s, simply legislating away white supremacy did not eliminate racial inequality.[9]

In the wake of Malan's 1950 legislative proposals, black Americans undertook some efforts on behalf of black South Africans. The CAA, reviving somewhat from its 1948 schism, in June 1950 informed people of the Malan government's "measures toward increasing the enslavement of the 10 million non-white people of that country," and of African protests against these measures. The council urged the UN to protect the rights of nonwhites. The NAACP reasoned that as the Justice Department had invoked the Internal Security Act of 1950 to bar entry into the United States to past and present members of foreign Communist, Nazi, Fascist, and other totalitarian parties, it should do likewise with the "totalitarian and anti-Negro" Nationalist Party. In the fall of 1950 it contacted Attorney General J. Howard McGrath concerning the matter. The NAACP did not possess enough clout, however, to overcome the strategic minerals and staunch anticommunism that the South Africans had to offer.[10]

The African American press also made calls for national and international action against the institution of apartheid. The *Amsterdam News*, declaring that racism by custom or by legislation no longer could be tolerated, counseled the United Nations to investigate the issue. If the UN found South Africa guilty of UN Charter violations, then it should expel South Africa and declare it an outlaw nation. The *Defender* advocated U.S. intervention on behalf of nonwhites in South Africa in order to prevent oppressed Africans from turning to communism. The *Afro-American* argued that Washington should give no more aid to the South African government and, further, should suspend support for Britain until London halted all support of South Africa. Given the post–World War II economic state of Britain, this would have been a weighty card to play. However, the U.S. government was not about to test the alliance with Britain over racial problems in South Africa. Nor were U.S. officials keen on establishing a precedent of countries pressuring other nations over racial questions when America's own racial affairs were hardly in order.[11]

Yet even as South African events in 1950 generated some activity across the Atlantic, there were notable limits on African American engagement. The appeal to invoke the Internal Security Act represented the extent of NAACP efforts. While the board of directors discussed the lack of a U.S. policy toward Africa and the Caribbean during their June 1950 meeting, nothing more came of it other than vague commitments to form a committee. No organization issued a call to action on the part of African Americans. For most, events in South Africa had little connection to the struggle of African Americans. Reading about South Africa in the CAA's newsletter *New Africa*, A. A. Marks of Memphis wrote to ask, "Why in the world would one worry about the racial conditions in Africa when we as a minority group catch hell here in this country? Chances are I'll never make it to Africa, therefore I am not in the least bit interested in what goes on over there, but very concerned about conditions here at home."[12]

If asked, black Americans generally still would voice a broad anticolonialism but at most as no more than a secondary concern. When black South Africans staged the National Day of Protest and Mourning on 26 June, it barely rippled through black America.[13] The lack of connection between the struggles helps explain why a regular columnist for the *Defender*, Albert Barnett, could write lightly about the Group Areas Act. On the heels of the day of protest, Barnett commented on what he found to be two interesting news items from Africa. The first one was that "our modern educational system and teaching methods are becoming increasingly effective in spreading the light of intelligence into dark places." The dark place in question: a school for blacks in East London, South Africa. The second item involved Malan finally receiving parliamentary approval for the Group Areas Act. "It's an interesting experiment, one well worth watching," opined Barnett. "With Whites, Blacks, and Mulattoes legally separated and knowing the proverbial 'attraction for the opposites,' one might well pose the question: 'Will there be any cheating, and if so, what will be the penalty?'" Nothing in the column suggested any connection between the plight of blacks in South Africa and the United States.[14]

U.S. Policy, South Africa, and African Americans

During the same period, the U.S. government framed its relationship with the new regime. Shortly after Malan's election the State Department generated a policy statement toward South Africa, the first for any area in Africa south of the Sahara. It defined three general objectives: to maintain and develop friendly relations between the United States and South Africa; to encourage South African bonds of sympathy with the Western powers and its continued participation in the United Nations; and to encourage the economic development of South Africa and the growth of its foreign trade. The policy statement recognized that race relations reigned as the omnipresent issue in South Africa and warned that unless a policy could be developed "on something other than a substratum of fear and hate," progress in South Africa "will be hampered and the development she has already achieved will be endangered." Even so, officials maintained much more interest in securing South Africa's support for the struggle against communism and in expanding markets for trade. At this point, and for a long time to come, strategic considerations trumped any concerns about racial policy.[15]

Officials saw much in South Africa that assured them it would make a staunch ally. As historian Thomas Borstelmann points out, the dominant impression Americans held of white South Africans immediately after World War II was of "English-speaking, Christian, capitalist, anticommunist Western allies who had carved a corner of European civilization on the 'Dark Continent.'" The United States and South Africa had been allies during both World Wars. Their economic connections were expanding. And, most importantly, as the nuclear age and the Cold War dawned simultaneously, geological surveys revealed that the world's largest undeveloped reserves of uranium ore capable of early commercial development existed in the soil of South Africa. Any number of factors—South Africa's wealth of gold and strategic minerals, its rapidly industrializing economy, its expanding trade with the United States, its strategic location on the sea lanes around the Cape of Good Hope, its historic ties to Great Britain and the Commonwealth, its zealous anticommunism—made the country a desirable ally.[16]

South Africa's strategic importance combined with U.S. officials' fears that South Africa under Malan would slip into isolationism to propel Washington to accept Pretoria's proposal that their respective legations be upgraded to embassies. Truman approved the action in November 1948, and on 1 March

1949 the Senate confirmed North Winship as the first American ambassador to South Africa. The Nationalists' stated intention of imposing apartheid plainly did not sway the U.S. decision.[17]

The State Department's response to the series of clashes and demonstrations in South Africa during the first half of 1950 made clear that Cold War geopolitical and economic interests would determine Washington's relationship with South Africa. In late January the arrest of an African man sparked a fray in the Newclare Township that resulted in the arrest of 600 Africans. Two weeks later, when an African resisted arrest for not carrying his pass, others came to his aid, and the confrontation escalated into three days of conflict in Newclare and neighboring Sophiatown. U.S. diplomatic personnel in South Africa apprised the State Department that the clashes stemmed from rising racial tensions. The U.S. consul general in Johannesburg, Sydney Redecker, wrote that the disturbances "grew out of the grievances of the natives against the white authorities" and were "the most serious to occur thus far against the established European authority of South Africa." Redecker cited "thoughtful observers" as feeling that "unless there is a drastic improvement in the economic and living conditions of the natives and the removal of the causes of their unrest, further and more serious disturbances may be in store for Johannesburg and South Africa." Potentially, he wrote, "conditions will build up for a serious social upheaval within the not distant future, which will rock all of South Africa." The political attaché in Cape Town, Joseph Sweeney, described the May Day disturbances as "uglier in mood than any in the recent past" and as evidence of escalating racial tension "which threatens the internal stability of the Union of South Africa." Sweeney believed that in the wake of the recent violence only three answers were possible for South Africa: compromise, further riots, or a police state. For further riots to be avoided, certain obvious steps needed to be taken on behalf of nonwhites: higher wages, health benefits, more housing, less stringent pass laws, and a greater role for blacks in South African life. Sweeney correctly predicted that none of these steps would be taken and that instead the Malan government intended to create a police state with an aim to "perpetuate White supremacy in an Afrikaans republic."[18]

U.S. diplomats in South Africa and State Department officials in Washington clearly knew of the escalating racial tensions in South Africa and of the South African government's movement toward a white supremacist police state. Indeed, the embassy in South Africa even assessed the greatest source of communist strength as "the restrictive and often repressive treatment of Natives" and found that "the legitimate grievances of Natives are legion and among the few persons who espouse these grievances the majority of vocal ones are Communists." Yet on both sides of the Atlantic, U.S. officials subsumed any concern over how South Africa's racial policies affected either the nonwhite population or the future of the country under their preoccupation with anticommunism. When at the start of 1951 the new American ambassador John Erhardt listed objectives for U.S. policy in South Africa, he concentrated on strengthening South Africa's support of the West, expediting the utilization of South Africa's strategic raw materials, and maintaining South African participation in the United Nations and the British Commonwealth. As for the racial divide, he advised that American influence should "cautiously and without giving offense" work to bring racial policies "closer to the general standards of Western democracies," and evoke a harmonious formula for the coexistence of whites and blacks.[19]

Cold War considerations unwaveringly dictated maintaining a strong alliance with white South Africa, with strategic desires eclipsing concerns about the long-term effects of the racial situation. This thinking flowed from the highest officials in Washington, where Secretary of State Dean Acheson bewailed "purists who would have no dealings with any but the fairest of the democratic states, going from state to state with political litmus paper testing them for true-blue democracy."[20]

Yet with South Africa's racial policies rearing their ugly heads in multiple forms, the country continued to receive worldwide attention. UN debates about South Africa's refusal to submit a trusteeship agreement for South West Africa (Namibia) and about South Africa's domestic treatment of Indians plainly showed that most of the world's nations opposed the white South African government's actions. After World War I, the League of Nations had assigned German South West Africa to South Africa as a mandate; since that time, South Africa had harbored designs on the territory. With the death of the League of Nations, the status of the mandate entered uncharted waters. In 1946 South Africa announced that it planned to annex the territory. UN member states unanimously disagreed, believing that the UN stood as the heir to the League and that South West Africa should be made part of the UN trusteeship system. By this point, India was turning into South Africa's most implacable international foe. India's links to South Africa traced back to the importation of thousands of indentured Indian workers in the nineteenth century. South Africa's racist treatment of people of Indian descent had in fact prompted Mohandas Gandhi to debut his nonviolent resistance in South Africa shortly after the turn of the century. In 1946, Gandhi once again had encouraged and supported South African Indians in a passive resistance campaign, this time against the Asiatic Land Tenure and Indian Representation Act. India's concern about the treatment of Indians in South Africa broadened into leading international condemnation of the entire white supremacist structure of South Africa.[21]

The Truman administration of course viewed the issues of South West Africa and South Africa's treatment of Indians as annoyances that detracted from the greater issue of containing communism. Yet what in Washington qualified as nothing more than a minor distraction stirred up antagonism and resentment by people of color around the world. When the State Department updated its Policy Statement for South Africa in March 1951, it had to acknowledge South Africa's "reactionary racial policies, and the difficulties which those policies have engendered in the UN." The statement noted that criticism voiced in the UN had the effect of aligning colored nations of the world against white South Africa while providing a useful subject for Soviet propaganda against the West. Allying with South Africa linked the United States to South Africa's racial policies, damaging American efforts to win the hearts and minds of Third World peoples. Cold War concerns and UN criticism thus prompted U.S. officials to try to influence the South African government "to adopt a more conciliatory attitude in the UN." Yet ultimately, U.S. officials reaffirmed the fundamental policy objective first articulated in 1948: "It is in our interest to maintain friendly relations with South Africa because of strategic considerations and also because South Africa represents a good market for our products."[22]

Through the early 1950s U.S. officials charted what they alternately termed a "middle course," a "middle position," or a "middle-of-the-road position" toward colonial areas in Africa.[23] In the case of South Africa, U.S. officials sought to promote friendship with the government by augmenting economic and military ties and working to soften worldwide condemnation of that country, while at the same time maintaining good relations with the Third World by not seeming to support South Africa's racial policies. What U.S. officials termed a "middle path," however, constituted little more than support for the ruling white power structure, at least until African independence became a foregone conclusion. Those in the U.S. foreign policy establishment talked incessantly about the dangers of "premature independence" and the need to preserve white rule for as long as possible. These officials preferred leaving the ruling white power structure in place, giving only lip service to African independence. Naturally the verbal gymnastics of the "middle course" created awkwardness and antagonism. More significantly, as Cold War strategic concerns continued to drive U.S. relations with South Africa, all those on both sides of the Atlantic who opposed continuing white minority rule were left more angry and disillusioned.[24]

During this crucial period of African policy development the potentially powerful domestic constituency for black Africa, black Americans, had fallen virtually silent or been rendered largely ineffective on the issue. One result of the stifling of international race consciousness among black Americans was that major civil rights organizations did not develop meaningful, Africa-oriented programs as integral parts of their overall operations. Their minimal institutional voice on African affairs, in turn, retarded the ability of African Americans to develop an effective constituency for Africa.[25]

The CAA remained the black-led organization most focused on the political and economic problems that Africans faced. But continuing government repression fed concerns in black America about associating with the left wing and protecting the domestic agenda from communist taint, thereby slowly strangling support for the CAA. In the late 1940s and the early 1950s its influence waned, and the CAA, fighting for survival, could do less regarding Africa.

The NAACP, still the leading voice of black America at midcentury, stood as the African American organization best positioned to act on behalf of non-white South Africans. Activists prodded it to speak out on African issues. Du Bois, for one, had worked hard to convince the NAACP to institutionalize an organizational framework for black American interest in Africa. When he returned to the NAACP in the mid-1940s, Du Bois had viewed his Department of Special Research as "a sort of foreign affairs department of the NAACP reviving and carrying on the work of the Pan-African Congresses." Du Bois never felt satisfied that the NAACP leadership properly appreciated or supported his work and felt that the NAACP particularly neglected issues concerning Africa. In December 1946 he had complained to Walter White, "Ever since my preliminary report on the work of this department, made in 1944, I have stressed in nearly every report to the board certain actions which we ought to take toward Africa. To this the board has paid no attention except in the case of my visiting the Pan-African Congress." Du Bois acknowledged that the NAACP had the liberty to ignore the unrest, agitation, and development of Africa and to take the position that "our problem has to do with the United States and that there we have more than enough to keep us busy and to use our available funds; and that we should leave the problems of Africa to some other organization." However, he continued, no other organization was "taking up this work as it should be performed." He assessed the CAA as being "well-equipped to study South Africa" but believed that practically no organization gathered material on the rest of Africa. Of course, months later the NAACP fired Du Bois, after which he became a CAA official.[26]

Adopting Du Bois's ideas would have created an institutional framework for the NAACP to actively pursue transatlantic issues. But the NAACP had other priorities at mid-century, with its leadership emphasizing anew its traditional domestic agenda. After Du Bois's departure, no person held specific responsibility to organize, promote, or lobby on issues relating to Africa. Africa as a peripheral concern meant that African issues easily fell through the cracks during this critical time for African liberation struggles and U.S. policy formation.

The Defiance Campaign

Given the ongoing anger about apartheid, reports of black unrest in South Africa inevitably continued to reach the State Department. In August 1951 an embassy official, Morris Dembo, met informally with a group of ten middle-class black South Africans to discuss their views of the situation. Dembo reported to the State Department on the three main points of discussion: the impossibility of compromise and the unavoidability of revolution; the fact that, despite shortcomings among black organizations, the struggle against oppression was developing and "the pot was bubbling"; and the disappointment with U.S. decisions that essentially supported South Africa at the UN. The report warned that blacks in South Africa assessed world developments in terms of the national black and white struggle and accordingly found it hard to resist communism because in white South Africa only the communists sided with racial equality. Dembo concluded that the observations typified black opinion in South Africa and warned of future trouble. Three months later, political attaché Sweeney reported that relations between blacks and whites in South Africa had deteriorated to "the lowest level" in the country's history and that "the present tension cannot continue indefinitely — it must be released somehow." He mentioned in passing that at a meeting of non-European leaders to begin on 15 December 1951, a campaign for mass protest might be mapped out.[27]

At the ANC's annual conference in December 1951, the meeting to which Sweeney referred, the organization adopted the report of a joint planning council that had convened representatives from the primary organizations of nonwhite groups in South Africa. This planning council included the ANC, representing blacks, and the South African Indian Congress (SAIC), representing Indians, with members of the Franchise Action Council (FRAC), representing Coloureds, invited as observers. The planning council's report called for a campaign of passive resistance against apartheid legislation unless the government immediately repealed the most onerous laws. The report provided a blueprint for these organizations to conduct the mass campaign, while defining the long-term goal as having democratic rights extended to nonwhites.[28]

In accordance with the adopted recommendations, ANC president-general James Moroka and secretary-general Walter Sisulu sent a letter to Prime Minister Malan declaring that if by 29 February 1952 the government failed to repeal specific discriminatory legislation, then on 6 April the ANC would launch the protest campaign. They targeted six specific laws for the initial campaign: the Pass Laws, the Group Areas Act, the Separate Representation of Voters Act, the Bantu Authorities Act, the Suppression of Communism Act, and Stock Limitation laws. Both the SAIC and FRAC pledged their support for a united campaign of noncooperation.[29] Malan, as expected, rejected the threat. The government, he warned, would "make full use of the machinery at its disposal to quell any disturbances and, thereafter, deal adequately with those responsible for inciting subversive activities of any nature whatsoever." Moroka and Sisulu sent a second latter regretting Malan's response and reiterating their plans to proceed with the Defiance Campaign.[30]

In March, after the government ignored the ultimatum's deadline, Manilal Gandhi staged a 21-day hunger strike. The son of the Mahatma Gandhi, Manilal hoped his action would spur a peaceful resolution. His hunger strikes, however, proved to be less effective than those of his father. With the South African government giving no ground, 6 April loomed as a day of confrontation.[31]

As the date approached, some protest leaders fretted about their preparedness for a full-fledged passive resistance campaign. They felt they needed to train more volunteers and raise more money for cushioning the burdens of jailed volunteers' families. The symbolic justice of launching protests on 6 April, the tercentennial of Dutch colonizer Jan Van Riebeeck's landing and a day white South Africans had proclaimed as one of celebration, still appealed. But eventually campaign planners decided to postpone mass action until 26 June, the anniversary of the 1950 National Day of Protest. The ANC and SAIC appealed to nonwhite South Africa to observe 6 April as a "National Day of Pledge and Prayer" as a prelude to the Defiance Campaign. Limited demonstrations on 6 April passed without incident.[32]

On 26 June national volunteer-in-chief Nelson Mandela led small groups of protesters into action. Their initial goal: to overflow the jails by forcing arrests on petty apartheid offenses. People of color walked into the white sections of post offices; they used white entrances and platforms at railway stations and boarded white railway cars; they entered locations without a permit; they stayed out at night without curfew passes. Thousands landed in jail, where they chose to serve prison terms rather than pay fines. In the first month, police jailed over 1,500 demonstrators for various petty offenses. Over 10,000 more stood prepared to keep the demonstrations going. By the middle of August, the arrest total climbed past 3,000; in early October, the total surpassed 5,600. The South African government arrested demonstrators at a rate of approximately 400 per week.[33]

In October the UN opened its annual meetings, where the emerging bloc of nonaligned nations intensified their attacks on South Africa's racial policies. India spearheaded the General Assembly's condemnation of apartheid and the effort to bring more pressure to bear on the Malan government. For its part, South Africa announced that it would brook no interference from the outside world. Racial policies, it claimed, were strictly an internal affair and accordingly not within the jurisdiction of any UN resolutions. When the General Assembly created a three-person committee to study South Africa's racial segregation policies in November 1952, South Africa swore any such commission would receive no cooperation.

The Defiance Campaign provided a nonviolent protest against white supremacy to which the entire world, including African Americans, could respond. In the tradition of Mahatma Gandhi, these black South Africans sought a peaceful method to end white injustice toward nonwhite peoples. Blacks defied a system that worked to keep them destitute economically, deny them their voice politically, and separate them socially. And while the campaign called on nonwhites in South Africa to do their best to defy segregation laws, it asked the worldwide community to support these endeavors.

Black America at the Time of the Defiance Campaign

As the Defiance Campaign appealed for support in 1952–53, a number of ongoing concerns shaped black America's engagement with Africa and, more specifically, with the Defiance Campaign. Some forces had a more recent history to them, such as the Cold War repression of leftist anticolonial activists, while other factors had a longer history, most particularly the still ongoing negative images of Africa that reinforced tendencies to keep a distance from Africa.

Textbooks, teachers, novels, movies, and any number of commentators still promoted images of Africans as primitive savages, thereby continuing to distort the perceptions that African Americans had of contemporary Africa. In January 1953, Dr. Marguerite Cartwright, an instructor at Hunter College in New York, described the scene when it came time for elementary schoolchildren to study Africa: "The entire continent is presented in the framework of howling savages and dense jungle. It is taught as though it were devoid of a historical past, a modern present, or a possible future. . . . There are no signs of civilization, no schools, no homes as we know them, no domestication of animals, no means of transportation other than by dugout canoes. Recreation consists of tribal wars, feasts, dancing to drumbeats, the bizarre and exotic." When *Life* magazine devoted a special issue to Africa a few months later, it introduced Africa south of the Sahara by declaring, "From the headwaters of the Blue Nile to the Cape of Good Hope, across 46 degrees of latitude and two thirds of a continent, many of Africa's 200 million still live in a jungle twilight of a primitive past."[34]

While some individuals and organizations, such as Du Bois and the CAA, worked to correct the racist images of Africa, and while the black press continued efforts to promote pride in African history, progress remained slow. Unfortunately, the African American press itself was not innocent of perpetuating negative stereotypes and turning Africans into exotic others. Articles such as the one the *Courier* offered its readers about a Swazi chief eating his brother in order to restore his prestige did little to redeem Africa. In fact, all too often the black press demeaned and exoticized Africa.[35]

In the face of such images and of the unquestioned priority of the domestic struggle, many black Americans saw little reason to dwell on Africa. Comments by two black American women highlight the consequences of such negative stereotypes. "To 90% of us the Africans are still savages. . . . I'm not curious about Africa, but I can't help that," declared one woman. "Maybe it's the fault of the American educational system. They make you curious about Europe and Asia, but never about Africa." Her companion offered a comparison to make her point: "There is no more in common between me and an African than [Franklin] Roosevelt and [Queen] Juliana though they were both of Dutch extraction."[36]

The musings of Era Belle Thompson, associate managing editor of the Johnson Publishing Company, publisher of magazines such as *Negro Digest* and *Ebony*, give further voice to feelings of disconnection. Sent to Africa in 1953 to gather material for the company, Thompson published an account of her trip upon returning. With her prior knowledge of the continent geared to concepts handed down by Livingstone and Stanley, she initially had little desire to undertake the journey. "Like most American Negroes, I was so busy shedding my African heritage and fighting for my rights as an American citizen that what happened to my 175,000,000 brothers beyond the sea was a matter for the missionaries. Had anyone called me an African I would have been indignant. Only race fanatics flaunted jungle ancestry or formed back-to-Africa movements. . . . I was proud of my red and white blood, ashamed of the black, for I grew up believing that black was bad, that black was dirty and poor and wrong. Black was Africa. I did not want to be African." Textbooks, movies, cartoons, magazine stories, all "made a shambles of my African background," and accordingly, she wrote, "as a child I began denying my forefathers, despising my motherland."[37]

Some black Americans consciously rejected any racially based connection to Africa, arguing in particular that as blacks in America asked the country to stop segregating and discriminating in racial terms, they should not themselves engage Africa in racial terms. Marjorie McKenzie, a columnist for the *Courier*, responded to a lecture by historian Rayford Logan by asking, "Should American Negroes adopt the hypothesis that the elimination of racial discrimination and segregation in the United States and the continent of Africa is a related problem which will be solved at the same time? This theory was advanced by Dr. Rayford Logan, professor of history at Howard University . . . . [Logan discounts] the meaning of American citizenship and the uniformity of our political system. He consigns us to think in racial terms, a practice we have asked our white friends to abandon as unhealthy. [Dr. Logan] has challenged us to deep consideration of a frightening idea."[38]

In backing universalist principles and domestic designs for integration, black American interest in Africa often became structured along nonracial paths. Of course, even as they promoted integration and the equality of mankind, black Americans could not avoid the racial uses others imposed. So when arguing that no government with an official antiblack policy should be permitted to stand, black Americans generally did so as a response to the racial categorization prescribed by others. Race was not unimportant; daily life proved that it was. Yet racial solidarity held minimal importance in delineating the contours of the relationship with Africa.

Black Americans who regularly engaged Africa and sought to end colonial domination there commonly used universalist, equalitarian ideas and arguments to call on America to follow its avowed national principles and values. This enabled black Americans to push for change while supporting the "American Way." The writings of sociologist and journalist Horace Cayton, one of the most international-minded among his peers, vividly illustrate such ideas. Cayton, the grandson of the black Republican senator Hiram Revels on his mother's side and of a slave on his father's side, grew up in Seattle as the son of a one-time newspaper publisher. For a while he ran with the wrong crowd and, after being caught for petty theft, ended up in a cruel reform school. After getting out, he worked and traveled before finally deciding to pursue his education. He eventually ended up on a fellowship at the University of Chicago, working with sociologist Robert Park in the 1930s. When his marriage fell apart, a depressed Cayton went to Europe, returning months later convinced more than ever that America was his home. Cayton then followed a series of teaching jobs and sociology projects to various parts of the country before publishing together with St. Clair Drake in 1945 a major work on black life in Chicago, *Black Metropolis*. Cayton's personal life remained a shambles, however, as he divorced his second wife and spiraled into depression. Eventually he climbed out of it, partly through his regular work as a columnist for the *Courier*.[39]

As the *Courier's* accredited correspondent to the UN, Cayton regularly wrote with sympathy about the struggle for freedom throughout the world, but at the same time he made clear his own position: "I am not taken in by any spurious notions about my African heritage. American Negroes are really just dark-skinned Americans. We are not held together by any idea of a common African background, history, or culture but rather by the opposition of white Americans. As a group we don't even resemble Africans. Culturally we are wholly American . . . this is our home, our country."[40]

Yet even as he felt disconnected from Africa, Cayton expressed strong interest in and support for the struggles of Africans. Cayton received letters from readers questioning why he harped on Africa, one of which specifically asked why he demanded acceptance in America on the one hand and pleaded the cause of Africa on the other. Cayton responded that black Americans now had little in common with their African brothers because slave owners had deliberately stripped blacks of all African culture. This process, Cayton argued, had rendered black Americans more American than other groups in the country. But the realization that race and color played an important part in the world meant that "partial identification" with Africa came from more than sentimental interest. Cayton carefully emphasized that interest in Africa did not mean disloyalty; there could be concern over imperialism and exploitation without losing allegiance to the United States. Indeed, he wrote, "Over and above all the sentimental identification because of race, there is a real and legitimate reason why both Negroes and whites should share the feeling of exultation in the fight which Africa is putting up for her freedom. It is the American way to act." Cayton's reasoning meant that he, and other black Americans, did not have to reconsider their own relationship with Africa in order to demand an end to colonialism in Africa.[41]

Even as Africans initiated and launched a widespread protest campaign, highly sophisticated African Americans still accepted that they would show Africans ways to handle discrimination and would lead them in gaining equality. That Africans were laying the groundwork for a new African American relationship with Africa had yet to be fully recognized. Bayard Rustin, serving as race relations director for the Fellowship of Reconciliation (FOR) and becoming a pivotal actor in the civil rights movement, offers a particularly notable case. With his interest in Africa stoked by the Defiance Campaign, in August 1952 he leapt at the chance to visit the continent for the first time. His trip, sponsored by FOR and the American Friends Service Committee, helped establish transatlantic links. At the same time, Rustin's responses also reveal telling ongoing attitudes. Among the articles he wrote based on this trip, one was entitled, "Africa Looks to Colored America." The piece argued that Africans had "astounding" admiration for African Americans and that many measured their progress through comparisons with black America. According to Rustin, the black GI in Africa during World War II had "encouraged his African cousin to stand up," and this became the major factor in "the victory over African servility."[42]

Just as important in shaping engagement with the Defiance Campaign were the newer forces generated by the pervasive influence of the continuing Cold War. Americans in general, and black civil rights leaders in particular, felt a need to display an overt "Americanism," which in turn affected their relationship with Africa. A 1952 reader opinion poll conducted by the *Courier* asked, "Are Negro leaders more cautious because of their fear over being branded as Reds?" The response: 70 percent said yes, 25 percent said no, and 5 percent were undecided. In its next poll the *Courier* asked, "Does the threat of communism materially aid the advance of the Negro toward full citizenship?" The response: 64.4 percent said yes, 32.7 percent said no, and 2.9 percent were undecided.[43]

Black Americans felt Cold War pressures, but as the *Courier* polls suggested, they also saw the Cold War as an opportunity to advance their own agenda. They knew that the treatment of minorities in America did more to damage the worldwide cause of democracy than any actions by the Soviets, and they took advantage of the leverage this afforded them.[44] Ties to liberation struggles in Africa, be they ties of condition or of race, seemingly held less promise. Moreover, any overt criticism of Democratic U.S. foreign policy, especially if echoed by communist advocates, risked appearing disloyal and thus endangered civil rights reform.

While most black leaders saw, and used, the communist threat as a means to advance the domestic agenda, some also recognized the potential for using fears of communism as a way to influence U.S. officials' thinking on colonialism in Africa. Thus, while the Cold War on the one hand choked African American links with Africa, it also opened up alternative ways to lobby on Africa. African Americans continued to play the "communist card" in an effort to push U.S. policy toward a more pro-African stance. They understood, as did colonized peoples in Africa, that any "middle path" was in actuality pro-white. They suffered no illusions over the fact that while the U.S. government verbally supported the right to self-determination, it concretely supported its European allies, the ruling colonial powers.

African Americans argued that colonial peoples did not want to turn to communism; however, with white regimes in Africa obviously not interested in granting freedom and with the United States turning a blind eye, people struggling for independence had to look toward the communist bloc for support. When A. Philip Randolph urged Eisenhower to make substantive changes on African policy, he concluded that only a philosophy of "freedom, fraternalism and friendship" could prevent millions of blacks from "being lured into the orbit of world Communism and keep them in the family of free men."[45] Walter White used similar anticommunist arguments when he lobbied the U.S. delegation to the UN. Organizing a petition that cited colonial problems throughout the African continent, White called for the U.S. delegation to take a course of action that would identify America with the aspirations of Africans. Indeed, he argued, the United States needed to bring into being a world of men whose freedom would give them the will to turn back despair and Soviet totalitarianism. On behalf of the NAACP, the Urban League, and church, labor, and civic organizations, White submitted the letter to the U.S. delegation in early December 1952.[46]

The black press similarly used anticommunist arguments in commenting on Africa. "We have repeatedly called attention to the criminal course of affairs in South Africa," expounded the *Defender* in one of a series of editorials on southern Africa, "and urged action by our government to bring pressure to bear on the Malan crowd and prevent racial war which is in the making. If we do not come to the aid of the oppressed native millions, they are certain to fall victim to the communists who will use them for their own ends. . . . The future of Africa is hanging in the balance and the lessons of current history, particularly in China, should force us to recognize that we cannot afford to stand idly by. . . . The oppressed of the world should look to Washington for help and not Moscow. It is our duty to make certain they will not look to us in vain. We should be guided by enlightened self-interest if nothing else."[47]

Using anticommunism undoubtedly worked as a way to engage policymakers' concerns, but it was fatally flawed by the fact that few officials in Washington could be convinced that long-term friendship with currently subjugated Africans compared to the immediate threat of the Soviet Union. In the specific case of South Africa, U.S. officials had decided that placing pressure on South Africa would cause deep resentment in that government, thereby adversely affecting relations with a country deemed a vital strategic ally. State Department officials feared that any outside pressure might even exacerbate the situation, and they repeatedly argued that no effort should be made to prod the South African government to soften its racial policies. In fact, when South African deputy prime minister and minister of finance Nicolaas Havenga visited the United States at the height of the Defiance Campaign, Secretary of State Acheson deliberately avoided broaching the topic of South Africa's domestic crisis.[48]

African American appeals to democratic principles also carried little force at the height of the Cold War. When the United States repeatedly sidestepped taking a stand at the UN against South Africa's racial policies, the *Amsterdam News* registered disappointment that, in its words, the U.S. delegation would not support the principle of human liberty. The monumental task of moving U.S. policy in a direction more favorable to black freedom struggles, however, would take more than the voices and political weight of black America.[49]

African American support for anticolonialism endured, but African Americans who had chosen to generally support U.S. anticommunist-driven foreign policy were left with few options. Using anticommunist-inspired arguments had little to no effect on reshaping African policy, yet criticism too vocal risked damaging a working relationship with Washington on domestic issues. In fact, in trying to maneuver through the Cold War minefield, black Americans sometimes accepted policies detrimental to Africans that they otherwise might have denounced. The abundant quantities of uranium in South Africa provided a vivid example of the tension. In the Cold War atomic era, South Africa's relatively rare lode of uranium held particular importance and therefore provided Washington a compelling reason for maintaining smooth relations with South Africa. In May 1953 the United States, Britain, and South Africa jointly opened a uranium plant in South Africa. The *Amsterdam News* remarked that in usual times Washington would denounce the extreme racialism and segregation of South Africa. But because these were not usual times, it noted, "our historic humanity is, in many instances, playing second or third fiddle to uranium deposits and our anti-Communist position." No call for a reordering of priorities followed, however. Instead, the *Amsterdam News* asked Americans to remain sensitive to the cries of the oppressed even as it implicitly went along with the national policy priorities.[50]

In accepting the parameters of the anticommunist framework, most African American leaders found they had only a narrow basis for connections with Africa at this time. Political expediency did not form the basis for a relationship of mutual respect and interest. In fact, political calculations illustrate once again how domestic concerns held primacy, and often drew attention away from African events. The Defiance Campaign's launch coincided with the heating up of the 1952 presidential campaign, starting as it did between the Republican and Democratic conventions. Truman had announced in late March that he would not run for another term, leaving the presidential race without an incumbent for the first time in a quarter century. During that time the Democrats seemingly had solidified their hold on the black vote. The racist Dixiecrat wing of the party, however, rendered any such hold tenuous. African Americans felt that the Democrats had much for which to answer, and they held a keen interest in the parties' nominees and their civil rights planks. So as Africans initiated the Defiance Campaign, the *Crisis* trained its editorial page not on South Africa but on what it labeled "The Single Issue." African Americans would vote only for a presidential candidate with a forthright civil rights platform, declared the *Crisis*, observing, "Negroes are tired of being second-class citizens, and are going to turn thumbs down on any candidate, Democrat or Republican, who hedges on this all important issue. In fact, for most Negroes it is the only political issue in the presidential race."[51]

African American Responses to the Defiance Campaign

Thus, as the Defiance Campaign commenced, the continuing legacy of the negative images of Africa and the blanketing Cold War paradigm helped shape and minimize African American connections with African struggles, as did the predominant universalist arguments and domestic orientation. It is in this context that African American responses to the Defiance Campaign should be seen. Yet even with the many influences working to mitigate links with Africa, African Americans still would respond to events in South Africa more vigorously than they had previously. The broader context makes more apparent how vital a stepping-stone the Defiance Campaign would be in reframing the African American relationship with Africa, with it ultimately serving as an influential model as African Americans initiated their own resistance in 1950s America.

The planning stages of the Defiance Campaign initially connected several individual African Americans with Africa via the worldwide peace movement. William Sutherland, a pacifist activist, learned of the plans to launch the Defiance Campaign while in Europe in 1951. Returning to New York, Sutherland informed George Houser and Bayard Rustin, cosecretaries for race relations with the Fellowship of Reconciliation, about the plan and urged them to commit FOR to the campaign. Rustin and Houser received the idea coolly at first, for they counted as their two primary obligations antiwar causes in the world at large and civil rights activism in the United States. Sutherland, however, mailed FOR literature to South Africa, initiating contact with ANC leaders. As a result, the ANC started writing to Houser and Rustin, who commenced work on a program to help the ANC campaign.[52]

Houser, Rustin, and others quickly grew concerned about the limited organized constituencies for Africa in the United States. A variety of pacifists, liberals, and religious leaders with connections to organizations such as FOR, the War Resisters League, and the International League for the Rights of Man therefore decided to create Americans for South African Resistance (AFSAR). Headed by the ministers Donald Harrington, George Houser, and Charles Trigg, AFSAR also included such notable black Americans such as Charles S. Johnson, Mordecai Johnson, Adam Clayton Powell Jr., A. Philip Randolph, Rev. James Robinson, Bayard Rustin, George Schuyler, and William Sutherland.[53]

AFSAR rapidly positioned itself as an avowedly noncommunist alternative to the CAA. When the CAA contacted AFSAR regarding mutual cooperation in mobilizing public support for the South African protesters, AFSAR firmly distanced itself. While surely people in the CAA represented many points of view, responded AFSAR, "there are many who are not by any means unsympathetic to the basic policies of the Communist Party."[54]

Clearly cooperation among organizations with ties to Africa would be riven by domestic considerations as well as "territorial" concerns. A short time later AFSAR would find the shoe on the other foot when, embarking on broadening its mission by turning itself into the American Committee on Africa (ACOA), it contacted the NAACP about cooperating more fully. NAACP board member Arthur Spingarn found himself "not too favorably impressed" with ACOA's backers, concluding that despite being persons of good will, these men had no apparent qualifications for the work involved and had little knowledge of Africa. Roy Wilkins concurred in Spingarn's tepid response and, apparently without seeing the irony, added, "Too bad the NAACP could not have developed an African committee for this work."[55]

Therefore, when the Defiance Campaign commenced, responses in America came from distinct quarters. The initial protest day, 6 April, prompted AFSAR to stage an afternoon rally at the Abyssinian Baptist Church. Speakers included the congressman Rev. Adam Clayton Powell Jr., the actor Canada Lee, and the AFSAR cochairmen, the Reverends Harrington and Trigg. Following the rally, a motorcade went to the South African consulate to help conduct evening demonstrations. For its part, the NAACP sent greetings and pledged unqualified support for the fight to ANC president Moroka.[56] The CAA, despite its ongoing debilitating fight with the government, sallied forth in support of the protesters. It staged an open-air mass meeting on the evening of 5 April on Harlem's corner of 126th and Lenox, at which hundreds of people rallied in support of the South African civil disobedience movement. The CAA called for two minutes of silence to be observed at noon on 6 April as a show of nationwide solidarity; for the rest of the week it coordinated picketing in front of the South African Consulate in New York City.[57] As head of the CAA, Robeson used the Defiance Campaign to encourage not only an internationalist vision in black America but also to urge black Americans to take lessons from South Africa's example:

> Imagine all sections of the Negro people in the United States, their organizational and programmatic differences put aside, joining together in a great and compelling action to put a STOP to Jim Crowism in all its forms everywhere in this land. Think how such an action would stir the whole of America, raising to a new high level the people's resistance to the mounting fascism which is bent upon wiping out the constitutional rights of ALL Americans. A dream? No. Look at the Union of South Africa. See there how the victims of an even more savage racist oppression . . . have solemnly determined that only by establishing a common front of united and resolute resistance can they escape absolute enslavement by the fascist Malan regime.[58]

African Americans explicitly compared segregation in South Africa and America and uniformly found apartheid worse. Benjamin Mays, president of Morehouse College, went so far as to declare apartheid "worse than anything that ever existed in the Southern United States." People connected white supremacy across the Atlantic in different ways. "Whether it takes the form of subtle distinctions insidiously woven into cleverly written laws, or unabashed insistence on segregation in the United States, or on apartheid, its South African counterpart," Mary McLeod Bethune pointed out, "know that discrimination is always justified — always 'necessary' — in the minds of its authors." In drawing such parallels between conditions in the two countries, such commentaries help establish the level of awareness necessary to create an environment in which African Americans would become more inclined to take action supporting black South Africans.[59]

Some in the black press demanded that the U.S. government take action. The *Defender* counseled the State Department to pressure Malan to prevent a racial war in the making. The *Amsterdam News* called on the government to use its influence to "stay the tyrannic hand of Malan." The *Afro-American* criticized Western leaders for condemning the "slavery" behind the Iron Curtain while doing nothing in South Africa about the "millions of natives [who] are not only held in abject slavery, but are stripped of every human dignity to which free men aspire."[60]

When the South African protesters launched their large-scale resistance in late June, they inspired more African Americans. The press searched to find appropriate ways to describe the protesters' mission. Most settled on comparisons to righteous crusades against great odds. The *Amsterdam News* compared the Defiance Campaign to the American Revolution. The *Afro-American* preferred parallels to Jesus Christ, John Brown, and Mohandas Gandhi, men who started with few in number and yet accomplished wonders. The *Afro-American* had no doubt that with steadfastness of purpose and dedication to a cause they knew to be just, the crusaders could not lose. Significantly, too, victory might mean more than justice in South Africa, for oppressed people and colonial powers were "anxious about the outcome of this drama." In drawing these comparisons, these papers established for civil protest in South Africa a noble worldwide pedigree; as black civil disobedience in the United States drew on the African efforts, it could and would share this lineage.[61]

Individuals and organizations rallied support for the resisters. The day after the formal launching of the Defiance Campaign, Du Bois sent to President Truman a petition signed by 160 African American leaders, including Charlotta Bass, Sidney Poitier, Paul Robeson, and Coleman Young. The petition, which Du Bois had initiated as plans for the Defiance Campaign had crystallized, called for the United States to go on record condemning South Africa's racist program as "a flagrant violation of human rights and a threat to world peace."[62]

The CAA then convened an "Emergency Conference on the Present Crisis in South Africa" at Harlem's Hotel Theresa on 24 July 1952, with the aim of developing plans for mobilizing black churches, civic and labor organizations, and the press to support the fight against fascist tyranny in South Africa. About sixty people attended. They agreed to conduct a campaign to collect 100,000 signatures on a petition that asked the U.S. government to denounce apartheid publicly and halt any assistance to South Africa. The petition also asked for donations, with the hope that $5,000 could be sent to aid the families of those arrested in South Africa. The campaign hoped to achieve its goals in seven weeks; however, in that time it collected just 3,800 signatures and $835. On 19 September the CAA sent an initial $900 to support the Defiance Campaign. It sent $600 more on 31 October and $500 more on 30 December, making a total of $2,000 by year's end. AFSAR, also trying to raise money, sent $1,500 by the end of 1952, then sent that much again by April 1953. Walter Sisulu, secretary-general of the ANC, sent a message of thanks through the CAA for "the moral and material support which our cause and the Campaign for the Defiance of Unjust Laws in particular has received from the Negro people of the United States."[63]

The "moral and material" support Sisulu referred to offers insight on the constantly evolving African American relationship. Sisulu probably had no way of knowing, but the material support generated by black America for the Defiance Campaign fell short of what had been raised seventeen years earlier during the Ethiopian crisis. Money raised, in real dollars, totaled less than half that raised for Ethiopia, and in much better economic times than had existed in the middle of the Great Depression. Attention by some never turned to the Defiance Campaign, and that of some others turned quickly away.[64] As seen, black America framed its views of Africa amidst any number of competing factors, so there should be little wonder that the extent and nature of the responses to the Defiance Campaign varied so greatly. Indeed, there was no simplistic Manichean choice of association and dissociation with Africa, but instead a variegated interest amidst an arena of approaches. The powerful influence of African liberation struggles was still in the germinal stages of shaping the black American relationship with Africa.

Thus, in the divergent responses, some ignored the Defiance Campaign while others reacted with deep emotion. These latter felt great frustration over the extent of black American support for the Defiance Campaign. A few people singled out the African American press for not doing enough to aid black South Africans. William Clarke of New York wrote to the *Courier* about his "pain and disappointment" at its failure to comment more on the South African situation. Charles Terrell, also of New York, asked the editors of the *Afro-American* how they could miss the biggest story of 1952 — the boiling ferment for independence among colonial peoples. The spark for his complaint: the previous week *Afro-American* editor Cliff Mackay had listed his top ten stories for 1952. Nothing relating to Africa made the list — but number nine was the Brooklyn Dodgers not winning the world championship.[65]

Other African Americans cast their nets more broadly and bemoaned the lack of community interest in the situation in Africa. Evangeline Johnson of New York City believed black Americans sympathized with their "blood brothers" in South Africa, but she lamented that they did little to pressure the

U.S. government to stop giving financial and moral support to Malan. She called on African Americans to "raise hell" against the lending of money to South Africa and to boycott anything from South Africa.[66]

Perhaps most telling were the African Americans who expressed anger at leaders for not devoting more attention to the colonial problem. "What is incomprehensible to me is the silence of most of our colored leaders in America," decried Jamie Suarez of New York City. Suarez believed that African American leaders were "remarkably stingy in their condemnation of those who oppress black peoples" and that they failed to condemn Malan because they focused so much on the Soviets.[67] The actions of black American leaders gave such accusations credence. Urban League executive director Lester Granger, citing events such as the Italian invasion of Ethiopia and the rise of Malan, lamented that the previous twenty-five years had seen a steadily worsening situation for blacks in Africa. He noted that the degeneration had proceeded with insufficient attention from the rest of the world, "and in the absence of any effective spokesmanship from the world's greatest body of educated, trained Negroes — the Negro population of the United States." To rectify this, he called for the formation of a mass organization composed of 5 million black and 10 million white Americans with a goal of guiding U.S. foreign policy to a more courageous and intelligent assertion of American attitudes toward Africa. Yet Granger himself had not mentioned Africa in his column for at least the previous sixteen months, and he did nothing to follow up and implement his idea. When labor leaders A. Philip Randolph and Frank Crosswaith organized a meeting to object to the treatment of Jews in the Soviet Union, Evangeline Washington of New York City asked why neither had done the same for the racial oppression suffered by blacks in South Africa.[68]

The Defiance Campaign plainly generated conflicting responses in black America. Among some, particularly the rank and file, the black South African protesters energized concern for and action regarding Africa, while among others, particularly the civil rights leaders, ongoing Cold War and domestic concerns mitigated responses. In 1952, black Americans offered an array of opinions and attitudes as they worked to frame their connections with Africa.

Events at the NAACP annual convention in June/July of 1952 captured some of the shifting tensions and views. The NAACP had not been standing by silently but had been working to halt loans to South Africa. In February 1951, Walter White had urged Eugene Black, president of the International Bank of Reconstruction and Development (IBRD), to reconsider the $50 million loan being made to South Africa. To support his case White cited South

Africa's vicious racial policies and defiance of the UN over South West Africa. Black replied that the loan papers had been signed already and, in addition, that the IBRD Articles of Agreement provided that loans should be made without regard to political and other noneconomic factors. Black further contended that the projects the IBRD had agreed to finance would benefit all peoples in South Africa. Correspondence continued between the two, with neither finding satisfaction in the other's responses.[69] In May 1952, attorney Roy Garvin informed White that South Africa planned to send a delegation to the United States to ask for a $19 million loan, partly financed through the IBRD. Garvin argued that a mass protest would be effective in an election year. White pursued the matter, seeking information on any and all loans made to South Africa since Malan took power and convincing the NAACP board of directors to approve sending a delegation to call on Black. Yet Black again rebuffed NAACP efforts, arguing that the projects financed by the 1951 loan had created jobs at a high level of pay and that this had helped black Africans more than anyone else.[70]

At its June 1952 annual convention the NAACP adopted its strongest position to date on South Africa. While before it had urged the U.S. government to use its influence to reverse the policy of apartheid, in 1952 the NAACP called upon the government to "use to the fullest extent every facility at its command to oppose the cruel and barbaric white supremacy doctrine of Malan and his government." It condemned the IBRD loans to South Africa and demanded that the government, the IBRD, the Export-Import Bank, and all private banks refuse to make any loans or extend any credit to South Africa as long as it continued its current policies. Finally, it pressed the government to take "more vigorous action" against the "cold-blooded" annexation of South West Africa, and to oppose with equal vigor similar threats against Bechuanaland (Botswana), Lesotho, and Swaziland.[71]

Convention delegates, not satisfied with mere resolutions, pushed the NAACP leadership to assume an even more active stance. Concerned over the lack of an institutional framework to support black South Africans, the delegates passed a resolution stating that "the problems of colored peoples of the world are similar to the problems of Negroes in the United States" and that the NAACP's program for first-class citizenship for all peoples "should assume an international role." Delegates directed the board of directors to set up a special committee to study the possibility of expanding the program of the NAACP to "include more active participation and cooperation with peoples in foreign lands" and "to organize an international department under the auspices of an international secretary."[72]

Yet the diasporic consciousness shown by these NAACP members did not find its counterpart in the board of directors. The committee of board members established to investigate the feasibility of the internationalist recommendation reported back in November that finances did not permit the creation of a department of international affairs. They believed that the staff already carried out the spirit of the resolution and should continue to do so to the limits of its time and ability. Even when the NAACP board of directors supported ideas in the conference room, they did not always implement them. At various times they backed proposals for holding a broad-based meeting with the aim of focusing attention on the situation in South Africa, organizing protests against apartheid, sending resolutions to appropriate government officials, and raising money for the resistance movement. Yet no meeting and no fundraising came to pass. However, ongoing events in Africa and pressure from rank-and-file voices in black America would push the liberal civil rights leadership toward a more activist engagement with contemporary Africa.[73]

The Defiance Campaign and Nonviolent Protest

The nonviolent resistance campaign in South Africa essentially had ended by early 1953. While the South African resistors managed to fill some jails and cause headaches for the government, nobody could argue that it resulted in improved conditions for blacks in South Africa. In fact, the government used the campaign to help justify further repressive measures. Rioting that erupted in Port Elizabeth, Johannesburg, Kimberley, and East London between 18 October and 10 November resulted in the deaths of about forty blacks and whites, and the injury of hundreds more. The government quickly blamed the campaign for the disorders. The ANC disavowed any connection between the campaign and the riots, and "call[ed] upon the African people to cease forthwith in any violent action." It claimed that the police deliberately provoked the riots, and reiterated its position that the ANC was conducting "a non-violent struggle against racially discriminatory, unjust laws."[74]

The violence however provided the excuse the government desired to crack down on the protesters. In the weeks following the riots the government passed harsh new laws mandating severe penalties for those who committed offenses as a means of protest. The Criminal Law Amendment Act intended to make the recruitment of volunteers extraordinarily difficult by providing that any person who committed an offense could be sentenced to a £300 fine, three years in jail, a whipping of ten strokes, or a combination of any two. Upon a second conviction, whipping or imprisonment as well as a fine became obligatory. Those convicted of using words or actions calculated to cause another person to commit an offense as a means of protest faced even stiffer penalties. Further, the Public Safety Act empowered the government to declare a state of emergency if it deemed public order seriously threatened. Under a state of emergency persons could be summarily arrested and detained, the only obligation being that their names be submitted to Parliament within thirty days. The arrests and/or bans of the campaign leaders, the harsh penalties, and the fear that Malan could use continuing resistance to convert more white voters to his "law and order" regime contributed to the decision to suspend the campaign.[75]

In April 1953 the white electorate of South Africa went to the polls, marking their first nationwide opportunity to reject or ratify the changes being made by the Nationalists. The results were unequivocal: the Nationalist Party more than doubled its majority in Parliament. Malan viewed this as a mandate to push faster and further his racial policies.

To most outside observers the Defiance Campaign seemingly had done nothing to mitigate or weaken apartheid. African Americans could not look to Africa and see an absolutely successful use of nonviolent direct action nor an example of Africans gaining independence and equality. Those looking for antiapartheid gains had to find signs of subtle yet significant results. The Defiance Campaign had helped convert the ANC into a mass movement and had expanded the number of firmly committed supporters. It had demonstrated both strong black unity and striking self-discipline as black South Africans sought to control their own destiny.[76]

The significance for African Americans also remained subtle yet real. The Defiance Campaign pushed African Americans toward a greater attention to Africa. People emphasized anew the importance of Africa. Calls issued forth for African Americans to learn more about Africa, in order to help correct false notions about Africans and to achieve a greater understanding of the complex events on the continent. Some of the press responded to, as well as encouraged, a swelling interest in Africa by printing lengthy series about Africa to educate and inform their readers. The *Amsterdam News* ran a ten-part series on South Africa by George E. Haynes, the first black American to get his Ph.D. from Columbia, a cofounder and former executive director of the Urban League, and in 1947 a traveler in South Africa for the YMCA. The *Courier* ran a four-part series on South Africa by Homer Jack, a Unitarian minister who would become closely involved with activism on behalf of black South Africa. Horace Cayton embarked on his own series covering all of Africa for the paper.[77]

Messages of racial unity that had been heard before, especially during the invasion of Ethiopia, but had been dampened by shifting attitudes and intervening events, mainly the Cold War, appeared more frequently. Letters to the editor expressed the view that as long as blacks in Africa remained subjugated, those in America would be held in contempt. Others discussed the connections between the struggle of blacks in Africa and America. Lawrence Jenkins of Mount Vernon, New York, argued that there would be no peace in the world until Africa was independent, and called on African Americans to organize "and give our support to our brothers in Africa in their fight for freedom."[78]

As an increasing number of black Americans emphasized the importance of contemporary Africa, most did so while being careful not to minimize their own Americanism. "It is beyond challenge that the principle goal of Negro Americans is to be accepted as good, loyal and equal citizens of this country," wrote Matthew Holden to *Defender* columnist Albert Barnett. "Nonetheless, the redemption of Africa is the hope of the Negro. So long as dark men in Africa are held in slavery, dark men in America will be held in contempt." Black Americans by and large accepted that while they fought for integration under a banner of universalist values, they also were a special people with unique historical experiences. The Defiance Campaign helped promote the African side of African American identity.[79]

With the Defiance Campaign invigorating interest in Africa, and stung by criticism of his lack of efforts on behalf of Africa, A. Philip Randolph wrote a lengthy letter to President Eisenhower in which he asked that an eleven-point program be presented to the British and French as the price for continued American aid. His wide-ranging proposals covered specifics such as supporting a UN investigation of "Fascist Malanism" in South Africa to broad changes including granting Africans the right to vote, giving them access to more arable lands, and dropping the color bar. Randolph pursued the matter by asking Eisenhower to meet with him and other leading African Americans. The White House sought counsel from the Office of African Affairs, which pointed out that while Randolph's views did not accord with the State Department's, "Randolph and his associates are influential citizens whom it is desirable not to offend." Even so, given Eisenhower's personal racial predispositions and Washington's Cold War concerns, Randolph's proposals stood little chance, and the White House avoided any meeting with Randolph.[80]

Other liberal black American leaders also started speaking with stronger concern about white supremacy in Africa. Outrage swept black America in 1953 when Max Yergan, completing his shift from leftist internationalist to Cold War hawk, declared his belief that while apartheid would not accomplish its objectives, "it is necessary to try to understand why South Africa acts as it does, and that our approach should be sympathetic and constructive." He commiserated with white South Africans' fear of being subsumed by the black majority and challenged those who criticized white South Africans to ask themselves what they would do under similar circumstances. Despite Yergan's claim that "the unity, the protection of the free world" motivated him, leading black Americans immediately condemned his comments. The civil rights leadership had adopted anticommunism but refused to take this to such extremes as defending white supremacy. Walter White personally excoriated Yergan and convinced the NAACP board to prepare a statement about this "exceedingly dangerous propaganda" that Washington could use as "justification for the actions of Malan." Lester Granger expressed shock and anger — to which Beatrice Davoen of Brooklyn responded that Granger did not go far enough, for, as she put it, Yergan had "betrayed every living black in the world." Labor leader Willard Townsend denounced Yergan as an apologist for the colonial powers. African American leaders still voiced a broad anticolonialism and maintained watch against white supremacy in Africa.[81]

Perhaps most strikingly, the Defiance Campaign offered to all a dramatic example of nonviolent direct action, an approach not widely advocated by African Americans at the time. As black America debated tactics to use in the struggle for equal rights and full citizenship, in the early 1950s many even advised against overt forms of protest. A year before the Defiance Campaign began, the *Defender* declared that in the fight for first-class citizenship "knuckle-busting, pressure group, mass action techniques" had been shelved because recent years had seen a profound change in public opinion on the race issue: "Almost every issue of Negro papers and periodicals in the last ten years has had occasion to hail some sensational item of progress in race relations." With the change in times, the *Defender* reasoned, "It would be foolish to break a door down to open it when a key to accomplish the same purpose was at hand. Today a committee of intelligent Negroes can get more results than a marching crusade of thousands could get a decade ago."[82]

The liberal civil rights leadership in particular favored less confrontational tactics, most notably legal action. The string of courtroom victories achieved by the NAACP on a range of issues — education, housing, voting — over the last decade had convinced many white and black leaders that mass action was not necessary, or even wise. Thus, when black South Africans started their mass protests, many black Americans were dismissing the relevance of this approach for their own situation. In July 1952 the *Courier* called for a "direct frontal attack" on racial segregation throughout the South, honing in on two tactics: legal action and media blitzes. There were no foot soldiers in this frontal attack. The *Daily World* had gone even further: "Mass action on the part of some individuals or organizations to achieve recognition or employment in industry without well organized machinery is an improper manner in which to approach a most delicate situation. Mass action, which in most instances stems from mob psychology, often runs contrary to logical reasoning and clear thinking."[83]

Marjorie McKenzie, the *Courier* columnist, specifically addressed whether a civil disobedience campaign like the one in South Africa would be useful in the domestic civil rights struggle. Civil disobedience, she argued, provided a weapon for helpless people who had no other avenues of protest or action, but it was inconsistent with democratic methods, goals, and ideals. McKenzie contended that therefore it was an inappropriate tactic for African Americans, who had the Constitution on their side and could utilize voting power to bring about solutions.[84]

Yet the Defiance Campaign, influencing not only the volume but also the character of African interest, helped reshape views about using mass action tactics. In direct contrast to McKenzie, other African Americans saw real lessons for black America. Horace Cayton commented that with the eyes of the world upon South Africa, what was happening might prove to be a lesson to people of color throughout the world, and noted, "It might even work in the United States and this possibility intrigues me." Events in South Africa prompted not only interest but also voices supporting the approaches used and their applicability in America. Surveying the landscape during the Defiance Campaign, the *Defender* wrote with respect about South Africa's freedom fighters, who had taken "advantage of the marvels of communication and the spirit of the time" to win a hearing before the world court of public opinion. The *Defender* believed that the jury of time would "prove the sagacity of native leaders and the end of rule by whites." The civil disobedience of black South Africans now appeared as a viable, even wise path to follow in fighting white supremacy.[85]

The Defiance Campaign may not have improved the situation of black South Africans, but for black Americans it offered an enduring example of oppressed Africans working to end discrimination, segregation, and inequality. Awareness of the Defiance Campaign permeated the community, even if at the time not everyone explicitly connected it to the African American struggle. African Americans, recognizing that more substantial gains in the post–World War II years would have to grind slowly through the courts and even more slowly through white intransigence, could turn to the example of black South Africans and their attempts to fight segregation and inequality through nonviolent protest. African Americans stood on the cusp of dramatic changes, including their own use of nonviolent direct action, and Africa helped drive these changes. Writing to the *Afro-American*, A. L. Foster expressed his hope that black leaders in the South would have the courage to follow the example of Africans and "defy the segregation laws of those whose political leaders are just as determined as Malan to enforce 'apartheid.'" A short time later, in places like Baton Rouge and Montgomery, African Americans would become convinced of the efficacy of nonviolent protest in the American South.[86]

4

KENYA

The Mau Mau and Revolutionary Violence, 1952–1956

Let me preface what I am going to say with this: I hate violence and injustice to any people, regardless of color or religion. I love peace, harmony and brotherhood so much that I don't even like the use of angry words.

But what to do when there is a drive against one; and when if one does not submit meekly, violence is used against him? Should he still keep his hands to his side? Or should he defend himself in whatever way he can?

Take the Kikuyus . . .

Joel Rogers, Pittsburgh Courier *(9 May 1953)*

Thousands of miles to the north of South Africa, other Africans offered a different example of resistance. While people of color in South Africa waged the Defiance Campaign against apartheid and the white minority government, in East Africa the Kenya Land and Freedom Movement, popularly known as Mau Mau, launched a war to overthrow white supremacy and to reclaim the land. The Defiance Campaign and the Mau Mau rebellion offered African Americans a stark contrast: the Defiance Campaign used nonviolent resistance in the Gandhian tradition; the Mau Mau used armed violence.

Violence, and particularly some of the more brutal killings, presented African Americans with a challenge. African Americans roundly criticized the colonial rule of Kenya and the handling of the Mau Mau revolt, and they supported the objective of black majority rule in Kenya. Yet was the murder of civilians, both white and black, whom one believed stood in the way of freedom and equality therefore justified? Responses to that question revealed how different groups of African Americans were debating the best path to follow in their own freedom struggle. Further, the Mau Mau clearly targeted not only white settlers but also the traditional Kikuyu leadership and other Kenyans perceived to be supporters of the colonial government. Mau Mau killings of Africans in fact far outnumbered those of white settlers: the Mau Mau killed 1,880 civilians, all but 58 of whom were African.[1] This aspect of Mau Mau also resonated in black America. Even as civil rights leaders condemned the Mau Mau and their actions, more militant voices spoke out in support of the Mau Mau and against the established African American civil rights leadership. Indeed, black elites' condemnation of Mau Mau spoke as much to their reading of its implication for their own situation as to their disagreement with Mau Mau tactics.

We see in responses to Mau Mau, then, how African Americans wrestled with the scope and meaning of their own freedom struggle. As black Americans grappled with different approaches to gaining rights and freedom, most at this time did not accept, let alone embrace, violence. Legal avenues, and then nonviolent protest, stood as the favored ways for effecting change in America. The Mau Mau insurgency, turning up the heat on simmering tensions within black America, widened the parameters of debate over how to combat white supremacy, and helped to foster a militant critique of the liberal civil rights leadership. In years to come, Mau Mau became embedded in African American consciousness as a powerful symbol of resistance — both to white supremacy as well as to the traditional civil rights leadership.

Mau Mau and a State of Emergency

During the colonization of Africa, most Europeans viewed the continent as climatically unsatisfactory for large-scale European settlement. Heat and disease, not to mention inhabitants who wanted to maintain their own authority and way of life, combined to make most parts of Africa forbidding. The Kenyan Highlands, however, gained a reputation as a place favorable for European settlement.

The British encouraged the emigration of white settlers to Kenya as a way to help pay for the railroad being built from the East African coast to Uganda. The British never wanted their colonization schemes to drain the Empire's finances, so the railroad, completed in 1902, needed passengers and cargo in order to pay for itself. Farmers in Kenya helped foot the bill by paying to ship out their goods as well as to import supplies. Offers of cheap land in vast quantities brought settlers to Kenya. After World War I, the Kenyan government schemed to attract demobilized veterans. The government overrode the rights of Africans long established in the area as the increasing number of settlers pushed more and more Africans off the land and onto reserves. This tactic benefited the settlers by freeing up land as well as ensuring a cheap labor supply. On the other hand, it increased bitterness among Africans, especially the Kikuyu, who populated the highlands that the settlers commandeered.[2]

During the crises of the worldwide depression in the 1930s and the world war in the 1940s, the Kenyan colonial state allowed and even promoted production by African peasants. In the 1930s, African production helped finance the colonial bureaucracy and the state subsidies to the white settler farming community; during World War II, peasant production provided exports to reduce the dollar deficit. Africans squatting on European-owned land also prospered during the war years, as colonial officials did not want to antagonize their labor force in the midst of hostilities.

The post–World War II years, however, brought an abrupt halt to the encouragement of African market-oriented agriculture. With the end of the war, the colonial government again worked to attract demobilized British veterans as well as British colonialists leaving India in the face of that country's impending independence. The burgeoning number of white settlers combined with racist colonial land policies to squeeze the growing African population onto reserves unable to support the people. The colonial government also reintroduced policies to restrict severely agricultural production by African squatters on white settlers' lands.

At the same time, a small population of Africans seemed to be advancing at the expense of their fellows. Chiefs created and given power by the colonial government increased their wealth and authority by solidifying their individual possession of land. Others involved with the colonial system, such as government employees, also sought to acquire land. Alien to Kikuyu traditions, this private land ownership tore at the fabric of the society. Younger Kikuyu with no access to land, along with displaced tenants and squatters, became greatly embittered. The disgruntled squatters evicted from European farms and tenant farmers who lost their small plots often drifted to Nairobi, where between 1941 and 1948 the population soared by 17 percent each year. Disaffection spread there, too, especially as during World War II urban Africans had not fared nearly as well as rural Africans, due to wages trailing inflationary price increases. After the war, prices continued to rise, unemployment grew, and crime became a serious problem.[3]

Emerging African politicians, particularly Jomo Kenyatta, spoke out against colonial policies but found themselves excluded by the colonial administration from the decision-making processes. Sir Philip Mitchell, the governor of Kenya from 1944 to 1952, believed wholeheartedly in the system of "indirect rule." During his tenure the Kenyan government became dependent upon African chiefs who were British appointees. Yet the political legitimacy and influence of the chiefs who worked with the British was declining in the face of rising African nationalism and militancy.

Frustrated, angry, and dispossessed, more and more Africans abandoned the advocates of constitutional politics and change in favor of more militant voices. The Mau Mau began in the late 1940s and, despite being banned by the British in 1950, grew rapidly. Central to the Mau Mau was the "oathing," during which, according to historian John Lonsdale, recruits "committed their life to the cause in swallowing a stew of mutton or goat, vegetables and cereals, sprinkled with soil, marinated in goat's blood, and watched by uprooted sheep's eyes transfixed on thorns."[4] The Mau Mau movement found a particularly receptive audience among the dispossessed squatters, the poor peasant and tenant farmers, the younger Kikuyu who had been transformed into a landless rural class as whites and Kikuyu elites increasingly privatized land, and the urban unemployed and destitute. Many of these people felt they had little to lose and much to gain by resorting to a campaign of violence. Not everyone joined Mau Mau, for divisions existed among the Kikuyu over what was considered legitimate action within the Kikuyu moral order and particularly over the question of following the path of armed struggle. Still, over time, militants became increasingly influential, events grew more volatile, and violence rose. The situation deteriorated rapidly over the summer of 1952, culminating on 7 October 1952 with the assassination of Chief Waruhiu, a prominent government supporter.[5]

On 20 October 1952, the recently appointed governor Sir Evelyn Baring declared an emergency, timed to coincide with the arrest of nearly 200 alleged leaders of the Mau Mau, including Kenyatta. More militant men than Kenyatta actually were the driving forces behind Mau Mau, but because he was Kenya's most visible nationalist, the colonial regime assumed Kenyatta's leadership of the rebellion. These arrests triggered a war that lasted nearly four years. During the first year alone the British had to bring in five battalions of British troops, six battalions of the King's African Rifles, and several squadrons of R.A.F. light and heavy bombers. These forces supplemented the thousands of members of the Kenya Police, the loyalist Kikuyu Home Guard, and the white settler's Kenya Regiment. Against these forces ranged the ill-equipped and barely trained Mau Mau. Nevertheless, for four years, periodically with striking success, the Mau Mau resisted the British.[6]

U.S. Policy, Africa, and African Americans in the Early 1950s

American officials in the early 1950s had little desire to end white minority rule, for they saw decolonization as being at odds with their over-arching objective of containing communism. Africans, however, viewed communism and anticommunism as far less important than the goal of removing colonial rule. As historian Thomas Borstelmann notes, for the majority of the world's population "the Cold War and the supposed dangers of communism were merely distractions from the historic opportunity provided by World War II for ending the European colonialism that had long dominated the lives of most of the world's people."[7]

In 1950 the State Department held in Mozambique a regional conference for Africa south of the Sahara. Looking beyond the geopolitical significance of South Africa to broader Africa, the meeting addressed problems confronting the United States in its political, economic, and cultural relations in the area. Its goal was to develop a preliminary statement regarding U.S. attitudes, objectives, and policies toward Africa. State Department officials actually characterized the conference as "an opportunity to lay the foundations for a restatement of American policy toward Africa," an acutely ironic phrasing since — as George McGhee, then assistant secretary of state for Near Eastern, South Asian and African Affairs, later admitted — at that time "no comprehensive U.S. policy had been formulated for Africa south of the Sahara."[8]

In preparation for the conference, the State Department consulted a panel of American experts on African affairs. Eleven nongovernmental panelists participated, including Ralph Bunche and Channing Tobias. The consultants suggested coupling the new program for technical assistance proposed under Truman's Point IV program with a bold reaffirmation of U.S. opposition to colonialism. "Such a definition," they urged, "would be a much more powerful weapon in our cold war with Russia than any tactical or *ad hoc* approach."[9]

In the end, however, the actual conference produced no bold new initiatives. Rather, participants focused on U.S. policy and Africa from the perspective of the colonial governments; they evaluated how colonial officials, not African peoples, viewed U.S. policies and actions. The summary of conclusions declared: "It was emphasized that one factor which must be borne constantly in mind is that the mass of indigenous people in Africa South of the Sahara know little about our foreign policies and probably care less." This belief, of course, assumed that Africans did not care how much the

United States was backing their colonial rulers. The attitude reflected in the summary provided little basis for State Department officials in Washington to promote a strong anticolonial line.[10]

As the State Department tried to form a consensus on general colonial policy, it produced a paper entitled "United States Policy Toward Dependent Territories." The paper advocated what essentially would be the "middle course" in subsequent years: the United States should recognize that it had "a profound interest" in the survival of its Western European allies, whose economic revival was seen as at least partly dependent upon their colonies. At the same time, the United States should continue its traditional sympathy and support for self-government by colonial peoples. Thus, when in December 1950 the Bureau of Near Eastern, South Asian, and African Affairs prepared its first five-year regional policy statement for Africa south of the Sahara, Western-oriented, anticommunist interests drove the objectives:

(1) Social, political, and economic advancement of the people of Africa as rapidly as practicable to convince them that their individual and national aspirations can best be achieved through continued association with the free nations of the world.

(2) Political and economic stability sufficient to resist domination by unfriendly movements or powers through subversion or aggression.

(3) Development of mutual understanding and cooperation by the United States and the colonial powers on questions relating to colonial policy.

(4) Maintenance of U.S. strategic interests, including access to strategic raw materials.

(5) Advancement of U.S. business interests, including the securing of nondiscriminatory treatment for U.S. nationals.

The colonial bias was unmistakable. The paper even added, "the metropolitan powers need reassurance from the United States that we are not purposefully working to bring about a premature according of political independence to the peoples of Africa."[11]

The policy statement recognized that "sympathy on the part of the American Negroes for the aspirations of the native peoples of Africa" could affect implementation of the objectives.[12] Yet a variety of ongoing factors — African Americans' traditionally weak voice on foreign policy, policymakers' racism, the Cold War's dampening influence, the repression of leftist voices on Africa, the focus by leading civil rights organizations on domestic affairs, the general acceptance by these organizations of Truman's Cold War foreign policies, the legacy of black American concerns about negative images of Africa — worked against African American influence during this critical period when the United States formed its basic policy framework for addressing the rising tide of nationalism in Africa.

U.S. policy, then, essentially accepted the continuance of white rule in Africa. Assistant Secretary of State McGhee in fact used a June 1951 speech before Northwestern University's Institute on Contemporary Africa to extol the virtues of development programs by colonial governments. He opined that a "vast ferment of cooperative activity in the development of Africa" pervaded the continent. He argued that for many Africans, "only slightly touched by modern civilization," the immediate problem was not political status but health, education, and economic concerns. McGhee concluded that "the peoples of Africa must realize that the greatest danger to the full realization of their economic, social, and spiritual development lies in the menace of Communist imperialism, which threatens the security of the entire free world and assures for the Africans as colonial peoples — not self-government but a dark future of political and cultural enslavement."[13]

Yet the rising tide of nationalism prevented the United States from fully supporting European interests without alienating Africans. Heavy-handed anticommunist rhetoric held little appeal for African nationalists, who felt that Washington should support concretely its rhetoric of freedom and democracy. Knowing that eventually the United States must deal with indigenous leaders in Africa, the question for Washington became how to handle growing African aspirations for independence while maintaining the strongest possible worldwide front against communist advances. Africa at mid-century may have seemed relatively tranquil compared to other trouble spots around the world, yet still the United States found itself unable to satisfy completely all parties with an interest in the continent.[14]

In mid-1952, with the Defiance Campaign in South Africa starting up and tensions in Kenya reaching the snapping point, American officials felt compelled to launch another round of internal debate over policy toward colonial areas. The debate focused not on priorities, for all agreed that keeping Africa allied with the "Free World" stood paramount. Rather, debate hinged on how best to achieve that goal, and it clearly demarcated competing positions within the State Department. One group, generally "Europeanists," argued that rapid decolonization would damage the overall anticommunist effort. They maintained that rapidly ending white rule would lead to weak, unstable indigenous governments that would be susceptible to Soviet or Chinese control. Further, accepting arguments that colonial markets remained important for European economic health, Europeanists argued that white rule in Africa remained necessary for strengthening Western European allies and enabling them to guard against communist gains. While recognizing that in the long run America's strength and security needed friendly relations with areas that some day would gain independence, these Europeanists maintained that immediate, even apocalyptic, concerns meant more. America's "long-term interests will have little meaning unless they are reconciled with our immediate security interests," they argued. "There would be little value in throwing our support to dependent peoples with a view to developing worthwhile democratic friends in half a century, if, by so doing, we might seriously jeopardize present American security and the continued survival of democracy itself."[15] Officials who felt that overemphasizing support for European allies created counterproductive short- and long-term consequences lined up to oppose this viewpoint. Often involved with the UN or Third World areas, these officials argued that continued white supremacy drove Africans to communism as their only means for liberation. In addition, undue support for colonial powers alienated hundreds of millions of formerly colonized people in countries such as India. These peoples could become a "third force" whose manpower and resources might be denied to the West in its struggle against communism or, even worse, might choose to ally with the Eastern bloc. U.S. interests lay, then, in more strongly supporting majority rule. A typical argument thus advised: " 'Premature independence' obviously is as bad as overdue autonomy. And experience has shown that Communism thrives on delayed and repressive colonial policy as much as on premature independence movements. The United States should condone or encourage neither."[16]

In truth, the apparent differences were more superficial than substantive. While the two sides disagreed on the weight that should be accorded European interests, neither side argued for substantive and material U.S. support for colonial liberation struggles. Both groups believed that the United States must generally follow the "difficult middle course." One high-ranking State Department official summed up the debate by declaring that while there existed differences of approach, "there is no disagreement on the basic proposition that both our long-term and our short-term interest require us to maintain the uncomfortable middle-of-the-road position." This position for broader Africa, of course, stood no more in the middle than did the U.S. position toward South Africa. When forced to choose between contradictory options, the virulent immediacy of Cold War anticommunist priorities held sway. White minority rule would be supported over African freedom struggles and black majority rule.[17]

Little changed from the Truman administration to the Eisenhower administration. Brenda Plummer notes that "the State Department during the Truman and first Eisenhower administrations maintained a Cold War hard line that placed it in the colonialist camp," while Thomas Noer argues that, in many ways, the rhetoric, style, and personalities of the Eisenhower administration made African policy seem even more conservative and hostile to African aspirations.[18] Henry Byroade, successor to McGhee as assistant secretary of state for Near Eastern, South Asian, and African Affairs, made clear that the new administration would maintain the emphasis on preventing communism from spreading in Africa, and do so by continuing support for European rule. Speaking in October 1953, Byroade acknowledged that "old-style colonialism" was on the way out and that much blood and treasure might be saved if the Western world hastened rather than hampered the evolution toward self-determination. Even so, he more forcefully stressed the threat of "the new Soviet colonialism." Declaring that "premature independence can be dangerous, retrogressive, and destructive," Byroade defended slow evolution toward independence over immediate independence. After surveying reasons why "premature independence" did not serve the interests of the West or of the colonized peoples themselves, Byroade finally justified the continuing colonial presence in Africa by declaring that "serious observers of the African scene agree that the European governments are making substantial contributions to the evolution of these peoples." For the Byroades of the world, the era of the white man's burden had not ended.[19]

The reports about the Mau Mau generated by U.S. diplomats in Kenya fed the stereotyped beliefs that already commanded thinking in Washington. The Mau Mau started receiving mention in consular reports as early as March 1951. Over the following eighteen months Vice Consul Robert Stookey not only pilloried the Mau Mau regularly, he even denigrated those Kikuyu who were resisting Mau Mau, informing Washington that the efforts by some Africans to resist Mau Mau through "white" magic instead of through cooperation with colonial officials "underlines the state of savagery, ignorance, and barbarism in which the vast majority of indigenous East African tribes remain."[20]

When Governor Baring declared the emergency and the war began, American diplomats clearly sided with the colonialists. Their language not only favored the metropole, it also reinforced prejudices and beliefs that supported continued colonial rule as the only viable path for Africa to follow. For example, the consulate reported that in the first five weeks of the state of emergency, the Kenyan government's efforts in "restoring law and order" were met by the Mau Mau "with additional shocking crimes." Further, it continued, "[d]espite stern measures taken to deal with the current unrest, lawlessness has continued, with resulting bloodshed, terrorism, and property losses." Not even the sanctity of Christmas could stop Mau Mau atrocities, according to Consul General Edmund Dorsz, who informed Washington that "Christmas Eve was another red letter day for the Mau Mau — 11 Africans murdered, including one woman and two children." This "Yuletide thuggery" underscored Dorsz's assessment of Mau Mau's spread during the previous months: "The purpose of the society (anti-foreign, anti-Christian), its ritual (pagan mumbo-jumbo) remained unchanged, but its membership and acceptance among the Kikuyu increased to such a point that a high police official estimated privately that over half the tribe were either members or sympathizers." Given Mau Mau's potency, he added, "fortunately nearly all of the firearms are in the hands of the forces of law and order." The Mau Mau, Dorsz concluded, at minimum had "retarded" orderly political development. In drawing his conclusion, Dorsz acknowledged that the Kikuyu held legitimate grievances, but he never fully considered what "orderly development" under colonial auspices had meant for the vast majority of dispossessed Africans.[21]

Given such reports and the general images of Mau Mau, African Americans had little chance to use events in Kenya to convince U.S. officials to reframe policy toward colonial Africa. More "legitimate" liberation struggles, such as that in Ghana, would have to sweep forward. In black America, however, the Mau Mau helped frame competing discourses on the direction of the domestic struggle.

African American Responses to Mau Mau

African Americans, seeing the Mau Mau rebellion coming on the heels of the Defiance Campaign, perhaps had a better understanding than Washington officials of the ferment for change in Africa. The *Courier* declared Africa the continent of the future, and black rule the future of the continent. This goal, it conceded, would not be reached smoothly or without turmoil; there would be controversy, cruelty, and bloodshed on the way.[22]

The Mau Mau war years provided plenty of cruelty and controversy. As Mau Mau fighters took the war to the whites of Kenya and to Africans perceived to be loyalists, the Mau Mau ability to resist British efforts to eliminate the movement led, in turn, to draconian actions and reprisals on the part of the British and white settlers. Historian John Lonsdale cites the following shockingly lopsided casualty figures: 164 troops or police killed by the Mau Mau, most of them African; 1,880 civilians killed by Mau Mau, all but 58 of them black; 12,590 Mau Mau (or Africans so described) killed in action or by hanging.[23]

Brutality by the British, the white settlers, and the Africans in their employ stiffened African American opposition to colonial rule. African Americans broadly criticized economic, social, and political repression in Kenya. In doing so, they denounced most harshly the land alienation that the Kikuyu had suffered at the hands of the white settlers. The *Courier*, focusing attention on "the terroristic system which led to the uprisings in Kenya," argued that the British needed to address "the just grievances of the Kikuyu people who number over a million and have been deprived of their fertile lands in favor of the white planters." Indeed, the Kikuyu had been subjected to "the worst features of South Africa's apartheid policy." Journalist Joel Rogers also used the comparison to South Africa, writing, "Nowhere in Africa, including South Africa, have the whites been so voracious as in Kenya. Grabbing all the best lands of the natives, they made virtual slaves of the latter." And on several occasions, the *Crisis* likewise traced the roots of the rebellion to land alienation.[24]

African Americans also criticized the British handling of the insurgency. Black papers wholly condemned the practice of "collective punishment," by which the British punished entire villages for allegedly aiding or harboring Mau Mau. The wholesale arrests, deportations, and use of "detention" and "rehabilitation" camps for Mau Mau suspects and prisoners also provoked outrage. The *Afro-American* lambasted the British for allowing the "ruthless and promiscuous slaughtering of Africans without any evidence of guilt" and decried collective punishment as "a page straight out of Hitler's book." The *Defender*, characterizing British operations as a campaign of terror, criticized the deportation of thousands of Africans to marginal areas and the brutality used to extort confessions from suspected Mau Mau prisoners. "Murder in Kenya! What's happening is far worse!" fired Joel Rogers to commence a series of articles. "It's massacre and terrorism, such as the twentieth century has not seen. The Royal Air Force . . . is bombing East Africans, their women and their children, from the air."[25]

African Americans roundly criticized the British prosecution of Kenyatta, during the course of which authorities bent and broke the law in order to convict Kenyatta of masterminding the Mau Mau. The *Afro-American* dismissed as farcical the criminal charges leveled against the nationalist leader for "inciting disaffection against the Kenya government." The paper argued that being oppressed, exploited, and "systematically robbed of their best land" had spawned the disaffection, not Kenyatta. British attacks on Kenyatta had the effect of solidifying his standing in black America as a black nationalist hero. The *Amsterdam News*, proclaiming that Kenyatta "upheld the African's right to determine his own way of life, which is one of the things our Founding Fathers fought for," announced, "In our book, Jomo (Burning Spear) Kenyatta is a black patriot and Africa could use more like him."[26]

At the same time, parts of black America felt great reluctance to support Mau Mau actions, for as Mau Mau fighters took up their weapons, the world press took up its pens. African Americans' limited access to events in Kenya forced them to rely on these press accounts to a great extent. The Mau Mau — with their blood oaths, secrecy, and deadly acts — were caricatured and stereotyped. Sensationalized accounts of the oathing claimed that even more disturbing acts occurred, including the drinking of menstrual blood and unnatural acts with animals. These accounts deliberately sought to portray the Mau Mau as savage and bestial, to be rejected and condemned. Publications such as *Time* magazine slanted coverage so that readers identified with the white settlers (who were developers of the land and upholders of "law and order") while they recoiled from the Mau Mau (who were savages and "terrorists"). Author Robert Ruark crafted a best-selling novel in 1955, *Something of Value*, based on these binary images. "In order to understand Mau Mau it is first necessary to understand Africa," Ruark declared in his foreword, "and the portion of Africa in which Mau Mau was allowed to flourish is only just fifty years old as we reckon civilization." Despite being just a decade removed from the Nazis and their concentration camps, Ruark continued on: "To understand Africa you must understand a basic impulsive savagery that is greater than anything we 'civilized' people have encountered in two centuries." Throughout the war the white settlers and the British made effective use of language to control characterizations of Mau Mau as primitive and bloodthirsty savages bent on rampage and destruction, as opposed to freedom fighters seeking justice and equal rights. "It is testimony to the effectiveness of this campaign of criminalization," according to historian Frank Furedi, "that the irrational image of Mau Mau still endures."[27]

Lurid depictions found their way into the African American press. An early *Defender* story on the Mau Mau wrote of "fanatic Africans" who "continue their bloody campaign to drive the white man out of all of Africa." Later articles called the Mau Mau a "small band of fanatic terrorists" and "cultists." An *Afro-American* correspondent also wrote of the "fanatic" Mau Mau, who came largely from "the primitive Kikuyu tribe" and showed "cold-blooded ruthlessness," striking "mercilessly, sparing neither women nor children." National Negro Publishers Association (NNPA) reports called the Mau Mau "an anti-white cult," while the Associated Negro Press (ANP) referred to "terrorist members of the anti-white Mau Mau cult." The similarity in these depictions suggests that these press agencies merely culled and repackaged wire service reports, but even so, they kept the descriptions, as did the newspapers when they ran the stories.[28]

Both the *Defender* and the *Daily World* ran a series of articles called "Turmoil in Africa," written by a Pulitzer Prize-winning white journalist, Malcolm Johnson. Concern over the imagery in Johnson's depictions prompted the *Defender* to write a cautionary editorial. It encouraged readers to read the series in order to examine issues from different perspectives yet warned against Johnson's reliance on what whites in Africa told him. Nevertheless, the paper ran the stories, in which Johnson described his trip into "dreaded Mau Mau areas" and to "primitive settlements where native tribesmen still buy their wives and sell their daughters in exchange for cattle." Johnson described the Mau Mau as a "secret native terrorist society sworn to drive out the whites or kill them to achieve black supremacy," and declared that the Mau Mau oath "expresses fanatical hatred of all whites and of the Christian religion."[29]

African American commentators also created unflattering images. Bayard Rustin depicted the Mau Mau as combining voodoo with modern political strategy. James Hicks, writing for the *Afro-American*, found it ironic that "while the world statesmen have been battling for years to avoid an open clash of the white against the black in more civilized areas of the world, the clash has suddenly come in an area where it was least expected — an uncivilized area of darkest Africa."[30]

The Lari massacre on 26 March 1953 in particular served to discredit the Mau Mau in the eyes of many around the world. This farming area had been deeply divided between African landowners loyal to the government and landless tenants who generally supported the Mau Mau. On the night of the massacre, Mau Mau supporters attacked loyalist households, burning, hacking, or shooting to death nearly one hundred men, women, and children. The Kenyan government invited reporters to the gruesome scene to witness the carnage, and their press reports and photographs helped paint a portrait of Mau Mau savagery. As the Mau Mau generally executed small attacks and raids, the massacre received all the more attention.

"Savage anti-white Mau Mau terrorists massacred an estimated 300 native territorial guards, their wives and children Thursday night in an orgy of burning, stabbing and shooting unequalled in ferocity in recent times," read those who glanced at the front page of the *Daily World*. The *Courier's* lead headline blared, "New Reign of Terror Launched by Mau Maus," while the

Defender told how Mau Mau "terrorists turned on their fellow tribesmen last Friday night and massacred an estimated 200 African natives." These media accounts did not report, however, that organized Mau Mau units apparently took no part in the massacre, or that in reprisal, vengeful security forces killed and mutilated hundreds of purported Mau Mau supporters. Also more or less buried was that on the same evening of the Lari massacre, Mau Mau units executed a relatively large-scale raid on a police post at Naivasha. During this well-planned and effective action they drove away the policemen and captured dozens of submachine guns, rifles, and ammunition and released close to 200 prisoners. The effectiveness of British efforts to control the image of the Mau Mau rebellion is seen in full relief here. Africans acting in a disciplined, effective manner did not fit the colonialist and Western media-preferred image of Mau Mau.[31]

Images of savage and primitive Mau Mau "terrorists" and "anti-white cultists" killing fellow Africans made it difficult for many African Americans to support the Mau Mau and its tactics. This reticence in part reflected a continuing reluctance to be linked with "savage" Africa. Further, the use of violence gave black Americans pause, especially violence against other blacks. The historian Rayford Logan commented at the time that even while black Americans criticized the harsh treatment meted out to the Mau Mau, "[they] have not approved of the excesses committed by some of the Mau Mau."[32]

Continuing Cold War pressures to support U.S. policy, even if that policy tended to favor colonial powers over African freedom, also helped shape African American responses to Mau Mau. Some black Americans, especially more conservative ones, took the anticommunism of the day as part of their core beliefs. Indeed, these black conservatives worried over being tied to a "radical" Africa and strongly believed in the paramount need to emphasize one's Americanness, not one's Africanness, when seeking equality in the United States.

Two of the most prominent and vocal voices for archly conservative, anticommunist black Americans had been at one time quite sympathetic to Africans: George Schuyler and Max Yergan. Schuyler had been an assistant editor for the outspoken monthly magazine *The Messenger* during the 1920s, after which he became a columnist, chief editorial writer, and then associate editor for the *Courier*, a platform from which he gave strong support for Ethiopia during the Italian invasion. Yergan had worked in South Africa as a representative of the YMCA and upon his return had helped found and served as executive secretary of the CAA. By the early 1950s, however, both men had become representatives of a staunchly conservative, anticommunist vein in black America. They did not necessarily command a broad base of support, but their viewpoint needs to be recognized, as does that of the CAA and its leaders.[33]

In his controversial 1953 interview, during which he offered sympathy for white South Africa, Yergan also went on to address the situation in Kenya. With anticommunist fervor clearly commanding his perspective, Yergan discounted British officials themselves stating that no communist influence lay behind the Mau Mau. Yergan believed that Africans' legitimate grievances had been "exploited" by Mau Mau leaders and declared the Mau Mau to be a "criminal, conspiratorial movement which, it seems to me, is so closely patterned after the Communist methods that they must have something to do with it." Yergan condemned the "murdering" of scores of blacks who "either broke the oath or refused to be intimidated." He believed the British wanted to make progress on African grievances, but that white settler fears and "complications from the relative backwardness of the African people" slowed them.[34]

Schuyler leapt to defend Yergan from those who denounced his remarks. In doing so, Schuyler even more acerbically criticized the Mau Mau: "Mau Mau is the Kenya-version KKK or Mafia which is for Africa for the Africans — in the rough." Mau Mau willingness to kill Africans who collaborated with white colonialists most affronted Schuyler, whose sympathy for the alleged black collaborators grew at least in part out of his own sense of embattlement at home. "The terrorists don't know that killing off capable Negro leaders will not solve the natives' problems." Further souring Schuyler on the Mau Mau was his belief that Jomo Kenyatta had communist connections, arising from two trips Kenyatta had taken to Moscow in 1929 and 1932.[35]

Leftist African Americans, conversely, tried to aid the black struggle in Kenya. The CAA, by now showing the strain from its debilitating battle with the federal government, still tried to rally support. On 24 April 1954 it sponsored a Conference in Support of African Liberation at the Friendship Baptist Church in New York City. A hundred delegates and observers attended the day-long session. In calling the meeting, the council clearly linked African Americans, Africans, and their struggles:

> The time has come when we in America must speak out and give support to our brothers who struggle for freedom in Africa. . . . Africa is our concern because our own security, our own democratic rights and the prospect of our preventing the use of American means and men in shedding the blood of Africans, depend on what happens in Africa today and tomorrow. . . .

Black Americans, struggling to wipe out the humiliation and degradation of second-class citizenship, know that racist doctrines of white supremacy are grounded in the lies which continue to be taught and disseminated concerning the "backwardness" of the African people. The Africans' advance to freedom means a death-blow to the myth of African inferiority and a tremendous impetus to the advance of black Americans toward the achievement of their full rights.[36]

Du Bois gave the conference's keynote address, in which he worried about the state of the African American relationship with Africa. He warned that the fight to restore and maintain colonialism had shifted from Asia to Africa, where, according to Du Bois, Europe and the United States had organized a determined last stand to perpetuate the color line in the world. He decried African Americans' lack of support for Africa and felt the reason for this to be clear: "Africa and its problems have never been popular in America. On the contrary, America for the most part has conceived her best interest lays in actions and policies which involved disaster and repression for Africa and her children. Consequently we American Negroes whose frantic endeavor has long been to be Americans in every right, thought, and action, have usually hastened to follow every wind of American opinion with regard to Africa." He counseled African Americans to be interested in the African situation, "for if colonial serfdom is maintained in Africa, the color line will not disappear in Afro-America."[37]

While seeking to aid African struggles in general, the conference largely focused on the Mau Mau revolt in Kenya. The conference adopted resolutions voicing the "strongest protest against the crimes committed by the British in Kenya" and calling on the UN to protect the people of Kenya against genocide. Conference participants formed an organizing committee to conduct a campaign of direct assistance to "the heroic peoples" of Kenya. The goal: in four months raise $5,000 to send to the Kenyan freedom fighters, along with quantities of dried milk, vitamin pills, and first aid supplies.[38] But by this time the CAA's leftist ties and the government's persecution had weakened its ability to generate support on African issues, while in addition many in black America felt ambivalent about how much they could support the Mau Mau. By September 1954 the Kenya Aid Committee had been able to collect and forward only $500 to the Kenyatta Defense Fund, that in addition to the mere $100 the CAA had sent to the Kenya African Union the previous year.[39]

Between these dramatically contrasting views existed a range of opinions about the struggle in Kenya. Many black Americans, condemning colonial rule and supporting the redressment of wrongs, sympathized with the Mau Mau. Black journalists generally offered relatively empathetic coverage of the Mau Mau, especially when compared to their white counterparts. The *Courier*, condemning the British for employing ever harsher measures in a bid to "exterminate by any means the native revolutionists," believed that the Kenyan government ignored the Kikuyu's just grievances and that "Mau Mau terrorism is a normal and understandable reaction to white aggression." The *Afro-American* described the revolt at times as a "desperate bid to obtain freedom" and a "momentous struggle for freedom."[40]

Various leading African Americans voiced strong opposition to colonial actions in Kenya. Congressman Adam Clayton Powell called for ending all U.S. aid to Kenya because of British "massacres" of Africans. Sidney Williams, director of the Chicago Urban League, urged organizations across the country to pass resolutions condemning colonialism, particularly in Kenya, and asked the U.S. government to deplore in no uncertain terms the various military, economic, political, and social devices being used to thwart Africans' heroic efforts to cast off colonialism.[41]

The Brotherhood of Sleeping Car Porters (BSCP) held a meeting in 1953 to protest and condemn the attacks against Africans in Kenya and South Africa. A. Philip Randolph, New York councilman Earl Brown, and Congressman Powell were among those who addressed the gathering. Soon afterwards, the BSCP introduced a resolution at the American Federation of Labor (AFL) convention stating that whereas "the fires of nationalism are raging and sweeping across the continent of Africa, in the forms of revolts and insurrections against the arrogant and ruthless domination of the white colonial government officials and selfish and greedy white settlers, who, with their guns and bombs, grab the choicest, most desirable and productive land and drive the natives into the worst part of the land known as the Reserves," the membership condemned imperialistic colonialism in Africa. The resolution also called for a trade union mission to Kenya and other parts of Africa "to investigate the terrorism of the settlers and colonial government leaders." The resolution further directed the AFL president to call upon President Eisenhower and Congress to cut off all economic aid and new loans to governments that planned to use such aid and loans in their colonies.[42]

Yet clearly an uneasiness about the Mau Mau pulsed through black America, and the use of violence as a means to an end became a central issue for African Americans as they responded to the revolt. The overarching goal of the Mau Mau—to end white minority rule—appealed to African Americans. At the same time, images associated with the Mau Mau, images propagated by the British and white settlers yet absorbed by black Americans, raised concerns about supporting the Mau Mau. Black Americans favored any erosion of white supremacy around the world, but at what price?

Following its initial 1953 resolution, the BSCP modified its position to make clearer its dissociation from Mau Mau tactics. While declaring that "it views with great horror and righteous indignation the ruthless, disgraceful and murderous bombing of the Mau Maus" in the effort to subjugate Africans "who are in revolt against the un-democratic and un-Christian expropriation of their choice land by white settlers," the BSCP also pointedly added that it did not approve of the policy of violence as an instrument of liberation on the part of native Africans in Kenya.[43]

Similarly, the 1953 NAACP Annual Convention passed a resolution on Kenya that stated, "We condemn the terrorist methods used against the Mau Mau and others who fight to abolish colonialism and racism," while at the same time affirming, "We view with alarm the terrorist methods of the Mau Mau in Kenya." The convention called upon the U.S. delegation to the UN to initiate a thorough and unbiased study of the struggle for equality in Africa, and for the UN to formulate a program of action that would be vigorously and speedily implemented. The resolution warned, "[T]he grim alternative to such action is either terrorism or surrender in despair to communism — either of which would be disastrous."[44]

Although prominent black American leaders generally sympathized with the just Kikuyu grievances and advocated that they be redressed, they would not condone the use of violence. Thus, when Randolph wrote to Eisenhower supporting African liberation, he condemned "the outrages perpetrated upon African natives, especially in South Africa and Kenya" and urged that pressure be applied so the British military would "immediately cease dropping bombs upon the peoples of the Kikuyu tribe of Kenya." At the same time, Randolph carefully distanced himself from Mau Mau violence, adding, "[T]he leaders of the African natives must be prevailed upon to see that violence and bloodshed cannot constitute a solution of their social, economic, and political problems."[45]

Other leaders distanced themselves even more sharply from Mau Mau actions. National Urban League head Lester Granger criticized Mau Mau violence as "an unforgivable orgy of bloody killings" and stated his preference for boycotts and civil disobedience. Walter White, still secretary of the NAACP, characterized Mau Mauism as a "ghastly evil."[46]

In the early 1950s, as always had been the case, no sweeping agreement existed in the arena of ideas about contemporary Africa. Not surprisingly, then, those articulating strong diasporic linkages criticized those who they felt showed insufficient pan-African sensibilities. In 1954 a reader of the *Amsterdam News* prompted an episode illustrative of the wide range of views. Signing off as "A Black Harlemite," the writer criticized the paper for supporting a war fund to help Koreans while ignoring Kenyans. Acknowledging that the letter conveyed the sentiments of others received, the *Amsterdam News* responded by publicly defining its position on Kenya. The paper pointed out that not all of the people in Kenya were black, and that Mau Mau and British armies alike butchered innocent black and white men, women, and children. The paper acknowledged the plight of Mau Mau supporters, who had been stripped of the choicest land and left in a state of economic slavery, but it also sympathized with the white settlers' argument that they had developed the land. The paper ultimately declared its support for a speedy end to colonialism but excused itself from doing much because, in its words, "We don't kid ourselves into thinking that we can shout loudly enough in Harlem to change these conditions overnight." Moreover, the editors emphasized that although they felt deep concern about human misery everywhere, they were "more concerned about the immediate problems that meet us at every turn right here in New York City," adding, "It's difficult to become carried away with citizenship problems that exist 7,000 miles away until those at home have been solved."[47]

The *Amsterdam News*'s emphasis on the struggle at home and concern for the position of whites as well as blacks in Kenya unmistakably displayed domestic priorities and a universalist outlook. At the same time, the "Black Harlemite" and the other readers who wrote to the paper reflected a more pan-African perspective in black America. Parts of black America were adopting more militant and nationalist positions, perceiving the liberal civil rights leadership as too cautious and too supportive of U.S. Cold War foreign policy, and advocating stronger ties to Africa and support for Africans.

The Mau Mau fighters pushed black Americans to consider more fully how extensively to use violence in resisting white supremacy, and a number of people reached the conclusion that the Kikuyu had been left with little recourse. Sociologist, professor, and pastor Gordon Hancock concluded that little moral difference existed between Mau Mau's own actions and white actions taken in suppressing the rebellion. "If it is evil for Mau Mau and non-Europeans to use violence and terrorism, by the same reasoning it is evil for Britain and South Africa to use those methods." Horace Cayton, who provided relatively sympathetic coverage of the Mau Mau throughout the war, sharply criticized those who highlighted the savagery of Africans while ignoring the exploitation of Africans and their relegation to the bottom of the economic, social, and political heap. Cayton contended that people should reserve judgment on the effectiveness of the Mau Mau program of terror as a political weapon, remarking that "any time that people are hopelessly oppressed and find no other means of expressing their dissatisfaction, they will resort to violence." Cayton explored the issue further shortly after the Mau Mau killed Tom Mbgetla, an African nominated for the Nairobi City Council. Cayton described the killing as the execution of a spy working to aid white exploiters and stated that while he did not believe in violence, "one must admit that Mbgetla had it coming."[48]

The difficulty of drawing the line at which one accepted violence as a political tool marked many black responses to Mau Mau. Cayton did not stand alone in personally denouncing violence while simultaneously justifying its use. Joel Rogers, for instance, emphasized his aversion to violence but explained Mau Mau killing of whites and "Uncle Tom" Kikuyus as part of the history of oppression. "The Mau Mau are doing precisely what whites, or any other group, racial or national, did when any stranger came in and sat on their necks." Others went further and lauded Mau Mau tactics. "Seldom have determined men so poorly armed — and apparently so loosely organized — accomplished so much by violence in so short a period," declared George McCray, a labor organizer for the BSCP. McCray lauded the Mau Mau revolt as "one of the most cleverly devised rebellions of the twentieth century." B. D. Davis wrote to the *Afro-American* urging black Americans to start "organizing aid to the Kenya Africans." Having weighed the different liberation struggles active in Africa, Davis concluded that the Mau Mau had it right: "Their cause is a beginning which can be more effective toward winning independence than the Gold Coast, Nigeria, or any other African area."[49]

Sociologist and pan-African scholar St. Clair Drake experienced the force of Mau Mau on people's thinking in early 1953 when he addressed an AME congregation in Chicago on what was happening in Africa. Drake described the situations in Kenya and South Africa, contrasting the means being used. Before he sat down, he concluded, "Since I am speaking in a Christian pulpit, I am sure that all of us hope that Africa can win its freedom the non-violent way and not be pushed into the Mau Mau way." The church's minister rose after Drake finished and, taking the podium, said that while he liked everything Drake said, "You don't treat Mau Mau right. I told my congregation this morning that if I was a young man I'd buy myself a boat ticket to Mombassy [*sic*]; and when I got there I'd buy myself a train ticket to Nairobi; and when I got off that train I'd buy myself the biggest, longest, panga knife I could find, and I'd run all up and down the sides of Mt. Kenya just cutting white people's throats."[50]

In the mid-1950s few black Americans saw Mau Mau violence as a model for achieving full equality in America, but the Mau Mau insurgency helped crystallize the tactical question and moved some toward accepting violence in principle. Accepting that the Mau Mau had the right to use violent means to fight white supremacy and oppression in Kenya held the distinct potential to grow into accepting that at some point violence could be necessary in the face of white intransigence in the United States. As the African American relationship with Africa evolved, the Mau Mau analogy grew in salience as southern whites remained defiant after *Brown v. Board of Education* tore down the legal basis of "separate but equal."

Significantly, too, the efficacy of violence was not merely a question of black against white. Many African Americans had a sophisticated enough understanding of the Mau Mau to recognize the importance of the violence directed against "collaborating" Kikuyu elders and elites. Wrapped in the Mau Mau goal of ending white supremacy was the issue of who would have power and leadership within the Kikuyu society. For African Americans, this issue became transmuted to who would lead the civil rights struggle, the shape that struggle would take, and what attendant changes might result within black America.

Increasingly, African American civil rights leaders found themselves under attack for their lack of action in regard to Kenya. After Randolph and fellow labor leader Frank Crosswaith convened a meeting at Harlem's Hotel Theresa protesting the treatment of Soviet Jews, letters to the African American press questioned the priorities of these men. "Have these men done as much for the Africans of Kenya and South Africa even though they are members of that race?" queried William Clarke of New York City. Clarke advocated a more pan-African perspective, concluding, "One must question the mentality of men who ignore the suffering of their own people to rush to the assistance of others." Reverend Ivan Harrison of Sneads, Florida, informed the *Afro-American* that the South needed a strong Mau Mau society to deal with "Uncle Toms." A self-described "Constant Reader" of the *Amsterdam News* wrote that African Americans needed a Mau Mau in order to get rid of all the crooked black American leaders and politicians.[51]

Ivan Harrison, William Clarke, and similar writers bring to the fore debate within black America over the traditional leadership and the disgruntlement that many felt with it. Showing plainly that parts of the black community adopted more militant and nationalist positions than did African American leaders, these writers' words could not have settled lightly on the elite civil rights leadership.

In the Aftermath of Mau Mau

By the end of 1954 the war had turned against the Mau Mau, and by 1956 the fight had been reduced to mopping up operations. Yet, the influence of Mau Mau would continue to resonate through both Kenya and black America. While the Mau Mau did not win the military war, black America saw the Mau Mau forcing change. At various times African Americans lauded the Mau Mau for halting the immigration of more "land-grabbing" white settlers, for forcing the British to discuss the future of Kenya with Africans, for making the British bring Africans into the Kenyan government, for changing the perception of Africans as passive and docile, for helping inspire other uprisings, and for upholding the right of Africans to determine their own way of life. Even George Schuyler admitted that the Mau Mau forced the British to appoint a black minister in the Kenyan government and inspired nationalists throughout Africa.[52]

The Mau Mau helped foster the belief that colonialism stood on shaky ground and that Africa might soon overthrow political discrimination, economic injustice, social deprivation, and white racism. The Mau Mau fed the growing awareness of and general respect for African struggles throughout black America. This, in turn, promoted fundamental shifts in the mid-1950s, as African Americans, hearing and seeing more about African liberation struggles, increasingly looked to contemporary Africa and found there inspiration and pride.

Because African Americans' diasporic consciousness historically had not differentiated areas of Africa, the confluence of the Mau Mau rebellion and the South African Defiance Campaign, along with the rise to power of Kwame Nkrumah in Ghana and unrest in the Central African Federation, caused African Americans to see the continent as "aflame" in revolt against white supremacy. The outbreak of the Algerian war for independence in late 1954 further fueled this impression, although at that time and even subsequently most African Americans felt less connected to North Africa. Even so, as the war in Algeria grew more protracted and brutal, and as the writings of Frantz Fanon gained readership and popularity, Algeria also contributed to the ongoing image of Africa as inexorably struggling for independence and kept at the fore questions about revolutionary violence.

From the beginning of the Mau Mau conflict, then, black Americans opened their papers and read front-page headlines such as "Africa Teeters Near Brink of Revolution; Violence Continuing" and "Racial Fires Flare as Africans Stiffen." Newspapers ran series on insurgent Africa, be it Malcolm

Johnson's appalling "Turmoil in Africa" in the *Defender* and *Daily World* or Horace Cayton's more favorable "Africa Series" for the *Courier*. In its editorial "Africa Awakes," the *Crisis* wrote that behind the headlines about the Defiance Campaign and the Mau Mau lay the story of an ascendant Africa. Political and economic conditions had caused Africans to rebel, and the *Crisis* concluded that African hostility in these countries was a time bomb that eventually would blast Europeans out of Africa. These feelings would only heighten as the 1950s progressed.[53]

The Mau Mau uprising particularly sharpened African Americans' awareness of the situation for blacks in Kenya, and that country would remain an area of special interest well after the defeat of Mau Mau on the battlefield. Its meaning, however, would vary widely for different groups within black America. Alternative interpretations of Mau Mau would reflect as well as help shape differing paths taken in the domestic struggle. The liberal civil rights leadership, facing attacks within black America and finding they needed to take a stronger stand on African issues in general and on Kenya in particular, sought to promote alternatives that eschewed violence and attacks on established black leaders. On the other hand, a more militant, nationalist African America found in the Mau Mau direct inspiration for shaping and conducting the black struggle.

While the liberal civil rights leadership may not have felt comfortable backing the Mau Mau, its growing interest in Kenya became concretely manifested through support for Kenyan leaders not linked to Mau Mau, such as labor leader Tom Mboya. Mboya, who not incidentally also found backers in the U.S. government, had risen steadily to prominence in Kenya. He first became active in labor organizing during the early 1950s. When the state of emergency began, he moved into politics by becoming the director of information and treasurer of the Kenya African Union (KAU) after the mass arrests of KAU leaders. When the government banned the KAU shortly thereafter, Mboya continued his upward movement by becoming general secretary of the Kenya Federation of Registered Trade Unions.

Mboya came to the United States in the fall of 1956 on a speaking tour sponsored by the American Committee on Africa. On this tour Mboya promoted, among other things, trade union support for Kenyan labor as well as American educational opportunities for Kenyan students. Mboya met with a host of labor leaders, including George Meany, Walter Reuther, David Dubinsky, and A. Philip Randolph. These meetings led to Mboya's success in securing an AFL-CIO grant of $35,000 toward building a trade union center in Kenya. Mboya also laid the groundwork for procuring scholarships and travel expenses for Kenyan students wanting to study in the United States.

Mboya's first trip to the United States started donations trickling in; in 1959 his second trip opened the spigot, and support flowed from whites and blacks. In response to Mboya's appeals, more than forty American colleges granted scholarships to eighty-one Kenyan men and women.[54]

The liberal civil rights leadership had few reservations about supporting Kenyan educational opportunities; indeed, this fit with a long tradition of Africans studying in the United States. Still, support for Kenyan students served as a way to foster a Western-oriented, democratic elite leadership class and marked the beginning of a new, more intensive phase, as the African American elite increasingly promoted funding African education in these years. Joining together on this burgeoning path of contacts, singer Harry Belafonte, actor Sidney Poitier, and Jackie Robinson, baseball star turned civil rights advocate and newspaper columnist, appealed for contributions to aid Kenyan students trying to reach the United States to study. They noted that a visit by the "brilliant African leader" Mboya had dramatized the urgent need for higher education for promising young Africans. The letter from Belafonte, Poitier, and Robinson, sent under the auspices of the African-American Students Foundation (AASF), appealed for money to help cover travel and other education-related expenses for Kenyan students receiving scholarships. A few months later, after the State Department refused to help fund AASF efforts, presidential candidate John F. Kennedy made the politically astute move of helping fund the program through the Kennedy Foundation, thereby solidifying support in a black America that was gauging politicians' views on race more and more through their views on Africa.[55]

Other African Americans helped sponsor individual African students. Lester Granger helped support two Kenyan brothers. P. L. Prattis, editor of the *Courier*, helped secure a scholarship for a Kenyan to attend the University of Pittsburgh. Martin Luther King Jr., who maintained a correspondence with Mboya, made multiple efforts to help students from Kenya. In an illustrative episode, Mboya informed King that Tuskegee had accepted a student named Nicholas Rabala but that Rabala needed nearly $1,000 for costs while at the school. King responded that he would be happy to provide some money and wrote to William Scheinman, president of the AASF, to say that he would assist Rabala for up to $1,000. Half of the money was to come from King's Dexter Avenue Baptist Church and half from the Southern Christian Leadership Conference (SCLC).[56]

King also met and corresponded with Dr. Julius Gikonyo Kiano, an economics professor and future Kenyan government minister. The two first met in Montgomery when Kiano accompanied Mboya on his 1959 visit to the United States. Afterwards, King informed Kiano that he had made definite arrangements to provide $20 a month for two Kenyan students' expenses and that he was talking to other ministers to assess what commitments they could offer. Three months later King wrote to Kiano with the good news that support had been secured for five Kenyan students to study at Alabama State College. The Montgomery Improvement Association would provide for two students, King's Dexter Avenue Baptist Church and Ralph Abernathy's First Baptist Church for one each, and a local club for one more. King believed that contracts to support three more students might be made with other local groups.[57]

Growing interest in Africa and a spreading feeling that diasporic struggles were linked certainly helped fuel support for Kenyan educational needs and for noncommunist labor leaders. The desire to develop alternatives to Mau Mau and all it implied did too. Through such mechanisms, African American civil rights leaders demonstrated their interest in and commitment to Kenyans without allying themselves with Mau Mau–style leaders and action. The civil rights community accordingly supported Mboya, promoted the development of an American-educated Kenyan leadership class, and in the early 1960s backed Thurgood Marshall's participation in the Kenyan constitutional talks.[58]

For a more militant black America, the Mau Mau did not embody a path to avoid but instead provided an example and a symbol to tap in one's own efforts. The Mau Mau insurgency helped push a younger generation of leaders toward more militant thinking. In 1953, for example, a young NAACP field secretary named Medgar Evers named his first son after Jomo Kenyatta. Indeed, the Mau Mau fed into a tradition of "armed self-reliance" that historian Timothy Tyson helps reconstruct in his analysis of Robert F. Williams, the North Carolina NAACP official who was censured and suspended by the national organization in 1959 for advocating armed self-defense.[59]

The Mau Mau rebellion embedded itself in the consciousness of black America and became a potent symbol of black resistance against both white supremacy and the established civil rights leadership. More militant black Americans praised the Mau Mau for pushing for dramatic, wholesale change and for standing up to traditional Kikuyu leadership and elites. The Mau Mau provided a sounding board that helped sharpen emerging tensions in black America — between a mass versus elite orientation in the civil rights movement and between acceptance of nonviolence versus armed self-defense as strategies of choice.

The meaning and symbolism of Mau Mau, both in terms of being more militant as well as being willing to overturn the traditional black leadership, would be echoed by people such as Malcolm X. As early as 1953, when canvassing the docks in Philadelphia while working to open a Nation of Islam temple, Malcolm X was referencing Mau Mau for his listeners.[60] Up to his death, Malcolm X used the Mau Mau analogy as a powerful encoded reference. "When the nations of Africa are truly independent — and they will be truly independent because they are going about it the right way — the historians will give Prime Minister, or rather, President Kenyatta and the Mau Mau their rightful role in African history," proclaimed Malcolm X at a Harlem rally in late December 1964. "They'll go down as the greatest African patriots and freedom fighters that that continent ever knew, and they will be given credit for bringing about the independence of many of the existing independent states on that continent right now."

Malcolm X understood and used the layered meanings of Mau Mau for African Americans. He linked the Mau Mau to his audience, exhorting them to realize that "you and I can best learn how to get real freedom by studying how Kenyatta brought it to his people in Kenya." "In fact," he argued, "that's what we need in Mississippi. In Mississippi we need a Mau Mau. In Alabama we need a Mau Mau. In Georgia we need a Mau Mau. Right here in Harlem, in New York City, we need a Mau Mau."[61]

5

GHANA
African Independence, 1957–1958

I think we American Negroes are now ready to look outside ourselves and so learn something of the vast continent of Africa of which Ghana is a tiny but dynamic example. Our wider knowledge of Africa would destroy for all time much of the propaganda which has passed for our history. . . . Ghana's independence will help the American Negro stand with added firmness in the fight against discrimination at home.

Maida Springer, Pittsburgh Courier *(13 April 1957)*

In the mid-1950s the vision of Africa being aflame with revolutionary fires spread through black America. The Defiance Campaign in South Africa and the Mau Mau in Kenya gave way to images of other struggles successfully achieving freedom. In particular, Ghana's movement to independence in 1957 pushed it to the vanguard of all liberation struggles. For African Americans, Ghana and Kwame Nkrumah, leader of the independence movement and the nation's first head of state, became powerful symbols that pushed African Americans to reconstruct their images of contemporary Africa and the terms of their relationship with it.

Ghana's success in attaining full independence while the domestic civil rights movement struggled for gains prodded African Americans to reassess their relationship with Africans. A wider, more international perspective developed within the black American freedom struggle, and African liberation struggles became a vital, although curiously underappreciated, force in promoting domestic civil rights efforts. As Ghana and Nkrumah became important symbols of independence and the ability to overcome, they simultaneously helped recast the "broad anticolonialism" that had characterized black American politics in recent years. African American anticolonialism, reshaped along more racially specific lines, took a particular interest in Africa, creating the conditions for the striking growth in the late 1950s and early 1960s of African Americans marking Africa as their special foreign policy concern.

Even more, as Africans overthrew colonial rule and took their place on the world stage, they overturned old stereotypes about African "primitiveness" and "backwardness." Feelings of indifference, ambivalence, or even superiority toward Africans decreased in black America; racial pride in Africa increased. For many African Americans, Ghana's independence came filled with portent. Long-held dreams might be fulfilled: Africa would return to its former greatness; a powerful African nation would rise to make the Western world accountable for its deeds; respect would grow for people of African descent everywhere.

African independence encouraged black Americans to reach out and expand their notions of ethnicity to include contemporary Africa. Indeed, Ghana's independence, followed by the accelerating pace of other African countries' gaining independence, provided a widespread, positive force for all African Americans to recast their images of contemporary Africa. As Nkrumah and Ghana promoted transatlantic connections, contemporary Africa soared not only as a source of political encouragement but also of social and cultural inspiration. This process brought the seemingly dual paths of universalist integrationism and racialist nationalism into greater balance and made Africa a cornerstone in black Americans' self-constructions of identity.

Nkrumah's Rise to Power

On 28 February 1948, police in Accra fired on a peaceful demonstration by ex–World War II servicemen, killing two and injuring several more. Days of rioting followed, during which dozens more died and hundreds were injured. The riots triggered a long chain of events that eventually led to Ghana's independence.

In June 1948, a Commission of Inquiry sent by Britain to the Gold Coast recommended that the existing constitution be scrapped as undemocratic and outmoded. Believing that it could maintain better control over the Gold Coast by effecting some changes and thereby keep the initiative out of the hands of Gold Coast nationalists, the British government acted upon one of the commission's recommendations and appointed a committee of Africans to draft proposals for a new constitution. The resulting constitution provided for a nationally elected assembly and an executive council consisting of three appointed ex officio members and eight representative members drawn from the assembly. Yet in these constitutional reforms the British reserved important powers, most prominently the right to appoint the ex officio members, who held the key portfolios of Defense and External Affairs, Finance, and Justice.

The British reservations of power meant that the new constitution fell short of the demands by Nkrumah and his followers for "self-government now," a demand that reflected Nkrumah's history of nationalist and pan-Africanist involvement. Nkrumah had left the Gold Coast as a young man in 1936 to attend Lincoln University in Pennsylvania. An historically black college, Lincoln had been established in 1854 to provide higher education for black men. Two South African students who enrolled in 1896 started Lincoln's long connection with educating Africans. In the next three decades, twenty-three Africans graduated. In the 1930s, African graduates included Nkrumah as well as Nnamdi Azikiwe, the Nigerian nationalist and future president. Nkrumah himself graduated sixth in the 1939 class of forty-six, then went on to study at Lincoln's theological seminary while simultaneously working on a master's degree in philosophy at the University of Pennsylvania.[1]

During the early 1940s, Nkrumah became increasingly active in the pan-African political arena. The African Students Association, founded in 1941, elected him president in 1942. In 1944 the CAA asked him to be a sponsor of its conference on Africa. The next year he took part in the NAACP's colonial conference, serving on the committee that drafted the resolutions. Nkrumah departed the United States for England in May 1945, a month after the NAACP conference. In England he became involved in the preparations for what would be the Manchester Pan-African Congress, playing a prominent role as organizing secretary. Two years later he returned to the Gold Coast to become secretary of the United Gold Coast Convention (UGCC), an African political party dedicated to achieving independence. In 1949, he split from the moderate, elite-oriented UGCC to form his mass-based, nationalist Convention People's Party (CPP).[2]

In January 1950, Nkrumah and his supporters embarked on a campaign of "positive action," which Nkrumah later defined as "the adoption of all legal and constitutional means by which we could attack the forces of imperialism in the country." The weapons, he wrote, were "political agitation, newspaper and educational campaigns and, as a last resort, the constitutional application of strikes, boycotts, and non-cooperation based on the principle of absolute non-violence, as used by Gandhi in India."[3] Amidst strikes and small-scale violence, the government declared a state of emergency and arrested Nkrumah for inciting "illegal" strikes. From prison, Nkrumah instructed his supporters to contest elections being held in accordance with the new constitutional guidelines.

Nkrumah's CPP won the February 1951 elections by an overwhelming margin, and Nkrumah himself was elected to be a member of the legislative assembly. In the week following the election the British authorities released him from his sentence and invited him, as head of the party receiving the most votes, to lead the Gold Coast's first African administration. Nkrumah assumed internal authority as "Leader of Government Business."[4]

Nkrumah, clearly no British lackey, now held more responsibility than any black African in colonial Africa ever had. Yet reaction in the African American press to this momentous step toward African rule was surprisingly subdued. Indeed, virtually none of the established African American newspapers covered the unfolding story in Ghana. The *Defender* and the *Daily World* did not report the events; the *Courier*, *Afro-American*, and the *Amsterdam News* each published only one or two small articles. These articles made more of Nkrumah's Lincoln affiliation than of the fact that this election and its results constituted a major step toward power being turned over to Africans. Even the CAA, while calling Nkrumah's release from prison and move to power a "great day of rejoicing," buried the story on page 5 of its newsletter.[5]

When Nkrumah came to the United States shortly thereafter, reaction also was lukewarm. Lincoln University president Horace Mann Bond invited Nkrumah to give the commencement address and receive an honorary doctorate at his alma mater. Bond wrote to inform the State Department of this arrangement and urged it to take measures to make the visit even more significant. Even though Nkrumah's visit was unofficial in nature, Assistant Secretary of State McGhee hosted a luncheon for Nkrumah. Of the original guest list of twenty, nine were black Americans, four of whom—Ralph Bunche, William Hastie, Channing Tobias, and Walter White—sent regrets. A few years later, when circumstances in the Gold Coast changed further and the importance of Africa to African Americans was exploding, the response to Nkrumah and his presence would be far different.[6]

In 1952 the Gold Coast constitution changed again. Under its provisions, the British governor-general no longer chose the leader of government business from the assembly; instead, the assembly itself voted for a prime minister, who ranked only behind the governor in authority. The executive council became known as the cabinet. With this change, which coincided with preparations for the Defiance Campaign in South Africa, African Americans began to take more notice of the situation. The *Courier* ran a front-page story praising Nkrumah for his "breathtaking" vigor and brilliance. Over the course of the following year Mary McLeod Bethune, Bayard Rustin, and Walter White put pen to paper to remark upon the positive example Nkrumah offered Africans.[7]

African Americans showed a growing interest in Nkrumah and what now seemed to be substantial progress toward Gold Coast independence. In the spring of 1953 the NAACP tried to convince Nkrumah to visit America to address the NAACP's annual convention. The NAACP also asked the State Department to declare the proposed visit as being in America's national interest, a move that held both symbolic and financial ramifications. The request placed the State Department in a difficult situation. Normally an unofficial visit such as this one would not receive that designation, yet the Bureau of African Affairs was, according to an internal memo, "under increasing pressure . . . from various quarters, including certain American Negroes in positions of some influence, to strengthen our ties with the Gold Coast." Further, the memo noted, "[The NAACP] seems to regard our reaction to the 'national interest' aspect of Nkrumah's visit as a test of the Department's attitude toward such African colonial areas as are approaching full self-government." The African desk therefore concluded that "in view of the delicacy of this case" the Department should stretch the point and certify the trip. The synergy created by Nkrumah, Africa, and African Americans was becoming more influential in the realm of international politics and race. In the end, Nkrumah decided that pressing concerns in the Gold Coast prevented him from visiting at the time, so instead he sent a message of goodwill and solidarity to the NAACP convention. In turn, the convention passed a resolution sending fraternal greetings to Nkrumah and the people of the Gold Coast.[8]

Nkrumah and the assembly continued to push for self-government and independence. In 1954 an amended constitution reduced or transferred many of the British governor's discretionary powers. Henceforth, the general population elected all assembly seats, and the prime minister chose the entire cabinet. The governor retained control only over defense and external affairs, and that only until the British Parliament passed an Act of Independence conferring full sovereignty upon the Gold Coast. In the June 1954 general elections the CPP won 72 out of 104 seats. Nkrumah became prime minister over a cabinet of his choosing and a now self-governing colony. These dramatic developments prompted the *Defender* to write that the 1954 election "opened wide the door to a brighter era for all Africa." The *Defender* in fact elevated Nkrumah and the Gold Coast to prodigious symbolic heights: "It would be morally sound to say that all Africa is casting its eyes upon the Gold Coast and Nkrumah. 'So goes the Gold Coast, so goes Africa' is the general feeling."[9]

Africans were not alone in casting their eyes toward the Gold Coast; so did people of color around the world. In doing so, black Americans wrestled more fully with the meaning of contemporary Africa. Developments in the Gold Coast led writer Richard Wright to pursue an interest in visiting Africa, a desire stoked by the urgings of long-time pan-Africanists George and Dorothy Padmore. In the spring of 1953, Wright corresponded with Nkrumah about traveling to the Gold Coast. This led to a ten-week summer visit for Wright — and autographed copies of *Native Son* and *The Outsider* for Nkrumah. Wright's reactions to the Gold Coast formed the basis for his book *Black Power*, published in 1954.[10]

Wright and his book stand as notable landmarks in black America's changing relationship with Africa. While *Black Power* offered smatterings of political analysis on the evolving case of black self-government, on the whole Wright commented only briefly on the effects of British colonialism and on Nkrumah's efforts to create a modern African political party and state. Finding himself frustrated with the CPP and its lack of support for his mission, Wright shifted his focus "to concentrate on the life of the people, which intrigues me no end."[11] The majority of *Black Power* consists of Wright's everyday experiences blended with his personal grappling over questions such as how "African" he felt and whether an essential African soul existed.

Wright, like many black Americans at the time, was struggling with the meaning and relevance of contemporary Africa for one's own self. "According to popular notions of 'race,' there ought to be something of 'me' down there in Africa. Some vestige, some heritage, some vague but definite ancestral reality that would serve as a key to unlock the hearts and feelings of the Africans whom I'd meet. . . . But I could not feel anything African about myself, and I wondered, 'What does being *African* mean?' " Wright never answered this question to his own satisfaction.[12]

Wright at times felt some essential racial connection, such as when he came across dancing that evoked what he knew from America; however, he fought any tendency to consider this as proof of an essential black being. Instead, this was something to turn over in his mind, a "riddle" as to "why black people were able to retain, despite vast distances, centuries of time, and the imposition of alien cultures, such basic and fundamental patterns of behavior." Most often Wright felt cut off, alienated from the Africans with whom he interacted. As his journey progressed, Wright moaned, "My money is melting under this tropic sun faster than I am soaking up the reality about me. . . . I'm of African descent and I'm in the midst of Africans, yet I cannot tell what they are thinking and feeling. And, without the help of either the British or the Africans, I'm completely immobilized." Wright quickly fell into a pattern of exoticizing and even casting aspersions on the actions and lives of Africans. According to Wright, for instance, marriage and adultery operated on a "cash and carry" basis, with some African chiefs even urging their wives to commit adultery in order to collect large sums of money in fines.[13]

Wright's faith in the superiority of Western thought and modernization remained unshakable, even in the face of disturbing historical evidence regarding Western ideas and action concerning Africa. Wright situated himself in a rational Western world and felt discomfited by a culture and life that he believed rested on irrational foundations. Ending his book with an open letter to Nkrumah, Wright urged the militarization of African life. Doing so would "atomize the fetish-ridden past, abolish the mystical and nonsensical family relations that freeze the African in his static degradation; it will render impossible the continued existence of those parasitic chiefs who have too long bled and misled a naive people; it is the one and only stroke that can project Africa immediately into the twentieth century!" Wright, who in earlier writings had held a despairing outlook on modern Western life, did pause to question his assumptions about pulling Africans out of the life that they had led. He even noted that he was literate, Western, industrialized, disinherited, and that he "felt each day the pain and anxiety of it." Yet in the end, he voiced few concerns about Africans taking this same path.[14]

Wright concluded that any sense of at-homeness in his travels "stemmed not from ties of blood or race, or from my being of African descent, but from the quality of deep hope and suffering embedded in the lives of your people, from the hard facts of oppression that cut across time, space, and culture."[15] And yet, Wright focused less on the political economy of colonialism and the various devastating effects of colonial rule than on the so-called "African personality" and his relationship to it. As Wright's biographer Michel Fabre concludes, "As an American and a Westerner, Wright had a difficulty identifying with the African vision of the world. . . . Africa turned out to be a foreign country, whose customs, emotions, and habits of thought disconcerted, even alienated him, and taught him that he was incurably American and Western."[16]

Wright and others clearly felt an ambivalence about how to incorporate the changing Africa into their lives. Wright himself knew it was important, wanted to help steer it, but could not fully integrate or understand it. Responses to his book indicate that others who recognized the significance of Gold Coast advances also still were negotiating the relationship of it to African American lives. Walter White, for example, in reviewing *Black Power*, declared that the Gold Coast offered the most important experiment in democratic living taking place anywhere in the world. With the Defiance Campaign in South Africa and the Mau Mau in Kenya struggling to make headway toward black rule, the path of "negotiated independence" in West

Africa seemingly held more promise. At the same time, White's review centered on the old warhorse, the threat of communism, arguing that the Gold Coast experiment potentially offered a hopeful path that would save Africa from communism.[17]

African Americans plainly understood that the Gold Coast changes had wider implications for Africa; at the same time, most still were wrestling with defining the full implications of these advances and how they connected to their own struggle. In the next few years, more and more African Americans would confront a changing Africa, and most did so through the prism of Ghana emerging onto the world stage. They did so, too, while absorbing momentous changes in America. In 1954 the Gold Coast elections came directly in the wake of the *Brown v. Board of Education* decision. The following years brought significant new developments in both the Gold Coast and America, for by the end of 1956 the British had promised independence for the Gold Coast and the Montgomery bus boycott had achieved success. Both the domestic black freedom struggle and the relationship with Africa were entering a new stage.

Reactions to Independence, 1957

On 6 March 1957 the Gold Coast became fully independent under the new name of Ghana. For the first time a modern African nation south of the Sahara had achieved independence from European rule.[18] African American responses to Ghana's independence reveal dramatically strengthening bonds of connection with contemporary Africa. And in a profound shift from the first part of the century, African Americans embraced modern Africa while drawing lessons from the contemporary African experience.

Of course, some in black America clung to long-established thought patterns. In particular, the never-ending questions over where to focus attention continued, and domestic issues and concerns remained paramount. On the day the Gold Coast attained formal independence, the lead headline in the *Defender* proclaimed: "Jail, Fines for Truman Aides." The story: two minor officials in the Truman administration, which had been out of power for four years, were convicted of income tax evasion. The one thing concerning Ghana's independence that made the front page was a photo of Vice President Richard Nixon being greeted by a Ghanaian cabinet minister. Indeed, the *Defender* saw the flotilla of dignitaries from the United States as the important story. Its coverage of Ghana's independence concentrated on the American notables in attendance rather than the import of independence itself.[19]

The brief encounter of Nixon and Martin Luther King Jr. in Accra in fact became a major story in black America, at times outweighing the significance attributed to Ghana and its independence. Nixon and Eisenhower had evaded southern blacks' entreaties to visit the South in order to find out for themselves about life under Jim Crow, so King's first ever face-to-face meeting with Nixon potentially held far-reaching significance. Biographer David Garrow says King asked Nixon at this meeting to come visit him in Alabama, where "we are seeking the same kind of freedom Ghana is celebrating." Although King received no promise that Nixon would visit him in the South, the meeting nevertheless generally received higher profile in the black press than any other single aspect of Ghana's independence. "The independence celebration at Ghana as a sovereign state was equally meaningful to Americans, though conceivably for a different reason," wrote the *Defender*. "It was there that Rev. Martin Luther King . . . met Vice President Richard Nixon at a reception given by Prime Minister Nkrumah."[20]

Lingering negative imagery of Africa also continued to permeate some thinking, impeding any reconfiguring of attitudes about Africa or movement toward making Africa an integral part of black American lives. Nkrumah himself undoubtedly merited praise; however, not all believed that the rest of the country, let alone the continent, had achieved the same level of accomplishment. Ghana's independence portended a new view of Africa, but some still questioned whether or not the promise had been fulfilled. The comments of Lester Granger reveal lingering doubts about African "progress." Granger, even while writing about the thrills of attending the celebrations and remarking on his sense of being at home and being accepted in Africa, observed that he was also struck by "the vivid contrast between twentieth century America and the dark continent only now emerging from the grip of the nineteenth century."[21]

Journalists and their newspapers also had not unfettered themselves completely from perceptions that black Americans had reached a higher level of civilization than Africans. Horace Cayton, who usually wrote sympathetically about the non-Western world's struggles, voiced his opinion that Nkrumah needed to stay in the British Commonwealth because its economic and military advantages were necessary for Ghana's "emergence from a primitive tribalism to a mature state." Louis Lautier, covering Nixon's trip and Ghana's independence celebrations for the *Afro-American*, managed to evoke an image of brotherhood while at the same time reinforcing the sense that African Americans were on a higher plane. "This capital is filled with dignitaries of color from all over the world. Robed tribal chiefs are solemnly shaking hands with their more sophisticated brothers from the United States."[22]

In line with these views that cast into doubt the advancement of Africans, for some the "natives" had not struggled for but had been "given" independence. The *Defender* even glossed over Britain's colonial exploitation and replaced the British stand against Hitler as that nation's "finest hour." "This is a glorious day for Africa. It is also Britain's finest hour. In removing the yoke of colonialism from the necks of the oppressed natives of West Africa, and in giving them independent dominion status within the great constellation of the British commonwealth, England has added a new chapter to the history of modern civilization."[23] Analyses in which British "statesmen" emerged heroically and Ghanaian "natives" merely received a gift dulled the agency and accomplishments of Africans themselves. Other African American papers likewise made little effort to connect their readers' struggle to the successful struggle in Ghana. For the *Daily World* and the *California Eagle*, independence in Ghana inspired only the hope that it would presage liberation for the entire continent; for the *New York Age*, it meant nothing more than an opportunity for more black Americans to become diplomats. Such coverage offered little basis for changing traditional ideas.[24]

So for some black Americans, Africa remained at a distance and its meaning had not changed much. They may have hoped that Ghana's independence foreshadowed independence for the entire African continent but felt personally that celebrations in Ghana were relatively unimportant. Clearly no single event, no matter how momentous, could change all long-established patterns of thought. When the Gold Coast became Ghana at the stroke of midnight on 6 March, all black American attitudes did not magically transform.

Yet recognition of this fact should not mask the profound shift that was taking place in black America. Ghana's independence forced black Americans to reassess their relationship with contemporary Africa and, in the process, to reassess the construction of their own identities. Africa, tossing off white rule and taking independence, no longer remained a place easily stereotyped as "backward" and needing to be "redeemed" or "uplifted." Africa's drive for freedom had moved further, faster, than that of black America. Africans, while transforming their continent, pushed African Americans to dismiss old notions and articulate new ideas. Ghana's independence helped transform the relationship of black America to Africa, laying the necessary groundwork for Africa, historical and modern, to become a more celebrated part of black American life. A new epoch of stronger connections between African Americans and Africa was at hand, with contemporary Africa as an inspirational element in African American lives.

The number of African American notables who attended the independence celebrations indicates the importance that they placed on Africa. Adam

Clayton Powell Jr. commented, "Nothing in my public life of 27 years has attracted the attention and attendance of colored American leadership as has Ghana."[25] Those who made the trip included Martin Luther King Jr., head of the Southern Christian Leadership Conference; Lester Granger, executive director of the National Urban League; A. Philip Randolph, president of the Brotherhood of Sleeping Car Porters and vice president of the American Federation of Labor; Ralph Bunche, United Nations undersecretary for special political affairs, representing Dag Hammarskjöld and the United Nations; Adam Clayton Powell Jr., congressman from New York; and Charles Diggs, congressman from Michigan; Horace Mann Bond, president of Lincoln University; John Johnson, president and owner of the Johnson Publishing Company; Dr. C. B. Powell, editor and publisher of the *Amsterdam News*; John Sengstacke, editor and publisher of the *Defender*; Claude Barnett, head of the Associated Negro Press; Shirley Graham Du Bois, representing W. E. B. Du Bois, whose passport had been revoked and not yet reinstated; William Sherrill, president of the Universal Negro Improvement Association; Rev. James H. Robinson, founder of Operation Crossroads Africa; and numerous religious dignitaries, representing the National Baptist Convention of the USA, Inc., the National Baptist Convention of America, the African Methodist Episcopal Church, the African Methodist Episcopal Zion Church, and the Christian Methodist Episcopal Church.[26]

Leaders from the broad spectrum of black America — religious, civil rights, labor, political, educational — made the pilgrimage, finding Ghana's independence important enough to leave their duties at home and make the lengthy and expensive journey to Africa. They perceived, in the words of Bunche, that independent Ghana "writes a new, glorious chapter to annals of freedom and democracy . . . [it] gives the only answer — and it is irrefutable — to the theories and practices of the racial factor in the equation of ability and capacity." As part of the journey, they paid homage to Nkrumah. Randolph declared Ghana's leader to be "a man of homely virtues, massive integrity, and a granite-like resolution to stand steadfast in the challenging enterprise of building a free nation," and all in all, "a sort of George Washington and Abraham Lincoln to his country." C. B. Powell broadened the analogy, proclaiming, "Ghana can now boast of the most astute and courageous leaders of the world. We believe that if Kwame Nkrumah does nothing else, he will go down in history with such leaders as George Washington, Lincoln, Roosevelt, Stalin, Gandhi, Nehru, and many others." Claude Barnett went so far as to write to Nkrumah after the independence celebrations about having "fallen prey to the psychological impact of 'Ghana.'" Barnett encouraged

Nkrumah to issue the command whenever he could be of service. The very fact that so many black leaders traveled to Ghana and said these things itself worked to advance connections with Ghana and Africa within African American communities.[27]

African Americans from all walks of life felt inspired by Ghana and made connections between the struggle for independence in Africa and the struggle for equality in America. Throughout the country African Americans sponsored and attended Ghana Independence Day celebrations. Readers of the *Amsterdam News* requested the words and music to Ghana's national anthem in such numbers that the paper had to publish a general announcement that no official copy had been released.[28]

Sidney Williams, former head of the Urban League's Chicago chapter, went so far as to declare Ghana's independence the most significant event for African Americans since emancipation. Prominent African Americans were visiting Ghana, he opined, because they believed it might be the answer to their hopes for a "big black nation" that would restore dignity and self-respect. Others agreed, hoping that Ghana would inspire all black Americans and that "the Negro leadership watching the birth of freedom in Ghana will return to this country strongly imbued with the spirit of Kwame Nkrumah who led the fight for the liberty of the Ghana people." "I am happy and proud when Africans reach their potential, because I believe this will automatically help me," remarked another African American. "The African in the next 25 years will do more to ease the stigma of color than the American Negro has done in the 99 years he has been free."[29]

The press coverage of events in Ghana reacted to as well as contributed to the strengthening of pan-African connections. The *Courier* in fact printed a special 32-page supplement titled "Salute to Ghana" in addition to large quantities of regular reports on the nation. In contrast to its coverage of the Gold Coast earlier in the decade, stories about Ghana no longer referred to the people as "natives" but as Africans or Ghanaians. Traditional customs no longer served as quaint tidbits on non-Western ways. The *Courier* focused attention on the Ghanaians gaining independence, as opposed to the British giving it, with the hope that in turn the Ghanaian example would help empower African Americans.[30] A front-page editorial emphasized the importance of Ghanaian independence:

[As] Ghana enters the society of free nations today, the event has a particularly pertinent significance for American Negroes. . . . Traced through the centuries, the majority of American Negroes are Ghanaians whose cultural roots have been destroyed, a new people who have lost touch with their original culture and civilization and have failed of full acceptance in the new society where they find themselves.

Are American Negroes an inferior people? Can they meet the full challenge of modern, Western civilization? We American Negroes look to Ghana to furnish the answers to these questions. . . .

Ghana's contributions, as a free nation, to peace, to art, to industry, to government, will be regarded by American Negroes as symbols of their own worth and potential. . . .

When we, American Negroes, shake hands with Ghana today, we say not only "Welcome!" but also, "Your opportunity to prove yourself is our opportunity to prove ourselves."[31]

Ghana provided roots to a people torn from their ancestral culture, roots that many believed had been irrevocably destroyed during the enslavement process. Even more, Ghana offered inspiration and redemption for African Americans. As the world marched forward, the course that Ghana took, and the achievements of that nation of 4.5 million people, promised to have a dramatic influence on the status and struggle of African Americans. The watching world would have proof of blacks' abilities. The pride of Ghana would be the pride of African Americans.

Significantly, the more internationalist press not only extolled Ghana as a source of racial pride and consciousness, it also identified and promoted specific links between African independence movements and the civil rights struggle in America. Africa now offered lessons, not debased people needing uplift. The *Courier*, for instance, saw in the Ghanaians ability to wrest independence from the British a straightforward example for African Americans. "It is our hope that the brilliant example of Ghana will spur us to close ranks similarly and pool our talents and resources so that we in the great American democracy may attain a larger measure of independence."[32]

African Americans often revealed a common duality of thought in making such connections. On the whole, they would have preferred that race and color not be defining factors in American life; and yet, they felt an affinity to Africa, an affinity most typically based on racial identification. The *Amsterdam News* account of Ghana's independence vividly illustrated this blending of integrationist and nationalist sensibilities. Identifying the "common bond between American Negroes and Ghana" as based on the fact that both "are striving for full freedom in that state that we already have," the paper declared, "It is not so much a question of color that we rejoice over Ghana as it is a question of freedom." Yet other words in the same editorial showed that the common bond also arose from race and color: "There is more than meets the eye behind the birth of the new nation of Ghana in the so-called dark continent of Africa. . . . To the millions of colored people around the world Ghana represents the first robin of spring after a long cold and dark winter."[33] The "first robin of spring" sang in March 1957, making clear that Ghanaian nationhood held much more weight than independence in Asia (as compared to Malaysia gaining independence the same year) or even North Africa (as compared to the Sudan becoming independent the previous year). Ghanaian independence held meaning as the first black African nation to cast off colonialism.

The *Afro-American* similarly reflected this duality of integrationist and nationalist thought when it used Ghana's independence to promote a profound change in thinking in what has been called the "name game." In its editorial "Proudly We Can Be Africans," the paper declared,

> We submit that it is time Americans took the designation "Negro" out of the shadow. With the increased importance of Africa in the world and the UN, those of us who are of African descent can take justifiable pride in the continent from which our forebears came. From now on we should refer to ourselves as Africans, rather than colored people or Afro-Americans or "Negroes" when such designation becomes necessary. The truth of the matter is that more than anything else we are Americans, which under ordinary circumstances should be designation enough for anybody. But the circumstances, as far as we are concerned, have not yet become ordinary.[34]

Providing another vital avenue for promoting new ties to the continent, religious leaders moved beyond the old role of sending missionaries to redeem Africans and articulated how an Africa gaining independence related to black America. The Reverend David Licorish provided one clear view of the transforming relationship. As the associate minister of the Abyssinian Baptist Church of New York City, Licorish took charge when Rev. Adam Clayton Powell Jr. left town. On 3 March 1957, with Powell in Accra, Licorish preached the day's sermon:

> At long last American Negroes are beginning to understand the ties of kinship which bind together the African people and American colored citizens. We sincerely hope and trust that this new nation in Africa will serve as a symbol to all colored peoples everywhere that freedom is possible for all. Ghana means that peoples everywhere must throw off the yoke of colonialism, servitude, and second-class citizenship and enter into the full ranks of the rights of freedom and equality. It means that a people

though downtrodden and held down by the shackles of servitude can rise and throw off the yoke of bondage. . . . It means that no people are permanent pawns in the hands of their masters.[35]

In drawing explicit parallels between the independence of Ghana and the struggle of African Americans, Licorish appropriated Ghanaian success as both a symbol and an inspiration for African American success.

Martin Luther King Jr. also believed that vital connections existed between the freedom struggle in America and the struggles in Africa. King, who felt a "very deep emotional feeling" over the birth of this new nation, first visited Africa for Ghana's independence celebrations. He flew over with Bunche, Powell, and Randolph and had a private lunch with Nkrumah. Coretta Scott King remembers that when she and her husband saw Accra, "We realized that we ourselves had been the victims of the propaganda that all of Africa was primitive and dirty." The independence ceremony thrilled King, but the next morning he fell ill, and Nkrumah had to send his personal physician to care for him. The Reverend Michael Scott, a devoted worker for African rights, visited him at his bedside. There King informed Scott about his growing conviction that "there is no basic difference between colonialism and racial segregation, although naturally there are surface differences." "At bottom," said King, "both segregation in America and colonialism in Africa were based on the same thing — white supremacy and the contempt for life."[36]

According to King biographer Lawrence Reddick, King's visit to Africa renewed his strength and faith, leaving him "inspired and more determined than ever to push forward the frontiers of freedom in his own native Southland." He departed the celebration feeling that it would "give impetus to oppressed peoples all over the world" and particularly that it would influence the situation in the American South.[37] Upon returning to Montgomery, King personally sought to spread such influence by preaching about his trip to Ghana and outlining for his congregation the "things that we must never forget as we ourselves find ourselves breaking aloose from an evil Egypt, trying to move through the wilderness toward the promised land of cultural integration." In his view, Ghana's independence held these lessons:

The oppressor never voluntarily gives freedom to the oppressed. You have to work for it. And if Nkrumah and the people of the Gold Coast had not stood up persistently, revolting against the system, it would still be a colony of the British Empire. . . . So don't go out this morning with any illusions. Don't go back into your homes and around Montgomery thinking that the Montgomery City Commission and that all of the forces in the leadership of the South will eventually work out this thing for Negroes, it's going to work out, it's going to roll in on the wheels of inevitability. If we wait for it to work itself out, it will *never* be worked out! Freedom only comes through persistent revolt, through persistent agitation, through persistently rising up against the system of evil.

King then drew three more lessons. One observed that "a nation or a people can break aloose from oppression without violence." Another clarified the truth that "freedom never comes easy": "It comes through hard labor and it comes through toil. It comes through hours of despair and disappointment." And his last lesson voiced King's belief that the black struggle in America was tied to those in Africa as well as to a broader, more universal sweep toward righteousness. In the end, while the road to freedom is difficult, "Ghana tells us that the forces of the universe are on the side of justice."[38]

As black Americans increasingly viewed Africa as important in its own right, rather than merely as a piece in a Cold War chess game, their anticolonialism was reshaped along more African-centered lines. The broad anticolonialism that for a decade commonly had been tied to anticommunist arguments shifted to a more specific anticolonialism tied to Africa. In this reframed anticolonialism, African Americans more often remarked on how liberation struggles in Africa aided the struggle in America rather than on how African Americans could aid and uplift Africans. Even more, liberal and internationalist African Americans started abandoning anticommunist rhetoric in their appeals for the decolonization of Africa. When Nixon, returning from Ghana, emphasized the need for America to get into Africa quickly to head off communist penetration, the *Afro-American* responded to his concerns by pointing out that Africans were not interested in the fight against communism and warned that if the United States was not in Africa to help Africans instead of the colonial powers, then it should stay home. Ghana, the most important symbol of an ascendant Third World for African Americans, pushed black Americans away from the Cold War–influenced anticommunist rhetoric and mindset of the early 1950s.[39]

Geopolitics, Africa, and African Americans

Nkrumah and Ghana marched in the vanguard of African liberation as British and French colonies throughout the continent moved swiftly toward independence. The sweep of events prompted French president Charles De Gaulle in early 1958 to devise a referendum designed to circumvent independence demands in French colonies: either vote yes on a new French Constitution, which would allow colonial autonomy within a Franco-African Community; or vote no, and all French economic, political, and military presences — and assistance — would be removed immediately. Under these terms only Guinea dared to try independence. Ghana's triumphal transition to independence, followed by Guinea's equally successful break, encouraged other colonies to press for increased autonomy and, often, for full independence.

The agitation for independence, and indeed the sheer number of independent countries, provoked a new sense of urgency about Africa in the meeting rooms of Washington during the last years of the 1950s. Inevitably, Cold War concerns loomed large. Mushrooming national liberation movements seemingly provided fertile ground for communist intrigue. Further, although the Soviets had shown little interest in Africa during Stalin's regime, after his death in 1953, policy shifted. The Soviets increasingly sought to influence Third World countries, and the growing competition for worldwide influence between the Soviets and the Chinese fanned communist activity in Africa.[40] Washington found that its "middle path" of acceding to continued colonial rule by anticommunist allies while verbally backing eventual self-determination and majority rule by Africans steadily grew more offensive to African nationalists, some of whom sought alternative supporters, communist or not, who offered stronger commitment to African liberation.

The tumultuous changes on the continent forced American officials to revisit policy toward Africa. In 1956 the National Intelligence Estimate (NIE) regarding Africa south of the Sahara — one of a continuing series of high-level reports created through interdepartmental cooperation among the Central Intelligence Agency (CIA), State Department, Army, Navy, Air Force, and Joint Chiefs of Staff — had to be revised. The preceding estimate, produced less than three years earlier, had identified the "chief problem" in Tropical Africa as the "increasing African discontent and demands for self-government." Yet the report reassuringly concluded that "The breakdown or overthrow of existing authority is nowhere imminent in Tropical Africa." The authors felt that the colonial powers would make the "adjustments" necessary to prevent discontent from erupting into large-scale revolt for at least a decade. Most believed that the colonial powers would hold out for an even longer period of time. Faced with other world problems, Washington had welcomed the illusion of stability in Africa through the maintenance of colonial authority. Few in Washington realized the depth of African nationalism, and even fewer prepared to deal with it.[41]

The revised 1956 estimate reflected the rapid changes occurring in Africa and the greater urgency about preparing for African independence.

The report predicted that Africans "will make increasing demands for self-government," that the result would be "an increasingly rapid emergence of new African states," and that "regardless of how political demands are handled," throughout Tropical Africa interracial tensions almost certainly would increase. The report warned that during the conflict between the metropoles and those demanding self-rule, the United States would be "bombarded" from both sides with demands for diplomatic and moral support.[42]

In late 1956 and early 1957 the time appeared ripe for rethinking policy toward Africa for a number of reasons. Washington's own strategic assessments indicated a need to shift policy toward a more active, pro-African independence stance. Indeed, the potentially flammable mix of race and international politics made it very difficult to cultivate friendships with newly emergent countries governed by people of color while at the same time essentially backing continued colonial rule over other people of color.

In addition to the independence of Ghana, other international factors pointed to the need to change policy. U.S. officials finished the 1956 NIE in the midst of the Suez crisis, triggered when Egyptian leader Gamal Abdel Nasser nationalized the Suez Canal. Britain, France, and Israel responded by attacking Egypt, outraging President Eisenhower, who had not been informed in advance. The willingness of the British and French allies to proceed independently on such a vital issue fostered U.S. officials' disposition to chart a more independent course of action on questions concerning these nations' colonies in Africa. U.S. desires for increased economic opportunities in Africa subtly reinforced these other pressures to depart from the traditional obsequience to the colonial powers' concerns.[43]

Domestic race relations and political concerns created additional pressure for a more pro-African policy. The black freedom struggle continued to be a public relations nightmare for U.S. foreign policy, with first Montgomery's bus boycotts and then the confrontations surrounding Little Rock's desegregation ravaging America's image abroad. When Nixon returned from his 1957 trip to Africa, he informed Eisenhower, "Every instance of racial prejudice in this country is blown up in such a manner as to create a completely false impression of the attitudes and practices of the great majority of the American people. The result is irreparable damage to the cause of freedom which is at stake." Revealing his ordering of priorities, Nixon recommended, "In the national interest, as well as for the moral issues involved, we must support the necessary steps which will assure the orderly progress toward the elimination of discrimination in the United States."[44]

Like their African counterparts, a growing number of African American voters were using a candidate's views on colonialism and decolonization as a barometer for views on racial issues in America. A politician who did not support black majority rule in Africa had a far more difficult time convincing black voters that he supported equal rights in America. Thus, with the 1960 presidential election guaranteed to have no incumbent, stronger support for African independence was viewed as a way to gain black votes. Indeed, as Brenda Plummer argues, Kennedy would compensate for his "demonstrably poor civil rights voting record" by using the Africa issue as a bridge to the black electorate. During the campaign Kennedy referred to Africa 479 times in his campaign speeches, charging repeatedly that the United States had lost ground to the Soviets in Africa because it had failed to address the needs and aspirations of Africans.[45]

Some increased attention occurred. In September 1956 the State Department created the new position of deputy assistant secretary of state for African affairs, and then in August 1958 finally established a separate Bureau of African Affairs with its own assistant secretary of state for African affairs. This structural change helped lend weight to the "Africanists" within the State Department. Sending Vice President Nixon to represent the United States at Ghana's independence celebrations itself manifested a growing concern with Africa. Secretary of State Dulles urged placing Nixon as head of the official U.S. delegation, noting that the emerging nations of Africa would "follow with particular attention the degree of interest and sympathy" that the United States accorded Ghana's independence.[46]

Nixon's three-week tour through the northern half of Africa after Ghana's independence left him championing increased attention to Africa. His report to Eisenhower detailed a series of recommendations for U.S. policy with Africa: that the Defense Department and the International Cooperation Administration give higher priority to their operations in Africa; that the State Department immediately strengthen qualitatively and quantitatively its representation in Africa, with the administration urgently considering requesting the necessary funds from Congress; that only the most highly qualified representatives be assigned to African posts; that planning commence for diplomatic relations with the emerging African states; and that aid and information programs be reviewed to gain the maximum political impact. Nixon specifically applied these recommendations to Ghana, adding that the United States must "follow most closely the evolution of this state, realizing that its success or failure is going to have profound effect upon the future of this part of Africa." Within months Robert Cutler, special assistant to the president for national security affairs, labeled Nixon the "father" of a new African policy.[47]

Nixon, however, fathered no fundamental change. While the foreign policy establishment recognized the rising unrest in Africa, this resulted in no policy breakthroughs. Washington officials who argued that siding with African nationalist movements served American interests by promoting friendlier ties with Third World peoples still found themselves up against immediate Cold War priorities and Western-oriented sensibilities. Throughout Nixon's report to Eisenhower his reasons for giving more emphasis to, as opposed to trans-forming policy toward, the African continent remained grounded in the anti-communist logic of the day. "The course of [Africa's] development, as its people continue to emerge from a colonial status and assume the respon-sibilities of independence and self-government, could well prove to be the decisive factor in the conflict between forces of freedom and international communism." Nixon favored U.S. support for newly independent countries in order to "alleviate the conditions of want and instability on which commu-nism breeds."[48]

Significantly, the support Nixon envisioned did not extend to nations that were still struggling to obtain independence. Thus, in August 1957 when the National Security Council (NSC) produced its first paper on Africa south of the Sahara, the attempt to follow the "middle path" still resonated. On the all-important issue of nationalism or colonialism, the report declared, "Pre-mature independence would be as harmful to our interests in Africa as would be a continuation of nineteenth-century colonialism, and we must tailor our policies to the capabilities and needs of each particular area as well as to our overall relations with the metropolitan power concerned." Within the year, the rapid rush of events in Africa compelled the NSC to issue a new report, yet aside from an increased emphasis on providing economic and technical assis-tance to emerging nations, the old "middle path" framework remained.[49]

A number of ongoing factors help explain the lack of actual change in African policies by the Eisenhower administration, as well as by subsequent administrations, even in the face of increasing nationalism and the imminent demise of colonialism throughout most of Africa. The seeming safety of backing colonial powers who were Cold War allies continued to override considerations of truly supporting African independence. Bureaucratic in-clinations also favored the Europeanists over the Africanists in the State Department. Behind these factors lurked the enduring prejudices of Amer-ica's highest officials. These men, by and large believing Africans to be back-ward and inferior, generally concluded that Africans actually benefited by remaining under colonial rule. While discussing U.S. policy toward Africa south of the Sahara, Eisenhower and Dulles agreed with each other that no country outside of South Africa had the capability of governing itself. Nixon, the "father" of a "new" African policy, felt it naïve to hope that Africa would be democratic and offered his opinion that perhaps the United States should develop military strongmen to offset communist development of labor unions. In making his suggestion, Nixon proffered his judgment that some people in Africa had been out of the trees for only about fifty years. Maurice Stans, director of the Bureau of the Budget, who had returned recently from a trip to the Belgian Congo, chimed in that he believed many Africans "still belonged in the trees." Such painfully obvious racial predispositions among these, the highest officials in the land, meant that truly shifting toward policies supportive of African independence faced enormous hurdles.[50]

Finally, the absence of a strong lobbying structure for Africa in the black American community also diminished the prospects for a fundamental shift in U.S. policy. While the CAA had operated during the Defiance Campaign and the Mau Mau insurgency, by the time of Ghana's independence it had shut down. Intense government harassment and repression during the Cold War had taken its toll on the organization. In May 1953 attorney general Herbert Brownell began proceedings before the Subversive Activities Control Board (SACB) to have the CAA registered as a communist-front organization. Five months later a grand jury had subpoenaed CAA director Alphaeus Hunton to appear. Public rebuttals and legal challenges by the CAA had done nothing to stop the steady government quashing of the organization. At the same time, the CAA's positions also had helped marginalize it in black America, contributing to its declining position. As most of black America had learned of and rejoiced over Nkrumah's rise, the CAA had questioned and even condemned his leadership. In a series of articles in 1954, the CAA newsletter *Spotlight on Africa* had questioned Nkrumah's lack of Marxian socialist commitment. In one of its more slanderous passages, the CAA, upset over Nkrumah's refusal to fully support communists, portrayed Nkrumah and rabid racist and apartheid architect Daniel Malan as bedfellows: "It is curious but not unfathomable that Malan and Nkrumah, two men who on most questions are worlds apart, should find common ground in their officially announced policy of keeping alleged Communists out of all government posts in their respective countries."[51] On 14 June 1955, in its dying stages and facing another round of investigation by the SACB, the CAA had voted to dissolve itself.[52]

The silencing of the CAA, marginalized as it may have been, left a large void in the leadership of organizational criticism of U.S. foreign policy. In the mid-1950s, a pair of organizations that focused on Africa somewhat filled the breach. The first, the American Committee on Africa (ACOA), came into being after the conclusion of the Defiance Campaign, when Americans for South African Resistance transformed itself into an organization with a broader scope. ACOA adopted as its main priorities helping the emergence of democratic self-governing states in colonial Africa and freeing Africans from exploitation, poverty, and racial discrimination. ACOA viewed its program as having two aspects: an educational one, which would disseminate information about issues in African countries and about the views of African leaders; and an active service component, which would undertake special projects of aid and development.[53]

ACOA offered African Americans one of the few organized alternatives for acting on their interests regarding Africa. African Americans involved with ACOA in the mid-1950s included Rayford Logan, who worked with the provisional committee to establish ACOA; Marguerite Cartwright, James Farmer, and Bayard Rustin, who participated in the executive board; and Adam Clayton Powell Jr., A. Philip Randolph, Channing Tobias, and Willard Townsend, who sat on the national advisory board. Even so, white liberals such as George Houser firmly controlled ACOA, and the organization generally targeted the more affluent, liberal white audience. ACOA included black American leaders but found it difficult to mobilize the people and resources of the African American community. The extent to which it could be a vehicle for African American concerns remained problematic, then, and African Americans would seek to create an alternative in upcoming years.[54]

The American Society of African Culture (AMSAC) also formed in the mid-1950s. Affiliated with the Paris-based Society of African Culture (SAC), AMSAC was a more culturally oriented, as opposed to politically oriented, organization. When the SAC journal *Présence Africaine* issued a call for the First World Congress of Negro Writers and Artists to be held in Paris in September 1956, French West Africans asked Richard Wright to contact black Americans about attending. Wright wrote to Roy Wilkins, who in turn contacted John A. Davis, then a political science professor at the City College of New York. Davis arranged for an African American delegation composed of himself; Horace Mann Bond, president of Lincoln University; James Ivy, editor of the *Crisis*; William Fontaine, professor of philosophy at the University of Pennsylvania; and Mercer Cook, professor of romance languages at Howard University. After they returned, these men formed the core of AMSAC.[55]

AMSAC, especially in its early years, followed a largely intellectual and academic program, in an effort to disseminate and promote African culture in a positive light. Davis described AMSAC's work as follows: "[It is] concerned with studying and disseminating information on the high culture of Africa in order to bring about an appreciation of the cultural validity of Africa among Africans, American Negroes, and the nations of the world.

This work has aimed at providing a sense of worth among American Negroes and Africans, a basis for respect from whites, and a basis for continental pan-Africanism."[56]

Overtly cultural objectives naturally held political undertones. Efforts to dispel negative images of Africa held ramifications that went beyond the cultural sphere, offering to black Americans a different vision of Africa and hence a different role for it in their lives. Further, insofar as cultural advancement and recognition intertwined with the political, economic, and social conditions of African countries, members of AMSAC concerned themselves with these areas too.[57] Still, throughout the late 1950s and into the early 1960s, political efforts and lobbying stood as secondary concerns, and political ramifications came as a by-product of cultural and intellectual pursuits. AMSAC remained an intellectually elite organization primarily concerned with African culture and, as such, it faced inherent limits as to how much it could mobilize black America when it came to African issues.[58]

Nkrumah's Visit, 1958

Nkrumah returned to the United States in 1958, stepping onto a black American stage largely devoid of popular, avowedly pan-African leaders and facing an audience primed by the African events of the preceding half dozen years to frame anew the position of Africa in their lives. The joy over Ghana's independence had worked to make African Americans take pride in contemporary Africa and promote the African side of their identity. As one would expect, African Americans needed time and buttressing events to negotiate old tensions and articulate new meanings as the relationship transformed. Nkrumah's visit in July 1958 played a vital role in the reconceptualizations.

Nkrumah's widely anticipated arrival as the head of an independent Ghana played a crucial and generally underappreciated part in helping shift the attitudes of black Americans.[59] The inspiration and pride sparked by Ghana's independence received concrete reinforcement during Nkrumah's stay. Anyone who picked up the *Courier*, the *Afro-American*, or even the *Defender*, saw Nkrumah being embraced by the nation's elite. That Nkrumah was black and African held deep meaning for black Americans.

Kicking off coverage of Nkrumah's trip, *Courier* staff writer Harold Keith found Nkrumah's welcome "perhaps the greatest reception ever accorded a visiting head of an African state." Vice President Nixon and Joint Chiefs of Staff chairman General Maxwell Taylor greeted Nkrumah at the airport. Nkrumah met with President Eisenhower, who then hosted a luncheon for him. Nixon and Secretary of State Dulles both held meetings and hosted dinners. Nkrumah addressed the House of Representatives and the Senate, as well as the National Press Club. Official Washington treated his visit with care and importance. The U.S. embassy in Ghana reported that upon his return Nkrumah offered his unsolicited appreciation of the "warmth" of the official and unofficial reception, saying that he had been "all but over-whelmed by hospitality." The *Afro-American* commented that Washington "rolled out the red carpet," while Du Bois wrote that Nkrumah was "treated as never a Negro had been treated by the government."[60]

When Nkrumah traveled to other parts of the country, he also found a warm reception. In New York, Governor Averill Harriman and the city's act-ing mayor hosted a luncheon at the Waldorf-Astoria. In Chicago, added late to Nkrumah's itinerary, the Civic Reception Committee headed by Claude Barnett rushed to celebrate properly the historic visit. Mayor Richard Daley met Nkrumah at the airport. The city then paraded Nkrumah in what the *Defender* described as "one of Chicago's most spectacular welcomes" and launched him on a whirlwind of receptions during his short stay. The *Courier* described Nkrumah as having been "feted, wined, dined and eulogized by the great and lowly, the rich and the poor, the masses and the classes."[61]

Black America pulled out the stops for Nkrumah. Nowhere was he greeted more spectacularly than in Harlem, where people lined his parade route and greeted him with adulation. Jackie Robinson, Roy Wilkins, A. Philip Ran-dolph, and Lester Granger headed the official entertainment committee. Ten thousand people jammed the reception sponsored by the Harlem Citizens' Committee of 100 and the Harlem Lawyers Association at the 369th AAA Group Armory.[62]

Ralph Bunche gave Nkrumah a rousing welcome that made explicit the ties between Nkrumah, Africa, and African Americans. "Welcoming you this evening, I cannot fail to recall that it was only in March last year that, on your invitation, I had the inspiring experience of witnessing in your capital, Accra, an event more impressive than any in my long experience." Bunche went on to recall when Nkrumah stood at the first meeting of Ghana's parliament:

> You were more, *much more*, than the leader and liberator of the people of Ghana; much more, indeed, than the spokesman for African Africa. . . . You, as a consequence of the successful upward climb of the people of Ghana under your dedicated leadership — whether you will it or not — represent spiritually and symbolically, all of us whose skins are pigmented, all the people the world over who have suffered from prejudice and dis-

crimination because of color or race, all who know the subjection of colonialism, all of the depressed and underprivileged, the scorned and the deprived. . . .

We salute you, Kwame Nkrumah, not only because you are the Prime Minister of Ghana of Africa, although that is cause enough. We salute you because you are a true and living representation of our best hopes and ideals: of the determination we have to be accepted fully as equal beings, of the pride we have held and nurtured in our African origin, of the achievement of which we know we are capable given only opportunity, of the freedom in which we believe, of the dignity imperative to our stature as men. . . . But above all, Mr. Prime Minister, we embrace you because *you and your people* and *we* are *brothers* — brothers *of* the skin and *beneath* the skin.[63]

Bunche's racialist emphasis is even more meaningful in light of his past opinions regarding the relationship with Africa. Bunche's longstanding interest in Africa can be traced back at least as far as his 1930s doctoral dissertation, which compared French administration of its colony of Dahomey to its League of Nations mandate in Togoland. At that time, he grounded his leftist internationalism in a class-based, not race-based, analysis. In the 1940s, even as he moved away from his leftism, he had argued that any Pan-African Congress must be broad enough in nature to address the issue of exploited groups not considered "Negro" and that perhaps such a conference should not even be limited to territorial African problems. Indeed, Bunche questioned the advisability of a pan-African movement, and thought that if such a movement carried on, it should be confined to Africans. His words in 1958, then, were all the more telling of the racialist emphasis taking place — a shift nurtured by Africa's independence — and of the increased blending of a racialist nationalism with liberal integrationism.[64]

On the evening following the Harlem reception, the NAACP, Urban League, and ACOA sponsored a 1,000-person dinner at the Waldorf-Astoria. The audience included ambassadors, senators, and congressmen, as well as representatives of Chase Manhattan Bank, New York Savings Bank, Pan American Airways, Mobil Overseas Oil, U.S. Steel, and Union Carbide. Never had the Waldorf's ballroom "glittered and throbbed more impressively," observed Raymond Talbert, a vice president for Mellon National Bank.[65] African American dignitaries included Thurgood Marshall, Mordecai Johnson, A. Philip Randolph, Jackie Robinson, Hulan Jack, Earl Brown, Adam Clayton Powell Jr., and Charles Diggs. Bunche, Roy Wilkins, and Lester Granger all paid tribute to the Ghanaian leader. "Between Little Rock, Arkansas, and

Accra, Ghana, 8,000 miles of land and sea stretch," proclaimed Granger, "but there is no more than the whisper of a bird's breath between the hopes and aspirations of the black citizens in Arkansas in the Deep South and the triumph and expectations of the black men and women of Ghana who walk the streets of Accra proud and tall." Wilkins affirmed the same sentiments: "As other loyal Americans look back upon their European homelands with affection and pride, so we look upon Ghana and the emerging nations of Africa. Your struggles and your successes have aided us in our trials and tribulations here." Wilkins's speech in particular helps illustrate the pervasiveness of the transformation taking place. Wilkins never had shown much interest in Africa, certainly less than had his predecessor Walter White. Yet here he tied black Americans to contemporary Africa and made clear that African successes echoed in America.[66]

Of course, Wilkins understood that he and the NAACP faced new challenges for leadership of the civil rights movement. In the ongoing scramble for leadership, the legitimacy bestowed by association with Nkrumah made it worth ensuring that one said the right things about the relationship with Africa. At the same time, the fact that these were "right" meant that they held meaning both for Nkrumah and for broader black America. Nkrumah, it should be noted, also sought legitimacy — for his leadership in the quest for pan-African unity. He called upon symbols of pan-Africanism, for example, evoking Marcus Garvey by establishing the Black Star Line shipping firm. He cultivated images of youth, power, and modernity, balanced by respect for tradition. Nkrumah consciously sought African American support for his pan-African vision.[67]

Nkrumah's visit and reception had a palpable impact on black America. In the late 1940s and early 1950s the two major black figures associated with Africa had been Du Bois and Robeson. Their leftist ideas had caused both to be hounded, pilloried, and persecuted. While their interest in Africa may not have been the root cause of their persecution, by no means was it disentangled from it. When Robeson fought the revocation of his passport in 1950, the State Department brief submitted to the Court of Appeals argued that even if the passport had been canceled solely because of Robeson's status as a spokesman for large sections of black Americans, the government believed that this "would not amount to an abuse of discretion in view of appellant's frank admission that he has been for years extremely active politically in behalf of independence of the colonial people of Africa."[68] When Du Bois sought to attend the independence celebrations in Ghana, the State Department denied him the right, despite (or, perhaps more accurately, because of) Du Bois's lifelong work for a free Africa. Even Nkrumah's personal appeal had made no difference. Yet now, a mere eighteen months later, a black African leader was receiving the red carpet treatment in Washington.[69]

The rising assertiveness and confidence generated by the civil rights movement itself augmented the growing turn toward contemporary Africa. The *Brown v. Board of Education* decision had, in the words of historian Harvard Sitkoff, "heightened the aspirations and expectations of Afro-Americans as nothing ever had before." "Nearly a century after their professed freedom had been stalled, compromised, and stolen," he wrote, "blacks confidently anticipated being free and equal at last."[70] In December of 1955 Rosa Parks kept her bus seat, and the Montgomery boycotts ensued. With the Civil Rights Act of 1957, Congress enacted civil rights legislation for the first time in three generations. Civil rights victories helped stir rising racial pride and consciousness in the African American community. As the civil rights movement progressed, grew more potent, and promoted black pride, it nourished conditions conducive to reworking the role of Africa in African Americans' identity.

Into this mix stepped Nkrumah, whose reception resonated not only with leaders like Bunche and Wilkins, but also with the person on the street. "For the first time in my life I was proud to be a Negro," wrote Maria Garden. "When I saw the reception and honor given to Ghana's Prime Minister, a jet black man, I got down on my knees and thanked God for the awakening of this day. All is not lost for us." Mary Gause-Bey, a reader of the *Defender* whose passion surpassed her lyricism, wrote a poem she entitled "Salute to Ghana." Praising the country and calling it an inspiration for African Americans, the poem's second stanza read: "Ghana, O' Ghana we bow in submission to you today / For having rolled the stone away / You are a sample and an example for us / That the way to victory is to keep making a fuss."[71]

Nkrumah rose ever higher in stature. "His accomplishments should be a spark of hope for colored people all over the world," Morris Williams wrote to the *Courier*. Williams, arguing that African Americans and Africans fought the same foe of racial prejudice, added, "We should receive some inspiration from this man whose plight, and the plight of his whole continent, was perhaps worse than ours." Russell P. Crawford wrote for the *Amsterdam News* that African Americans "would do well to emulate his [Nkrumah's] example in our own struggle here in America" and chided American black leaders for being too timid when the masses stood ready to assert their rights. Mrs. Minnie Cartwright, a retired nurse in Chicago, wanted Nkrumah's presence exploited even more extensively. She urged that Nkrumah be given the opportunity to see the South Side and "the people who need his inspiration the most." Even some of those who had shown only mild interest in Ghana's independence the previous year became wildly enthusiastic about Nkrumah. The previously unstirred *Defender* now became swept up in Nkrumah's triumphal tour, declaring, "Those who heard Ghana's Prime Minister Nkrumah during his brief visit to Chicago came away tingling with inspiration."[72]

In his role as head of state, "voice for Africa," symbol of a rising Third World, and world leader, Nkrumah prodded African Americans to defy the Cold War political climate and question how extensively they should support U.S. foreign policy. Personally gravitating away from the West, Nkrumah and his nonaligned pan-Africanist positions made African Americans reconsider their own positions and adopt more independent, critical stances. While Nkrumah did not spark a particularly cohesive rallying behind a pan-African diasporic unity, his presence and powerful image encouraged African Americans to expand the parameters of mainstream political discourse. The *Defender*, for example, sharply departed from the hardline anticommunism it had preached throughout the Cold War and praised Nkrumah for his policy of neutralism. Nkrumah was positioning himself, the *Defender* argued, where he could arbitrate conflicting world interests, and through "tact, diplomacy, and political skill, Dr. Nkrumah is proving that the white man has no monopoly on wisdom."[73]

Nkrumah's visit further promoted a broader trend toward balancing the liberal integrationism so dominant in the previous decade with a rising racialist nationalism that was at least partly tied to contemporary Africa. The symbols of Nkrumah and Ghana strengthened the shift toward pride in Africa and things African. While some in black America continued neither to connect the struggles in Africa with that in America nor to search for deeper links between black peoples in the two lands, more and more African Americans increased their interest in Africa, developed appreciative views of Africa, and expanded their sense of African ethnicity. As James Baldwin remarked, "I'd be astonished if anybody reacted to newsreels or movies of Africans the way I did. Now there is pride. The shot of Nkrumah getting off his plane has an effect on all the other images. It takes a certain sting out of the African savage."[74]

Substantive and Symbolic Connections

Providing tangible evidence of the flowering African connections, Ghana's independence accelerated the emigration of African Americans to Africa. For African Americans desiring to return to the ancestral homeland, Ghana stood as a particularly favored destination. The fact that many of those enslaved had come from West Africa provided additional impetus to those who believed they could return to reconstitute an identity lost when their ancestors were torn from Africa. While most could not definitively trace their roots to Ghana itself, that was not the point. In the diasporic consciousness, specific locality played little role compared to the African totality.

The emigration reveals powerful nationalist impulses at work in black America and suggests that contemporary Africa had become a crucial element in the construction of more and more African Americans' identities. Longtime pan-African proponents Du Bois and George Padmore were perhaps the two most prominent leaders who emigrated to Ghana. Padmore became Nkrumah's adviser on African affairs in late 1957. In October 1961 Du Bois arrived, to coordinate work on his longstanding goal, the publication of an Encyclopedia Africana. Du Bois assumed Ghanaian citizenship and lived out his days in his adopted nation.[75] Others, ranging from the well-known to the obscure, also headed to Ghana. When Maya Angelou arrived in 1962, she found four basic groups of African American expatriates in the country: some forty-plus families who wanted to melt into the landscape, mainly as teachers and farmers; those who came under the aegis of the U.S. government; a miniscule business community; and a cadre of "political emigrés." Impassioned and dedicated to Africa, the members of this last group felt they would be the first accepted by Ghanaians; they then planned to "hold the doors open until all Black Americans could step over our feet."[76] Especially enticing to this group of black nationalists was Nkrumah's pan-Africanist background and vision, a vision that sought to purge the continent of artificially created boundaries established by Europeans and promised to create a united and powerful Africa with which the world, especially the white world, would have to reckon. Nkrumah himself actively encouraged the emigration of African Americans who possessed skills to offer and who wanted to help build pan-African dreams.[77]

The actual experiences of individuals who went to Ghana, as well as other parts of Africa, often ended up serving as a crucible in which individuals reflected on how African or American they were. Wrestling with their feelings and, of course, reaching their own personal conclusions, many found, somewhat as did Richard Wright, that they could not find a simple, essential sameness between themselves and the Ghanaians with whom they interacted. The relationship was far too complex. Angelou voiced some of the conflicting emotions when she wrote of her initial vision of what Ghana would be like: "We would work and produce, then snuggle down into Africa as a baby nuzzles in a mother's arms. I was soon swept into an adoration for Ghana as a young girl falls in love, heedless and with slight chance of finding the emotion requited." As time went on, Angelou saw more expatriates arrive, often with expectations that could not be met. "The need to believe in Africa's maternal welcome was painfully obvious. They didn't want to know that they had not come home, but had left one familiar place of painful memory for another strange place with none."[78]

Those who went to Ghana found that few simple answers existed in this relationship. "[Y]ears of bondage, brutalities, the mixture of other bloods, customs and languages had transformed us into an unrecognizable tribe," decided Angelou. And yet, Africa still was in African Americans, and Angelou concluded that blacks in America "had never completely left Africa." Others who ventured to Ghana experienced a similar range of emotions. As perhaps should be expected, there would be no single answer about the meaning of Africa in the ever-changing relationship of African Americans to it.[79]

Of course, the overwhelming majority of black Americans never physically set foot on African soil. All in all, relatively few African Americans actually uprooted their lives in America and went to Ghana, despite Nkrumah's invitations. Some visited, and others worked there for a short time, but only a very few ever obtained citizenship or lived there on a permanent basis. During Malcolm X's visit in 1964, one expatriate numbered the African American community in Ghana at 300. But as St. Clair Drake made clear, there was and continues to be a widespread psychological return to Africa, one not predicated upon physical relocation. Increasing numbers of African Americans found positive meaning from Africa, even though they did not actually return to the continent. For many, the success of Ghana brought into more equal balance the dual visions of full integration and equality in American life along with affirmation of a black identity.[80]

Ghana and Nkrumah framed the surging and widespread importance of contemporary, independent Africa for African Americans. Although African Americans in the late 1940s and early 1950s generally were disconnected from Africa while they focused on shaping an identity that would allow them to integrate fully into America, in the late 1950s they were pushed by Nkrumah and Ghana to transform their use of Africa. Ghana's independence and early years of statehood under Nkrumah made African struggles important symbols of the ability to overcome and achieve success during a crucial period in the civil rights struggle. Through both their actual deeds and their role as potent symbols, Nkrumah and the Ghanaian people fostered the increasing importance of Africa among African American leaders and the wider community. In so doing, Ghana helped prompt a shift toward a wider, more international perspective within the civil rights movement. And with

African nations attaining full independence while the U.S. civil rights movement still struggled for gains, African Americans had to reassess their relationship with Africans. Racial pride stemming from things African increased,
while notions of indifference or superiority toward Africans decreased. Providing a positive force that encouraged African Americans to recast their
images of Africa and to view contemporary Africa as a source of political,
social, and cultural inspiration, Nkrumah and Ghana reconfigured African
Americans' diasporic consciousness. The Year of Africa in 1960 would ce-
ment the transformation.

6

THE YEAR OF AFRICA
Lows, Highs, and Corners, 1960

What is happening in America and in South Africa is that the vision of human equality has caught new fire. The tired old cliches of gradualism are being burlesqued by the quietly valorous acts of the Negro people everywhere who will no longer accept the proposition that there are any second-class children of God.

Chicago Defender *(13 April 1960)*

The paramount fact, however, was not so much the substance or the rationale of the speech. What really stood out in bold relief was that an unmistakably black man [Kwame Nkrumah] had attained sufficient stature and prestige to ascend the rostrum of that great international body. . . . That in itself is history of the first magnitude.

Chicago Defender *(9 October 1960)*

The United Nations declared 1960 to be "The Year of Africa." No fewer than seventeen countries—Benin (Dahomey), Burkina Faso (Upper Volta), Cameroon, Central Africa Republic, Chad, Congo (People's Republic of), Congo (Zaire), Gabon, Ivory Coast, Madagascar, Mali, Mauritania, Niger, Nigeria, Senegal, Somalia, and Togo—gained independence during those twelve months. The UN admitted more than a dozen African states as new members. The single most striking event of the year, however, was not the independence of any one country, but the massacre of sixty-nine unarmed protesters at Sharpeville by South African police. For Africans and African Americans, the year swung between glorious heights and shocking depths. In the case of the Congo, exultation and despair came wrapped in one package.

The slew of African nations gaining independence mixed with news about, and anger over, the Sharpeville massacre and the neocolonial machinations in the Congo to keep the continent a prominent feature in the lives of African Americans. The events of 1960 strengthened links between African Americans and the worldwide struggle against white supremacy, while doing so on a more Africa-centered basis. The combination of all this helped ensure the turning of a corner: an Africa once marginalized as a place to uplift and redeem had transformed African American views of it and become instead a source of inspiration and pride, as well as a special international concern for African Americans.

Spring Lows: The Sharpeville Massacre

After the Defiance Campaign ended, ANC-led opposition to apartheid continued. Expanding on ties made during the protest campaign, the ANC moved in a multiracial direction, forging closer relations with Indians, Coloureds, and leftist whites in the struggle against apartheid. The convening of the Congress of the People on 25–26 June 1955 highlighted the ANC's move toward multiracialism. Participants included whites from the heavily communist Congress of Democrats, Indians, and Coloureds; representatives from the Liberal and Labour Parties attended as observers. Central to the meeting was the adoption of the Freedom Charter, which essentially restated longstanding ANC aims while adding economic nationalization as a principle. The charter also committed the ANC to a policy of multiracialism, as opposed to "pure" African nationalism. The preamble endorsed the position that "South Africa belongs to all who live in it, black and white."[1]

The Nationalist Party government in South Africa, for its part, continued to implement apartheid and institutionalize a police state in order to more thoroughly control South African society. Imprisonment and banning orders circumscribed opposition leaders' activities and silenced their voices. Repression, however, proved a double-edged sword. While critics found themselves facing increasingly stringent government sanctions, the ever harsher apartheid laws and diminishing avenues of protest generated rising frustration throughout the country's black majority.

The ANC's closer ties with non-Africans, most particularly the white left, did not go unopposed. A growing "Africanist" faction argued that Africans would have to fight alone to achieve maximum strength in the struggle, a claim rejected by most prominent ANC leaders as chauvinistic and racialistic. At the regional Transvaal ANC conference in November 1958 the dispute boiled over. ANC president Albert Lutuli's address to the meeting warned against developing a "dangerously narrow African nationalism, which itself encourages us to go back to a tribalism mentality." The Africanists decided the time had come to split from the ANC and establish their own organization.

The Africanist movement formalized itself as the Pan Africanist Congress (PAC) in April 1959.[2]

Robert Sobukwe, the guiding Africanist intellectual and president of the PAC, argued that Africans had the numbers to bring South Africa to a halt. To do so, Africans first needed to transform themselves psychologically. He argued that Africans must abandon a slave mentality and begin to believe in their inherent worth; only then would they be prepared to make an uncompromising demand for their rights as citizens and humans. Organizing the struggle along multiracial lines, Sobukwe argued, eroded the latent nationalist sentiments of the African masses. The mere presence of whites and Indians in leadership positions undermined the Africans' sense of self-reliance, because most Africans had been conditioned to think of these groups as superior. The PAC prescription for change lay in a doctrine of exclusive African nationalism, which would inspire Africans to undertake the sacrifices needed for the revolutionary confrontation that the PAC envisioned.[3]

The PAC found its greatest appeal among the relatively politicized and impatient urban working-class youth, who yearned for militant action. PAC leaders soon realized, however, that to attract and hold more followers they needed to produce some concrete results. At its first annual conference in December 1959, the PAC adopted a proposal for an anti-pass campaign, during which members would refuse to carry passes and would submit themselves for arrest.[4] The proposal followed a similar resolution by the ANC, which had announced its intention to launch an anti-pass campaign on 31 March 1960, the anniversary of anti-pass demonstrations in 1919. Hoping to steal a march on the ANC, the PAC scheduled its own campaign for 21 March. On 16 March 1960 Sobukwe wrote to Major-General Jans Rademeyer, Commissioner of Police, informing him that the PAC planned to begin a "sustained, disciplined, nonviolent campaign." On 18 March, as the PAC circulated flyers in the street, Sobukwe publicly announced the campaign at a press conference. The ANC declined a PAC invitation to join the demonstrations, saying that they could not support an action for which they were not properly prepared and which had no reasonable chance of success. Instead, the ANC planned to carry on its own program.[5]

On Monday, 21 March, the anti-pass campaign commenced with decidedly mixed response. No demonstrations took place in the major cities of Durban, Port Elizabeth, and East London; negligible protests occurred in Johannesburg. But in Sharpeville, an African location thirty-five miles from Johannesburg on the outskirts of the Vereeniging industrial complex, demonstrations and submissions for arrest did take place. After several hours, with the crowd size and the tension mounting, police nerves snapped. No order to shoot and no warning shots were given before a line of police commenced firing. As the demonstrators ran, the police shot dead 69 Africans and wounded 186 more. Most victims were shot in the back as they fled.[6]

While Sharpeville became a lightning rod for world criticism, it was not the only place where police actions left Africans dead, nor did it create the greatest sustained domestic protest. In two Cape Town locations, Langa and Nyanga, large crowds also gathered as thousands refused to report to work. Police dispersed crowds in Langa in the morning, but even more returned in the late afternoon. Despite a government order banning large meetings, by 5:30 P.M. about 10,000 had assembled. The police arrived in force, launched a baton charge without warning, and, in the effort to disperse the crowd, used firearms, killing two demonstrators. Full-scale rioting erupted and raged for several hours, marking the start of three tense weeks.[7]

The government refused to make concessions, arguing that doing so would only prompt further demands from Africans. Nevertheless, in an effort to bring the situation under control, the government temporarily suspended pass-related arrests. When ANC president Lutuli called for 28 March to be a nationwide, stay-at-home day of mourning for the Sharpeville and Langa victims, the prospect of a general strike by Africans loomed large. On that day, several hundred thousand workers stayed away from their jobs. In Langa alone, 50,000 blacks listened to funeral orators call for continuing the strike until the government met African demands.[8]

Two days later the government made clear it would offer no reforms and instead would give no quarter in ending African resistance. It declared a state of emergency and assumed broad powers to act against all forms of alleged subversion. These powers included the authority to arrest and detain indefinitely any person suspected of antigovernment activity. Early that morning police began conducting nationwide swoops to arrest leaders and supporters of the campaign. In Langa and Nyanga, police beat up striking workers and began a systematic roundup of known PAC leaders.

From that point on, the government spared no effort in crushing all manifestations of rebellion. The police opened fire at thousands of African demonstrators in downtown Durban, killing three. Other outbreaks of protest and pass burning also met with swift retaliation. The police and military cordoned off Langa and Nyanga, where they permitted strikebreakers to leave in the morning and then staged house-to-house raids. Police seized anything resembling a weapon and assaulted workers with clubs and whips. Commissioner of Police Rademeyer called the campaign one of "intimidation of the intimidators." On 7 April the police lifted the pass laws suspension, and the next day the government banned the ANC and PAC under the terms of the newly passed Unlawful Organizations Act. The government broke the strike by the second week of April. When the now underground ANC called for Africans to stage a week-long stay-at-home starting 19 April, the campaign received no popular support. Instead, demoralized African workers lined up at government offices to replace their burned passes.[9]

Responses to Sharpeville

In the wake of the massacre at Sharpeville, the South African government faced a political crisis of unprecedented magnitude. South Africa's simmering racial problems splashed across the world's media in front-page stories and grisly photographs. Condemnation poured in from every corner of the world, and international isolation seemed an imminent reality.[10] The U.S. government found itself in the predicament of supporting a regime reviled throughout the world while trying to convince that same world of its commitment to freedom and democracy.

Washington had continued its staunch backing of the South African government throughout the 1950s. The careful and cushy handling that State Department officials gave the South African government can be seen even in the State Department's response to the relatively benign proposal made by Mason Sears, U.S. representative to the UN Trusteeship Council, that the American embassy's Fourth of July celebrations in South Africa be integrated. In an atmosphere of rising African nationalism, Sears promoted this idea as "a very little thing to do [that] would have a very happy effect upon millions of Africans all over the continent." The Southern African Affairs desk came out strongly against Sears's proposal as overly provocative, and the idea went nowhere.[11]

When the "disturbing course of race developments" prompted the embassy in South Africa to recommend that Washington take a more active concern in the growing racial tensions, the embassy based its advice on fears for the strategic and economic interests of the United States throughout the continent, not concerns for the conditions of the black majority in South Africa. American officials wanted to keep South Africa as a bastion of anticommunism and a reliable supplier of strategic minerals. Not surprisingly, given the U.S. track record vis-à-vis South Africa, the embassy staff concluded, "It is in the interest of the United States that White leadership be preserved, or at least indefinitely prolonged, in South Africa."[12]

Such attitudes certainly dovetailed with the predilections in Washington, where the chief executive's racial biases left him unswayed by concerns about fundamental human rights in Africa. An episode indicative of Eisenhower's thinking about Africans occurred just a few weeks after the Sharpeville massacre, when the National Security Council discussed the Congo's impending independence. CIA director Allen Dulles reported that the Belgians' "frantic efforts" to form a viable government had been handicapped by the existence of more than eighty Congolese political parties. Eisenhower quipped that he did not know so many people in the Congo could read. Eisenhower felt most comfortable with the status quo, and harbored tremendous suspicion about the changes sweeping Africa. "In flood force, the spirit of nationalism had grown in all Africa," Eisenhower would write of that period. "The determination of the peoples for self-rule, their own flag, and their own vote in the United Nations resembled a torrent overrunning everything in its path, including, frequently, the best interests of those concerned."[13]

However, the rapid emergence of independent African states as part of a rising Third World, along with the East-West struggle for world opinion and increasing pressure for civil rights at home, had prodded the Eisenhower administration toward at least appearing less supportive of South Africa's racial practices. In late 1958 the United States for the first time supported a UN resolution, albeit a weak one, criticizing South Africa's racial policies. Always before the United States either had opposed or abstained on all resolutions critical of South Africa. The shift was slight and cautious but evident to South Africa. Sharpeville carried the potential to damage the relationship much more.[14]

Upon hearing news of the massacre, the State Department quickly released a statement: "The United States deplores violence in all its forms and hopes that the African people of South Africa will be able to obtain redress for legitimate grievances by peaceful means. While the United States, as a matter of practice, does not normally comment on the internal affairs of governments with which it enjoys normal relations, it cannot help but regret the tragic loss of life resulting from the measures taken against the demonstrators in South Africa."[15] Yet even that mild rebuke went too far for Eisenhower, who questioned Secretary of State Christian Herter about the statement. Herter claimed that he had heard nothing about the statement until after it had been made to the press, that he regarded it as a breach of courtesy between nations, and that he was "furious" about it. He explained that a bureau chief had proposed a statement, and the press office had released it without checking at the top policy level. Eisenhower grumbled that "the fat was in the fire" and decided that now they would have to call in secretly the South African ambassador to tell him that although recent events distressed the United States, it regretted having made a public statement. Eisenhower added that if it were his decision, he would find another post for the bureau chief involved. Top officials in Washington plainly felt unwilling to forsake a tight relationship with the white South African regime, and the diplomatic personnel in South Africa reinforced their inclinations. U.S. Ambassador Philip Crowe wrote that the "police had no choice under the circumstances," and that he believed the State Department statement actually had contributed to the very tense atmosphere.[16]

For a president so unconcerned with Africa, Eisenhower maintained an unusually active interest in the diplomatic aftermath of the massacre. The UN Security Council quickly took up the matter, and Eisenhower personally ensured that UN ambassador Henry Cabot Lodge worked to keep any resolution condemning South Africa as mild as possible. The resolution the Security Council passed on 1 April, with American affirmation, blamed the South African government for the shootings and called upon it "to initiate measures aimed at bringing about racial harmony based on equality." Herter termed the draft of the resolution "surprisingly mild"; Eisenhower viewed it as "mighty tough." To underscore the U.S. position after Sharpeville, State Department officials assured the South African embassy that it had no intention of recalling the American ambassador or of boycotting South Africa in any way. Given the response of key officials on the scene and in Washington, African Americans faced tremendous difficulty in using Sharpeville to move U.S. policy; but the events themselves took on high meaning for black America.[17]

Contacts between black Americans and black South Africans did not end after the collapse of the Defiance Campaign, but at first they remained somewhat tenuous. Connections would deepen as African independence struggles increasingly influenced African American thinking during the course of the decade. In March 1953, ANC secretary-general Walter Sisulu wrote W. E. B. Du Bois to suggest convening a Pan-African Congress in the near future. Sisulu felt that Du Bois, in his capacity as "President of the Pan-African Congress," would be the logical person to call for such a meeting. Du Bois, ever the pan-African supporter, responded by conveying his deep interest. Yet he worried that realizing the goal of holding a congress would be difficult in the current international climate. He felt it probable that he himself could not even obtain a passport to attend. Sisulu persisted in his efforts but never succeeded in launching a meeting.[18] In time, ANC efforts to organize the Congress of the People in South Africa drew away Sisulu's energies from the task of convening a Pan-African Congress. Communication across the Atlantic regarding the Congress of the People reflects the continuing shadow of the

Cold War and how in the mid-1950s the environment remained a difficult one for promoting contacts. In response to Sisulu's efforts to enlist African American support for the ANC and the Congress of the People, Walter White, fearful of any NAACP involvement with leftist organizations, wrote to Ralph Bunche asking him to ascertain whether Sisulu, or any organization with which Sisulu associated, had communist links.[19]

Some black leaders worked with the avowedly noncommunist ACOA to keep lines of contact open. After the arrest of 156 persons in South Africa in December 1956, which triggered the more than four-year-long Treason Trial, black Americans supported ACOA efforts to raise money for the defendants' legal defense and their families.[20] It would be through ACOA that Martin Luther King Jr. extended his growing interest in and contact with Africa. Returning from Ghana, King took as a special interest the situation in South Africa. The tradition of Gandhism, the nonviolent protest campaigns during the 1950s, and the leadership of Albert Lutuli made the struggle in South Africa ideologically appealing. When ACOA campaigned for a worldwide Day of Protest to be held on 10 December 1957, Universal Human Rights Day, King acted on his growing conviction that black Americans and black South Africans were involved in essentially the same struggle and became the campaign's U.S. national vice chairman. The campaign, seeking to heighten awareness of apartheid and to pursue action against it, urged people to sign a "Declaration of Conscience" that denounced the racial situation in South Africa and demanded that the South African government honor its moral and legal obligations as a signatory to the UN Charter and the Declaration of Human Rights. ACOA also encouraged people to organize demonstrations in their own communities in order to build public opinion as a force for change.[21]

As King involved himself more and more with African issues, he frequently collaborated with ACOA. In the years 1959 and 1960 alone he wrote the introduction to an ACOA pamphlet on South West Africa, sent out appeals for ACOA's Africa Aid and Defense Fund, and acted as honorary chairman of the ACOA-sponsored Africa Freedom Day in 1960.[22] In January 1960 King wrote to Enoch Dumas of *Drum* magazine in South Africa, "I have done a considerable amount of reading on the whole of Africa and I have taken particular interest in the problems of South Africa because of the similarities between the situation there and our own situation in the United States."[23]

The bloody massacre at Sharpeville provoked even greater passion regarding the racial situation in South Africa, while also heightening concern with affairs on the continent in general. African Americans reacted to the massacre with horror and outrage and sharply condemned the South African regime. "The shockingly brutal slaughter of more than 100 men, women and children by the police of the Union of South Africa in the past twenty-four hours warrants a re-examination of the relations of the United States of America with that nation," NAACP secretary Roy Wilkins wrote to Secretary of State Herter. "The butchery reported when Africans invited arrest in protest against the law requiring the carrying of passes is unmatched except by the wholesale killings of the Hitler regime in Nazi Germany." Wilkins called upon Washington to recall the American ambassador and cut off all economic aid and commercial relations. "In [the NAACP's] opinion, there has never been a more justifiable reason for withdrawing recognition of a country. The Union of South Africa, through this callous and murderous action against its own citizens has forfeited its right to recognition by the leader of the Free World nations." Wilkins urged a prompt severance so that the world's people would not conclude that the United States condones "wanton slaughter as an instrument of state power."[24]

The black press decried the "barbaric action" and the "dastardly, contemptible, unwarranted show of white supremacy by South African whites." "The wanton slaughtering of men, women and children in Sharpeville and elsewhere in South Africa has shocked the conscience of the world into realizing the extent bestiality is resorted to in order to perpetuate a vicious antiracial system," declared the *Defender*. "The appalling loss of blood brings into sharp focus a segregative policy that is being pursued in blood."[25]

As African Americans bitterly denounced the South African police and government, they highlighted the protesters' fortitude and valor. "Truly the natives showed their courage while the South African government sent in jet fighters and light bombers," wrote the *Daily World*, contributing to the widespread portrayal of South African protesters as heroic figures nobly fighting against all odds. "Despite a widening pool of blood, the Africans unharmed continued to face armored cars, sub-machine guns with a stoicism that had the quality of Spartan courage," added the *Defender*. The *Afro-American* noted that fears of suffering did not prevent Africans "armed only with sticks and stones from standing up to machine guns, tanks and jet fighter planes in South Africa."[26]

The State Department condemnation of South Africa's deadly handling of the protests rang hollow to black America, who knew all too well how cheap talk could be. The "most singular" aspect of the State Department's Sharpeville statement, contended the *Courier*, was that the administration did not express similar outrage over the arrest of peaceful student picketers or the massive southern defiance of school desegregation. The *Defender* made clear its own view that the administration followed a double standard, pointing out that no comparable expression of outrage had come forth while blacks had been molested and jailed for peacefully demonstrating against inequality and injustice in the American South. Indeed, while the State Department's "mild protest" seemed to be a step in the right direction, the *Afro-American* doubted the statement's sincerity. If the U.S. government truly wanted to censure racism and violence, it argued, then it would do so in places such as Alabama.[27]

Black Americans explored ways to bring pressure to bear on both the U.S. and South African governments. Adopting a tactic first used during the Defiance Campaign, and used again more successfully two decades later, black Americans picketed in front of South African consulates. Picketers included the New York chapter of the Negro American Labor Council, led by A. Philip Randolph and Cleveland Robinson, and ministers from the AME Church.[28]

African Americans also urged boycotts of South African goods. Declaring that "prayers and pronouncements will not suffice in this instance," the Council of Bishops of the AME Church adopted a four-point program in response to Sharpeville, including a call for UN sanctions and boycotts of South African goods. Congressman Adam Clayton Powell Jr. called for suspending all trade with and credit for South Africa and for the AFL-CIO to urge its longshoremen not to unload South African goods. In short order, the International Confederation of Free Trade Unions (ICFTU), which included the AFL-CIO, set a boycott to start 1 May and to last for two months. The NAACP wrote to numerous grocery organizations, "In view of the massacre of Africans and their continued oppression, the time has come to cease importation, handling and sale in this country of South African products." The NAACP urged in particular ending commerce in South African rock lobsters, arguing that dealing only in lobsters caught in American waters and processed by American workers would achieve both a patriotic and a humanitarian goal.[29]

Roy Wilkins invited Oliver Tambo, deputy president and highest-ranking exiled leader of the now banned ANC, to speak at the NAACP's annual convention in June 1960. As Wilkins explained in his invitation, "Our people are keenly interested in the struggle in South Africa and in the very fine work that has been done by the African National Congress. An address by you giving a firsthand account of the situation in South Africa and the ways in which our brothers are combating the restrictions and cruelties imposed upon them will be welcome by our delegates." Even though Tambo could not make the trip, the convention passed a resolution far stronger than previous ones on South Africa. Delegates called upon the U.S. government to press for prompt UN action on complaints brought against South Africa, "including if necessary military intervention by the United Nations to stop the violation of fundamental human rights." They further urged the government "to welcome the oppressed people of South Africa to America to live."[30]

AMSAC, stepping into a more clearly political realm, condemned the massacre. John Davis declared that "there are times . . . when men of culture can no longer confine their interests to things cultural."[31] ACOA sent strongly worded telegrams to Eisenhower urging condemnation of the massacre and the recall of the American ambassador in order to "make American condemnation of South African racist policies clear to the world." ACOA also appealed for money to aid the victims of South African repression. Sponsors of ACOA's Africa Defense and Aid Fund included Harry Belafonte, Lorraine Hansberry, Mordecai Johnson, Martin Luther King Jr., Benjamin Mays, F. D. Patterson, A. Philip Randolph, Jackie Robinson, Hope Stevens, and Roy Wilkins. This fund sent $15,000 to help the survivors of Sharpeville and other victims of the state of emergency.[32]

As part of its efforts, ACOA called an Emergency Action Conference for 31 May and 1 June at the Carnegie International Center in New York. Cooperating sponsors included AMSAC, the NAACP, Americans for Democratic Action, the Jewish Labor Committee, the Amalgamated Clothing Workers of America, the International Ladies Garment Workers Union, and United Auto Workers Local 23. Over 300 persons attended. Jackie Robinson, hoping an ACOA-organized campaign might result in more effective American participation in worldwide efforts to stamp out racism, chaired the conference. "I see the struggle against race supremacy and racial inequality as world-wide," Robinson declared. "The fight against Jim Crow here is part of the same struggle in South Africa."[33]

The ACOA conference made numerous recommendations for Americans to follow in the fight against apartheid, many of which would be included in future antiapartheid efforts. Indeed, the workings of this conference helped pave the way for antiapartheid efforts in the years to come. The conference concluded that boycotts of South African goods should occur on two fronts: labor unions should refuse to unload South African ships or handle South African goods, and consumers should refuse to buy South African products. The conference requested American tourists, athletes, and performers not to participate in tours and programs in South Africa, or if they did go, to take every opportunity to protest apartheid while there. It discouraged private investment in South Africa until that nation honored the UN Declaration of Human Rights and urged businesses with investments already there to use their position to oppose apartheid.

Conference participants called on the U.S. government to take multiple actions. The president and Congress should declare U.S. policy as unequivocally opposed to apartheid, actively work to separate South West Africa (Namibia) from South Africa, and vigorously pursue South African compliance with UN resolutions pertaining to apartheid. The State Department should integrate social functions and personnel at its South African embassy and consulates and provide aid to escapees from South Africa and South West Africa in a manner comparable to that given Hungarian refugees. The federal government should not purchase gold or strategic material from South Africa when an alternative source of supply existed and should ban imports from South Africa in accordance with laws prohibiting the importation of goods made by forced or convict labor. The conference called upon the Export-Import Bank and other financial institutions to reconsider the conditions under which they lent money to South Africa and asked Congress to consider legislation withholding financial privileges to businesses that practiced racial discrimination in South Africa. Finally, the conference recommended that a South Africa Emergency Campaign be established out of the Emergency Action Conference in order to implement the resolutions of the conference, to defend arrested South Africans, and to aid their families. ACOA offered to organize the campaign, with the immediate aim of raising $100,000.[34]

Internationally aware, African Americans understood that others besides the United States helped support the South African regime. African Americans particularly condemned the Western powers for not pressing South Africa to change its racial policies. The *Amsterdam News*, for example, argued that the South African police and military had forced Africans into involuntary servitude by brutally beating workers to break the stay-at-home. Questioning how long the West would tolerate brazen slavery by one of its allies, the newspaper argued that "it is simply a prostitution of national virtue for any nation — and that includes our nation — to engage in any type of international affairs with South Africa while she is bathed and soaked in the blood of an innocent, defenseless people."[35]

African Americans felt that the Western allies possessed the ability to pressure South Africa into at least moderating its racial policies; they also recognized the Western reluctance to intervene forcefully with a staunch anticommunist friend. Therefore, some rested their hopes on potential UN action. Horace Cayton voiced his wish that the growing potency of black power on the world scene, particularly in the Afro-Asian bloc at the UN, would prod the UN to bring more pressure to bear on South Africa. Others urged the UN to take specific action, such as commissioning an investigation of South Africa's policies or, as the AME Church demanded, expelling South Africa from the world body.[36] But with the Western powers reluctant to take action against South Africa, African Americans and their allies in the UN found they had little ability to effect powerful action. Even after Sharpeville, African Americans had trouble overcoming the entrenched influence of strategic concerns and the Cold War on official U.S. policy.

Even so, the *Amsterdam News* editors firmly declared that they had no intention of letting up or closing their eyes and "pretending that the horrible situation existing in South Africa is not there." Just a half dozen years earlier the paper had defended its inaction regarding Kenya by stating, "It's difficult to become carried away with citizenship problems that exist 7,000 miles away until those at home have been solved," and had added, "We don't kid ourselves into thinking that we can shout loudly enough in Harlem to change these conditions overnight." African struggles had caused striking shifts in black America.[37]

Sharpeville and Sit-Ins

The horror of the Sharpeville massacre obviously contributed to African Americans' impassioned responses; so did the timing. Seven weeks before the massacre, four students from North Carolina Agricultural and Technical College walked into a Woolworth's in downtown Greensboro and asked to be served at the lunch counter. The launching of sit-ins helped reinvigorate the civil rights struggle. When the Sharpeville massacre occurred seven weeks later, the sit-in movement had spread to fifty-four cities in nine states. As protests rocked South Africa, black students in America formed the Student Nonviolent Coordinating Committee (SNCC), which became the spearhead of a burgeoning popular movement across the American South.[38]

The sit-ins energized the movement at home and riveted attention on the domestic situation, which to some degree reinforced the focus on the domestic situation among African Americans. The *Courier* reminded readers that while it abhorred what happened in South Africa and appreciated the State Department bulletin regarding the massacre, "our first concern is with what is happening right here to our sons and daughters, our families and friends who remain the victims of racial insult, segregation and discrimination 97 years after Emancipation. We would like to hear more officially expressed outrage over THAT."[39]

Yet even as they felt a chronic tension over where to focus their energy and resources, by and large African Americans now saw the struggle against white supremacy in a global context. African Americans across a broad political spectrum made connections between the struggle in America and the struggles in Africa, reshaping their relationship with Africa while rebuilding their anticolonialism on a very Africa-centered basis. A. Philip Randolph's emotional homage to the South African protesters and their role in the worldwide fight against white supremacy is illustrative. As the "great world of color" burst into flames for freedom, Randolph declared, "This crucial struggle of Africans for freedom is pertinent to, and tied up with the whole fight of Negroes in America today for the status of free men. These black gods and comely goddesses that lie slain upon their own lands have not only given up their lives for their own liberty, but also for the freedom of the Negroes of African descent on the North and South American continents."[40]

On the most obvious level, the protests in the American South and South Africa had no cause-and-effect connection: South African protesters did not launch their action because of sit-in campaign inspiration, nor did sit-ins commence because of an event in Africa. Yet African Americans knew of apartheid's brutality, and most believed that America practiced a version of apartheid with its own segregative and discriminatory laws. Events on the two sides of the Atlantic melded together: the militancy of student protesters in the South seemed to parallel that of antiapartheid protesters in South Africa; the intransigence of white southerners seemed matched by that of Afrikaners. African independence struggles and Southern sit-ins seemed part of a growing transatlantic militancy for change.

As they saw the lengths to which whites in South Africa would go to prevent blacks from gaining equal rights and citizenship, more African Americans came to appreciate fully the international dimension and depth of the problem. White supremacy was a worldwide phenomenon and the struggle against it a worldwide endeavor. The *Crisis*, declaring that rebellion against the twin evils of racial prejudice and discrimination had spread across Africa and the American South, placed the meaning of these events in a global context. The world had become small, and what happened in one corner affected the destiny and welfare of peoples everywhere: "American Negroes take courage and hope from an independent Ghana and Guinea; revolts in the Congo stiffen the resolve of Africans in South Africa. Everywhere the colored peoples are resolved that the arrogance and the domination of whites must go."[41]

Once again, the fight against white supremacy had taken on a more transnational character, yet one that differed from the early 1940s. The fight for freedom and equality had been rebuilt, with class-based, economically driven anticolonial critiques of the 1940s replaced by a more explicitly racialistic pan-Africanism. Even in the broad sweep of the advancing Third World, the more international outlook animating black America focused squarely on Africa.

Sharpeville heightened interest in Africa and prompted people to see connections between the struggles in South Africa and America far more than had been the case during the Defiance Campaign less than a decade before. As Lester Granger put it, "The thermometer of Negro interest in African affairs has steadily climbed during the past eight years. It hit peak with the South African massacre of hundreds and possibly thousands of peaceful demonstrators by the Verwoerd government."[42] African Americans regularly stressed connections between the sit-ins in the South and the protests in South Africa. The *Defender* reminded readers that despite the distance between Dixie and South Africa, events in both places embodied the same things: the explosion of black resentment against generations of white supremacy and a surging demand for a place in the sun. "The white people in the southern part of the United States and the white people in the southern part of Africa are both engaged in a war they cannot win," vowed the *Amsterdam News*. The following week the *Amsterdam News* ran a political cartoon portraying a black man on a cross and two white men plunging spears into his side. The white man labeled "USA" thrust a spear tagged "Sit-In Arrests"; the white man labeled "S. Africa" thrust a spear tagged "Passbook Laws." Even the *Daily World*, historically loath to connect black Americans with Africa, proclaimed, "It will be seen that the situation in the Union of South Africa is much akin to some of the problems encountered by Negroes in this country."[43]

Further, as black Americans wrestled with their own increasing militancy, the confluence of events made the actions of blacks on both sides of the Atlantic more acceptable. Increasing militancy at home seemed all the more reasonable and necessary when viewed internationally. The South African government's deadly response to nonviolent African demonstrators provided a grim reminder that white supremacy would not give way easily. "What is actual in South Africa is potential wherever the notion of white supremacy exists," wrote Gordon Hancock, who felt that events in South Africa should concern all foes of white supremacy. "What is happening in South Africa is a grim reminder that the same thing could happen here."[44]

The events of Sharpeville and its aftermath offered black Americans a potent analogy as they debated how best to conduct the struggle for equal citizenship. The African protests not only exemplified the sacrifices that some would nobly make in the struggle for freedom and equality, they served as an important way station in African Americans' movement toward more militant methods. Indeed, frustration with events in South Africa combined with a rising sense of militancy to prompt more African Americans to accept violence against the white regime in South Africa. When the banned ANC and PAC announced their intention to launch armed resistance against the apartheid regime, even nonviolence stalwarts such as Martin Luther King Jr. did not speak against it. When a white farmer named David Pratt attempted to assassinate South African prime minister Hendrik Verwoerd, the *Defender* and the *Afro-American* portrayed Pratt as a modern John Brown. The *Defender* sanctified Pratt's action with the thought that he "might have been driven by a divine spirit to put an end to the wanton massacre of helpless Africans" and described Pratt's effort as "a blow on behalf of African freedom."[45]

While nonviolence still commanded the respect of most African Americans, those who saw parallels between white South African and white American responses to black demands for equal citizenship also could see parallels for black responses when whites resisted black equality. Indeed, African American acceptance of violence as a method of opposing white supremacy in South Africa suggested that time and continued white intransigence in America would lead more African Americans toward accepting the same in the United States. The *Afro-American*, frustrated with white resistance to peaceful change, assayed the sit-ins in the South and the carnage of Sharpeville. The paper remonstrated with moderates who feared that the sit-ins would lead to violence, declaring, "In our social system, it is the moderates who are most to blame for segregation and discrimination. They advocate a peaceful status quo." The *Afro-American* lamented that "the sad truth is that in some instances violence is the only answer to oppression." As evidence, it offered the African countries that had won independence, "but only through riots and resistance and agitation such as goes on in South Africa today."[46] Sharpeville and its aftermath not only energized African American concerns with Africa and helped reconfigure African American anticolonialism on more racialistic lines, it continued the trend of contemporary African freedom struggles ratcheting higher the acceptance of more forceful methods of protest in the domestic black freedom struggle.

Autumn Highs: Africa on the World's Stage

Sharpeville would remain a defining nadir when African Americans surveyed events in Africa. Yet, on the other hand, as the Year of Africa progressed, the continent welcomed nation after nation to independence. During the summer alone, as many nations as existed in all of South America established independence: in June, the Congo, Madagascar, Mali, and Senegal; in July, Somalia; in August, Benin, Burkina Faso, Central African Republic, Chad, Congo (Brazzaville), Gabon, Ivory Coast, and Niger.[47] The rapid and fundamental changes occurring on the continent placed Africa in the news on a regular basis, and helped fuel African Americans' burgeoning interest in Africa.

The collective peak of the year came at the fall UN General Assembly meetings, when more than a dozen new African nations gained entry to the world organization. Even the casual observer could see that the sheer number of non-Western nations entering the UN had the potential to redefine the orientation of the organization, even to tilt the General Assembly in a direction less favorable to Western interests. Africa seemed poised to become a force in world affairs. The *Defender* looked at the General Assembly meetings and proudly proclaimed that a "new voice" had "lifted itself above the clatter of the General Assembly," heralding it as "the voice of New Africa — the Africa which is seething with nationalism and whose speedy rise out of the dust of colonialism has bewildered the white world."[48]

Africa's speedy rise, particularly in the context of the continuing Cold War, forced U.S. officials to consider the continent more carefully than at any time since World War II. In fact, President Eisenhower's address to the General Assembly on 22 September 1960 concentrated on Africa and on arms control. Eisenhower proposed a program for the international community to follow that he argued would protect newly emerging African nations from outside pressures that threatened their independence and sovereign rights: (1) all countries in the UN should pledge to respect the African peoples' right to choose their way of life and the course they followed; (2) the UN should help African countries maintain their security in order to avoid a wasteful and dangerous arms competition on the continent; (3) the UN should help newly developing African countries shape their long-term modernization programs; (4) an "all-out" UN effort should help African countries promote educational activities they might want, with America contributing to such an effort; and (5) all countries should support the UN peacekeeping force in the Congo and the establishment of a UN fund for the Congo. This last proposal aimed to defuse the escalating Congo crisis. Given his previous level of involvement with the continent, the struggle for the loyalty of the emerging nations of the world undoubtedly pushed Eisenhower to devote much of his speech to Africa. This address came, the *Defender* noted, from a man for whom previously "Africa was not on the map."[49]

African Americans witnessed the president devoting large parts of his UN address to Africa, the African contingent at the UN growing in size and strength, and African dignitaries and diplomats performing on the world stage. "For the first time in world history," according to the *Defender*, "black men hold in their hands the necessary weights with which to tip the scales in the direction wherein lies their vested interests and equity." The excitement and allure of the power of Africa swept along even the conservative, southern-oriented *Daily World*. Its managing editor celebrated the "glorious day for the black nations, which are now admitted and being welcomed into full membership of the United Nations Assembly." "Ethiopia is truly stretching forth her wings," he continued, "and black people are proving to others that they are somebody. The era is wonderful and the times most exciting."[50]

Central to the events in New York, particularly for African Americans, was Kwame Nkrumah's return to the United States. A star-studded array of Communist-bloc, Western-bloc, and nonaligned leaders — including Eisenhower, Nikita Krushchev, Fidel Castro, Jawaharlal Nehru, Marshal Tito, and Gamel Abdel Nasser — could have overshadowed Nkrumah's attendance at the opening of the General Assembly. But African Americans treated Krushchev as one might a relatively minor world figure, and Castro's stay in Harlem carried less weight with black America. Nkrumah's significance extended far beyond that of a man who led a nation comprising only 2 percent of the people in Africa; Nkrumah came across as Africa's spokesman.[51]

In this symbolic role, Nkrumah's lengthy address to the General Assembly held special importance. His speech contained five major points: he supported an end to all colonial rule; he urged support for Patrice Lumumba's Congolese government and called on the UN to use only African nations and troops to create an African solution to the Congo problem ("Africa for Africans!"); he recommended that African nations avoid military alliances with countries outside Africa; he supported the admission of communist China to the UN; and he called for a revised UN Charter with a permanent seat for an African nation on the Security Council.[52]

Almost everything Nkrumah said stood at variance with U.S. positions, which prompted Secretary of State Herter to denounce Nkrumah for making "a bid for the left-wing group of African states" and for being "very definitely in what you might call the Communist camp."[53] Uniformly and across political lines African Americans rebuked Herter. The *Afro-American* declared, "The insulting attempt of Secretary of State Christian Herter to smear Dr. Nkrumah with the tar of communism did no harm to Ghana's brilliant president." The *Amsterdam News* termed Herter's comments "intemperate and ill-advised" and noted that the remarks "will not contribute to the betterment of our already shaky relations with the new African states." The *Defender* stated that nothing in Nkrumah's speech suggested that his approach to African affairs was communistic and chided Herter for driving people and nations into the communist camp with "trite and offensive" talk. The *California Eagle* attacked Herter's comments as evidence of "the paternalistic attitude of white America when it deals with peoples of African descent," going on to observe, "Mr. Herter was guilty of an excursion into international McCarthyism that can only breed distrust for the United States and its role in Africa."[54]

Contemporary Africa's importance to African Americans had grown to the point that the words of a leftist nationalist politician openly warning against alliances with the West and supporting the admission of communist China to the UN had broader black America defending him and attacking the U.S. Secretary of State. Africans and their successes challenged liberal African Americans to question the thinking behind their general acceptance and support of U.S. foreign policy during the previous decade. Africa aided African Americans in their breaking down of Cold War strictures, and the actions of Nkrumah, the most visible of the new generation of African leaders, held particular symbolic import.

African Americans, in the midst of publicly defying white supremacy in America, lauded Nkrumah for doing the same in the international arena. The managing editor of the *Courier* drew entirely different lessons from Nkrumah's speech than had Secretary of State Herter:

At the week's end these facts had been recorded in history:
1. No longer will Africa accept global decisions affecting her people unless she is in on the policymaking.
2. Africa is determined to maintain an already declared policy of "positive neutralism" and confident she can give birth to her own ideology.
3. Africa will play a prominent role in determining whether or not Red China will enter the United Nations.

These are the things which must cause a total revision of the earth's power structure. Global power politics will no longer be played by white men of East and West alone: The brown, black and yellow men of the world will now have a say in what is to be. History has dictated this situation.[55]

Nkrumah stood for all of Africa, and as Nkrumah had overthrown British rule in Ghana, Africa would overturn Western dominance as a whole. Black America cheered Africa's activism in forcing Western nations to set a place for it at the world power table. "They [Westerners] looked upon the Ghana Prime Minister's address with mixed feelings of dismay and anger, all of which was laced with a good bit of fear," opined one writer in discussing the "white world's" reaction to Nkrumah's speech.[56] The belief in heightened African power infused that writer, and other African Americans, with black pride. Contemporary Africa became part of African America.

Indeed, Nkrumah's presence in New York held profound meaning, particularly for a renewed black nationalism. Conditions in black America, particularly the universalist and integrationist agenda of the World War II and Cold War years, had helped mute the black nationalists' message. But black nationalism now surged again. Domestically, frustration over white intransigence generated nationalist sentiment. Internationally, African independence promoted stronger affinity for Africa and black nationalism. When Nkrumah made a trip to Harlem while at the 1960 UN meetings, black nationalists claimed a prominent presence. Nkrumah spoke at a rally in front of Harlem's Hotel Theresa, where a crowd laced with a strong black nationalist contingent greeted him with shouts of "Long Live Nkrumah!" Nkrumah thrilled the crowd with his evocation of "the solid bond we feel between the people of Africa and the Afro-Americans in this country." Other speakers at the rally included James Lawson, head of the United African Nationalist Movement, Carlos Cooks of the African Nationalist Pioneer Movement, and Malcolm X of the Nation of Islam, as well as Adam Clayton Powell Jr. and Rev. James Robinson.[57] Nkrumah's star would maintain a special luster for black cultural and political nationalists in subsequent years. As Malcolm X shared after visiting Africa in May 1964, "In Ghana — or in all of black Africa — my highest single honor was an audience at [Christiansborg] Castle with Osagyefo Dr. Kwame Nkrumah."[58]

Turning A Corner

Images of Africa had changed. No longer was contemporary Africa a negative image from which to dissociate, nor was it simply a place needing "civilization" or freedom from colonial subjugation. Fraternity with and pride in things African swept through black America. The image of a free and independent Africa animated the diasporic consciousness of African Americans. That Nkrumah toured America and spoke before the UN in his traditional kente cloth showed to the world the pride he had in being African. After Nkrumah "electrified" delegates with his address to the General Assembly, the *Defender* felt that while Nkrumah's words had logic and relevancy, the fact that an unmistakably black man had given that speech "really stood out in bold relief."[59] The wave of independent African nations, and the attendant growth of African diplomats on the world stage and in the streets of America, buttressed these images and had a visceral effect on African

Americans. As one put it, "Africa provides me today with a kind of proud identification with ancestors. It causes you to swell up with pride just to see an African on the podium of the UN, Africans who have to be consulted in the decision-making process in the world."[60]

As contemporary Africa's importance grew in black America, African Americans more and more related the independence movements and their successes to their own lives. Nkrumah and Ghana, followed increasingly by other leaders and nations in insurgent Africa, pushed black America toward using Africa in their fight against white supremacy. Liberation struggles provided an example and an inspiration for those fighting for civil rights and full equality. On the most basic level, the success of Ghana, then of Guinea in 1958, and then the explosion of independent countries in 1960 prodded black Americans onward in their quest. In 1961 Martin Luther King Jr. would write, "The liberation struggle in Africa has been the greatest single international influence on American Negro students. Frequently I hear them say that if their African brothers can break the bonds of colonialism, surely the American Negro can break Jim Crow." Theologian James Cone argues that King's enduring optimism during the bus boycotts, sit-ins, and March on Washington was "linked with the success of anticolonialist movements in the Third World."[61]

Beyond inspiring black Americans to continue the struggle, the sweep of African independence boosted the pride and confidence that African Americans felt in their heritage and themselves. Successful liberation struggles helped cast aside negative images of Africa, offering examples of black men and women running their own countries. James Farmer, national director of the Congress of Racial Equality (CORE), believed strongly in the power of this influence: "As the African freedom fight got under way and reached its first successful culmination in the independence of Ghana, and as other nations fought for and gained independence, American Negroes began to take a fresh look at Africa through more hopeful eyes; they saw and were impressed by the proud black people who represented those nations. . . . People began studying African art, African culture, African dance, and African history. American Negroes were at last getting somewhere in their quest for identity, their search for roots." Farmer felt sure that it was no accident, then, "that the emergence of the new nations of Africa coincided with the civil rights revolution in the United States."[62]

African successes provided the sense that black Americans were not an isolated and outnumbered minority but part of a sweeping global majority. While certainly not a new idea, the undeniable advances made by Africans in ridding themselves of white supremacy animated the belief as it coursed throughout black America. "Montgomery Negroes could correctly visualize themselves as an integral part of the struggle for freedom throughout the world," wrote Norman W. Walton, an African American history professor at Alabama State College, in April 1957. "The Negroes of Montgomery spoke of freedom and democracy in Africa and Asia. They seem to bear personal witness to the struggle in Africa, through the eyes of their leader, Rev. M. L. King, who made the trip to Africa in March, 1957, to witness the birth of the Negro State of Ghana." One sees here the immediate and powerful effect of the transnational linkages being made between African and American freedom struggles.[63]

While offering positive inspiration, Africa's rapid progress also increased frustration with the pace of change in America. As Manning Marable points out, the contradiction between a "free" Africa and its "unfree" descendants in America "was an immediate and important parallel." Example after example of successful independence struggles provided a gauge against which black Americans could compare their own civil rights struggle. In the words of Martin Luther King Jr., "The nations of Asia and Africa are moving with jet-like speed toward gaining political independence, but we still creep at horse-and-buggy pace toward gaining a cup of coffee at a lunch counter."[64]

Thus in multiple and intertwined ways the national liberation movements in Africa registered with black Americans, contributing to the advance of their own freedom struggle. In writing their histories of the civil rights movement in America, scholars have tended to understate this influence.[65] That African Americans saw black men and women demanding and receiving their freedom, running their own countries, and playing important roles on the world stage should not be underestimated. Such scenes transformed their images of Africa, so they could draw inspiration and pride not just from historic Africa but now also from contemporary Africa.

A particularly tangible manifestation of the changed thinking came with the civil rights leadership's decision to finally develop a political framework for institutionalizing the relationship with Africa. As the 1960s began, no organization of and by and for blacks had as its central aim addressing political issues regarding Africa and U.S. policy toward Africa. When the venerable *New York Age* had criticized the African-American Institute for placing only one black American on a new committee of eighteen people that it formed in 1959, the *Age* pointed out, "More disturbing than this, however, is the appalling lack of any effective antidote to the African-American Institute. Other than the desperately-needed American Society of African Culture and the well-intentioned American Committee on Africa, there are no intelligently organized efforts among Negroes to achieve a better understanding between themselves and Africans."[66]

Yet with Africa assuming a stronger importance in African American consciousness, more African Americans sought ways to institutionalize the relationship with independent Africa and aid the liberation of colonized Africa. Notably, this included liberal civil rights leaders, who during the late 1940s and early 1950s typically had adopted Cold War priorities and followed an integrationist agenda in which Africa played a limited role. Dual emotions helped fuel their increasing dissatisfaction with the organizational alternatives available: frustration over the white supremacy that parts of Africa still faced, along with hope generated by the rise of independent Africa. One finds, then, multiple efforts by people whom scholar Martin Kilson has called "pragmatic activists" to create a structure controlled by African Americans that focused on Africa and could rally black America to press for a revised U.S. policy toward Africa.[67]

Hearkening back to Du Bois's postwar efforts, some activists sought to turn the NAACP into a more pan-African-oriented body. Before he returned to head CORE, James Farmer briefly served as program director for the NAACP. During that time Farmer met with African diplomats to discuss the relationship of independent Africa to the color question in America and the role that the NAACP could play in the worldwide freedom struggle. He also discussed with NAACP staffers the possibility of establishing a liaison relationship between the NAACP and Africans and found the staff responsive. Farmer therefore decided to convince Roy Wilkins of the merits of this course of action, noting that "many friends" of the NAACP "have long desired that the Association extend its influence in international affairs." Farmer emphasized that "American Negroes are also apparently more 'Africa conscious' than at any previous time in this nation's history," noting, "Recent events have stimulated this unparalleled awareness, pride, and concern." He recognized that the Association "might not desire to go as far as establishing an 'International Desk' at this time"; in that case, he advised taking at least minimal steps to expand its international focus. Farmer correctly perceived that Wilkins did not want formal internationalization of NAACP efforts. Wilkins would be persuaded, however, to cast his and the organization's weight behind the creation of a new African-oriented entity.[68]

Frustrated that organized political efforts regarding Africa were falling beyond the scope of current black organizations, other African Americans tossed about the idea of creating a new organization. A. Philip Randolph had ruminated about such a need since his attendance at Ghana's independence.

He regretted the "lack of information among Negroes themselves about Africa," but a number of additional concerns motivated Randolph's interest in Africa. Primarily he sought to end colonialism because of the economic slavery that the system bred. Randolph long had viewed the labor movement in an international perspective, and he very much wanted the trade union movement strengthened in Africa. He corresponded with African labor leaders such as Tom Mboya and used his positions as head of the BSCP and member of the AFL-CIO Executive Council to promote projects that aided the development of an African labor movement. Various enterprises in which Randolph played a role included establishing an AFL-CIO program to train African labor leaders in the United States; building a trade union educational center in Kenya; building a labor college in Uganda; aiding the defense of Kenyan labor leaders on trial for publishing defamatory material and for conspiracy; urging labor to support ACOA's South Africa Defense Fund; and bringing Mboya to the United States on a speaking tour. Randolph also sought to build AFL-CIO pressure on the Republicans and Democrats to come out in favor of increased aid to newly independent African states. Playing a familiar Cold War card, he warned that the West would be unable to halt the spread of communism in Africa so long as the people stood unconvinced of the sincerity of the Western powers.[69] So from a racial, labor, economic, and political perspective, Randolph grew convinced of the need to promote transatlantic links, and accordingly he increased his African-related commitments. After initially declining to become a board member of ACOA in the mid-1950s, by decade's end he was working more and more on ACOA's behalf, speaking at ACOA's Africa Freedom Day celebrations and signing appeals for the Africa Defense and Aid Fund.[70]

At the same time, Randolph pursued his hopes for creating an African American organization that would be helpful in Africa's struggle toward freedom and independence. In a 1958 letter to George McCray, he described the motivation behind this goal: "The Negroes in America should know more about African nationalism so that they may exert some influence on the political and government machinery in this country to help the African nationalist movement, not only because it is right, but because of enlightened self-interest." Randolph proposed forming an organization that would develop contacts with African nationalist groups and work to obtain public and private sector support for programs on behalf of Africa. He then discussed the prospect with fellow labor leaders such as Ted Brown, assistant director of the Civil Rights Department of the AFL-CIO and director of research and education for the BSCP; George McCray, president of Chicago Local No. 1006 of the American Federation of State, County and Municipal

Employees, AFL-CIO; and Maida Springer of the International Ladies Garment Workers Union (ILGWU).[71]

Characteristically, Randolph initially dreamed of a mass organization that would promote awareness of and identification with Africa as well as influence policy toward Africa. He became convinced that such a group could "fill the vacuum of interest and activity in the Negro community with regards to Africa," a vacuum into which he felt nationalists and Black Muslims already were moving. Randolph believed that AMSAC did not fulfill this role, for, as he put it, "it does not go deep enough into the struggles of Africa for liberation and independence." AMSAC, in return, saw the potential for a political wing to its cultural focus. As for ACOA, Randolph, working as part of its national advisory board, helped convince ACOA leaders that increased African American participation in influencing U.S. policy toward Africa could only aid Africa's, and ACOA's, endeavors.[72]

Efforts to create an Africa-oriented organization controlled and operated by black Americans bore fruit in 1961–62. A series of meetings about holding a conference of African American leaders on the topic of Africa resulted in the American Negro Leadership Conference on Africa (ANLCA), which met for its first major conference at Columbia University's Arden House in November 1962.[73] The "Big Six" of the civil rights leadership constituted the Call Committee: James Farmer, Congress of Racial Equality; Dorothy Height, National Council of Negro Women (NCNW); Martin Luther King Jr., Southern Christian Leadership Conference; A. Philip Randolph, Brotherhood of Sleeping Car Porters; Roy Wilkins, NAACP; and Whitney Young, National Urban League.[74] The Call Committee invited approximately seventy-five organizations to sponsor the conference, about half of which chose to do so. African American business, civil rights, educational, fraternal and sorority, labor, professional, religious, and social organizations received invitations. By the time of the Arden House conference the list of sponsors included Alpha Kappa Alpha Sorority; Alpha Phi Alpha Fraternity; ACOA; AMSAC; BSCP; CORE; Delta Sigma Theta Sorority; Gandhi Society for Human Rights; Improved Benevolent Protective Order of Elks; NAACP; NCNW; National Medical Association; National Newspapers Publishers Association; National Urban League; Negro American Labor Council; Operation Crossroads Africa; Phelps-Stokes Fund; SCLC; SNCC; The Bible Way Church of Our Lord Jesus Christ; The Links, Inc.; Trade Union Leadership Council; United Automobile, Aircraft and Agriculture Implement Workers of America; United Steelworkers of America; and the Western Christian Leadership Conference.[75]

Delegates came from across the nation, including New York, Philadelphia, Baltimore, Atlanta, Birmingham, Oklahoma, Pittsburgh, Cincinnati, Detroit, Chicago, Los Angeles, San Francisco, and Washington, D.C. In addition to the call and planning committee members, representatives from each of the sponsoring organizations attended. Individuals ranged from Ella Baker of SNCC to Smallwood Williams of the Bible Way Churches Worldwide, from Aaron Brown of Alpha Phi Alpha to Daniel Watts of the black nationalist Liberation Committee for Africa.[76] Reporters came from the Associated Negro Press, the *Afro-American*, the *Courier*, *Jet*, the *New York Times*, the Voice of America, and the United States Information Agency, representing the black press, the daily press, and the government media.[77]

The ANLCA sought to use the collective weight of these people and organizations to raise interest in America about the situation in Africa, to educate people about Africa, and to influence U.S. policy toward the continent. The near universal support of the organization indicates just how important contemporary Africa and its freedom struggles had become to the civil rights leadership and to the struggle in America. Even as voter registration drives, civil rights demonstrations, and confrontations over integrating higher education occupied the attention of black America, African American leaders cleared their schedules to take part in the ANLCA's efforts. The civil rights leadership had shown concern with Africa in the past, but this attempt to create an organization for lobbying on behalf of African causes and interests marked a new chapter in the relationship with Africa. Galvanized by African liberation struggles and frustrated by colonial and neocolonial machinations and the lack of firm U.S. backing for a free Africa, African American leaders had adopted a broader pan-African perspective.

Indeed, even while its call to the conference acknowledged domestic priorities, the civil rights leadership showed how markedly it had shifted toward the idea that the freedom struggle had powerful transatlantic connections on which it should act. The "Big Six" wrote: "The American Negro community in the U.S. has a special responsibility to urge a dynamic policy on our own country. Although we have a serious civil rights problem which exhausts much of our energy, we cannot separate the struggle at home from that abroad." Ideas of African American exceptionalism — what Du Bois had called "race provincialism" — gave way to links across the ocean.[78]

The ANLCA would operate for the next half dozen years yet would struggle to maintain its momentum amidst the political and social upheavals of the 1960s. The never-ending struggles of the domestic civil rights campaign, the splintering of the nonviolent direct action coalition, and the difficult complexities of an independent Africa made the continuance of the ANLCA an ongoing travail. Eventually it fell apart over the Biafran war in Nigeria. Its very formation and existence, however, shows how two interrelated arguments became broadly accepted, animating a broader pan-African vision and a stronger African American interest in U.S. policy toward Africa. The first of these was that the struggles in America and in Africa were linked; the second, that black Americans could help create a policy more favorable to Africans, one that would benefit both Africa and America. The powerful influence of African liberation efforts washed westward across the Atlantic, influencing the African American struggle for freedom and, reciprocally, convincing the civil rights leadership that America could better support African peoples and nations.

In forming the ANLCA, African American civil rights leaders sought to institutionalize a political relationship with independent Africa. They made it clear that African issues concerned them and that their voices would need to be consulted when U.S. officials addressed African issues. In doing so, these "pragmatic activists" reflected a black community that had expanded the conception of its own identity to embrace contemporary Africa. In years to come, organizations such as TransAfrica would carry on this political tradition. At the same time, starting with the Congo crisis, events in Africa worked to shape the predominant energy of that relationship toward aiding those fighting for independence rather than those struggling against neo-colonial machinations and internal turmoil.

7

CONGO

Independence, Black Nationalism, Leftism, and Splintering, 1960–1961

According, then, to what I take to be the prevailing view, these rioters were merely a handful of irresponsible, Kremlin-corrupted provocateurs. I find this view amazing. It is a view which even a minimal effort at observation would immediately contradict. One has only, for example, to walk through Harlem and ask oneself two questions: Would I like to live here? and, Why don't those who now live here move out? . . .

The time is forever behind us when Negroes could be expected to "wait." What is demanded now is not that Negroes continue to adjust themselves to the cruel racial pressures of life in the United States, but that the United States readjust itself to the facts of life in the present world. One of these facts is that the American Negro can no longer, nor will he ever again, be controlled by white America's image of him. This fact has everything to do with the rise of Africa in world affairs.

James Baldwin, on African American protests at the UN *following Patrice Lumumba's death,* New York Times Magazine *(12 March 1961)*

Exactly in the middle of the Year of Africa, amidst the explosion of newly liberated African nations, the Congo celebrated its independence from Belgium. The euphoria that commenced on 30 June 1960 proved short-lived, as the country almost immediately plunged into crisis. Belgians, Americans, Soviets, UN officials, and factions of Congolese quickly turned the country into a maelstrom of neocolonial intrigue and Cold War politics. For months the country lurched from one crisis to another, with the tumultuous events keeping the Congo situation at the forefront of world affairs.

Like most people around the world, African Americans viewed postindependence events in the Congo with alarm. Few doubted that the Belgians deliberately stoked the chaos in order to regain authority in the country. The secession of the mineral-rich Katanga province confirmed for most that the West remained determined to control at least the most strategically vital parts of that nation. Violence in the Congo, particularly coming on the heels of the massacre just a few months earlier at Sharpeville, offered black Americans more evidence of white intransigence. At the same time, the sight of Africans resisting white supremacy inspired African Americans to defend the legitimacy of black independence.

Many African Americans, although certainly not all, rallied behind Congolese prime minister Patrice Lumumba, who stood at the center of the complex swirl of events. Few in the world knew much about him when the Congo gained independence; yet as Lumumba moved into the spotlight, people could hardly be neutral about his galvanizing presence. In the months following independence Lumumba would be portrayed as a communist, a nationalist, an opportunist, a hero, and as truthful, dishonest, unstable, charismatic, and messianic. To critics he loomed as a demon embodying their worst fears; to supporters he represented the best hope for keeping the Congo together as a black-ruled country. Whether one supported his objectives, denounced his alliances, or felt exasperated at his actions, one had to confront his presence. This was as true for black Americans as it was for world diplomats.

In the crucible of the Congo crisis, Lumumba's black nationalism and ever more pronounced leftism pushed black Americans to wrestle with these issues in their evolving relationship with Africa as well as in their own lives and the domestic freedom struggle. In the horror and outrage that followed the Sharpeville massacre, African Americans had defined issues in stark black-white terms; few differentiated the black nationalist creed of the PAC from the multiracialism of the ANC. The Congo crisis, and particularly the figure of Lumumba during it, forced black Americans to address more fully the diversity of African movements — and, by implication, their own range of political alternatives.

As always, black Americans did not respond with one voice to events in newly independent Africa, and Lumumba's star-crossed fate provided a canvas for drawing out and defining a dizzying array of attitudes. To some in black America, Lumumba became a black nationalist hero; others, including many civil rights leaders, remained wary of him and his actions. Indeed, this reticence prompted some in the broader community to condemn the mainstream civil rights leadership for not taking a strong enough stand in favor of Lumumba. African American responses to the Congo crisis and to Lumumba reveal how issues such as black nationalism, leftist thought, and militancy created fissures in black America.

In its denouement, then, the Congo crisis helped chart a course toward focusing attention and support on nations that were still fighting minority rule as opposed to independent countries that were facing neocolonial machinations. The complexities of the Congo crisis made African Americans abundantly aware that newly independent African countries faced a variety of subtle and not-so-subtle problems and, further, that in facing these problems Africans themselves did not speak with one voice. African Americans, who traditionally failed to disaggregate Africa, now faced enormous difficulties in differentiating between competing African personalities and factions. The chosen recourse generally was to focus attention on more easily defined struggles of still colonized African peoples fighting against white regimes, an approach that had the added benefit of helping a splintering civil rights coalition maintain more cohesion as it faced a new Africa.

Background to Independence

At the 1884–85 Berlin Conference, the major European powers agreed to allow Belgium's King Leopold II to establish rule over the "Congo Free State" as his personal empire. In order to exploit the Congo's vast resources, Leopold granted leasing rights in the Congo to private concessionaire companies. These companies embarked on a horrific rape of the Congo. One of the most notorious was the Anglo-Belgian India-Rubber Company (ABIR), founded in 1892, which received a concession four times the size of Belgium, with exclusive rights to exploit all forest products for thirty years. In exchange for helping to enforce the company's rule in the area, the state was given a 50 percent share in ABIR. In lieu of paying taxes, the local population was forced to collect wild rubber. The ABIR agent for an area would list all men in villages under his control and assign them each a rubber quota. In time, women and children also were forced to fulfill quotas. Villagers of any age who fell behind were flogged, imprisoned, mutilated, and/or shot. The intensity of rubber harvesting quickly exhausted the available supply. By 1906 the entire ABIR concession was devoid of rubber.[1]

Reports of the gruesome atrocities inflicted against the population of the Congo Free State, in ABIR's concession and elsewhere, began filtering out in the early 1890s. Exposure of the concessionaires' activities by people such as the African American historian George Washington Williams, an early and vocal critic who traveled to the Congo in 1890, and reformer E. D. Morel, author of the graphic 1906 exposé *Red Rubber*, led to spreading international condemnation. When Roger Casement, British consul to the Congo Free State, traveled up the Congo River in 1903 to investigate personally the stories of abuse, he collected evidence typified by one man's testimony: "We tried, always going further into the forest, and when we failed and our rubber was short, the soldiers came to our town and killed us. Many were shot, some had their ears cut off; others were tied up with ropes around their necks and bodies and taken away. The white men at the posts sometimes did not know of the bad things the soldiers did to us, but it was the white men who sent the soldiers to punish us for not bringing in enough rubber."[2]

International disapprobation, along with growing African resistance, helped convince Leopold to hand over the Congo Free State to the Belgian government in November 1908. By that time the Congo had become one of the most devastating killing fields of modern times. Before the institution of the Congo Free State, estimates placed the Congo region's population at 20–30 million; the official census taken in 1911 revealed only 8.5 million people remaining.[3]

European colonial powers followed different ideas about the best way to govern their territories, as well as how best to avert independence for African nations. The Belgians built their regime largely on the premise that by meeting Congolese social and economic needs, there would be no political unrest. Casting their colonial rule as enlightened paternalism, they believed they could insulate the Congo from the African nationalism emerging elsewhere on the continent. Belgian efforts to prevent political agitation included restricting general education to the primary level and allowing no African representation in political affairs.

As British and French colonies moved toward independence, Brussels gave no indication that it would accept any change in the Congo's status. Congolese independence in fact seemed a remote possibility prior to 1956, when a group of Congolese published a manifesto, *Conscience Africaine*, endorsing a thirty-year plan for independence. This document marked the first formal demands for independence by the Congolese; previous Congolese agitation had centered on social and economic issues. The moderate proposal, voiced in the atmosphere of change sweeping the entire continent, led to escalating demands for independence. Political parties mushroomed throughout the Congo. Joseph Kasavubu, a leading voice for accelerating independence, led the most significant regional party, the Alliance des Bakongo (Abako). Moise Tshombe headed the other major regional party, the Confederation des Associations Tribales du Katanga (Conakat). Both Kasavubu and Tshombe favored a federal system that would give them greater power. The leading party with national, rather than regional, designs was the Mouvement National Congolais (MNC). Originating in August 1956 from the Congolese who issued *Conscience Africaine*, the MNC became formally organized and more politically active in 1958 under the leadership of Patrice Lumumba.[4]

The engaging but at times volatile Lumumba came from a relatively small ethnic group in the central part of the Congo. His formal schooling extended only to the primary level, but under the Belgians even that put him ahead of the vast majority of Congolese. He worked as a postal clerk in Leopoldville (Kinshasa) and then as a postal accountant in Stanleyville (Kisangani). He wrote articles on politics and became involved in a Congolese trade union of government employees. In 1956 the Belgians arrested him on embezzlement charges, for which he spent a year in jail. After his release, he became more involved in politics. With little chance to build a political party based on ethnic ties, Lumumba moved to make the MNC the leading nationwide Congolese party. His trip to the All-African Peoples Conference in Accra in December 1958 exposed him to African nationalists from around the continent and inspired him with Pan-African visions.

Talk about immediate independence by the rapidly growing MNC and the multiplying regionally based political parties shocked the Belgians, who considered the Congo a "model colony." In January 1959, riots broke out in Leopoldville after an Abako meeting was banned. The riots left dozens, perhaps even hundreds, of Congolese dead and the Belgians shaken. Faced with a choice of repression or concession, Belgium chose the latter course, inspired in large part by images of the French war still raging in Algeria. They announced that the Congo would move toward independence. Yet at the same time, Belgium's long effort to prevent the growth of a Congolese leadership class bore bitter fruit. At the time of the January 1959 riots, not a single Congolese could be found in the three highest grades of civil administration. The effort to Africanize the civil service in the following year advanced only six Congolese to the second- and third-highest grades, where they joined the approximately 4,500 Europeans in the top three grades. By independence, Congolese university graduates totaled sixteen, a number that included no doctors, lawyers, or engineers. The 24,000-man Force Publique, the army, did not have a single Congolese officer.[5]

A congress of Congolese political parties led by the MNC met in April 1959 and demanded independence by 1961. Abako, which had refused to attend the congress, responded by demanding independence by March 1960. Amidst the escalating demands, the Belgian Minister for the Congo announced in December 1959 that independence would come in 1960. A roundtable conference in January and February 1960 hammered out the details, and set the actual date for independence as 30 June 1960.[6]

African Americans warmly received the announcement of this firm independence date. The *Afro-American* applauded the Congolese for "forc[ing] the Belgians to mark the freedom date of June 30, 1960 on their calendars."[7] Congo's independence, however, came amidst impending independence for over a dozen countries in Africa, and so did not rank as a singularly special event; certainly it did not provoke the same emotion as Ghana's independence. In the months following the Brussels announcement, the progress of Congo preparations intermingled with news about other nations on the continent moving toward independence. Joy and celebration greeted independence day, with small celebrations such as the one the Kongo University Committee hosted at Harlem's Hotel Theresa bringing out a few dignitaries. Still, at this point Congo's independence carried no particular emphasis.[8]

The Crisis

In the May 1960 parliamentary elections Lumumba's MNC and its allies won 40 of the 137 seats. This left the MNC well short of a ruling majority, but far ahead of the plethora of other parties, none of which won more than 13 seats.[9] Enormous difficulties marked the efforts to create an effective government, but after much maneuvering Lumumba became prime minister by putting together a coalition of twelve parties. Kasavubu, leader of Abako, assumed the more ceremonial position of president. While the Belgians hesitated to support Kasavubu because of his history of nationalist agitation, they worried more and more about what they perceived to be Lumumba's increasing radicalization. On independence day, Western concerns about Lumumba heightened. Hearing the Belgians congratulate themselves on their reign, Lumumba responded by scathingly denouncing Belgian rule: "[Ours] was a noble and just struggle, an indispensable struggle to put an end to the humiliating bondage imposed on us by force. Our lot was a painful eighty years of colonial rule; our wounds are still too fresh and painful to be driven from our memory." Lumumba hammered home his theme by recounting, in the presence of Belgian King Badouin, those wounds and humiliations. Ralph Bunche, representing the UN at the independence celebrations, described the speech as "a hard, anti-colonial, we are free now statement," one that left Belgian officials shocked, some with tears in their eyes.[10]

The Congo's shaky political situation started to fall apart a few days after independence, when members of the Force Publique, the old colonial army, mutinied on 5 July at a base ninety miles outside Leopoldville. Soldier dissatisfaction spilled over after the Belgian commander General Émile Janssens announced there would be no change in the soldiers' rank or pay as a result of independence. Lumumba calmed the soldiers by promising all of them a promotion of one full rank and the Africanization of the officer corps, but unrest already had spread to Leopoldville. Belgian refugees fleeing into the capital told wild stories of rapes and shootings, triggering panic and European flight. The sight of roaming Congolese soldiers, no longer under the command of Belgian officers, heightened white fears. On 8 July the British and French embassies ordered the evacuation of all nonessential personnel. Masses of European civilians fled across the Congo River to Brazzaville. Essential services and economic activity collapsed as the Europeans decamped, a bitter testament to the Belgian policy of excluding Congolese from all but the lower echelons of work.

The imposition of a curfew calmed Leopoldville, but by then mutiny, panic, and disorder had spread to other parts of the country. Lumumba and Kasavubu spent the next several days flying around the country, trying to persuade mutinous troops to return to their barracks. Bunche, who had intended to stay for a few weeks to advise the new government and to explore requirements for UN assistance, made plans to extend his visit. He telegrammed UN secretary-general Dag Hammarskjöld that the situation looked virtually hopeless, that the government had no control anywhere, and that troops were drinking openly and trying to recapture the power they had held in the immediacy of their uprising. "[T]his is the toughest spot I've ever been in," Bunche wrote to his wife Ruth. "Even Palestine was safe by comparison."[11]

In Belgium, sensational stories of Congolese running amok caused mounting demands for a restoration of order. The Belgian government sent reinforcements to bases in the Congo. On 10 July, Belgian troops went into action in response to a request by Moise Tshombe, now president of Katanga Province, to restore order in Elizabethville (Lubumbashi) after the killing of six Europeans. On 11 July, Lumumba and Kasavubu flew to Luluabourg, where they found the situation so precarious for Europeans that they agreed to a limited intervention by Belgian troops. That constituted the first and last time they agreed to rely on Belgian assistance. A few hours later they learned that the Belgians had bombarded the port of Matadi, killing a number of civilians. Over the next week the Belgians intervened in more than twenty places. As they did so, Lumumba and Kasavubu desperately cast about for a way to replace the Belgians.[12]

U.S. ambassador Clare Timberlake, fearing that Belgian intervention created antagonism that played into Soviet hands, urged the Congolese leaders to request UN assistance. Timberlake saw it as a way to restore order under a UN umbrella, and Washington supported this approach. While Washington categorically opposed using U.S. troops, it also feared that the potential backlash against the Belgians could help unite the Congolese behind a communist regime. Lumumba and Kasavubu sent their first request to the UN on 10 July, at which point Hammarskjöld believed assistance could be handled without a formal meeting of the Security Council. Two days later the Congolese leaders sent a second request, asking for the "urgent despatch" of UN troops to protect the Congo from external aggression — namely, the Belgians. On 13 July, Lumumba and Kasavubu broke diplomatic relations with Belgium and sent a message to Moscow asking the Soviets to monitor the situation carefully in case the Congolese needed assistance to stop Western aggression. Soviet premier Krushchev sent a sympathetic reply, though without committing to any specific support. With the situation deteriorating and the prospect of an East-West confrontation growing, Hammarskjöld called an urgent meeting of the Security Council.[13]

The thorny issue of Katanga added to the complexity of the crisis. Claiming that he was blocking communist control of the Congo (or at least Katanga), and bolstered by the presence of Belgian troops, on 11 July Tshombe declared Katanga to be independent. Katanga, and the other secessionist province of South Kasai, held the vast majority of the Congo's incredible mineral wealth. More than 20 percent of the Congo's GNP and 60 percent of its exports came from mining, and more than 75 percent of the country's mining production came from Katanga, making it vital to the viability of the nation. The Congo in 1959 had produced a tenth of the "Free World's" copper, half of its cobalt, and more than two-thirds of its industrial diamonds. Strategically vital uranium deposits joined with cobalt and tantalum reserves, vital for the aerospace industry, to heighten Katanga's strategic importance. The United States and its NATO allies had direct and vital investments at stake, and feared any "loss" of Katanga's riches.[14]

Officials in Brussels and Washington did not necessarily favor a Katanga secession, even under a pro-Western Tshombe. They feared that the rest of the Congo would collapse without Katanga's riches, opening the door to Soviet exploitation of the situation. Just before independence, American officials had made clear to Tshombe that the United States did not desire the fragmentation of Africa, that it hoped he would work within the framework of the Congo government, and that if Lumumba attacked a secessionist Katanga the United States would stand aside. Amidst the problems following independence, however, U.S. officials wavered in their commitment to a unified Congo. They did not want to take the lead in recognizing an independent Katanga, knowing that black Africa would view this with tremendous bitterness, but thought it possible that if other countries recognized Katanga, then the United States might also do so. At the very least, they hoped to insulate Katanga from the disorder engulfing the rest of the Congo.[15]

U.S. officials most of all did not want Katanga to be under communist control, and warnings that the communists viewed the Congo as a fertile field seemed to be coming true. Congo's independence came during a tense period in U.S.-Soviet relations, occurring shortly after the Soviet downing of a U-2 spy plane and the collapse of the May summit between Eisenhower and Krushchev. As U.S. officials saw another charismatic leftist leader appealing to Moscow, they feared a repetition of the recent Cuban experience. Lumumba became the focus of attention in Washington, where he was cast as an African Castro with Kasavubu his reluctant accomplice. That an African leader such as Lumumba would turn to the Soviets with little advance warning seemed increasingly plausible. Lumumba's mercurial shifts indeed convinced key officials that he operated under Soviet guidance. CIA director Allen Dulles termed Lumumba "a Castro, or worse."[16] Yet even as Dulles made his assessment, others minimized the extent of communist influence in the Congo and of Lumumba's alleged communist leanings. Hugh Cumming, director of the Bureau of Intelligence and Research for the State Department, found "no substantial or convincing proof of direct Communist involvement" in the postindependence travails. Cumming argued that Lumumba himself provided the best description of his views: "We are not Communists, Catholics, or Socialists. We are African nationalists. We reserve the right to be friendly with anybody we like according to the principles of positive neutrality."[17] In the atmosphere of 1960 Washington, however, the fact that Lumumba asserted his right to establish friendly relations with anyone made him suspect. Washington above all wanted a unified Congo friendly toward the West, but how to achieve that in the chaos of postindependence Congo was unclear. For the moment, the United States decided to support a UN mission to straighten out the situation.

The Security Council met during the night of 13 July, and by 6:30 the following morning Hammarskjöld started the UN Congo operation in motion. The UN dispatched a force drawn from countries outside both the Western and the Communist blocs. The first troops arrived in Leopoldville late on 15 July; within two weeks the force totaled over 11,000 men. At this point, both superpowers fully supported a UN peacekeeping force: Washington felt it could restore order without allowing the Soviets to make inroads; Moscow viewed it as the best way to remove Belgian troops, thus assisting the Lumumba government while earning the gratitude of other African states.[18]

Less than forty-eight hours after the first UN troops arrived, Lumumba and Kasavubu issued an ultimatum stating that they would ask the Soviet Union to intervene if UN forces did not remove all Belgian troops by midnight of 19 July. They based the demand on Bunche having said that Belgian forces would leave upon the arrival of UN troops. The ultimatum prodded the Belgians to announce that their troops would be out of Leopoldville by 23 July. However, the summary demand antagonized Bunche and other UN officials. It also seemingly linked Lumumba more closely to the Soviets while in turn increasing pressure on Krushchev to defend Lumumba's interests. Lumumba had not tied himself or the Congo to the communist bloc, but his actions further increased Western concern about Lumumba being either a communist "dupe" or an actual communist. On 19 July the American embassy in Brussels recommended that the United States try to remove Lumumba from office, maintaining that because Lumumba had "maneuvered himself into a position of opposition to West, resistance to United Nations and increasing dependence on Soviet Union," it therefore was prudent "to plan on basis that Lumumba government threatens our vital interests in Congo and Africa generally." "A principle objective of political and diplomatic action," the embassy concluded, "must therefore be to destroy Lumumba government as now constituted."[19]

Friction steadily increased among all parties over resolving the Congo crisis, and in particular over handling the Katanga secession. The Katanga issue especially outraged Lumumba, who saw Belgian industrialists carving a puppet state from his country. He worried, too, that losing Katangan revenues would create economic instability in the rest of the country, further spreading the contagion of secession. Lumumba wanted Katanga immediately returned to central government control, even if that meant UN troops had to use force. Hammarskjöld, for his part, worked for the intermediate objective of getting Belgian troops out of Katanga and UN troops in. Hammarskjöld achieved his objective on 12 August when he finally entered Elizabethville with 240 Swedish UN troops. Yet Lumumba exploded in fury that Hammarskjöld had gone in without him and that the actual secession had not been ended forthwith. Hammarskjöld's refusal to use military means to quash the secession intensified Lumumba's distrust of Hammarskjöld, the UN, and the West. The fact that Hammarskjöld took only white troops to Katanga escalated Lumumba's anger and suspicions. He vociferously attacked both Hammarskjöld and the UN, and on 15 August Lumumba wrote to Krushchev requesting that the Soviets supply him with transport planes and crews, trucks, weapons, and other equipment so that he could invade and end Katanga's secession. Krushchev, casting his lot with Lumumba, sent limited military aid, consisting of planes, crews, technicians, weapons, and ammunition.[20]

The rift between Lumumba and Hammarskjöld, followed by the arrival of Soviet aid, sent shock waves through Washington. U.S. efforts to use the UN to preempt the Soviets had not worked, and Lumumba seemed to be increasingly dependent on communist advisers and aid. U.S. officials became determined not only to keep the UN in the Congo, but also to find a way to remove Lumumba from leadership. It now appears virtually certain that the CIA in early September sent an assassin to eliminate Lumumba by poisoning his toothbrush. Yet before the plan could be executed, Lumumba already had been forced from power.[21]

In the wake of Lumumba's appeal to the Soviets, Kasavubu took action himself. Prone to indecision, after several weeks of hesitation he drove to the Leopoldville radio station in the evening of 5 September and announced that he had dismissed Lumumba. He named Joseph Ileo, a moderate federalist with close ties to the Catholic church and the West, to form a new government. Kasavubu also asked the army to lay down its weapons and called on the UN to maintain law and order in the Congo. Lumumba responded swiftly. In less than an hour he had taken to the radio denying Kasavubu's right to dismiss him. He denounced Kasavubu as a traitor who was aiding Belgian and French imperialists and proclaimed that Kasavubu would continue no longer as head of state. On 7 September Lumumba addressed the Assembly, which then voted to annul both Kasavubu's dismissal of Lumumba and Lumumba's dismissal of Kasavubu. The next day Lumumba won a victory in the Senate, where after two hours of oration he received a 41–2 vote supporting him. On 13 September the two houses of Parliament, meeting together, voted 88–25 to give Lumumba "special powers." In response, on 14 September, Kasavubu adjourned parliament for a month, claiming that it had acted illegally.[22]

During this turbulent period, U.S. officials worked hard to swing Joseph Mobutu, Lumumba's private secretary before his boss appointed him army chief of staff, over to Kasavubu's side. Hours after Kasavubu's announcement adjourning parliament, Mobutu seized power in the name of the military. He pledged to "neutralize" Kasavubu, Lumumba, Ileo, and other politicians until the end of the year. He called on Congolese university students and graduates to run the government. He expelled the Soviet and Czechoslovakian embassies. When the CIA alerted Mobutu to an alleged plot on his life a few days later, Mobutu swung decisively in favor of the Western-backed Kasavubu. He told U.S. embassy officials that he would arrest Lumumba and work to transfer power to an Ileo-Kasavubu government by the end of October. Mobutu was unable to arrest Lumumba, however, for Lumumba stayed in his house under UN protection. Therefore, a cordon of Mobutu's soldiers prevented Lumumba from leaving the house, thus restricting his access to Leopoldville or the nation.[23]

African Americans Respond to the Initial Crisis

Even before the crisis flared, many whites had been questioning the readiness of Africans for self-government. African Americans vociferously rejected such voices. In March 1960, when noted liberal champion Eleanor Roosevelt suggested that nationalism was moving too rapidly in Africa, Bunche took sharp issue with her. "I know of no absolute criteria for determining when the people are ready for independence," Bunche declared. Rather than questioning the pace of nationhood, Bunche suggested people instead should ask what the international community could do to help newly independent people.[24]

Detecting rumblings of trouble before independence, the *Defender* warned that elements hostile to Congo independence were painting purposefully gloomy pictures of the personal struggles between Lumumba and Kasavubu, the breakdown of local administration, and of an imminent reversion to tribalism. Given all the forces working against Congolese statehood, the *Defender* felt that if the nation survived it would justify beyond question the capacity for African self-government throughout Africa. On the other hand, if the Congo disintegrated, European resistance to emancipation in the rest of Africa "could stiffen into horrified rigidity."[25]

African Americans rightly worried that colonial powers looking for any excuse to maintain their control for as long as possible would take the Congo as a "test case." As Emmett Marshall put it in a letter to the *Afro-American*, black Americans worried that the Belgians wanted the Congolese to fail so as "to try to discredit black leadership everywhere and for all times." African Americans suffered no illusions about the interests of the colonial powers or of international investors, and they insisted on the right of all people to freedom and self-determination. "We contend that every man, whether he is born a slave or a monarch, is ready for, and entitled to, freedom," argued the *Amsterdam News*. "And we flatly reject the colonial theory that a white nation must tutor a black nation for years on end before the people of the black nation are ready to be free. There are those who would like to use the rioting in this new state as an excuse for the white man to move back in and regain control of the Congo. We reject fully this type of thinking." The

Amsterdam News further argued that if some African states initially failed to measure up to international expectations, the failure should not be laid at the feet of the Africans but rather at the feet of the Western world, which for so long held Africans in thrall. "The white man has played the role of God Almighty in Africa for far too many years. And, as Prime Minister Nkrumah has said: 'If after 90 years of teaching, the pupil fails to pass his tests, perhaps we should blame, not the pupil, but the teacher.' "[26]

In numerous letters and articles African Americans expressed sympathy for the "growing pains" of the new Congo state. They commonly attributed these pains to the legacy of the colonial past, a particularly brutal legacy in the case of the Congo. They also offered numerous examples of the early problems experienced by Western countries. The *Eagle* noted that violence and rebellion had been a part of early U.S. history; Joel Rogers pointed to the actions of the oppressed against their oppressors in the aftermath of the French and Russian Revolutions; P. L. Prattis argued that no part of the world had seen more bloodshed than Europe. Such arguments emanated from across the political spectrum. The liberal and strongly pro-African *Afro-American* declared, "It is too much to expect a new and inexperienced government, no matter how determined, to straighten out overnight the accumulated mess of a hundred years of misrule." The conservative *Daily World* commiserated that a certain amount of "disorganization and reorientation" should be expected after a nation subjected to rule and domination by another power finally wins its freedom and immediately faces self-government. The *Defender* contended that if disorders and uprisings signaled incompetence, then no country since the dawn of civilization could escape criticism. Achieving a stable political balance takes a long time, it argued, and the new government should be entitled to make mistakes because growth develops through practice and experience. The *Defender* concluded, "To condemn a nation which is hardly two weeks old because of its faltering steps is both unfair and inadmissible. Rome, as the saying goes, was not built in a day."[27]

The Congo crisis also elicited responses that sought to help the Congolese. In these remarks, one hears as well echoes of the popular anti-imperialism of previous confrontations with white colonialism. Mrs. John Stewart of Chicago wrote to Roy Wilkins that, just as Jews went to Israel, black Americans should go and help the Congolese organize their country. She wanted the NAACP to facilitate this, arguing that the necessary money could be garnered from private sources or even the federal government. Marvin Robinson, a CORE field secretary, called upon black Americans to volunteer for nonviolent services in the Congo. Nationalist groups such as the United Sons and Daughters of Africa also sought volunteers for the Congo. Still others used the Congo as a springboard to broaden their vision to all of Africa. "Most of us are so tired of trying to pretend we are white folks," wrote Amos Gilliam of Tarboro, North Carolina. "[W]e need to go back to our own people — a lot of us are well-educated — and we would be the backbone of the new governments in Africa." Frances Walters proposed forming a pool of 75,000 black American technicians from which Africa could draw. Declaring that whites had failed in Africa because they failed to train Africans, Walters wrote, "We, the black peoples of the earth, now have the opportunity to rectify this mistake. We can take culture, education, mechanical know-how to Africa. . . . Only we can do it, for the whites have failed." Notable, too, is that even as African Americans saw Africans liberating themselves and running their own countries, letters such as these reveal the persistence of old ideas and assumptions about black Americans' playing a leading role in Africa.[28]

African Americans no doubt felt that blame for the Congo's troubles should be placed squarely on Belgian colonial misrule and postcolonial machinations. In the run-up to independence, the *Defender* had called Belgian governance a "classic example of rapacious colonialism" and had pilloried the Belgians for failing to foresee the need to prepare the Congolese for responsible self-government. The *Afro-American* concurred, lamenting that "Despite more than 100 years of rule in the Congo during which the Belgian rulers have made themselves the richest people in the world out of rubber, diamonds and minerals, the Africans have been so neglected that many of them are still primitive with no education and the barest necessities of life."[29]

As troubles spread in the weeks after independence, more and more voices joined the chorus of criticizing Belgium while sympathizing with the Congolese. Councilman Earl Brown of New York argued, "In truth, it is a wonder that the Congolese have been able to do as well as they have after generations of Belgian brutality and thievery." Mrs. Luvenia Cowles wrote to the *Amsterdam News* that while she regretted the violence in the Congo, she felt that the Belgians now reaped what their cruel rule had sown. Joel Rogers picked up this imagery when he asserted that, "In short, the recent terrifying experiences of white women and children [in the Congo] arise from the evil seeds sown there by the Belgians themselves."[30]

African Americans widely believed that if the Congolese were not "ready" for independence, that lack of readiness clearly stemmed from Belgian misrule. Jackie Robinson regularly denounced the Belgians for failing to provide the training and arrangements necessary for a smooth transfer of power. The *Crisis* argued that the Belgians had made no pretense of preparing the Congo for ultimate self-government, and the *Eagle* asserted its belief that "Belgium deliberately refrained from training Congolese in the art and responsibility of self-government and both sides must suffer temporarily." Conducting person-on-the-street polls on the hotly debated question of who held responsibility for chaos in the Congo, the *Afro-American* and the *Defender* found that those questioned uniformly traced the blame back to the Belgians.[31]

Condemning the Belgians for not "preparing" the Congolese for independence was a problematic position, however, for it seemed to accept that Africans in fact were not ready to run their own countries. Perhaps mindful of this implication, African Americans stressed all the harder the effects of Belgium's dastardly postindependence intrigue. Most believed that the Congo would have worked out any problems in a reasonable manner had the Belgians not reintroduced troops to the Congo and conspired to prod Katanga to secede under the puppet rule of Tshombe.

This argument broke sharply from coverage in the mainstream American press, which accepted Brussels' claim that it sent soldiers into independent Congo to protect Europeans from rampaging Congolese. Headlines across the United States screamed about the savage Congolese raping white women and committing uncounted atrocities. "With a primeval howl, a nation of 14 million people reverted to near savagery, plunged backward into the long night of chaos," *Time* magazine blared. *U.S. News & World Report* informed its readers, "There is little sign here that the 13 million Congolese can be restrained from tearing their newly independent country apart. Panic has seized most of the 100,000 whites, mainly Belgians, still in this country. Clearly they are in mortal danger." And *Newsweek* made plain that the Belgians needed to intervene: "Exactly one week after the Congo was born as a nation, it exploded with violence and horror. Masses of terror-stricken whites were fleeing by plane, by riverboat, by train, and by convoys of trucks and cars. Behind them, drunken mobs were roaming at will, shooting, looting and raping. Overnight, the savagery spread from Leopoldville. . . . The Belgian government was forced to act fast." In order to seal the case, pictures of black mobs and panicked whites accompanied the stories.[32]

This style of coverage continued throughout the subsequent weeks. In September 1960 a reporter described for readers of *U.S. News & World Report* his travels deep into the Congo. He recounted how a Canadian radio technician and a Tunisian UN employee had been tied to benches while Congolese "put a huge pot of water to boil over a fire" and concluded, "Only the last minute intervention of a Congolese officer saved the two UN employees from a horrible fate. The territory around Luluabourg is cannibal country." The reporter then proceeded to offer his broader analysis of the situation. After describing the Congolese National Army as "a wild mob of soldiers" who "terrorized" the country, beating whites as "almost hourly occurrences," he opined that with the help of the Russians, Lumumba planned to use this army "to conquer the rich and orderly province of Katanga." Finally, the reporter insidiously wrapped together his themes of barbaric primitiveness and communist advances in his conclusion: "What is certain, when you get deep inside the Congo, is that jungle law still rules much of the country which Moscow's Communists hope to turn into their first Red outpost in black Africa."[33]

As in the case of Kenya a decade before, the white press offered stereotypical images of primitive and savage Africans, now freed from the civilizing hand of whites, embarking on bloodthirsty rampages. Such a portrayal provided the needed justification for the Belgian decision to send in troops and keep them there. The African American press struggled to offset this coverage with analysis more sympathetic to the Congolese. Yet limited resources and reliance on mainstream wire reports made the task extremely difficult. An *Afro-American* correspondent, Charles Howard, in fact publicly expressed his conviction that a plot existed among the Euro-American press to wreck the Lumumba government.[34]

Black Americans strongly questioned Belgian motives behind sending more military personnel into the Congo, decrying the hypocrisy of the whole affair and arguing that the Belgians' presence only worsened the situation. The *Amsterdam News*, for example, wrote that the "glaring, garish headlines" carried by the daily press led readers to believe that the only thing happening in the Congo was the assault of white women and the murder of white men. Joseph Watkins, a reader of the *Courier*, summed up the frustration of many when he pointed out that white papers now blared headlines about Africans raping white women but had been entirely silent when during the colonial era whites raped, tortured, and murdered Congolese men, women, and children.[35]

As the situation in the Congo worsened, even blunter assessments of Belgian activity took hold. The *Afro-American* accused the Belgians of spreading atrocity stories as a ruse in order to justify holding on to the last shreds of an empire. To reclaim power, "they need a pretext — a smoke-screen," the paper claimed. "This need explains the screaming headlines of rioting, looting, rape and murder which for the past weeks have been front-paged in the Western World by a press that's either gullible or prostituted."[36] In early August the Belgians released a report that claimed mutinous Congolese soldiers raped over 200 European women after independence. The Belgians declared that this report exonerated their decision to place and keep troops in the Congo. The *Afro-American* conceded that atrocities had taken place but derided the Belgian case. Comparing the 213 rape cases to the mutilation and murder of 8 million Congolese by the Belgians, the *Afro-American* asserted that the Belgians shed crocodile tears. The real reason for the Belgian soldiers' presence was not to "protect the virtue of a handful of white women, but to stand watch over the continued rape of the Congo's natural resources."[37]

Black America had little patience for Belgian claims that the Congo needed its presence; they had even less for the intrigue and conspiracy they perceived behind Katanga's secession from the Congo. Jackie Robinson, for one, argued that because the Belgians had acted so dishonorably in refusing to provide the education, training, and experience needed for a smooth transfer of power in the Congo, Belgium should expect no sympathy for "such a blatant attempt at recouping through military force and a puppet secessionist government what it lost through its own ineptitude."[38] African Americans understood the West's enormous desire to maintain control over Katanga's vast natural resources and saw that an independent Katanga under a pro-Western Tshombe held enticing prospects for Western business and military interests. African Americans scathingly condemned Tshombe's actions, as well as Belgian support for him. While at least one reader of the *Afro-American* preferred the analogy to Judas, to most African Americans Tshombe was an "Uncle Tom," enabling Belgian and other Western interests to maintain their control over the Congo's precious resources. Proclaiming that "greedy Belgian whites have combined with Congo Uncle Toms to prevent any easy transit of the Congo government from slavery to independence," the *Afro-American* advised that Abraham Lincoln had the answer to the problem of secession. The *Defender* concurred, summing up what for most African Americans seemed self-evident: "Beneath the secession movement which is rocking the central government at Leopoldville is Belgian treachery and machination."[39]

Patrice Lumumba as Player and Symbol

Facing the somewhat delicate situation of not wanting to appear to condone any atrocities but wanting to protect black majority rule in the Congo, African Americans generally favored the UN's initial entry into the Congo. The UN, acting at the request of a sovereign Congolese government, would defuse a difficult situation and then leave—posing no threat of colonial subjugation to the Congo. This approach in some respects built on the old arguments made by Du Bois, White, and others, to use the UN to oversee an end to colonialism and colonial intrigue. The fact that Ralph Bunche initially acted as the UN point man made it seem an even better option. The

Afro-American described the initial UN decision to send troops into the Congo as "just and apropos."[40]

Yet supporting a unified, black-ruled Congo with the interim help of the UN would not finalize the issue for African Americans, for the Congo's problems were not neatly resolved. In the months that followed, black Americans confronted what would become a common scenario: as Africans struggled to cast off colonial rule, many of them turned to leftist ideologies and alliances with the communist world. In Lumumba's case, the Katanga secession, as well as anger over the apparent machinations of the Belgians and the other Western powers, propelled this turn. Yet Lumumba's courting of Soviet support cut against the staunch anticommunism that leading black American liberals and conservatives had followed throughout the Cold War. In the Congo, and later in other African countries, these African Americans had to decide how to balance their anticommunism with their support for African leaders struggling against colonial and neocolonial domination of their countries.

As Lumumba grew frustrated that UN troops neither served as his support personnel nor acted swiftly to suppress the Katanga secession, he also posed challenging questions about multiracialism, black nationalism, and pan-Africanism. Lumumba first called for the withdrawal of all UN troops, then for the withdrawal of just the white UN troops. The latter call in particular contradicted the nonracialist, integrationist objectives of civil rights leaders. When Lumumba changed course once again and allowed white troops to stay, the issue momentarily subsided, but the circumstances surrounding Lumumba's death soon would revive it. Supporting independence for African countries had been a relatively straightforward affair before the postindependence crisis in the Congo. Now it became more complex. The Cold War, decolonization, black nationalism, economic exploitation, leftism — all intertwined in a complex, sticky mess in the Congo.

Black American perceptions of Lumumba and responses to his actions sharpened growing differentiations in the relationship with contemporary Africa and the struggle in America. An increasingly militant swath of black America gave unquestioning support to Lumumba. The *Afro-American*, perhaps the most militant of the mainstream black press at the time, faithfully backed Lumumba. It supported Lumumba's demand that all white UN troops be withdrawn from the Congo, labeling Hammarskjöld "stupid" for sending them into the Congo in the first place. It branded Tshombe a "turncoat quisling," Kasavubu "a tool of his former colonial masters," and Mobutu "a creation of Belgian and American interests." It portrayed Lumumba, on the other hand, not as a communist but as a devoted nationalist who Western interests wanted to keep out of power because he was "so stubbornly, so patriotically pro-Congo."[41]

In this perspective, Lumumba was first and foremost a patriot trying to keep the Congo together and defend its best interests. However, by interpreting the Congo's best interests differently than did Western business and military leaders, he had incurred their disfavor. Western opponents of Lumumba and genuine Congo autonomy therefore had used the rioting following independence as an excuse to return to the scene, and then sought to remove Lumumba from power by labeling him a communist. While Lumumba's opponents seized upon his turn toward the Soviets to bolster their attacks, to his black American defenders this gambit reflected Lumumba's lack of options more than anything else. Indeed, Lumumba patently could not seek help from Western powers, for they were intertwined with the very economic interests that wanted to continue plundering the Congo.

Appreciating the force of nationalism more than most in Washington, these African Americans realized that leaders who were not pro-Western did not ipso facto have to be communist. The *Defender* credited Lumumba and his nationalism for forcing the world to address Africa and her situation: "[His] fanatical nationalism, his impatient and pyrotechnic diplomacy may have jarred the orthodoxy of Western politics to its roots, but there is no question but that the effusive Congolese Premier has drawn attention to his country on a dimension that could not possibly have been attained under other circumstances." The *Defender* accepted the possibility that Lumumba's actions may have brought the world closer to the brink of war but insisted, "The pendulum had to swing to the extreme to achieve desired results. The great powers were obliged to undergo self-introspection. And the United States, after deep meditation, decided to extend a helping hand to the black continent." Lumumba's approach held risks, and all that he stood for may not have met with favor, but the ultimate result — the world taking notice and Eisenhower even proposing increased economic and social programs — might not have come to pass otherwise. No longer, thought the *Defender*, could U.S. policy be "one of aloofness and indifference." Ultimately, of course, Lumumba might have been better off with an aloof United States.[42]

Lumumba's supporters blamed his troubles with the UN on the unwillingness of that body to support his legitimate government as fully as it should, no doubt due to the influence of Western interests. Much of the initial African American support for UN intervention melted away. Less than six weeks after the first UN troops arrived on the scene, the *Defender* declared the failure to resolve the Congo crisis a failure for Secretary-General Hammarskjöld, and urged him to step down "in the interest of international goodwill and peace." By October the paper argued that "it can scarcely be denied" that Hammarskjöld's initial efforts in the Congo "had the deplorable result of contributing greater confusion to what already had prevailed." The UN's handling of the Congo crisis in fact was seen to have tragically undermined the authority of a legitimate Lumumba government. Alphaeus Hunton, the former stalwart CAA leader then living in Africa, blasted the "coalition of imperialist and pro-imperialist forces in the U.N. attempting to push aside Lumumba, who unquestionably enjoys the widest support among the Congolese, and hand over the Congo into the safe hands of Kasavubu, Mobutu and Company. It is a shame upon the United Nations! It is an insult against the Congolese and Africans generally!"[43]

The plight of the Congo, on the heels of the Sharpeville massacre, plainly resonated in black America. That white opinion leaders tried to paint Lumumba as politically "suspect" made little difference to most rank-and-file African Americans. Partly this was because by mid-1960 it seemed that unwavering support of anticommunism had not done enough to advance the domestic social and political movements for change. But even more, the engagement with Lumumba helped black Americans break the bounds of Cold War thinking. As much as the Western powers increasingly cast Lumumba as a leftist ideologue, for black America what stood out more was the image of a black man struggling to unite an African country against white neocolonial intrigue. African liberation struggles, then, should not be situated in anticommunist terms but instead as black struggles against white supremacy, which accordingly should be supported as best as possible.

That said, Lumumba's actions clearly concerned a substantial minority of black Americans who felt uneasy with his militantly nationalistic rhetoric and increasingly leftist tilt. Lumumba's embrace of the Soviets especially created concern. While the civil rights leadership generally declined to see Lumumba as an out-and-out communist, it felt reluctant to embrace measures or people that seemed too extreme. The NAACP leadership largely fell silent as a result of the quandary. They did little to generate support for Lumumba, and hoped that the UN would resolve the Congo crisis.[44] When members implored the organization to work on behalf of the Congolese, Roy Wilkins responded by emphasizing the limited resources and domestic priorities of the NAACP: "[W]e sympathize very greatly with the Africans and we will do all we can to help them. However, our main job remains over here and we must continue all our efforts until we are successful in the United States." The primacy of the domestic struggle combined with the treacherous shoals of the Congo crisis to keep efforts oriented toward the struggle in America.

Yet the NAACP found that it faced the same situation with its international views as it was experiencing with its domestic programs: the national leadership more and more exuded a relative cautiousness that helped contribute to the movement of frustrated and increasingly militant blacks away from the organization.[45]

African Americans who felt conflicted over whether to or how extensively to support Lumumba often walked a careful path by arguing that upholding the legitimacy of a black government in the Congo and the wishes of the Congolese voters meant supporting Lumumba's right to govern. Within this framework, one could still criticize Lumumba's actions without undermining black independence. The *Amsterdam News*, for example, disparaged Lumumba's attempt to fire Kasavubu and his threat to do battle with UN forces. "Black people around the world," it declared, "are almost as embarrassed over the antics of Premier Patrice Lumumba and President Kasavubu of the Congo as they were proud of them when they first emerged as leaders of an independent black state in Africa." Yet at the same time, the *Amsterdam News* maintained that if the UN had acted forthrightly and supported Lumumba as it should have against the Belgians, then the world would not be on the brink of war over the internal politics of the Congo. It reinforced the validity of Lumumba's claim to office, adding, "We are convinced of the rightness of his cause." By arguing that Lumumba, as the legal ruler, should be in power, African Americans could resolve the dilemma that Lumumba posed by focusing on the issue of his legitimacy to govern and skirting the issue of communism. African Americans then could support Lumumba's desire, and their own, to see a strong and independent Congo with colonial influences removed, while distancing themselves from Lumumba himself.[46]

Other, more conservative voices, unequivocally criticized Lumumba. Disturbed by Lumumba's apparent communist leanings, Benjamin Mays, longtime president of Morehouse College, criticized Lumumba's "wild irresponsible statements" about inviting the Russians into the Congo. Staunchly anticommunist African Americans worried about the hand of the Soviets behind Lumumba's actions, and others joined Mays in gauging the changing Africa with Cold War anticommunism still a determinative factor. Lester Granger, nearing the end of his tenure at the Urban League, used his weekly column to criticize both Lumumba and the black Americans who uncritically supported him: "We shrugged off impatiently the warning of those who offered plain proof that Lumumba was either a communist stooge, or captive, or willing adherent. We continued to insist that Lumumba was a 'patriot' — was ceaselessly striving for unity in his fledgling nation — and did so even after he began knocking off those on his side but critical of his methods . . . now we know that colonialism has no monopoly on scoundrelly leadership." Granger hoped black Americans, learning that there was a difference between anticolonialism and freedom, were "maturing" and turning away from Lumumba.[47]

Granger's comments indicate, too, that African American responses to Lumumba reflected not only different groups in black America, but also changing views over time. Some of those who initially welcomed Lumumba warmly became disillusioned as Lumumba turned away from the UN and toward the Soviets. Criticism of Lumumba by people such as Granger picked up pace after Lumumba's request for Soviet military aid in mid-August and then accelerated even further after the exchange of dismissals by Lumumba, Kasavubu, and Mobutu in mid-September. Granger had stood and praised Nkrumah during his visit in 1958, symbolically embracing contemporary Africa; two years later, however, Lumumba had become too radical a figure for him.

Entering a new era, black Americans faced not so much the issue of incorporating into its life a contemporary Africa that was demanding and taking freedom — this largely had been done — but instead they were faced now with the challenge of unraveling the meanings of a fragmented, complex Africa. Granger did not feel compelled to endorse Lumumba simply because he was the legitimately elected leader of a black African country. His response to Lumumba portended future conundrums and conflicts for black America in responding to independent Africa.

The Death of Lumumba

Lumumba and the Congo crisis generated intense debate at the fall 1960 General Assembly meetings. Most parties had believed initially, for their own reasons, that the UN offered the best hope for a favorable solution. But the early widespread backing of a UN presence had not meant agreement on exactly how UN forces should handle their mission. In the complexity of the Congo crisis, the devil was in the details. Nkrumah, for example, believed that with the Congo facing the real prospect of ending up as a Cold War battlefield, the Congolese needed the UN to achieve a favorable resolution. Nkrumah urged the UN to support a fully unified Congo under the duly elected government of Lumumba as prime minister, and in doing so to draw its peacekeeping contingent entirely from African nations. Other African leaders supported the goal of a united Congo with secessionist Katanga returned, yet they less enthusiastically backed Lumumba. U.S. officials also supported a unified country but desired a multiracial UN force and, more importantly, a pro-Western regime. That increasingly appeared to imply a Congo without Lumumba. The Soviets, for their part, attacked the UN mission more and more stridently while supporting Lumumba more vociferously. African Americans thus confronted a complex, shifting situation in which the Congo crisis had evolved beyond a simple case of good African freedom fighters versus bad colonial regimes. For African Americans who had long urged the Eisenhower administration to adopt a more pro-African position, the problem was determining exactly what was "pro-African."

Increasingly, African American views on the Congo and on the UN mission there reflected their own positions on the freedom struggle in America. African Americans who felt they could work within the system, to pressure America to uphold its principles, tended to support UN efforts with a minimum of criticism. Liberal, pragmatic activists felt fairly satisfied with the stated position of the UN and with United States support for the UN effort. The growing barrage of attacks that the Soviets trained on Hammarskjöld and the UN operation further muted their potential criticism of UN policy and action. Civil rights leaders and organizations made little extra effort, then, to alter UN or U.S. policy on the Congo. Yet the pace and results of UN efforts, especially as Lumumba's relationship with the organization soured, frustrated a second, increasingly militant camp of black Americans. As time dragged on, these African Americans became disturbed by the UN's inability to effect a resolution of the crisis. They felt the UN needed to more fully support Lumumba, and that the United States needed to use its weight to steer the UN in that direction. The *Afro-American*, for example, steadily questioned whether America was doing enough to help the Congolese escape their seventy-five years of oppression under the Belgians and accused the United States of merely working to protect its interests in Katanga. The paper in fact lumped together the United States and its Belgian "co-conspirators" and blasted "Belgian and American interests" for "desperately trying to continue their exploitation of Congo gold." Domestic and international events mutually reinforced each other in shaping black Americans' perceptions and their increasingly sharp critiques of global efforts to maintain white supremacy.[48]

Tensions at the UN came to a head over whether to seat the Lumumba or the Kasavubu delegation to the world body. On 8 November, Kasavubu addressed the General Assembly and proclaimed his right, as head of state, to name Congo's delegation. Lumumba supporters conversely argued that Lumumba still served as the duly elected prime minister with the support of an illegally dismissed parliament. On 22 November, intense lobbying by the

United States produced a 53–24 majority vote, with 19 abstentions, to seat the Kasavubu delegation.[49]

Five nights later Lumumba made his fatal decision to slip out of his house in Leopoldville and head toward Stanleyville, his base of power. Not until the next afternoon did anyone realize that he had left. According to a close colleague, the General Assembly vote to seat the Kasavubu delegation convinced Lumumba that the UN would no longer protect him, despite UN assurances that his status had not changed. Lumumba planned to stump the countryside and raise popular support to sweep himself back into power as the undisputed leader of the Congo. After four days of frantic searching, Mobutu's soldiers captured Lumumba and a number of his supporters.[50]

Kasavubu and Mobutu imprisoned Lumumba at the Thysville military base, where he once again worked his oratorical magic. On 13 January the garrison mutinied, demanding higher pay. Rumors spread that a freed Lumumba led the disaffected troops. But by evening, pay raises had quieted the troops, and Lumumba was back under lock and key. Kasavubu and his advisers decided to act. On 17 January they delivered Lumumba to Tshombe in Elizabethville, ostensibly to prevent any future escape. Katanga soldiers and their Belgian officers then murdered Lumumba and his two companions, most probably as soon as they arrived, and undoubtedly with the knowledge (and perhaps even the participation) of Tshombe and his Minister of the Interior Godefroid Munongo.[51]

For over three weeks Katanga officials kept up a smokescreen about the status of Lumumba. As rumors circulated, black Americans signed petitions demanding his release. Then, on 10 February, Katanga officials announced that Lumumba and his companions had overpowered their guards and escaped from prison. Any uncertainty about Lumumba's disappearance ended on 13 February when Katanga Radio announced that Lumumba and the others had been killed by unnamed hostile villagers. Munongo defiantly proclaimed, "If people accuse us of killing Lumumba, I will reply, 'Prove it.'" People throughout the world felt small need for proof; little doubt existed that Tshombe and his cohort had murdered Lumumba.[52]

Anger over the murder swept black America, which saw the charade for what it was. African Americans had any number of targets at which to aim their wrath. Few had any doubts about Belgian involvement. In the words of the *Defender*, Kasavubu and Mobutu were "two unconscionable puppets of the Belgian government — who should be liquidated as rank traitors."[53] African Americans also questioned the extent of U.S. involvement, with many condemning it for at minimum not pushing for better protection of Lumumba. The *Afro-American* went further, flatly blaming the United States for the death, arguing that Kasavubu and Mobutu acted as American stooges who delivered Lumumba into the hands of Tshombe.[54]

Citing its failure to protect Lumumba and end the Katanga secession, black Americans also directed their anger at the UN. The *Eagle*, while primarily blaming Tshombe, Mobutu, and Kasavubu for the murder, additionally criticized the UN for permitting the arrest of Lumumba and his transfer to Katanga. Others took even stronger positions on UN complicity. "His death was the international lynching of a black man on the altar of white supremacy," wrote James Hicks, the *Amsterdam News*'s executive editor. "The lynching was staged before the world under the auspices of the UN." Emmett Marshall wrote to the *Afro-American* that he believed Lumumba had been crucified on a cross of racism by the white world. He accused the UN not only of allowing Lumumba to fall into the hands of his enemies, but of being unable to stand up for justice for black men. The archivist and historian L. D. Reddick painted the scene in stark terms: "I feel that the UN was criminally negligent in not protecting him."[55]

African Americans clearly decried the circumstances surrounding Lumumba's death and worried that they would harm the march toward black freedom. "The Congo murder of Patrice Lumumba is as disturbing to colored Americans as it is to the diplomats of the United Nations," declared the Reverend Fred Shuttlesworth. "Becoming increasingly more interested in world affairs, and especially concerned and anxious about the progress of the newly emerging African nations, we view as alarming and despicable any developments or impediments which stand in their way of freedom, dignity, and unity." For Shuttlesworth and others, Lumumba was no remote figure in distant Africa, but part and parcel of the African American struggle against white supremacy. This view prevailed despite Lumumba's alleged communist ties. Indeed, many reiterated that Lumumba had been deliberately tarred with being a communist in an effort to remove him. The popular radio minister Bishop Smallwood Williams faulted U.S. officials for failing to see the difference between nationalism and neutralism on the one hand and communism on the other. He chastised them, too, for failing to realize that the similarity of African and Soviet policy statements stemmed from African influence on the communists, not the reverse. African Americans recognized that the anticommunist rhetoric used to smear and stifle legitimate avenues of protest and change in America was also being used in Africa.[56]

The slain Lumumba symbolized for broader black America the struggle of African nationalism and freedom against continued white exploitation and oppression. Even former critics praised him for refusing to compromise or diminish the Congo's freedom. Although not all felt at ease with his politics, black America largely embraced Lumumba as a martyr, praising his stand against continued Belgian exploitation and for a unified Congo. Mary Phillips of Lemont, Illinois, extolled his efforts in obtaining freedom from the Belgians, adding that branding Lumumba a communist could not change the fact that he was the legitimate ruler of the country. Eugene Johnson of New York City lauded Lumumba for refusing to accept independence with strings attached. Eduardo Sprinkle saluted Lumumba as a "savior" of Africa.[57]

The UN "Riots"

Demonstrations sparked by news of Lumumba's death erupted throughout the world. Thousands of people took to the streets in Brussels, Paris, London, Amsterdam, Moscow, Cairo, Accra, Washington, Chicago, and New York. Some Western commentators, pointing to Lumumba's leftist links, denounced the demonstrators as communist-inspired. This allegation enraged many African Americans. The *Defender* called the condemnations of pro-Lumumba demonstrations "a studied exaggeration, designed to smear all those who are in sympathy with Lumumba and the cause of African freedom." It pointed out that "The white press has always been quick to smear Negro leaders who dare speak out against social injustice, and who have the guts to denounce in forceful language the areas where democracy has failed." The *Defender* accepted that perhaps an element of Soviet activity might have been involved but argued that no evidence existed that the Soviets guided the protests. Rather, the demonstrations stood as a testimony to the "spirit, dedication and valor" of Lumumba.[58]

Two days after the announcement of Lumumba's death came the most dramatic demonstration by African Americans. The UN Security Council had been called into session to discuss the ramifications of Lumumba's death and the Soviet charges of Hammarskjöld's complicity in the murder. As Adlai Stevenson, President Kennedy's newly appointed ambassador to the UN, stood addressing the council, protesters took action. In the official version of events, repeated by the white press, approximately twenty-five African Americans had obtained public gallery tickets and had seated themselves inside when sixty more rushed in to join them in launching an angry, shouting demonstration. United Press International (UPI) reported that "[a] screaming group of men and women, most of them American Negroes . . . fought with guards with their fists and chains in a wild melee in the corridors." A group of them had broken through the back door "on signal," and those in the gallery "immediately joined the wild demonstration." *Newsweek* described "a flying wedge of some thirty Negroes [who] overpowered the two blue-uniformed U.N. guards and stormed through the entrance of the packed public gallery" to join about thirty others planted throughout the gallery. Black nationalists James Lawson and Daniel Watts, however, both disclaimed this version of events, instead claiming that the riot began when UN guards rushed demonstrators who stood up for a silent protest.

Whatever the spark, in the ensuing melee more than two dozen people, including eighteen guards, sustained injuries. The UN cleared visitors from all public sections and closed the building for the first time in its history. Demonstrations continued throughout the day. That evening approximately 200 demonstrators, mostly African Americans, marched along the north side of 42nd Street toward Times Square. When they refused a police order to halt, mounted police charged to disperse them. For two days the UN building remained closed. As a precaution when it reopened, two dozen New York Police Department detectives joined the security detail for the UN.[59]

Black nationalist figures and groups — such as James Lawson and the United African Nationalist Movement, Daniel Watts and the Liberation Committee for Africa, On Guard, the Cultural Association for the Women of African Heritage, the United Sons and Daughters of Africa, and the Universal African Legion — predominated among the demonstrators. Communists played little if any role; indeed, protesters actually prevented the black communist Benjamin Davis from joining the demonstrations.[60] However, in the rush to find communist involvement, critics overlooked the leading roles played by both black nationalists and community outrage. Press accounts painted the demonstrators as pro-communist lackeys willing to help the Soviets undermine the UN. The *New York Times* offered the most interesting bifurcated coverage. Although its reporting mentioned the nationalist groups involved, its editorial about the protests fixated on the communist angle: "The disgraceful scenes that took place at the visitors' gallery at the United Nations Security Council were in keeping with what the Communists and their dupes have been doing in widely separated parts of the world. They were not spontaneous. They were deliberate, organized, and apparently paid for." The *Times* offered no evidence for its accusations. The House Un-American Activities Committee (HUAC) believed it could remedy the lack of evidence and announced its intention to launch an investigation of the organizations involved in the demonstration to expose their communist inspiration.[61] The fact that disturbances occurred around the world could have been taken as powerful evidence of the depth of outrage over Lumumba's murder; yet instead of accepting this context, most white Americans viewed the demonstrations as evidence of a sinister Soviet plot. This portrayal not only obscured the depth of black anger and militancy, it also allowed Americans to avoid any examination of the deeper issues raised by the whole Congo crisis.

Not surprisingly, black Americans themselves differed in their views of the protests at the UN. Indeed, black responses to the UN demonstrations further demarcated the widening rifts within black America over the scope and meaning of the domestic freedom struggle, as well as over the relevancy of Africa.

Conservative voices, stressing their traditional Americanism and desire for full integration, focused intently on the issue of communism in the Congo and in the UN protests. This group recognized the pervasiveness of domestic anticommunism, and worried that the stain of communism would impede black progress in America. They never had felt comfortable with Lumumba's politics, and although they objected to his murder, they believed that the protesters' response to news of his death went too far. The *Daily World* called the "violent demonstration" nothing short of "a disgraceful spectacle which will not help the cause of our race." Echoing Washington's claim that the demonstrations obviously were well planned, because they took place exactly while Stevenson was at the podium, the *Daily World* concluded that communists had inspired the protests. The *Daily World* warned black Americans not to be duped by communists, and reminded readers that "those who create unnecessary tensions and disorders hurt our true interests and they should also remember such action aids the Communists." Others echoed these concerns. "The riot of American Negroes in the United Nations gallery aided the Communist agitation in the Congo and betrayed the cause of the Congolese," wrote John Henry to the *Amsterdam News*. He urged people to repudiate revolutionary violence and demagogues who "betray" the sure progress of minorities in America. An enduring faith that black Americans could achieve full citizenship by working within the structures of American society underscored such statements. Africa remained primarily a foreign land, most useful for prodding America to accelerate the pace of domestic change via the argument that America needed to improve its racial situation to prevent harming relations with the world's emerging nations.[62]

Yet conservative commentary carried far less weight in black America than that of the much more encompassing liberal civil rights leadership and supporters. Liberal activists had moved away from seeing events in Africa strictly in terms of the anticommunist paradigm. Emphasizing the importance of African independence movements and the broader struggle against white supremacy, they promoted an independent Africa and a U.S. policy supportive of black Africa. Still, while they deplored the murder of Lumumba, many of these liberal activists remained wary of black nationalism, leftism, and militancy. They worried about possible negative fallout from the actions of the demonstrators, and distanced themselves from the events at the UN. The prominence given to the alleged role of communists in the UN protests weighed heavily on their responses. Roy Wilkins's statement on behalf of the NAACP emphasized the shock and horror caused by the murder of Lumumba, pointing out, "It is natural that American Negroes should add their protest against those developments in the Congo which have produced a crime of this nature. Too many of our citizens and public officials have failed to appreciate the deep and warm feeling American Negroes have toward the efforts of Africans to achieve freedom from colonialism." Yet Wilkins then attempted to isolate the UN protests from mainstream black Americans: "Many reporting agencies, by labeling the disturbances at the United Nations February 15 as activity of 'U.S. Negroes,' created a misleading picture of the position of American Negro citizens. Observers, including New York police officials, estimated the number of demonstrators in the UN at less than 100. Obviously, this raucous handful cannot be said to represent either the sentiment or the tactics of American Negroes."[63]

Ralph Bunche and other prominent black Americans endorsed this position. Bunche deplored the riots, and tendered an apology to his UN colleagues for the conduct of his fellow citizens. Manhattan borough president Edward R. Dudley declared the demonstration "unwarranted and disgraceful." "This particular group no more represented the American Negroes[,] 20 million of them, than George Rockwell of the American Nazi Party represents 160,000,000 white Americans," wrote P. L. Prattis of the *Courier*. "Nor would have all Negroes embarrassed their country by staging a violent demonstration at the United Nations even though most Negroes probably deplore the murder of Patrice Lumumba."[64]

Yet with the engagement with contemporary Africa pushing African Americans to define and redefine their positions both on Africa and on domestic issues, many African Americans were moving farther and faster than the traditional civil rights leadership. Those who condemned the protesters faced an intense barrage of criticism from black Americans who were increasingly militant and focused on ties to Africa. A more militant black America could abide neither the slow pace of change at home nor the cornering and killing of Lumumba abroad. The liberation struggles in Africa had invigorated the belief in the intertwined fate of people of color throughout the world and had trained it particularly on Africa. "One wonders why you and other 'Negro leaders' who so quickly apologized for the protest said little or nothing about the part in which the west (United States, Belgium and the other western powers) played in the murder of Lumumba," Jimmy McDonald of New York wrote to Wilkins. He continued:

> To me, those who speak for me should be a part of the Negro community, and I don't mean in color, but in the aspirations of the Negro people. Such as the people who are going to jail in the South, the women who lay down in front of a train in South Africa, or who live in a tent in Fayetteville, and last but not least the child who goes to school under the protection of a Federal Marshal. In closing, sir, let me say that in the future when you are apologizing, do not attempt to apologize for the man on the block because we are tired of scratching when we don't itch, tired of laughing when we want to cry and moreover tired of saying yes when we mean NO.[65]

Bunche also received scathing attacks. Columnist James Hicks, declaring that while he did not approve of the actions at the UN he did not feel them unwarranted, condemned Bunche and all others who felt the need to apologize to white people for the demonstrations. His stance received ringing endorsement from readers of the *Amsterdam News*.[66] Others wrote directly to Bunche to make their feelings known. "Why apologize for the demonstration of your 'fellow citizens' at the U.N.?" queried Venia Stampers of Sacramento. "Why not apologize for your own 'scandalous conduct' — the betrayal of your black fellow man in helping the white man maintain his stronghold in the Congo." R. Weston of Philadelphia castigated Bunche as an Uncle Tom, declaring, "You, especially you, cannot call the black people to account for actions pursuant to the task of restoring to the ex(?)-slaves [sic] of the American master race the honor of an African heritage."[67]

Some within the civil rights leadership of course recognized the increasing militancy underway in black America, particularly in regard to Africa. Martin Luther King Jr., reflecting that African leaders were popular heroes on most black college campuses, observed that "many groups demonstrated or otherwise protested when the Congo leader, Patrice Lumumba, was assassinated" and charged that "the newspapers were mistaken when they interpreted these outbursts as 'Communist-inspired.' " Still, the Congo presented black Americans with a complex crisis that forced them to consider anew their relationship to Africa and, in doing so, clearly led to a widening of the already divergent views in black America's approach to modern Africa.[68]

The civil rights struggle in America was not monolithic, nor were views of the relationship with Africa. For black Americans, the exact meaning and importance of Africa varied, and the need to confront Lumumba's nationalism, leftism, and death helped to further demarcate differences. Conservative gradualists saw first and foremost communism and racialist nationalism and thus rejected Lumumba. Liberal, pragmatic activists embraced a free contemporary Africa yet struggled to balance the desire to support and promote an independent black Africa with wariness about Lumumba. An increasingly militant segment of black America found in Lumumba a black nationalist hero who had worked unwaveringly to save his country from Western economic exploitation, neocolonialism, and dismemberment — a view that reflected the rising tide of domestic militancy and interest in broader pan-African ties, which in coming years would seep more deeply into both cultural and political realms.

In the Wake of the Protests

As might be expected, any number of commentators in white America continued to minimize the growing restlessness and militancy in black America and the relationship of these sentiments to events in Africa. After the death of Lumumba, *Newsweek* purported to examine the meaning of the rise of independent black Africa to African Americans by conducting "scores" of interviews. After giving a short survey of responses, *Newsweek* blithely concluded, "Responsible Negroes want no part of the 'black nationalism' movements that have proliferated in the Negro community in recent years."[69]

James Baldwin eloquently exposed the fallacy of *Newsweek*'s position by bringing to light the depth and shape of African Americans' feelings in the wake of the UN demonstrations. Baldwin did not doubt that pro-communists and professional revolutionaries protested at the UN that day. He insisted, however, that this was not the most threatening concern; to the contrary, he wrote, "Their presence is not as frightening as the discontent which creates their opportunity. What I find appalling — and really dangerous — is the American assumption that the Negro is so contented with his lot here that only the cynical agents of a foreign power can rouse him to protest." Baldwin pointed out that when the South had trouble with black Americans, it blamed "outside" agitators and "Northern interference"; when the North had trouble, it blamed the Kremlin.

Baldwin identified a different source for the mounting unrest of black Americans: Africa. He noted that his generation had been taught to be ashamed of Africa, either directly, by being told it had never contributed anything to civilization, or indirectly, by watching "nearly half-naked, dancing, comic-opera cannibalistic savages in the movies." The younger generation, however, had witnessed the advent of Africa on the world stage. A free Africa destroyed the power of whites to control black American identities, "for it meant that they were not merely the descendants of slaves in a white, Protestant, and Puritan country; they were also related to kings and princes in an ancestral home, far away." "And this," Baldwin argued, "has proven to be a great antidote to the poison of self-hatred."[70]

For millions of black Americans, contemporary Africa became a positive inspiration. An expanded notion of ethnicity, encompassing blacks on both sides of the Atlantic, heightened both interest in and concern for the ancestral continent. Events in Africa held meaning, be they the joyful outpourings from African nations gaining independence or the painful, sometimes deadly, progress toward true freedom. If, historically, frustration and disillusionment had driven some African Americans to seek a stronger relationship with Africa, clearly now a new basis for the relationship pervaded broader black America. Disillusionment and anger with America certainly were involved, but beyond this the hope and pride generated by contemporary Africa resonated in black America.

At the same time, events in the Congo made it abundantly clear that Africa's new freedom remained tenuous at best. Neocolonial threats, Cold War maneuvering, and internal rivalries undermined the struggle of newly independent African countries to maintain real independence. Some African leaders increasingly turned to the Communist bloc for support; still others adopted totalitarian control. In the case of nations still seeking independence, the intransigence of remaining colonial regimes forced liberation struggles to ratchet ever higher their use of armed resistance, which likewise disposed many of them to turn to the Communist bloc. All this created dilemmas in black America and striking differences of opinion over the appropriate responses.

The Congo crisis became a crucial force, then, in helping frame African Americans' ensuing discourse about Africa. Even as the Congo crisis made plain that independent Africa posed enormous complexities, African Americans found that they could circumvent the knotty dilemmas by emphasizing instead the struggles of still-colonized Africa. The relatively straightforward, and of course still profoundly important, freedom struggles offered a clearer cast of heroes and villains. Furthermore, African Americans found that bringing attention to bear on liberation movements that were fighting readily identified proponents of white supremacy offered a much more effective rallying point than did independent countries that were struggling to combat subtler enemies — economic, political, and cultural conundrums that had no ready-made solutions. Unity in supporting African independence struggles came more easily when it was black versus white; indeed, that unity could even help hold together a splintering domestic civil rights struggle. In the years following Lumumba's murder, then, African Americans tended to focus on the travails of liberation struggles as opposed to the trials of newly independent Africa. Yet doing so meant that even as African Americans began to recognize the realities and intricacies of independent Africa, they found they could skirt full engagement with these complexities by focusing on ongoing liberation struggles.

EPILOGUE

When most of [the young Black students born during World War II] were finishing high school, Nkrumah was walking in the United States — tall, Black and proud. Sekou Touré, with his penetrating eyes, had said 'hell no' to Charles De Gaulle. Images of black men in flowing African robes, sitting at the United Nations and carrying on the business of their governments, had a profound effect on the consciousness of these Black babies born during World War II. These new African realities disproved the old Hollywood images of black people as servants of Tarzan and rifle carriers for the Europeans. A new generation of Blacks was emerging.

James Forman, High Tide of Black Resistance *(1967)*

Lumumba's death, of course, did not end the Congo crisis. For years to come the dizzying array of actors and events roiling the country would continue to wreak havoc on the lives of the Congolese people. Not until Mobutu launched his second coup in October 1965 did the situation stabilize, though at the cost of having a kleptocratic authoritarian install himself as president-for-life.

Four months after Mobutu's second takeover, a military coup in Ghana ousted Nkrumah from leadership. As the 1960s had progressed, Nkrumah faced troubles and challenges within Africa that had weakened his carefully cultivated image of "spokesman for Africa." His Pan-African political vision received little support among other African nations as they became independent. Indeed, just weeks after the Ivory Coast gained independence, Prime Minister Felix Houphouet-Boigny remonstrated that Nkrumah believed he had "descended to earth to liberate the African masses."[1] Few leaders of national liberation struggles willingly diluted the new powers that their nations had gained by enrolling in an inchoate, Ghana-centered, Pan-African structure. Even as Nkrumah's grandiose personal ambitions alienated him from other African leaders, he encountered mounting difficulties at home. These centered on the nation's deteriorating economy, his increasing authoritarianism, and his promoting a cult of personality. In February 1966, Nkrumah left Accra for Hanoi, via Beijing, on a peace mission to help end the Vietnam War. Less than a decade after Nkrumah's crowning glory of ringing in Ghana's independence, a military coup toppled him from power while he was out of the country. He died in exile, in Sekou Touré's Guinea, six years later. African Americans plainly faced new challenges in engaging contemporary Africa, confronting a varied, complex Africa in which sorting through the charges and countercharges among African rivals posed enormous difficulties.[2]

The ever-changing relationship of African Americans and Africa had undergone fundamental transformations between the 1930s and the 1960s. The expanded role and influence of contemporary Africa in African American lives can be traced back to black America's responses to the Italo-Ethiopian War, which had energized widespread African American interest in the continent and had broadened many black Americans' notions of ethnicity to include contemporary Africans. To advance their objectives, African Americans protested, lobbied, and worked with national governments and international organizations, thereby internationally politicizing their expanded constructions of identity. Still, change had not been universal, nor had it been immediate for all. Numerous debates continued to animate discourse about contemporary Africa. The cultural memory of a negatively stereotyped Africa, concern over where to focus energies and resources, the shape of America's domestic politics and foreign policy during the early Cold War — all these and more had shaped the evolving relationship. Yet African liberation struggles, particularly during the 1950s, had made a profound impression in African American minds, and events in Africa had reshaped the African American relationship with Africa. "The rise of the African peoples to the status of free nations has inspired Americans of African descent and others of our fellow citizens who love freedom for freedom's sake," wrote Roy Wilkins to Kwame Nkrumah and the All-African Peoples Conference at the end of 1958. "The emergence of independent African states and the struggle of other peoples to attain that state have aided us in our crusade in this country." Six months later, Martin Luther King Jr. told the publishers of *Dissent*, an African publication in Southern Rhodesia (Zimbabwe), "Although we are separated by many miles we are close together in a mutual struggle for freedom and human brotherhood. We realize that injustice anywhere is a threat to justice everywhere. Therefore, we are as concerned about the problems of Africa as we are about the problems of the United States."[3]

African Americans had turned to contemporary Africa and included it in their lives for a number of positive reasons: for the inspiration it provided for the struggle in America; for a sense of solidarity, be it from a common sense of oppression or from a shared heritage; for the pride and confidence that came from seeing black men and women win their freedom and run their own countries. Individuals weighed these reasons differently, but all contributed to Africa becoming a more celebrated part of African American lives. A transforming Africa had enabled black Americans to reject old negative images of Africa, rethink ideas about redeeming and uplifting Africa, and embrace contemporary Africa. Association with Africa reached new heights. The visible adoption of African dress and performance styles in the late 1960s reflected transformations that unfolded during the late 1950s and early 1960s.

Yet black America faced an Africa that continued to change, and in some respects it became even harder to address the new dynamics. As the list of assassinations and coups d'état in Africa grew longer and longer, African Americans faced questions they had trouble answering: as Nkrumah shifted from nonalignment toward the communist bloc, as he more stridently criticized the United States, and as he promoted an autocratic cult of personality, how should black America respond? In the wake of Nkrumah's overthrow, given the starkly contrasting images of Nkrumah as liberation leader and Pan-African icon with those of a corrupt, authoritarian megalomaniac, whom should African Americans support?

African Americans faced a situation in which failing to disaggregate Africa became increasingly problematic. The historic imagining of Africa as a more or less unified whole could not be sustained in a world of radical nationalists, authoritarian strongmen, military coups, and democratic hopefuls. Africa would not lend itself to undifferentiated views. Internecine African conflict particularly created problems. The clarity of vision when every right-thinking person favored the Ethiopians over the Italians could not be matched when Ethiopia claimed sovereignty over Eritrea and part of Somalia while the Eritreans and Somalis sought self-determination and independence. The dispute between the Ethiopians and the Eritreans festered for decades, periodically flaring with bloody violence: who should one support in such a conflict? Or, returning to the Congo, how should African Americans decide which faction to support in the ongoing turmoil in the post-Mobutu Congo?

The unrelenting complexities of independent Africa made it simpler to focus attention on the parts of Africa that seemingly offered fewer complications. As the 1960s moved into the 1970s and 1980s, African Americans attended most sharply to areas where black freedom fighters fought with whatever weapons they could muster against white minority regimes that used skullduggery and violence to hold onto white supremacy. Concentrating on nations still engaged in liberation struggles as opposed to already independent countries enabled African Americans to continue building transatlantic bridges while finessing the task of addressing the complexities of contemporary Africa.

Engaging an Africa that was still struggling for independence also helped build and sustain a broader coalition of forces in black America. As the 1960s progressed, the civil rights struggle faced enormous pressures, not only from outside the movement but from within it. Militants, liberal activists, and conservative gradualists had differing views on events in America. Africa had sharpened these differentiations as black Americans confronted the meanings and implications of African liberation movements for their own lives and struggle. The implications of the use of violence in particular had pushed African Americans in divergent directions. Yet Africa also could be used as a unifying force. People who differed over the course of the struggle in America or the source of the woes in independent Africa could rally together around the injustices in the parts of Africa still enduring white minority rule.

African Americans most obviously found common ground and worked collectively in the fight against apartheid. Indeed, as almost all the rest of Africa achieved independence and then struggled through seemingly intractable postcolonial problems, African Americans focused more and more on South Africa. In the 1980s and 1990s, black America stood in the vanguard of creating and sustaining the international antiapartheid campaigns of the day. African American political clout in fact became instrumental in getting sanctions against South Africa passed by Congress over the objections of President Reagan. It was during this time, too, that Nelson Mandela — the one-time radical with ties to Castro in Cuba and Qaddafi in Libya, the one-time leader of the ANC's armed wing, Umkonto we Sizwe, the once nearly forgotten prisoner — became a legend who bridged all divides in black America.

Mandela's name resonated throughout America, black and white, drawing out people from the leadership and from the street in praise and support of this man. Mandela's triumphal visit to the United States in 1990 marked an especially moving moment in black America's embrace of contemporary Africa. For black America, Mandela transcended being an African leader and became an African American leader as well. Receiving Mandela as one of their own, African Americans saw him presenting to white America a symbol not only of what an African could be but of what an African American could be. Then, nearly a century after Ethiopian Emperor Menelik II's 1896 defeat of the Italians at Adowa, a turning point that had kept alive the flame of African independence in the country with which African Americans would begin to forge a new relationship with contemporary Africa, Mandela's 1994 election as president of South Africa signaled the formal culmination of Africa's political liberation from white supremacy.

Yet even as Mandela became the emblem of a free Africa and the apotheosis of African American dreams about contemporary Africa, his triumph also marked the last point at which African Americans could focus on the appealing simplicity of black and white politics in Africa. With black majority rule coming at last to this final white supremacist state, African Americans found they no longer could channel their focus away from the complex political, social, and economic realities of contemporary Africa. African Americans, having recast their relationship with contemporary Africa in the middle of the twentieth century, found at the end of the century that a new chapter had opened as they engaged a fully independent, ever-changing Africa.

NOTES

Abbreviations

BSCP Records	Records of the Brotherhood of Sleeping Car Porters, Library of Congress, Washington, D.C.
DF	Decimal File, subdivision of Central Files, RG 59
Drake Papers	St. Clair Drake Papers, Schomburg Center for Research in Black Culture, New York
Du Bois Papers	*Papers of W. E. B. Du Bois*, microfilm collection of W. E. B. Du Bois papers
FRUS	*Foreign Relations of the United States*, document collection of the U.S. Department of State
GOF	General Office File, subdivision of NAACP/LC
Hunton Papers	William Alphaeus Hunton Papers, Schomburg Center for Research in Black Culture, New York
LC	Library of Congress, Washington, D.C.
MLK/BU	Martin Luther King Jr. Papers, Mugar Memorial Library, Boston University, Boston, Mass.
NAACP/LC	Papers of the National Association for the Advancement of Colored People, Library of Congress, Washington, D.C.
NAACP Papers	*Papers of the National Association for the Advancement of Colored People*, microfilm collection of NAACP
NUL Records	Records of the National Urban League, Library of Congress, Washington, D.C.
Randolph Papers	*Papers of A. Philip Randolph*, microfilm collection of A. Philip Randolph papers
RG 59	Record Group 59, U.S. Department of State Records, National Archives, Washington, D.C.
Schomburg CCF	*Schomburg Center Clipping File*, microfiche collection of Schomburg Center for Research in Black Culture, New York

Note: Citations to microfilm sources include reel and frame numbers, separated by a slash (e.g., *Randolph Papers*, 3/442–43). Citations to the *NAACP Papers* include part number, supplement or series number (if any), and reel/frame numbers (e.g., *NAACP Papers* 11, ser. A, 30/701; *NAACP Papers* 1, 1951–55 suppl., 5/182).

Introduction

1. "Helping Ethiopia," Editorial, *Pittsburgh Courier*, 20 July 1935, 10.

2. "The *Courier* Salutes Ghana," Editorial, *Pittsburgh Courier*, 9 Mar. 1957, Ghana Suppl., 1.

3. Ndibe, "Can African Americans Save Africa?"

4. See, for example, George Fredrickson's *Black Liberation* and his earlier *White Supremacy* and James Campbell's *Songs of Zion*.

5. Two of the most important books are Brenda Gayle Plummer's *Rising Wind: Black Americans and U.S. Foreign Affairs, 1935–1960*, which masterfully surveys the breadth of African American involvement with foreign affairs during these years, and Penny Von Eschen's impressive and incisive *Race against Empire: Black Americans and Anticolonialism, 1937–1957*, which reconstructs a vital slice of diasporic intellectual and political engagement with the fight against imperialism. Other important works in the limited yet expanding literature include Tyson, *Radio Free Dixie*; Borstelmann, *Apartheid's Reluctant Uncle*; Dudziak, "Josephine Baker, Racial Protest, and the Cold War"; Skinner, *African Americans and U.S. Policy toward Africa*; De-Conde, *Ethnicity, Race, and American Foreign Policy*; Lauren, *Power and Prejudice*; Dudziak, "Desegregation as a Cold War Imperative"; Horne, *Black and Red*; Hunt, *Ideology and U.S. Foreign Policy*.

6. A sampling of sources that propound this thesis includes Jacobs, *African Nexus*, 5; Anosike, "Africa and Afro-Americans"; W. B. Helmreich, *Afro-Americans and Africa*, xxi; Weisbord, *Ebony Kinship*, 211; Redkey, *Black Exodus*, 1; Hill and Kilson, *Apropos of Africa*, 3; Emerson, *Africa and United States Policy*, 53; Emerson and Kilson, "The American Dilemma in a Changing World," 1079.

7. Lemann, "Black Nationalism on Campus," 32; Duignan and Gann, *United States and Africa*, 251.

8. Finkle, "Conservative Aims of Militant Rhetoric," 693–94; "The Negro in Print," *Newsweek*, 19 Apr. 1954, 96. In the late 1950s, circulation started suffering due to competition from large metropolitan papers that increasingly targeted black readers and hired away the best journalists, from the growing numbers of magazines aimed at African Americans, and from the charms of television. In the 1960s, readership declined further, as the mainstream press did not always reflect the heightened militancy of many African Americans; in contrast, circulation of alternative publications such as the *Black Panther* and *Muhammad Speaks* rose sharply. Hogan, *Black National News Service*, 235–36; Wolseley, *Black Press*, 56.

9. Myrdal, *American Dilemma*, 909, 923–24.

10. W. E. B. Du Bois, "The American Negro Press," *Chicago Defender*, 20 and 27 Feb. 1943, 13; Myrdal, *An American Dilemma*, 909–10; Lee, "Does the Negro Press Speak for Most Negroes?"

Prologue

1. Moses, *Wings of Ethiopia*, 141, 154.

2. Ibid., 154–55, quote on 155; Moses, *Afrotopia*, 26; Campbell, *Songs of Zion*, 74–75; Fredrickson, *Black Liberation*, 67–69. For fuller treatments of Blyden and Crummell, see Lynch, *Edward Wilmot Blyden*; Moses, *Alexander Crummell*.

3. Campbell, *Songs of Zion*, 96. See also Gaines, "Black Americans' Racial Uplift Ideology as 'Civilizing Mission'"; Redkey, "The Meaning of Africa to Afro-Americans," 11–19.

4. Campbell, *Songs of Zion*, 74.

5. Fredrickson, *Black Liberation*, 61–80, Turner quote on 78; Campbell, *Songs of Zion*, 77–88; Moses, *Golden Age of Black Nationalism*, 202–3; Redkey, *Black Exodus*. Other emigration activists included, for example, Chief Alfred Sam, who organized emigrants from the all-black towns of Oklahoma. His efforts created a wide stir in these areas, and, with his direction, in 1913 and 1914 several score of African Americans went to Africa. R. A. Hill, "Before Garvey: Chief Alfred Sam and the African Movement."

6. Campbell, *Songs of Zion*, 83; Turner quoted in Redkey, "The Meaning of Africa to Afro-Americans," 16. See also Fredrickson, *Black Liberation*, 75–80; W. L. Williams, *Black Americans and the Evangelization of Africa*, esp. 85–124; Angell, *Bishop Henry McNeal Turner and African-American Religion in the South*.

7. Fredrickson, *Black Liberation*, 55–56, quote on 56.

8. Crummell quoted in W. L. Williams, *Black Americans and the Evangelization of Africa*, 134; Gaines, "Black Americans' Racial Uplift Ideology as 'Civilizing Mission'"; Fredrickson, *Black Liberation*, 69, 79; Campbell, *Songs of Zion*, 84–86; Plummer, *Rising Wind*, 12.

9. Quoted in McCarthy, *Dark Continent*, 77–78. For more on literature catering to and buttressing stereotypes, see Hickey and Wylie, *An Enchanting Darkness*, 179–233; Borstelmann, *Apartheid's Reluctant Uncle*, 9; Gruesser, *White on Black*.

10. McCarthy, *Dark Continent*, xvi–xvii; Roosevelt, *African Game Trails*, x, 2. For more on travelers' accounts, see Hickey and Wylie, *An Enchanting Darkness*, 135–73, esp. 156–59 on Roosevelt.

11. Quote in Hickey and Wylie, *An Enchanting Darkness*, 135; McCarthy, *Dark Continent*, 5.

12. W. L. Williams, *Black Americans and the Evangelization of Africa*, 104–24, quotes on 105, 107.

13. Quoted in Isaacs, *New World of Negro Americans*, 128. This book has flaws and should be used carefully. The interviews never appear as a whole, so the context cannot be verified; also, the interviews were neither systematic nor representative of black America as a whole. However, the book provides a valuable record of leading black Americans' reactions to Africa as the relationship underwent fundamental changes. For more on African American reactions to missionary accounts, see Logan,

"The American Negro's View of Africa," 218; Chick, "American Negroes' Changing Attitude toward Africa," 532.

14. See Isaacs, *New World of Negro Americans*, 170–80, quote on 170. For more on movies creating negative images of Africa, see Borstelmann, *Apartheid's Reluctant Uncle*, 9.

15. For reproductions of textbook pictures of "The Races of Man," see Hunt, *Ideology and U.S. Foreign Policy*, 49–50.

16. P. L. Prattis, "Sociological Aspects of the Newly-Emerging Nations in Africa," 1961, box 144–20, folder 6 "Speeches," Prattis Papers, Moorland-Spingarn Research Center, Howard University, Washington, D.C.; Isaacs, *New World of Negro Americans*, 9. See also McCarthy, *Dark Continent*, 126–34.

17. For a discussion of the usage of the term "tribe" in relation to modern Africa, see "If It's Africa, This Must Be a Tribe," *Africa News* 33 (18 June 1990): 13.

18. Hansberry quoted in Isaacs, *New World of Negro Americans*, 285. Another person recalled, "The worst thing anybody could say to you in addition to calling you a 'black nigger' was 'black African'" (171).

19. Du Bois, *The World and Africa*, viii. See Rogers, *World's Great Men of Color*; Rogers, *100 Amazing Facts about the Negro*. For a recent article discussing these men and other African American scholars who held transnational historical perspectives during this era, see Kelley, "But a Local Phase of a World Problem."

20. Marable, "Pan-Africanism of W. E. B. Du Bois," 196. Examining what he terms the "scholar's dilemma" in African American writing about Africa, Elliott Skinner finds a continuing tension between two types of work: that with an ethical neutrality at its core and that with a desire to defend and promote the accomplishments of Africa. Skinner, "Afro-Americans in Search of Africa." See also Moses, *Afrotopia*, 21–23. For a recent version of this debate about scholarship in black studies, see Henry Louis Gates Jr., "A Call to Protect Academic Integrity from Politics," and Manning Marable, "A Plea That Scholars Act Upon, Not Just Interpret, Events," *New York Times*, 4 Apr. 1998, B11–B13.

21. Defining the exact nature of pan-Africanism sparks scholarly disagreement. The differentiation George Shepperson made in 1962 between Pan-Africanism as a politically oriented unification movement and pan-Africanism as a cultural and intellectual drive to promote memories of African origins and solidarity among African peoples serves as a useful reference point. While any choice has its trade-offs, this book uses "pan-Africanism" as a broadly inclusive term for the interconnectedness of diasporic communities and "Pan-Africanism" to refer more specifically to politically oriented movements, as in the formal Pan-African Congresses. See Drake, "Diaspora Studies and Pan-Africanism," 349–59; Geiss, *Pan-African Movement*, 3–8; Esedebe, *Pan-Africanism*, 1–3.

22. Du Bois, "The Conservation of Races," (1897), in Foner, *W. E. B. Du Bois Speaks*, 73–85, quotes on 79, 81; Fredrickson, *Black Liberation*, 72–74.

23. Du Bois, "The Conservation of Races," 79.

24. Du Bois, *Darkwater*, 68. In a 1944 article surveying historical developments in

the struggle for black freedom, Du Bois wrote of the 1920s that he "had emerged with a program of Pan-Africanism, as organized protection of the Negro world led by American Negroes." It would be the following year, at the 1945 Manchester Pan-African Congress, that the reality of Africans leading their own struggles fully hit Du Bois. Du Bois, "My Evolving Program for Negro Freedom," 60.

25. Fredrickson, *Black Liberation*, 149–51; quotes on 150. On Du Bois and his efforts at the Versailles Peace Conference, see also Marable, "Pan-Africanism of W. E. B. Du Bois," 199–202; Plummer, *Rising Wind*, 15–19; Lewis, *W. E. B. Du Bois*, 561–80; Fierce, *Pan-African Idea in the United States*, 208–14; Geiss, *Pan-African Movement*, 234–40.

26. For more on Du Bois and the Pan-African Congresses of the early 1900s, see Lewis, *W. E. B. Du Bois*, 248–51, 561–78; Marable, "Pan-Africanism of W. E. B. Du Bois," 202–8; Marable, *W. E. B. Du Bois*, 99–107, 119–20; Fierce, *Pan-African Idea in the United States*, 199–214; Geiss, *Pan-African Movement*, 176–98, 234–62.

27. "Constitution of the Universal Negro Improvement Association," in Hill and Kilson, *Apropos of Africa*, 185; Drake, "Diaspora Studies and Pan-Africanism," 353; Fredrickson, *Black Liberation*, 152–61.

28. Boley, *Liberia*, 32–44.

29. Ibid., 45–60; Schuyler, *Slaves Today*; Plummer, *Rising Wind*, 225.

30. Over time, a number of scholars have commented on how the overwhelming nature of the primitive images of Africa caused black Americans to react negatively to the continent. See, for example, McCarthy, *Dark Continent*, 146–47; Emerson, "Race in Africa," 169; Hooker, "The Negro American Press and Africa in the 1930s," 44–45; Emerson and Kilson, "The American Dilemma in a Changing World," 1061; Farmer, "An American Leader's View of African Unity," 71; Isaacs, *New World of Negro Americans*, 105–7; Ivy, "Traditional NAACP Interest in Africa," 230.

31. W. E. B. Du Bois, "A Forum of Fact and Opinion," *Pittsburgh Courier*, 25 Apr. 1936, sec. 2, 1.

32. Fredrickson, *Black Liberation*, 5–6, 26.

33. Bunche quoted in Urquhart, *Ralph Bunche*, 55; Robeson quoted in Stuckey, *Slave Culture*, 339.

34. Floyd Calvin, "Ethiopian Crisis Gives Race Stake in Internationalism," *Pittsburgh Courier*, 14 Sept. 1935, 5.

Chapter One

1. Ottley, *"New World A-Coming,"* 111.

2. Franklin and Moss, *From Slavery to Freedom*, 385. Historians from John Hope Franklin to John Henrik Clarke have argued that the Italo-Ethiopian War made black Americans more internationally minded. See Clarke, *Marcus Garvey and the Vision of Africa*, 326–27.

3. Emperor Menelik II died in 1913. His grandson, Lidj Yasu, then ruled, but a group of leading Ethiopians overthrew him in 1916 in favor of Menelik's daughter,

Zauditu. Selassie became Prince Regent at that time, and when Zauditu died in 1930, Selassie proclaimed himself emperor. However, because Selassie had no close blood relationship to Menelik, some Ethiopians favored continuing the line of descent through closer relatives of Menelik. Coffey, *Lion by the Tail*, 11–12.

4. Kelley, "This Ain't Ethiopia, But It'll Do," 16.

5. For a thorough and thoughtful discussion of the U.S.-Ethiopian exchanges, see J. E. Harris, *African-American Reactions to War in Ethiopia*, 1–18, quote on 11.

6. In a sermon delivered at a meeting of the Fraternal Council of Negro Churches in Cleveland, Ohio, Bishop James Bray of the Colored Methodist Episcopal Church preached that the Ark of the Covenant lay in Ethiopia. "Ethiopia: A Challenge to World Christianity," 21 Aug. 1935, *Schomburg CCF*, 001,654-2.

7. Raboteau, *Fire in the Bones*, 42–43; Forrest Cozart, New York, to the Editor, *Baltimore Afro-American*, 30 Nov. 1935, 4. For helpful interpretations of religious connections, see Scott, *Sons of Sheba's Race*, 10–17; and J. E. Harris, *African-American Reactions to War in Ethiopia*, 19–20.

8. Francis Baker to the Editor, *Baltimore Afro-American*, 3 Aug. 1935, 6; "Did Haile Selassie Pray Too Much?" *Atlanta Daily World*, 9 May 1936, 2. See also Barney Page, Chicago, to the Editor, *Chicago Defender*, 14 Sept. 1935, 16; and James Webb, Chicago, to the Editor, *Chicago Defender*, 1 Feb. 1936, 16.

9. "Is Ethiopia Stretching Forth Her Hand?" *Chicago Defender*, 20 July 1935, 10; "Race Churches Protest Aggression of Mad Italy," *Chicago Defender*, 27 July 1935, 24; "Race Churchdom Protests Aggression by Italians," *Chicago Defender*, 3 Aug. 1935, 24; "Beale Street Has All-Night Prayer for Ethiopia," *Baltimore Afro-American*, 3 Aug. 1935, 2; "Church News," *New York Amsterdam News*, 3 Aug. 1935, 6; "Black Peoples Learn of True Racial Status," *Chicago Defender*, 4 Jan. 1936, 1; "Ethiopia Gets Check for $100 from Pilgrim," *Chicago Defender*, 11 Jan. 1936, 24; "Ethiopian Envoy Insulted by Two Chicago Hotels; Barred," *Chicago Defender*, 1 Feb. 1936, 1; Walter Blair, Harlem, to the Editor, *New York Amsterdam News*, 7 Mar. 1936, 12; "Churches Giving Ethiopians Help," *New York Amsterdam News*, 18 Apr. 1936, 11; "Churchmen Denounce Mussolini War Policy," *Pittsburgh Courier*, 31 Aug. 1935, sec. 2, 10; "Baptists Ask Government to Save Ethiopia," *Pittsburgh Courier*, 14 Sept. 1935, sec. 2, 10; "Baptists Ask U.S. to Help Halt Il Duce," *New York Amsterdam News*, 7 Sept. 1935, 1; "Ethiopia Seeks Negro Doctors," *New York Amsterdam News*, 20 July 1935, 1.

10. "Troops Mass for War," *Chicago Defender*, 13 July 1935, 1. For a brief period before the war started, some black Americans believed that Japan would enter the conflict decisively on Ethiopia's behalf.

11. "Rocking the Cradle of Christianity," Editorial, *Atlanta Daily World*, 5 Oct. 1935, 4; "Italians Beaten, Flee," *Baltimore Afro-American*, 18 Jan. 1936, 1; B. B. Susaye to the Editor, *Chicago Defender*, 4 July 1936, 16.

12. Bethune Robinson to the Editor, *Pittsburgh Courier*, 25 Jan. 1936, sec. 2, 2; Alexander Keys to the Editor, *Chicago Defender*, 9 Nov. 1935, 16. See also the following letters to the editor: Edward Jones, Philadelphia, *Baltimore Afro-American*,

28 Sept. 1935, 6; G.E.L., Los Angeles, *Pittsburgh Courier*, 18 Jan. 1936, 10; Mabel Gully, Denver, *Pittsburgh Courier*, 29 Feb. 1936, 10; William Gilliam, Seattle, *Pittsburgh Courier*, 28 Mar. 1936, 10; W. Linton Blair, Harlem, *New York Amsterdam News*, 2 May 1936, 12.

13. Cable Lockey to the Editor, *Chicago Defender*, 24 Aug. 1935, 16. For examples of other letters to the editor referring to Ethiopians as "brothers," see W. A. Domingo, Harlem, *New York Amsterdam News*, 20 July 1935, 12; Frank Ferrell, *Chicago Defender*, 14 Sept. 1935, 24; Eugene Williams, Pratt City, Ala., *Chicago Defender*, 23 Nov. 1936, 16; Thornton Wester, Cleveland, *Pittsburgh Courier*, 27 July 1935, sec. 2, 2; Willie Berry, Birmingham, *Pittsburgh Courier*, 21 Sept. 1935, sec. 2, 2; Charles Harris, Philadelphia, *Pittsburgh Courier*, 18 Jan. 1936, sec. 2, 2; Benjamin Hawkins, Trenton, *Pittsburgh Courier*, 2 May 1936, sec. 2, 2; William Atkinson, Bridgeport, Conn., *Pittsburgh Courier*, 2 May 1936, sec. 2, 2; Margurite Cole, Paducah, *Pittsburgh Courier*, 20 June 1936, 10; Mason White, Washington D.C., *Baltimore Afro-American*, 30 Nov. 1935, 4; Mrs. Janie Davis, Jonesboro, N.C., *Baltimore Afro-American*, 16 May 1936, 4.

14. A Constant Reader to the Editor, *Pittsburgh Courier*, 30 Nov. 1935, sec. 2, 2; Harry Rooks, Omaha, to the Editor, *Chicago Defender*, 2 Nov. 1935, 16; Mrs. Wimley Thompson to the Editor, *Chicago Defender*, 10 Aug. 1935, 16.

15. On whites spreading such ideas, see Scott, *Sons of Sheba's Race*, 19, 32; J. E. Harris, *African-American Reactions to War in Ethiopia*, 1.

16. "War Pictures Show Up the Scientists," Editorial, *Baltimore Afro-American*, 16 Nov. 1935, 6; Du Bois, "Inter-Racial Implications of the Ethiopian Crisis," 83. Every newspaper discussed this issue. See, for example, "Ethiopia Scotches a Lie," Editorial, *Pittsburgh Courier*, 30 Nov. 1935, 10; "J. A. Rogers Tells Why We Should Help Ethiopia," *Pittsburgh Courier*, 20 July 1935, 4; "Rugged Ethiopian Hills to Halt Italy — Rogers," *Pittsburgh Courier*, 11 Jan. 1936, 6; "Are Ethiopians Colored?" Editorial, *Baltimore Afro-American*, 12 Oct. 1935, 6.

17. Actions by some African Americans in Ethiopia apparently constituted a secondary problem. Col. John Robinson, the black American aviator who traveled to Ethiopia to aid its cause, wrote to Claude Barnett, head of the Associated Negro Press, "I really believe that the higher Abyssinian wants the American Negro but [Hubert] Julian, Dr. Young, and Dr. Mest have made some bad examples." John Robinson to Claude Barnett, 3 June 1935, box 170, folder 9, Claude A. Barnett Papers, Chicago Historical Society, Chicago.

18. The debate over the race of the Ethiopians and whether Ethiopians, specifically the Amharic elite, rejected a racial affinity to African Americans has a related scholarly counterpart. William R. Scott argues that this was a major controversy during the war and devotes one of three parts in his book to the issue. Scott argues that the controversy raged unresolved throughout and long after the end of the war and that it proved deleterious to pro-Ethiopian relief efforts. Scott, *Sons of Sheba's Race*, 165.

However, Scott's support for this argument rests largely on the responses of three suspect witnesses: Hubert Julian, the disgraced aviator who after his departure from

Ethiopia soon found his way to Italy; Marcus Garvey, who came to personally despise Selassie, perhaps because he saw himself being eclipsed by Selassie as a race leader in the minds of many blacks; and Willis Huggins, a stalwart Garveyite whom Scott himself implicates for skimming donations for Ethiopia for his own personal use. On the whole, Scott offers little evidence of African Americans actually being alienated by Ethiopian attitudes toward them. To the contrary, during the war years one finds much evidence to refute the idea of this being a deleterious controversy. On this score, Joseph E. Harris offers much in establishing links between Ethiopians and African Americans in his book, *African-American Reactions to War in Ethiopia*, esp. 153–59.

19. See Wesley Freeman, Palestine, Tex., to the Editor, *Pittsburgh Courier*, 11 Apr. 1936, 12; Eugene Dodson, Kansas City, to the Editor, *Pittsburgh Courier*, 16 May 1936, sec. 2, 2; James Taylor, Huntington, W.Va., to the Editor, *Baltimore Afro-American*, 28 Dec. 1935, 6.

20. For more on the lack of influence by African Americans, see Challenor, "Influence of Black Americans on U.S. Foreign Policy toward Africa"; Skinner, "Black Leaders as Foreign Policymakers"; M. D. Morris, "Black Americans and the Foreign Policy Process"; Duignan and Gann, *United States and Africa*, 344–49.

21. Schraeder, *U.S. Foreign Policy toward Africa*, 2–5; Dickson, *U.S. Foreign Policy towards Sub-Saharan Africa*, 3.

22. Chief of the Division of Near Eastern Affairs (Murray) to the Under Secretary of State (Phillips), 17 Dec. 1934, *FRUS*, 1934, 2:768–69; Secretary of State (Hull) to the Chargé in Ethiopia (George), 18 Dec. 1934, *FRUS*, 1934, 2:769–70. For Secretary of State Cordell Hull's account of and reasoning behind skirting involvement in mediating the clash, see Hull, *Memoirs*, 1:418–43.

23. For details on the maneuvering involved in the Neutrality Acts of 1935 and 1936 and of Roosevelt's response to the Italo-Ethiopian crisis, see Dallek, *Franklin D. Roosevelt and American Foreign Policy*, 101–21. See also Hull, *Memoirs*, 1:410, 467–68.

24. Cornelius Williams to Franklin D. Roosevelt, 31 July 1935, RG 59, DF 1930–39, 884.113/99.

25. Walter White to Cordell Hull, Secretary of State, 21 Mar. and 11 Apr. 1935, *NAACP Papers* 11, ser. A, 30/579, 583.

26. Resolution on Italy and Ethiopia, 1935 Annual Conference, *NAACP Papers* 1, 9/852; Monthly Report by Walter White, Executive Secretary, July 1935, *NAACP Papers* 1, 5/1888; NAACP Press Release, 3 July 1935, *NAACP Papers* 11, ser. A, 30/683.

27. Secretary of State to Chargé in Ethiopia (George), 5 July 1935, *FRUS*, 1935, 1:725.

28. Walter White to Rayford Logan, 8 July 1935, *NAACP Papers* 11, ser. A, 30/695; Memorandum from White to the Board of Directors, 9 July 1935, ibid., 30/701; White to Manley Hudson, 10 July 1935, ibid., 30/702; Raymond Leslie Buell, President of the Foreign Policy Association, to White, ibid., 30/717.

29. Memorandum from Walter White to Charles Houston and Roy Wilkins,

15 July 1935, *NAACP Papers* 11, ser. A, 30/718; Wilkins to White, 16 July 1935, ibid., 30/721; Houston to White, 16 July 1935, ibid., 30/723; Lewis Gannett to Walter White, 15 July 1935, ibid., 30/742; Rayford Logan to White, 16 July 1935, ibid., 30/740; Manley Hudson to White, 25 July 1935, ibid., 30/768.

30. Secretary's Report for July 1935, *NAACP Papers* 1, 5/1895.

31. Memorandum from Walter White to Roy Wilkins, 12 July 1935, *NAACP Papers* 11, ser. A, 30/689; Walter White to Cordell Hull, 17 July 1935, ibid., 30/733; "Aid for Ethiopia," *New York Amsterdam News*, 13 July 1935, 12; State Department to Walter White, *NAACP Papers* 11, ser. A, 30/750; Memorandum by the Secretary of State, 22 Nov. 1935, *FRUS*, 1935, 1:826–33.

32. On Huggins's trip, see Ross, "Black Americans and Haiti, Liberia, the Virgin Islands, and Ethiopia," 338–39. On NAACP contact with the League, see, for example, NAACP to the League of Nations, 12 Apr. 1935, *NAACP Papers* 11, ser. A, 30/594; NAACP to the League of Nations, 13 Dec. 1935, *NAACP Papers* 11, ser. A, 30/886.

33. Walter White to Maxim Litvinov, USSR Foreign Secretary, *NAACP Papers* 11, ser. A, 30/628; White to Miss Frances Williams and Charles Houston, 11 June 1935, ibid., 30/650–51. For more on the NAACP pressure and the Soviet position, see Scott, *Sons of Sheba's Race*, 124–27; and Plummer, *Rising Wind*, 49–50.

34. William Bullitt, Ambassador to the USSR, to Cordell Hull, 6 July 1935, RG 59, DF 1930–39, 765.84/451; Secretary of State to Chargé in Ethiopia (Engert), 12 Sept. 1935, *FRUS*, 1935, 1:751–52; Secretary of State to Ambassador in the United Kingdom (Bingham), 27 Sept. 1935, *FRUS*, 1935, 1:767–68.

35. Secretary of State to Ambassador in the United Kingdom (Bingham), 14 Oct. 1935, *FRUS*, 1935, 1:775–76.

36. Murray for the Secretary of State to Mr. Kepler Hoyt, 29 Jan. 1936, *FRUS*, 1936, 3:40–41; Chargé in Ethiopia (Engert) to Secretary of State, 29 Jan. 1936, ibid., 3:42; Chargé in Ethiopia (Engert) to Secretary of State, 12 Feb. 1936, ibid., 3:42–48; Minister Resident in Ethiopia (Engert) to Secretary of State, 20 Mar. 1936, and Secretary of State to Minister Resident in Ethiopia, 27 Mar. 1936, ibid., 3:50–51.

37. "Helping Ethiopia," Editorial, *Pittsburgh Courier*, 20 July 1935, 10.

38. "Why Go to Ethiopia?" Editorial, *Chicago Defender*, 27 July 1935, 1. Other papers also opposed aid for Ethiopia. The *Daily World* proclaimed the raising of money for Ethiopia to be "alright for sentimental purposes" but wrong to do, because it did not jibe with Roosevelt's call for strict neutrality. "The Negro in This Italo-Ethiopian Crisis," Editorial, *Atlanta Daily World*, 20 Oct. 1935, 4.

39. "God Needs No Poison Gas; Deacon Prays for Ethiopia," *Baltimore Afro-American*, 24 Aug. 1935, 5; Kelly, Buffalo, N.Y., to the Editor, *Baltimore Afro-American*, 7 Sept. 1935, 6; "Watching the Big Parade," *Baltimore Afro-American*, 12 Oct. 1935, 6.

40. "Rhino-Eating Tribe Armed by Selassie," *Baltimore Afro-American*, 7 Sept. 1935, 3; "Italy Termed Baby Killer," *Baltimore Afro-American*, 26 Oct. 1935, 1; "Ethiopian Wounded Flee Red Cross Hospitals," *Baltimore Afro-American*, 4 Jan.

1936, 3; "First and Exclusive Pictures from a Grim and Threatening Battle Front," *Pittsburgh Courier*, 10 Aug. 1935, sec. 2, 1; "Law of Self-Preservation Forces Ethiopia into War," *New York Amsterdam News*, 12 Oct. 1935, 5; "Poking Fun," *Atlanta Daily World*, 1 Nov. 1935, 6. For cartoons, see, for example, "Bungleton Green" in the *Chicago Defender* during the month of September 1935.

41. "Ethiopia, the Golden Calf," Editorial, *Chicago Defender*, 2 Nov. 1935, 16. The following year the *Defender* began a new advertising campaign that promoted its widespread distribution. The hook read, "Subscribe NOW . . . for the *Chicago Defender* — The Only Race Newspaper Circulated in Every Civilized Country in the World." The *Chicago Defender* did not circulate much in Africa. Advertisement in the *Crisis*, Oct. 1936, 290.

42. Carrie Wilkins Elliott to the Editor, *Baltimore Afro-American*, 27 July 1935, 4; Harry Douglass, Jackson, Mississippi, to the Editor, *Pittsburgh Courier*, 6 July 1935, sec. 2, 2.

43. William Bishop to the Editor, *Baltimore Afro-American*, 24 Aug. 1935, 6; Frank St. Clair, Chicago, to the Editor, *Baltimore Afro-American*, 28 Sept. 1935, 6; Thomas Smith, Bethlehem, Pa., to the Editor, *Baltimore Afro-American*, 18 Jan. 1936, 6; Taschereau Arnold, "It's Now Time to Look at Ourselves," *Atlanta Daily World*, 2 Nov. 1935, 2. See also the following letters to the editor of the *Baltimore Afro-American*: Joseph Hardesty, Annapolis, 10 Aug. 1935, 4; Meeba Ficklin, St. Louis, 24 Aug. 1935, 4; Eugene Ely, Baltimore, 21 Sept. 1935, 6; and Raymond Watkins to the Editor, *Chicago Defender*, 21 Dec. 1935, 16.

44. "The Negro in This Italo-Ethiopian Crisis," Editorial, *Atlanta Daily World*, 20 Oct. 1935, 4.

45. " 'Bomber' Is Best Copy of 1935," *Atlanta Daily World*, 1 Jan. 1936, 1.

46. Scott, *Sons of Sheba's Race*, 38–68.

47. S.M. to the NAACP, 26 May 1936, NAACP Administrative Files, box C-297, folder "Ethiopia — 1936," NAACP/LC; Robinson, "African Diaspora and the Italo-Ethiopian Crisis," 60.

48. For more on the idea that being a black nationalist and a universalist cosmopolitanist are not mutually exclusive, see Fredrickson, *Black Liberation*.

49. "War Activities Quicken Harlem Trade Interests," *Pittsburgh Courier*, 26 Oct. 1935, sec. 2, 1.

50. For letters to the editor of the *Courier*, see, for example, Isadore Henderson and E. B. Nyobholo, *Pittsburgh Courier*, 3 Aug. 1935, sec. 2, 2. For letters to the editor of the *Defender*, see, for example, Taylor Lynn, Chicago, 10 Aug. 1935, 16; Samuel Bruce, Oakland, Calif., 17 Aug. 1935, 16; H. C. and Lillian Kirk, Sheffield, Ala., 21 Sept. 1935, 16.

51. See Buni, *Robert L. Vann*, 221, 246–47; "Here's Ethiopian Pronouncer . . . ," *Chicago Defender*, 3 Aug. 1935, 12; "Haile Selassie and Joe Louis Proved Biggest Names in News of the World," *Chicago Defender*, 4 Jan. 1936, 10.

52. "Volunteers Needed — Where?" *Pittsburgh Courier*, 27 July 1935, 10; "A Light

in the East!" *Chicago Defender*, 20 July 1935, 16. See also "Hands Across the Sea," *Pittsburgh Courier*, 13 July 1935, 10.

53. George Wood to the Editor, *Pittsburgh Courier*, 27 July 1935, sec. 2, 2. Frank Ferrell to the Foreign Editor, "Would Send Civilian Corps to Assistance of Ethiopia," *Chicago Defender*, 14 Sept. 1935, 24; George Terry to the Editor, *Pittsburgh Courier*, 17 Aug. 1935, sec. 2, 2. For other letters, see *Pittsburgh Courier*, 27 July 1935, sec. 2, 2, for a full page of letters; Cable Lockey, Lockland, Ohio, to the Editor, *Chicago Defender*, 24 Aug. 1935, 16; John Thomas to the Editor, *Pittsburgh Courier*, 21 Sept. 1935, sec. 2, 2; Peter Johnson, Albany, Ga., to the Editor, *Chicago Defender*, 28 Sept. 1935, 16; Tom Jones, Lake Placid, Fla., and Willie Berry, Birmingham, to the Editor, *Pittsburgh Courier*, 19 Oct. 1935, sec. 2, 10; Harry Rooks, Omaha, to the Editor, *Chicago Defender*, 2 Nov. 1935, 16; Alexander Keys to the Editor, *Chicago Defender*, 9 Nov. 1935, 16; Forrest Cozart, New York City, to the Editor, *Baltimore Afro-American*, 30 Nov. 1935; William Johnson, Jacksonville, to the Editor, *Chicago Defender*, 7 Dec. 1935, 16; Neville McGee, Harlem, to the Editor, *Pittsburgh Courier*, 25 July 1936, 12.

54. "*Courier* Scoops Country Again; Emperor Talks," *Pittsburgh Courier*, 13 July 1935, 2; "Here's Why U.S. Citizens Can't Fight for Ethiopia," *Pittsburgh Courier*, 20 July 1935, 45; "U.S. Law Blocks Enlistment," *Pittsburgh Courier*, 20 July 1935, 1.

55. Americanus, Baltimore, to the Editor, *Baltimore Afro-American*, 27 July 1935, 4; Caldwell Jones, Los Angeles, to the Editor, *Baltimore Afro-American*, 7 Sept. 1935, 6.

56. Plummer, *Rising Wind*, 46; "10,000 Protest Mussolini's War in East Africa," *New York Amsterdam News*, 28 Sept. 1935, 3; "Effigy of Duce Torn at Meet," *Pittsburgh Courier*, 5 Oct. 1935, 1; "Dr. Huggins Tells 2,000 of Ethiopia," *Baltimore Afro-American*, 14 Sept. 1935, 12; Address by Walter White at Madison Square Garden, 25 Sept. 1935, *NAACP Papers* 11, ser. B, 35/2. For information on other rallies, see "Citizens Stretch Forth Hands to Ethiopia in Mass Meetings," *Pittsburgh Courier*, 20 July 1935, 5; "20,000 Parade in Harlem to Preserve Peace," *Pittsburgh Courier*, 10 Aug. 1935, 5; "Consul General in Talk," *Chicago Defender*, 16 Nov. 1935, 5; "Chicago Aroused by War Threats," *New York Amsterdam News*, 13 July 1935, 3, and 22 Feb. 1936, 10.

57. Rogers's writings included such passages: "Sotted with disease, these men [Italian soldiers] have not stopped at ravishing pretty, innocent young black girls . . . they are even satiating their lust on nuns and the wives of Coptic priests!" "Babies, Women Slaughtered as Italy's 'War of Conquest' Rages in Ethiopia," *Pittsburgh Courier*, 12 Oct. 1935, 1; "Rogers Exposes War Atrocities; Girls, Nuns Raped," *Pittsburgh Courier*, 23 Nov. 1935, 1.

58. "The Conquering Lion of Judah," *Chicago Defender*, 19 Oct. 1935, 1; "Italians Seek Vast Empire, Huggins Says," *New York Amsterdam News*, 31 Aug. 1935, 1.

59. The cartoonist Jay Jackson sent his character "Bungleton Green," seen in the *Chicago Defender*, to Ethiopia, as did the cartoonist Holloway, who sent "Sunnyboy

Sam," seen in the *Pittsburgh Courier*. George Schuyler offered readers of the *Pittsburgh Courier* the serialized "Ethiopian Murder Mystery — A Story of Love and International Intrigue," which started its run on 5 Oct. 1935, sec. 2, 1. Langston Hughes's "Ballad" may be found in the *Chicago Defender*, 9 Nov. 1935, 16. Hughes also penned a song, with music by Thelma Brown, in which he used the theme of racial solidarity. "The New Ethiopian Marching Song Stirs Coast," *Baltimore Afro-American*, 7 Sept. 1935, 3. For the Christmas card, see "Here's *Afro*'s Christmas Card to All Its Readers," *Baltimore Afro-American*, 28 Dec. 1935, 5.

60. "The Frantic Fascists," Editorial, *Pittsburgh Courier*, 11 Jan. 1936, 10; "The Great Italian Flop," Editorial, *Pittsburgh Courier*, 4 Apr. 1936, 10; "Fooling the World," Editorial, *New York Amsterdam News*, 4 Apr. 1936, 12. The press's ability to keep Ethiopia winning until faced with its actual capitulation prompted *Baltimore Afro-American* writer Ralph Matthews to make this comment in his war postmortem: "But there is one fine thing about the whole affair that will go down as a remarkable achievement of colored journalism. Up to the last, the better headline writers kept Ethiopia winning." Ralph Matthews, "Manhattan Merry-Go-Round," *Baltimore Afro-American*, 16 May 1936, 4.

61. "Pan-American Reconstruction Group Seeks $10,000,000 to Aid Ethiopia," *Pittsburgh Courier*, 5 Oct. 1935, 4; Wilbur Douglaston to the Editor, *Baltimore Afro-American*, 3 Aug. 1935, 6.

62. On the front page of the *Chicago Defender* for the period 1933–38, extending well before and after the Italo-Ethiopian War, Louis appeared in a photograph or his name appeared in a headline eighty times. Selassie came in second, with twenty-four. In third, with twenty appearances, was Chicago's own congressman, Oscar DePriest, the first African American congressman since 1901. For examples of the African American press putting Louis and Selassie on the same lofty level, see "Youth Takes Its Place," *Chicago Defender*, 5 Oct. 1935, 16; "Haile Selassie 1st, Now Joe Louis; Who Next?" *Chicago Defender*, 27 June 1936, 14; George Schuyler, "Views and Reviews," *Pittsburgh Courier*, 27 June 1936, 10; Ralph Matthews, "Manhattan Merry-Go-Round," *Baltimore Afro-American*, 16 May 1936, 4.

63. William Johnson, Jacksonville, Fla., to the Editor, *Chicago Defender*, 7 Dec. 1935, 16. See also Albert Caldwell, New York, to the Editor, *Pittsburgh Courier*, 28 Dec. 1935, sec. 2, 2; "White Imperialism Trembles," Editorial, *Pittsburgh Courier*, 29 Feb. 1936, 10.

64. "World Turns Eyes on Ethiopia," *Chicago Defender*, 24 Aug. 1935, 1; Walter White statement for the *New York Amsterdam News*, 3 Oct. 1935, *NAACP Papers* 11, ser. A, 30/834; E. A. Abbott to the Editor, *Chicago Defender*, 26 Oct. 1935, 16. See also "Japan Arming Ethiopia," *Pittsburgh Courier*, 10 Aug. 1935, 1; "Race Transcends Religion," Editorial, *Pittsburgh Courier*, 28 Sept. 1935, 12; "The War Has Begun," Editorial, *Pittsburgh Courier*, 12 Oct. 1935, 10; "White Imperialism Trembles," Editorial, *Pittsburgh Courier*, 29 Feb. 1936, 10; "Was the World Sincere?" Editorial, *Chicago Defender*, 7 Sept. 1935, 10; "Natives May Chase Missionaries Out

of Africa," *Chicago Defender*, 2 Nov. 1935, 24; "Sad Spectacle," Editorial, *Crisis*, Sept. 1935, 273.

65. "Ethiopia Against the World," Editorial, *Crisis*, Aug. 1935, 241.

66. "Rescuing Italy," Editorial, *Chicago Defender*, 25 Jan. 1936, 16; "Ethiopia Appeals in Vain," Editorial, *Pittsburgh Courier*, 13 July 1935, 10; "Have the White Powers Reached an Agreement?" Editorial, *Pittsburgh Courier*, 2 Nov. 1935, 10; "We Ask the Question Again!" Editorial, *Pittsburgh Courier*, 25 Jan. 1936, 10; "The International Squeeze-Play," Editorial, *Pittsburgh Courier*, 21 Mar. 1936, 10; Paul Socker, Brooklyn, to the Editor, *New York Amsterdam News*, 20 June 1936, 14. See also "Justification for Mussolini's Onslaught Given in Flimsy Excuse by Davanzati," *Chicago Defender*, 12 Oct. 1935, 5; "The Ousting of Laval," *Chicago Defender*, 1 Feb. 1936, 16. Letters to the press also discussed the idea of a conspiracy. See Dr. Joe Thomas, Cleveland, to the Editor, *Pittsburgh Courier*, 20 July 1935, sec. 2, 2; Smith Shannon, Kansas City, Mo., to the Editor, *Pittsburgh Courier*, 18 Jan. 1936, sec. 2, 2; Darius Irby, New York, to the Editor, *Pittsburgh Courier*, 25 Jan. 1936, sec. 2, 2; Mrs. Lizzie Moss, Midland, Pa., and Mose Early, Albany, Ga., to the Editor, *Pittsburgh Courier*, 1 Feb. 1936, sec. 2, 2.

67. "War Activities Quicken Harlem Trade Interests," *Pittsburgh Courier*, 26 Oct. 1935, sec. 2, 1; "300 Extra Cops Do 'War Duty' in Harlem," *Baltimore Afro-American*, 12 Oct. 1935, 11; Asante, "The Afro-American and the Italo-Ethiopian Crisis," 178; "Getting Together," Editorial, *New York Amsterdam News*, 3 Aug. 1935, 10. On boycott calls, see, for example, "Aid for Ethiopia," Editorial, *New York Amsterdam News*, 13 July 1935, 12; Irvin Gordon, Baltimore, to the Editor, *Baltimore Afro-American*, 3 Aug. 1935, 6; Aubrey Willacy, Washington, D.C., to the Editor, *Baltimore Afro-American*, 10 Aug. 1935, 4; "Birmingham Italians Facing Store Boycott," *Pittsburgh Courier*, 2 Nov. 1935, 2; Theophilus Lewis, "Sketchbook," *New York Amsterdam News*, 3 Aug. 1935, 10.

68. Letter to the Editor, *Pittsburgh Courier*, 14 Mar. 1936, sec. 2, 2; Letter to the Editor, *Pittsburgh Courier*, 21 Mar. 1936, sec. 2, 2.

69. "No Princess," Editorial, *Baltimore Afro-American*, 27 July 1936, 4; White to H. Albert Smith, December 1935, *NAACP Papers* 11, ser. A, 30/875; J. E. Harris, *African-American Reactions*, 51; Ross, "Black Americans and Haiti, Liberia, the Virgin Islands, and Ethiopia," 333.

70. "Black People Learn of True Racial Status," *Chicago Defender*, 4 Jan. 1936, 1; "Selassie's Messenger Speaks to 4,000 in New York City," *Baltimore Afro-American*, 4 Jan. 1936, 12; NAACP Administrative Files, box C-297, folder "Ethiopia—1936," NAACP/LC; Plummer, *Rising Wind*, 52. In Chicago, for example, one church donated $94.50, another $106, and another pledged $100. "Ethiopian Envoy Insulted by Two Chicago Hotels; Barred," *Chicago Defender*, 1 Feb. 1936, 1.

71. Joseph E. Harris's book *African-American Reactions to War in Ethiopia* does a thorough and penetrating analysis of the Ethiopian Research Council (ERC). On the other hand, Harris promotes the importance of the ERC to a level that tends to

exclude the contributions of other organizations. For more information on these other organizations, see Ross, "Black Americans and Haiti, Liberia, the Virgin Islands, and Ethiopia," 328–52; Scott, *Sons of Sheba's Race*, 105–20; Plummer, *Rising Wind*, 47–52; as well as Harris, 63–75. Cities besides New York and Washington, D.C., also had aid organizations. Leading African Americans in Atlanta, for example, formed the Atlanta Committee for the Aid of Ethiopia, headed by Jesse O. Thomas, secretary of the southern region of the National Urban League. Its aim was very "establishment"-oriented — to help the Ethiopian Red Cross through the American Red Cross. "Atlanta Ethiopia Committee Organized," *Atlanta Daily World*, 17 Oct. 1935, 1; and "Atlanta Committee to Help Ethiopian Red Cross to Meet This Evening," *Atlanta Daily World*, 23 Oct. 1935, 1.

72. Consul-General John Shaw used the $350 figure in correspondence relating to the sending of volunteers to Ethiopia. John Shaw to Mrs. S. M. Brito, 30 Oct. 1935, *NAACP Papers* 11, ser. A, 30863.

73. "The Phantom Ship," *Pittsburgh Courier*, 7 Mar. 1936, 10; "Let Your Money Talk" and "Duce's Little Trick," Editorials, *New York Amsterdam News*, 14 Mar. 1936, 12; "Rain Wanted," Editorial, *Pittsburgh Courier*, 14 Mar. 1936, 10; "Haiti, Liberia and Sanctions," Editorial, *Pittsburgh Courier*, 25 July 1936, 10.

74. "Courier Authorized to Collect Funds for Ethiopia," *Pittsburgh Courier*, 18 Apr. 1936, 1. Shaw's letter was published in the *Pittsburgh Courier*, 2 May 1936, sec. 2, 2; "Honor Roll Contributors to Ethiopia," *Pittsburgh Courier*, 16 May 1936, sec. 2, 2. A few hundred dollars arrived in the first six weeks, a total of $328 by 6 June; during the next six weeks donations withered, with only an additional $51 contributed. "Honor Roll Contributors to Ethiopia," *Pittsburgh Courier*, 6 June 1936, sec. 2, 2, and 25 July 1936, sec. 2, 2.

75. "United Aid for Ethiopia Asked," *New York Amsterdam News*, 5 Oct. 1935, 11.

76. For a concise synopsis of the involvement of Julian and Robinson, see J. E. Harris, *African-American Reactions to War in Ethiopia*, 54–60; see also Scott, *Sons of Sheba's Race*, 69–95. Robinson returned to Ethiopia after Selassie regained power, while Julian many years later ended up being arrested for smuggling guns to Moise Tshombe in Katanga. RG 59, Lot and Office Files, 250/63/10/4, Bureau of African Affairs, Office of Central African Affairs, Country Files, 1955–63, box 7, "Hubert Julian."

77. "League Hears Selassie Hit at Treachery" and "Louis and Marva Deny Love Row Caused K.O. by German," *New York Amsterdam News*, 4 July 1936, 1.

78. "Ethiopia Will Get a New Hospital Unit," *Pittsburgh Courier*, 11 Jan. 1936, 2; "Medical Men Ship Full Unit to Haile," *Pittsburgh Courier*, 18 Jan. 1936, 3; "U.S. Aid for Ethiopia Shipped," *Chicago Defender*, 30 Nov. 1935, 2; "Aid for Ethiopian Sick and Wounded," *New York Amsterdam News*, 18 Apr. 1936, 11; "Honor Roll Contributors to Ethiopia," *Pittsburgh Courier*, 25 July 1936, sec. 2, 2; Ross, "Black Americans and Haiti, Liberia, the Virgin Islands, and Ethiopia," 340–54.

79. White to the International Press Service, 19 Sept. 1935, *NAACP Papers* 11, ser. A, 30/825.

80. At times the NAACP sent additional telegrams of protest. However, after the summer of 1935, Ethiopia did not appear in the reports of Walter White or on the agenda of the board of the NAACP. White and the board of directors instead regularly discussed domestic topics, including the Costigan-Wagner antilynching legislation, other antilynching efforts, the Angelo Herndon case, and the Scottsboro case. See the Secretary's Reports and the Board of Director's Minutes for October 1935–May 1936, *NAACP Papers* 1, reels 2 and 5; Walter White to Joseph Byrnes, Speaker of the House, 28 Jan. 1936, NAACP Administrative Files, box C-297, folder "Ethiopia – 1936," NAACP/LC.

81. The war had "a profound and irreversible impact on Afro-Americans," according to Brenda Plummer. "U.S. domestic and foreign policy required a basic overhaul. Assigning Afro-Americans a stake in the war . . . signified a recognition of their debut as actors on a new world stage, where history would remake racial, ethnic, and international relations." Plummer, *Rising Wind*, 81.

82. Memorandum by the Chief of the Division of Near Eastern Affairs (Murray) to the Secretary of State, 1 Aug. 1936, *FRUS*, 1936, 3:213–14; The Ambassador in the United Kingdom (Bingham) to the Secretary of State, 5 Aug. 1936, *FRUS*, 1936, 3:214–15; The Ambassador in the United Kingdom (Bingham) to the Secretary of State, 10 Aug. 1936, *FRUS*, 1936, 3:216; Secretary of State to the Ambassador in the United Kingdom (Bingham), 1 Sept. 1936, *FRUS*, 1936, 3:216–17; Memorandum of Telephone Conversation between Mr. Alling and Mr. H. Murray Jacoby, RG 59, DF 1930–39, 884.001 Selassie 1/353; Memorandum of Conversation between Mr. Murray and Mr. Alling and the Rev. Wm. Sheafe Chase, 8 Sept. 1936, RG 59, DF 1930–39, 884.001 Selassie 1/341. I owe much here to the excellent chapter detailing the mission in J. E. Harris, *African-American Reactions to War in Ethiopia*, 104–19.

83. DeConde, *Ethnicity, Race, and American Foreign Policy*, 108.

84. "Answer with Your Money," Editorial, *New York Amsterdam News*, 4 Jan. 1936, 8.

85. "Ethiopian Tragedy to Prove Spur For Negro Unity, Observers Hold," *New York Amsterdam News*, 9 May 1936, 1; "The Fascist Victory," Editorial, *New York Amsterdam News*, 9 May 1936, 12.

86. Asante, "The Afro-American and the Italo-Ethiopian Crisis," 181.

87. "Learning from the Ethiopians," Editorial, *Pittsburgh Courier*, 16 Nov. 1935, 10; "Mussolini's Three Days," Editorial, *Pittsburgh Courier*, 2 May 1936, 10; " 'Listen, My Children'," Editorial, *New York Amsterdam News*, 30 Nov. 1935, 8; "To the Race Teachers and Professors," Editorial, *Chicago Defender*, 3 Aug. 1935, 16.

Chapter Two

1. Several historians note that the drive for independence in India especially impressed African Americans: Plummer, *Rising Wind*, 89–96 and 123–24; Von Eschen, *Race against Empire*, 28–32; R. Harris, "Racial Equality and the United Nations Charter," 141.

2. Roark, "American Black Leaders," 255–57; DeConde, *Ethnicity, Race, and American Foreign Policy*, 144; Solomon, "Black Critics of Colonialism and the Cold War," 205–7.

3. For Robeson quote, see Hill, *The FBI's RACON*, 47. Robin Kelley writes about the connections African Americans made between the Spanish Civil War and the Ethiopian war in his essay "This Ain't Ethiopia, But It'll Do," 6–20.

4. Wynn, *The Afro-American and the Second World War*, esp. 39–59; Lawson, *Running for Freedom*, 14–20; W. A. Jackson, *Gunnar Myrdal and America's Conscience*, 235–36; Meier, "Toward a Synthesis of Civil Rights History," 212; Norrell, "One Thing We Did Right," 65–80; Klarman, "How *Brown* Changed Race Relations," 91. Harvard Sitkoff recently has brought into question the "militancy" of the war years while not questioning the long-term effects of the war. See Sitkoff, "African American Militancy in the World War II South."

5. Lauren, *Power and Prejudice*, quote on 136–37; W. A. Jackson, *Gunnar Myrdal and America's Conscience*, xviii–xix; Sosna, *In Search of the Silent South*, 202. Carl Degler argues that the Nazis' racial policies had tremendous impact on scholarly thinking in America, undermining concepts and terms such as "heredity," "biological influences," and "instinct" and helping to ensure the triumph of culture as an explanatory concept. Degler, *In Search of Human Nature*, 203–15.

6. Ottley, *"New World A-Coming,"* iii.

7. Roark, "American Black Leaders," 253–62, quote on 255. See also Von Eschen, *Race against Empire*, 22–43; Horne, *Black and Red*, 19–24; Franklin and Moss, *From Slavery to Freedom*, 406; DeConde, *Ethnicity, Race, and American Foreign Policy*, 144.

8. Council on African Affairs, *Proceedings of the Conference on Africa*; Von Eschen, *Race against Empire*, 73–74; Geiss, *Pan-African Movement*, 367, 382–83. For more on colonial peoples and the Atlantic Charter, see Plummer, *Rising Wind*, 83–85; and Von Eschen, *Race against Empire*, 25–28.

9. Von Eschen, *Race against Empire*, 57–60.

10. For more on the CAA, see Lynch, *Black American Radicals and the Liberation of Africa*; Lynch, "Pan-African Responses in the United States to British Colonial Rule in Africa in the 1940s"; Von Eschen, "African Americans and Anti-Colonialism, 1937–1957"; Von Eschen, *Race against Empire*.

11. Von Eschen, *Race against Empire*, chaps. 2–3, quote on 40. On African Americans blending radical internationalism and black nationalism in this period, see Robin Kelley, "This Ain't Ethiopia," on black volunteers in the Spanish Civil War; and Gerald Horne, *Black and Red*, on W. E. B. Du Bois.

12. Council on African Affairs, "The Job to Be Done" (pamphlet), n.d. [Aug. 1943], *Schomburg CCF*, 001,262.

13. For some of the recent scholarship on African Americans and the Communist Party during the Popular Front era, see Smethurst, *The New Red Negro*; Mullen, *Popular Fronts*; Fairclough, *Race and Democracy*; Kelley, *Hammer and Hoe*; Naison,

Communists in Harlem. On African American attitudes toward communists in re-gards to foreign affairs, see Plummer, *Rising Wind*, esp. 31–32, 56–57.

14. Plummer, *Rising Wind*, 107.

15. For more on the issue of human rights and racial discrimination at the Dumbar-ton Oaks Conference, see Lauren, *Power and Prejudice*, 147–50; Plummer, *Rising Wind*, 117–21. On the Dumbarton Oaks Conference in general, see Schild, *Bretton Woods and Dumbarton Oaks*.

16. Horne, *Black and Red*, 28; Board of Directors Minutes, 13 Feb. 1945, *NAACP Papers* 1, 3/448; W. E. B. Du Bois to Roy Wilkins, 28 Feb. 1945, *NAACP Papers* 14, 6/355; Wilkins to Du Bois, 2 Mar. 1945, *NAACP Papers* 14, 6/357; Wilkins to Du Bois, 13 Mar. 1945, *NAACP Papers* 14, 6/358; Board of Directors Minutes, 12 Mar. 1945, *NAACP Papers* 1, 3/460; Director of Special Research Report (Du Bois), 13 Feb.–12 Mar. 1945, GOF, ser. A, box 240, folder "Du Bois, William E. B., General 1945"; Director of Special Research Report (Du Bois), 12 Mar.–9 Apr. 1945, GOF, ser. A, box 240, folder "Du Bois, William E. B., General 1945."

17. Invitation to Colonial Conference, n.d. [Mar. 1945], *NAACP Papers* 14, 6/349; NAACP Press Release, 12 Apr. 1945, ibid., 6/352. Horne, *Black and Red*, 28–30; Plummer, *Rising Wind*, 133; Von Eschen, *Race against Empire*, 76–77.

18. Petition to Franklin D. Roosevelt and Edward R. Stettinius, n.d., box 30, folder "Pan-African, 1920–1949," Spingarn Papers, LC.

19. Secretary's Report (White), May 1945, *NAACP Papers* 1, 7/26; NAACP Press Release, 10 Apr. 1945, *NAACP Papers* 14, 19/52; Walter White to Franklin D. Roosevelt, *NAACP Papers* 14, 19/81.

20. NAACP Press Release, 2 May 1945, *NAACP Papers* 14, 18/25; NAACP Press Release, 10 May 1945, ibid., 18/550; Walter White to the Board of Directors, 9 May 1945, ibid., 18/58; Roy Wilkins to NAACP Branch Offices, 3 May 1945, ibid., 19/175–76.

21. Walter White to Edward Stettinius, 18 May 1945, *NAACP Papers* 14, 19/261; NAACP Press Release, 17 May 1945, ibid., 18/211; Walter White to the Committee on Administration, 28 May 1945, ibid., 18/340; Press Release, 21 June 1945, ibid., 18/320; Press Release, 28 June 1945, ibid., 18/321; "San Francisco," Editorial, *Crisis*, June 1945, 161. For more on African American attitudes toward and actions at the San Francisco conference, see Plummer, *Rising Wind*, 125–65; R. Harris, "Racial Equality and the United Nations Charter," 126–48; Horne, *Black and Red*, 33–39; Lauren, *Power and Prejudice*, 150–58.

22. Director of Special Research Report (Du Bois), 2 Jan.–10 Feb. 1945, 1940–55, GOF, ser. A, box 240, folder "Du Bois, William E. B., General 1945"; Director of Special Research Report (Du Bois), 12 Mar.–9 Apr. 1945, ibid. On Padmore, see Hooker, *Black Revolutionary*; Padmore, *Pan-Africanism or Communism?*

23. Board of Directors Minutes, 9 Apr. 1945, *NAACP Papers* 1, 3/469; W. E. B. Du Bois, "The Pan-African Movement," n.d. [Apr.–May 1945], box 30, folder "Pan-African Movement, 1920–1949," Spingarn Papers, LC.

24. Board of Directors Minutes, 9 Apr. 1945, *NAACP Papers* 1, 3/469; Board of Directors Minutes, 11 June 1945, ibid., 3/493; Board of Directors Minutes, 7 July 1945, ibid., 3/501; Walter White to W. E. B. Du Bois, 11 Apr. 1945, *NAACP Papers* 14, 3/599; Du Bois to White, 12 Apr. 1945, *NAACP Papers* 14, 3/600; White to Channing Tobias, 19 Apr. 1945, *NAACP Papers* 14, 3/601; White to William Hastie, 4 June 1945, *NAACP Papers* 14, 3/605.

25. Minutes of the Pan-African Congress Committee Meeting, 12 July 1945, *NAACP Papers* 14, 3/616–19.

26. Walter White to Mary White Ovington, 19 July 1945, box 30, folder "Pan-African Movement, 1920–1949," Spingarn Papers, LC; Subcommittee to Walter White, 17 July 1945, *NAACP Papers* 14, 3/650–52; William Hastie to White, 17 July 1945, *NAACP Papers* 14, 3/653; W. E. B. Du Bois to White, 20 July 1945, *NAACP Papers* 14, 3/598.

27. See Gbadegesin, "Kinship of the Dispossessed," esp. 224–34.

28. Walter White to W. E. B. Du Bois, 31 July 1945, *NAACP Papers* 14, 3/679; Board of Directors Minutes, 10 Dec. 1945, *NAACP Papers* 1, 3/551.

29. For more on the preparations for and convening of the Manchester Pan-African Congress, see Geiss, *Pan-African Movement*, 387–408; Von Eschen, *Race against Empire*, 45–54; Plummer, *Rising Wind*, 152–58; Du Bois, *The World and Africa*, 243–45; Horne, *Black and Red*, 25–32; Marable, "Pan-Africanism of W. E. B. Du Bois," 209–12.

30. Committee on Pan African Affairs to the Board of Directors, 10 Sept. 1945, *NAACP Papers* 14, 3/690; Board of Directors Minutes, 10 Sept. 1945, *NAACP Papers* 1, 3/506–7; Du Bois to the Secretary and the Pan-African Committee, 3 Oct. 1945, box 30, folder "Pan-African Movement, 1920–1949," Spingarn Papers, LC.

31. W. E. B. Du Bois to Walter White, 14 Nov. 1946, GOF, 1940–55, ser. A, box 241, folder "Du Bois, William E. B., General 1946."

32. Plummer, *Rising Wind*, 157–59; Von Eschen, *Race against Empire*, 52–53. These episodes render highly problematic Von Eschen's contentions that at this time the CAA was "the most visible African American group seeking to influence the direction of American foreign policy," and that "despite its left-wing radicalism, the CAA stood at the center, not at the margins, of black American opinion on colonialism" (69–70).

33. Rosenman, *Public Papers and Addresses of Franklin D. Roosevelt*, 9:672; Dallek, *Franklin D. Roosevelt and American Foreign Policy*, 281–84; Borstelmann, *Apartheid's Reluctant Uncle*, 12–14. Other officials also engaged in anticolonial rhetoric. In July 1942, Secretary of State Cordell Hull said, "In this vast struggle, we Americans stand united with those who, like ourselves, are fighting for the preservation of their freedom; with those who are fighting to regain the freedom of which they have been brutally deprived; with those who are fighting for the opportunity to achieve freedom. We have always believed—and we believe today—that all peoples, without distinction of race, color, or religion, who are prepared and willing to accept the responsibilities of liberty are entitled to its enjoyment." Nielsen, *The Great*

Powers and Africa, 247. For further discussion on U.S. anticolonial expressions during World War II, see Louis and Robinson, "The United States and the Liquidation of the British Empire in Tropical Africa," 32–37.

34. Wood, "From the Marshall Plan to the Third World," 205; Nielsen, *The Great Powers and Africa*, 246–49.

35. Hunt, *Ideology and U.S. Foreign Policy*, 106–16; for a fuller discussion of America's historical ambivalence about revolutions, see 92–124, 159–70.

36. On the split nature of American thinking on colonialism before the end of World War II, see Borstelmann, *Apartheid's Reluctant Uncle*, 12–16; and Noer, *Cold War and Black Liberation*, 15–17.

37. Leffler, *Preponderance of Power*, 142–46; LaFeber, *America, Russia, and the Cold War*, 49–58, 68–69; Gaddis, *United States and the Origins of the Cold War*, 346–52; Fried, *Nightmare in Red*, 66–72.

38. Heale, *American Anticommunism*, 137–38; Sullivan, "Southern Reformers, the New Deal, and the Movement's Foundation," 97–98; Fried, *Nightmare in Red*, 70–71; Theoharis, "Threat to Civil Liberties," 266–98; LaFeber, *America, Russia and the Cold War*, 58; Gaddis, *United States and the Origins of the Cold War*, 352.

39. Wood, "From the Marshall Plan to the Third World," 201–14; Kent, "British Policy and the Origins of the Cold War," 148–49; Borstelmann, *Apartheid's Reluctant Uncle*, 58–59; Nielsen, *The Great Powers and Africa*, 251–54.

40. Nielsen, *The Great Powers and Africa*, 249–50; Borstelmann, *Apartheid's Reluctant Uncle*, 77; Louis and Robinson, "The United States and the Liquidation of the British Empire in Tropical Africa," 33, 40–41.

41. Exceptions to this included the independent nations of Liberia and Ethiopia, both of which had U.S. diplomatic missions, and to some degree strategically important countries such as South Africa.

42. Policy papers prepared by the Bureau of Near Eastern, South Asian and African Affairs: "Future of Africa," 18 Apr. 1950, *FRUS*, 1950, 5:1526 n; "Regional Policy Statement on Africa South of the Sahara," 29 Dec. 1950, ibid., 5:1588, 1590. For a discussion of the Western prejudices of officials in the U.S. State Department in the middle of the twentieth century, see Borstelmann, *Apartheid's Reluctant Uncle*, 39–41.

43. George C. McGhee, "Africa's Role in the Free World Today," *State Department Bulletin* 25 (16 July 1951): 98.

44. Plummer, *Rising Wind*, 1, 35.

45. Ethiopia, occupied for five years from 1936 to 1941, regained its autonomy under Emperor Haile Selassie during World War II.

46. Leffler, *Preponderance of Power*, 75–77; Rivlin, *The United Nations and the Italian Colonies*, 9–14; Ralph Bunche to Walter White, 17 June 1949, *NAACP Papers* 14, 10/589.

47. On U.S. officials' concern with communist takeovers through the ballot box in both Italy and France, and their extensive efforts to prevent such an occurrence, see Leffler, *Preponderance of Power*, 121–22, 189–98, 206–7, 213–14; Maier, "Hege-

mony and Autonomy within the Western Alliance," 160–61. For the British position, see Louis, "Libyan Independence, 1951"; Kent, "British Policy and the Origins of the Cold War"; Rivlin, *The United Nations and the Italian Colonies*, 17–26.

48. NAACP News Release, 9 Sept. 1948, *NAACP Papers* 14, 6/886; NAACP Press Release, 9 Sept. 1948, ibid., 6/891.

49. Fredrickson, *Black Liberation*, 150–52, quotes on 150; Plummer, *Rising Wind*, 116.

50. Quoted in Geiss, *Pan-African Movement*, 383 n. 87.

51. Walter White to Members of Congress, 29 Apr. 1949, *NAACP Papers* 14, 10/172. On Roy Wilkins's support for this position, see NAACP Press Release, 28 Apr. 1949, ibid., 10/427. For more on the issue of South-West Africa, see Chapter 3.

52. Walter White to Poppy Cannon White, 10 Oct. 1948, box 12, folder 111, Walter White and Poppy Cannon White Correspondence, Beinecke Library, Yale University, New Haven, Conn.; Confidential Statement to the U.S. Delegation to the UN, 17 Oct. 1948, *NAACP Papers* 14, 15/675; Walter White to Thurgood Marshall, 11 Oct. 1948, *NAACP Papers* 14, 15/434; Walter White Report to the NAACP, 19 Oct. 1948, *NAACP Papers* 14, 15/468. After White departed Paris, Jay Krane of the CIO wrote to praise him for the work he did at the Paris meetings: "There's no one here who can or is willing to carry the ball, in terms of continuous pressure, as you did." Krane to White, 26 Oct. 1948, *NAACP Papers* 14, 10/6.

53. "Petition to the United States Delegation to the United Nations Concerning the Disposition of Libya, Eritrea, and Italian Somaliland," *Spotlight on Africa*, 28 Sept. 1948.

54. NAACP Letter to Multiple Organizations, 29 Mar. 1949, *NAACP Papers* 14, 10/253; "Statement Adopted by a Conference Called by the NAACP in Support of an International Trusteeship for the Former Italian Colonies and Southwest Africa and for the Independence of Indonesia," box 30, folder "Pan-African, 1920–1949," Spingarn Papers, LC; Walter White to Warren Austin, U.S. Representative to the UN, et al., 13 Apr. 1949, *NAACP Papers* 14, 10/109; NAACP Press Release, 13 Apr. 1949, *NAACP Papers* 14, 10/405; White to Henry Lee Moon and Roy Wilkins, 19 Apr. 1949, *NAACP Papers* 14, 10/143; NAACP Press Release, 13 Apr. 1949, *NAACP Papers* 14, 6/901.

55. "Americans Must Demand Just Decision on Italian Colonies in Interest of Peace," *New Africa* 8, no. 4 (Apr. 1949): 1.

56. Henry Lee Moon to Don Irvin et al., 5 Apr. 1949, *NAACP Papers* 14, 10/104–6; Henry Lee Moon to George Streator, 22 Apr. 1949, ibid., 10/144–47; Roy Wilkins to St. Clair Drake, 25 May 1949, ibid., 10/574; NAACP Press Release, 26 May 1949, ibid., 10/435; Abdullah Issa to Walter White, 1949, box 3, folder 99, Walter White and Poppy Cannon White Correspondence, Beinecke Library, Yale University.

57. White to Congressmen, 29 Apr. 1949, *NAACP Papers* 14, 10/172; NAACP Press Release, 28 Apr. 1949, ibid., 10/427; A. Philip Randolph to Dean Acheson, 12 Apr. 1949, *Randolph Papers*, 3/442–43.

58. Warren Austin to Walter White, 6 May 1949, *NAACP Papers* 14, 10/555.

59. Roy Wilkins to Dean Acheson, 15 Sept. 1949, *NAACP Papers* 14, 10/625; Wilkins to Harry Truman, 28 Sept. 1949, ibid., 10/637; Wilkins to Trygve Lie, 29 Sept. 1949, ibid., 10/626; State Department to Wilkins, 29 Sept. 1949, ibid., 10/639; Rivlin, *The United Nations and the Italian Colonies*, 42–62; NAACP Press Release, 26 May 1949, *NAACP Papers* 14, 10/494.

60. The NAACP annual conventions, for example, passed resolutions supporting the Marshall Plan, Point Four, NATO, and the Korean War in 1948, 1949, and 1951. Roark, "American Black Leaders," 263–64. For one perspective on how the growing Cold War dampened the militancy of the NAACP leadership, see Horne, *Black and Red*, 50–111.

61. Financial Reports, 1945–47, n.d., box 1, folder 18, Hunton Papers; Selected Financial Records of the Council on African Affairs, 1948, *Du Bois Papers*, 61/711.

62. On the 1948 internal struggles of the CAA, see Letter from John Latouche, Mary Church Terrell, and Henry Arthur Callis to Paul Robeson, 15 May 1948, box 1, folder 17, Hunton Papers; and Letter to Members of the Council from W. A. Hunton, 7 July 1948, box 1, folder 19, Hunton Papers. On the hiatus in its African activities, see Paul Robeson to Unknown [fragment of letter], 26 May 1948, *Du Bois Papers*, 61/770. On Hunton's position, see W. A. Hunton to the Editor, *New York Times*, 21 June 1948, box 1, folder 17, Hunton Papers. The summary of Schieffelin's position is drawn from "Reminiscences of William Jay Schieffelin (1949)," 77–78, in the Oral History Collection of Columbia University, New York. On the rupture in general, see Duberman, *Paul Robeson*, 330–33; Lynch, *Black American Radicals*, 38–39; Von Eschen, *Race against Empire*, 115–16.

63. Minutes of the Council on African Affairs, 25 Mar. 1948, *Du Bois Papers*, 61/748, 752; Duberman, *Paul Robeson*, 333.

64. Plummer, *Rising Wind*, 188–89. Looking at it from another angle, in comparing the post–World War II course of the communist parties in the United States and South Africa, George Fredrickson makes the point that despite massive repression in both countries, the Communist Party of South Africa weathered it, while the Communist Party of the United States did not: "The most significant factor accounting for the contrast of fortunes was that the American communists faced strong competition from an interracial liberalism that appeared to be the wave of the future, whereas the South African party did not." As a result of the partial successes and advances during and immediately after the war years, he writes, "the gradualism and liberalism of the NAACP seemed vindicated, and the communist claim that capitalism and racial equality could not coexist lost credibility." Fredrickson, *Black Liberation*, chap. 5, quotes on 222–23.

65. Duberman, *Paul Robeson*, 324–30, 341–62; quotes on 342.

66. Ibid., 341–62, quote on 342; "Robeson Speaks for Robeson," Editorial, *Crisis*, May 1949, 137; Robeson, *Here I Stand*, 29–30.

67. On the events at Peekskill and Robeson's ongoing fight to get his passport restrictions lifted, see Duberman, *Paul Robeson*, 364–74, 388–463.

68. "Mr. Robeson's Passport," Editorial, *Pittsburgh Courier*, 19 Aug. 1950, 8; Robert Alan, "Paul Robeson — the Lost Shepherd," *Crisis*, Nov. 1951, 569–73. Penny Von Eschen cites a U.S. diplomat in the Gold Coast writing to the U.S. State Department earlier in the year suggesting that just such a disparaging article be written, preferably by a black American. Von Eschen, *Race against Empire*, 127–28. Gerald Horne presents "Alan" as the pen name of a well-known New York journalist who was "a mole in the service of the FBI." Horne, *Black and Red*, 207.

69. For more on the repression of Du Bois and Robeson, see Marable, *Race, Reform, and Rebellion*, 27–29; Horne, *Black and Red*, 201–21. For more on the Civil Rights Congress, see Horne, *Communist Front?: The Civil Rights Congress*. The U.S. government tried to silence nonleftist critics of American race relations, too, although the cases of this are less well documented. See Dudziak, "Josephine Baker, Racial Protest, and the Cold War."

70. Klarman, "How *Brown* Changed Race Relations," 88–90; Shepherd, *Anti-Apartheid*, 62; W. A. Jackson, *Gunnar Myrdal and America's Conscience*, 278; Roark, "American Black Leaders," 266–67; Sitkoff, *Struggle for Black Equality*, 16–18.

71. "Flag Day," Editorial, *Atlanta Daily World*, 10 June 1948, 6.

72. W. E. B. Du Bois to Walter White and the Board of Directors, 7 Sept. 1948, *NAACP Papers* 11, 15/331; White to Du Bois, ibid., 17/66.

73. For more on the Du Bois ouster, see Horne, *Black and Red*, 75–82, 97–111.

74. Roark, "American Black Leaders," 260–63; Von Eschen, *Race against Empire*, chaps. 4–6, esp. 109.

75. "Keep an Eye on the Communists," Editorial, *Crisis*, Apr. 1948, 105; "The NAACP and the Communists," Editorial, *Crisis*, Mar. 1949, 72; "Robeson Speaks for Robeson," Editorial, *Crisis*, May 1949, 137; "Annual Convention Resolutions," *Crisis*, Aug.–Sept. 1950, 522–23; "Annual Convention Resolutions," *Crisis*, Aug.–Sept. 1951, 475–76; "Annual Convention Resolutions," *Crisis*, Aug.–Sept. 1952, 446.

76. Du Bois offered twelve points on which he would base the article: the conceding of the capability of blacks to receive the highest education; the minimizing of race differences; the fact that race amalgamation was no longer regarded as necessarily evil; the start of factual, scientific study of races; the increasing black population and its improving health; the decreasing illiteracy and increasing college enrollment for black Americans; the shifting of occupations from farming and domestic service to trades and professions; the receiving of recognition in academic circles, the arts, literature, sports, and science; the large increases in the numbers of teachers and nurses, and the small increases in the numbers of doctors, lawyers, and dentists; the successful fight for political and civil rights, with twenty-three cases having been won before the Supreme Court from 1915 to 1948; the near elimination of lynching; the courting of the black vote by all parties, who no longer could buy it simply with appointments and purchase; and the black presence in the labor movement and social uplift movements in the United States. W. E. B. Du Bois to the Editor of *American Magazine*, 12 July 1948, *Du Bois Papers*, 61/371–72; Du Bois to

the Editor of *American Mercury*, 12 July 1948, ibid., 61/373–74. Holt, "Afro-Americans," 17.

77. "Truman to the NAACP," Editorial, *Crisis*, Aug. 1947, 233; *Public Papers of the Presidents of the United States: Harry S. Truman*, 1948: 121–26.

78. On Truman's conversion to supporting a civil rights agenda, see Plummer, *Rising Wind*, 167–216; Dudziak, "Desegregation as a Cold War Imperative," 77–80; Sitkoff, "Harry Truman and the Election of 1948"; Lawson, *Running for Freedom*, 32–38; Marable, *Race, Reform and Rebellion*, 25; Wynn, *The Afro-American and the Second World War*, 117–21.

79. Lauren, *Power and Prejudice*, 187–95, Marshall quote on 190; Dudziak, "Desegregation as a Cold War Imperative," quote on 62–63; Borstelmann, *Apartheid's Reluctant Uncle*, 64–67.

80. *Public Papers of the Presidents of the United States: Harry S. Truman*, 126; "United States Policy toward Dependent Territories," 26 Apr. 1950, *FRUS*, 1952–54, 3:1097; "Regional Policy Statement on Africa South of the Sahara," 29 Dec. 1950, *FRUS*, 1950, 5:1598; Minutes of the Board of Directors, June 1951, *NAACP Papers* 14, 13/781. See also Borstelmann, *Apartheid's Reluctant Uncle*, 64–65, 141.

81. Sitkoff, *Struggle for Black Equality*, 16. See also Dudziak, "Desegregation as a Cold War Imperative," 103–13.

82. Quoted in Dudziak, "Desegregation as a Cold War Imperative," 110–11. See also Emerson and Kilson, "The American Dilemma in a Changing World," 1073; Meier, "Toward a Synthesis of Civil Rights History," 216–17. James Baldwin would write of the *Brown* decision, "Most of the Negroes I know do not believe that this immense concession would ever have been made if it had not been for the competition of the Cold War, and the fact that Africa was clearly liberating herself and therefore had, for political reasons, to be wooed by the descendants of her former masters." J. Baldwin, *The Fire Next Time*, 100–101.

83. Randolph quoted in Marable, *Race, Reform, and Rebellion*, 21; NAACP quote in Dudziak, "Desegregation as a Cold War Imperative," 111 n. 287.

84. For example, Gerald Horne declares that "the price for Truman's support was steep — an abandonment of militant action, especially in the arena of foreign policy." Horne, *Black and Red*, 92. Penny Von Eschen likewise argues that moving to protect civil rights by grounding its justification firmly in anticommunism and support of U.S. foreign policy was done at a "very high" cost. Von Eschen, *Race against Empire*, 120, 186.

85. Plummer, *Rising Wind*, 210–12; Fredrickson, *Black Liberation*, 267.

86. Brooks, *The Negro Press Re-Examined*, 35, 120.

87. "Civil War in the NAACP," Editorial, *Pittsburgh Courier*, 25 Feb. 1950, 16; "Don't Sign Peace Ballot," Editorial, *Baltimore Afro-American*, 10 June 1950, 4. For other examples of the intense anticommunism of the African American press as exhibited in mid-1950 alone, see "The NAACP Board Meeting," Editorial, *Chicago Defender*, 6 May 1950, 6; "Calling the Red Bluff," Editorial, *Chicago Defender*, 8 July 1950; "Don't Be A Sucker," Editorial, *Chicago Defender*, 29 July 1950, 6;

"Crushing Soviet Lies," Editorial, *Pittsburgh Courier*, 29 Apr. 1950, 14; "FEP Begins at Home," Editorial, *Pittsburgh Courier*, 1 July 1950, 14; "Mr. Robeson's Passport," Editorial, *Pittsburgh Courier*, 19 Aug. 1950, 8; "The Phony Peace Drive," Editorial, *Pittsburgh Courier*, 26 Aug. 1950, 6; "Who'll Start the Next War?" Editorial, *Baltimore Afro-American*, 25 Feb. 1950, 4; "The NAACP and Communism," Editorial, *Atlanta Daily World*, 25 June 1950, 4.

88. For examples of such reasoning in the African American press, see "Tragic Happenings," Editorial, *New York Amsterdam News*, 29 Apr. 1950, 8; "Keep an Eye on Africa," Editorial, *Chicago Defender*, 5 Aug. 1950, 6.

89. Walter White to Helen Reid, 20 Oct. 1949, box 6, folder 174, Walter White and Poppy Cannon White Correspondence, Beinecke Library, Yale University; Walter White to Poppy Cannon White, 11 Oct. 1948, box 12, folder 111, ibid.

90. "Crushing Soviet Lies," Editorial, *Pittsburgh Courier*, 29 Apr. 1950, 14; "Now for Army Equality," Editorial, *Atlanta Daily World*, 26 May 1950, 4; "Both Parties Guilty of Ducking FEPC," Editorial, *Baltimore Afro-American*, 27 May 1950, 4. See also "Another Phony Crusade," Editorial, *Pittsburgh Courier*, 5 Aug. 1950, 14; "Setting a Poor Example," Editorial, *Baltimore Afro-American*, 22 July 1950, 4; "Moving Forward," Editorial, *Chicago Defender*, 29 Apr. 1950, 6; "Foreigners React to American Prejudice," Editorial, *Crisis*, Feb. 1951, 103.

91. Roy Wilkins to Walter White, 9 May 1951, *NAACP Papers* 14, 13/779.

92. Plummer, *Rising Wind*, 210, 218. Plummer in fact points out that the Cold War generally helped weaken attachments to an internationalist ideal and reasserted the primacy of the individual nation-state as the guarantor of civil rights.

Chapter Three

1. "S. Africa Captured by Rabid Racists," and "Polygamy in Africa, Ancestor Worship in China on Way Out," *Baltimore Afro-American*, 5 June 1948, 12; "S. Africa Captured by Rabid Racists," Editorial, *Baltimore Afro-American*, 12 June 1948, 4; "From Bad to Worse," Editorial, *Crisis*, July 1948, 201; "South Africa Steps Backward," Editorial, *Chicago Defender*, 12 June 1948, 14; *Atlanta Daily World*, 16 May–29 June 1948; Paul Robeson to W. E. B. Du Bois, 26 May 1948, *Du Bois Papers*, 61/770.

2. "Landmark in Negro Progress," Editorial, *Pittsburgh Courier*, 12 June 1948, 6.

3. Quoted in Thomas Karis, "Joint Action and the Defiance Campaign, 1950–1952," 2:404 n. 4. For background on apartheid legislation and practice, see Study Commission on U.S. Policy Toward Southern Africa, *South Africa: Time Running Out*, 48–167; Meredith, *In the Name of Apartheid*, 54–62.

4. Lodge, *Black Politics in South Africa*, 33–34; Karis, "Joint Action and the Defiance Campaign," 2:405–7; Borstelmann, *Apartheid's Reluctant Uncle*, 147–49.

5. "Report of the Joint Planning Council of the African National Congress and the South African Indian Congress," 8 Nov. 1951, in Karis and Carter, *From Protest to Challenge*, 2:460; Karis, "Joint Action and the Defiance Campaign," 2:407–10;

Lodge, *Black Politics in South Africa*, 34–36; Borstelmann, *Apartheid's Reluctant Uncle*, 149–51.

6. Willard Townsend column, *Chicago Defender*, 29 Nov. 1952, 11.

7. "Keep an Eye on Africa," Editorial, *Chicago Defender*, 5 Aug. 1950, 6. See also "The Blockheads in Britain," Editorial, *Chicago Defender*, 18 Mar. 1950, 6.

8. "Hate in S. Africa Challenges World!" Editorial, *New York Amsterdam News*, 24 June 1950, 1; "S. Africa Should Be Next," Editorial, *Baltimore Afro-American*, 20 May 1950, 4. The same comparison would be used in years to come, as when the *Amsterdam News* called apartheid "the worst racist system that contemporary times have known," and the *Defender* declared that South Africa's racial laws "go beyond anything witnessed in Nazi Germany or the darkest period in the history of Mississippi." "S. Africa Arrests Gandhi," Editorial, *New York Amsterdam News*, 13 Dec. 1952, 16; "King George and Dr. Malan," Editorial, *Chicago Defender*, 26 Jan. 1952, 10.

9. For an insightful discussion on shifting views about racism, see Von Eschen, *Race against Empire*, chap. 7, esp. 153–59.

10. "Council Warns of Fascist Menace in South Africa," CAA Press Release, 16 June 1950, box 2, folder 3, Hunton Papers; Henry Lee Moon to Walter White, 20 Oct. 1950, *NAACP Papers* 14, 4/670; NAACP Press Release, 9 Nov. 1950, *NAACP Papers* 14, 4/671; NAACP Press Release, 26 Oct. 1950, *NAACP Papers* 14, 2/112. Alphaeus Hunton also wrote a short pamphlet for the CAA on the continent's struggles, entitled *Africa Fights for Freedom*.

11. "Hate in S. Africa Challenges World!" Editorial, *New York Amsterdam News*, 24 June 1950, 1; A. M. Wendell Maillet, Foreign News Editor, "Attlee Weakness Seen Cause of Seretse Woe," *New York Amsterdam News*, 22 July 1950, 15; "The Blockheads in Britain," Editorial, *Chicago Defender*, 18 Mar. 1950, 6; "Keep an Eye on Africa," Editorial, *Chicago Defender*, 5 Aug. 1950, 6; "Great Britain Has a Nerve," Editorial, *Baltimore Afro-American*, 1 Apr. 1950, 4.

12. Board of Directors Minutes, 22 June 1950, *NAACP Papers* 14, 13/717–18; "African Natives Are Right," Editorial, *Baltimore Afro-American*, 25 Feb. 1950, 4; "S. Africa Should Be Next," Editorial, *Baltimore Afro-American*, 20 May 1950, 4; A. A. Marks to W. A. Hunton, n.d. [July 1950], and W. A. Hunton to A. A. Marks, 6 July 1950, both in box 1, folder 16, Hunton Papers.

13. On the limited press coverage, see "Mourning Day Protests New S. African Jimcrow," *New York Amsterdam News*, 3 June 1950, 5; "Africans to Protest New Racial Bills," *Chicago Defender*, 10 June 1950, 1; "Fearful South Africa Ends Silent, Stay-at-Home Strike," *New York Amsterdam News*, 1 July 1950, 19; "65% Stop Work on 'Protest Day' in Africa," *Atlanta Daily World*, 9 July 1950, 1. For more on the Day of Protest, see Borstelmann, *Apartheid's Reluctant Uncle*, 149–51.

14. Albert Barnett, "Two Interesting News Items from Faraway Africa," *Chicago Defender*, 22 July 1950, 7.

15. Policy Statement of the Department of State, 1 Nov. 1948, *FRUS*, 1948, 5:524–32.

16. Borstelmann, *Apartheid's Reluctant Uncle*, 48–50, quote on 48.

17. Memo by Acting Secretary of State (Lovett) to President Truman, 23 Nov. 1948, *FRUS*, 1948, 5:532.

18. Consul General in Johannesburg (Redecker) to Department of State, "Serious Native Riots in Johannesburg," 17 Feb. 1950, *FRUS*, 1950, 5:1809–13; Joseph Sweeney (for the Chargé in South Africa Connelly) to Secretary of State, "May Day Riots on the Rand," 8 June 1950, ibid., 5:1824–26.

19. Sweeney (for Ambassador in South Africa Erhardt) to Secretary of State, "Communist Influence in South African Trade Unions," 3 Oct. 1950, *FRUS*, 1950, 5:1834–35; Ambassador in Union of South Africa (Erhardt) to Dominion Affairs Officer, Office of British Commonwealth and Northern European Affairs (Shullaw), 30 Jan. 1951, *FRUS*, 1951, 5:1428–29.

20. Acheson, *Present at the Creation*, 379.

21. For U.S. relations with South Africa and the issue of South West Africa, see Borstelmann, *Apartheid's Reluctant Uncle*, 77–78, 106–7, 121–22, 161–62; Noer, *Cold War and Black Liberation*, 25–26, 31–32. For relations between India and South Africa in the years immediately following World War II, see Lauren, *Power and Prejudice*, 167–71; Kapur, *Raising Up a Prophet*, 129–32. For more on African American interest in South West Africa and the treatment of Indians in South Africa, see Von Eschen, *Race against Empire*, 83–93.

22. "Department of State Policy Statement," 28 Mar. 1951, *FRUS*, 1951, 5:1433–42, quotes on 1433–34.

23. Draft Memorandum Prepared in Office of Dependent Area Affairs in combination with the Office of UN Political and Security Affairs, 8 May 1952, *FRUS*, 1952–54, 3:1111–15, "middle course" quote on 1114; Hickerson (Assistant Secretary of State for UN Affairs) to Matthews (Deputy Under Secretary of State), 13 May 1952, ibid., 3:1116–17 for "middle position"; Perkins (Assistant Secretary of State for European Affairs) to Matthews, 4 June 1952, ibid., 3:1118 for "middle-of-the-road position." Historians Thomas Noer and Thomas Borstelmann have examined the evolution of U.S. efforts to follow a "middle path," taking as a prime exemplar the need to carve out a policy toward South Africa while noting that the issue had to be confronted throughout the continent. See Noer, "Truman, Eisenhower, and South Africa: The 'Middle Road' and Apartheid"; Noer, *Cold War and Black Liberation*, 1–60; Borstelmann, *Apartheid's Reluctant Uncle*, esp. 139–44 and 177–79.

24. For a superb account of U.S.–South African relations during the 1940s and early 1950s, see Borstelmann, *Apartheid's Reluctant Uncle*. See also Noer, *Cold War and Black Liberation*, 15–60.

25. See Kornegay, "Black America and U.S.–Southern African Relations," 138–44.

26. Director of Special Research Annual Report, July 1945, GOF, 1940–55, ser. A, box 240, folder "Du Bois, William E. B., General, 1945"; Memorandum from W. E. B. Du Bois to Walter White, 2 Dec. 1946, GOF, ser. A, box 241, folder "Du Bois, William E. B., General, 1946."

27. Third Secretary of Embassy in Union of South Africa (Dembo) to Department of State, "Race Conflict and the Native Outlook," 2 Aug. 1951, *FRUS*, 1951, 5:1448–49; Joseph Sweeney (for Ambassador in Union of South Africa Gallman) to Department of State, "Native Unrest," 9 Nov. 1951, ibid., 5:1460–62.

28. "Report of the Joint Planning Council of the African National Congress and the South African Indian Congress," 8 Nov. 1951, in Karis and Carter, *From Protest to Challenge*, 2:458–65. See also Karis, "Joint Action and the Defiance Campaign," 2:412–14; Kuper, *Passive Resistance in South Africa*, 99–106.

29. "Letter Calling for Repeal of Repressive Legislation and Threatening a Defiance Campaign," 21 Jan. 1952, in Karis and Carter, *From Protest to Challenge*, 2:476–77; A. J. Siggins, "Along the Colonial Front," *Atlanta Daily World*, 15 Jan. 1952, 6; "Africans Rising Against Bias," *Pittsburgh Courier*, 19 Jan. 1952, 19; "South Africa's White Rulers Warn Blacks Against Protest," *New York Amsterdam News*, 2 Feb. 1952, 3; "Natives Warned Against White Supremacy Protest," *Atlanta Daily World*, 7 Feb. 1952, 4; Kuper, *Passive Resistance*, 99–111.

30. Karis, "Joint Action and the Defiance Campaign," 2:414 n. 34; "Letter Replying to Letter from Prime Minister's Office and Statement of Intention to Launch Defiance Campaign," 11 Feb. 1952, in Karis and Carter, *From Protest to Challenge*, 2:480–82.

31. "South Africans To Continue Fight for Rights," *Atlanta Daily World*, 4 Mar. 1952, 2; "April 6 To Be Crucial Day in South Africa," *Atlanta Daily World*, 3 Apr. 1952, 8; "Gandhi's Son Begins Fast Against African Segregation Edicts," *Baltimore Afro-American*, 15 Mar. 1952, 3; "Gandhi Protests 'Jimcrow'; Fasts," *New York Amsterdam News*, 15 Mar. 1952, 7.

32. Karis, "Joint Action and the Defiance Campaign," 2:416–17; "Gandhi Ends Protest Fast in South Africa," *Baltimore Afro-American*, 5 Apr. 1952, 5; "South Africans Stage Strong Protest Against Race Laws," *Atlanta Daily World*, 8 Apr. 1952, 6; "S. Africa Fights Back," *New York Amsterdam News*, 12 Apr. 1952, 1.

33. "Political Cops Raid Homes in S. Africa," *New York Amsterdam News*, 2 Aug. 1952, 2; "Jail More South Africans," ibid., 9 Aug. 1952, 16; "S. Africa Jails 600 Non-Whites," ibid., 23 Aug. 1952, 16; "Arrests Continue in S. Africa; 5,600 Jailed," ibid., 18 Oct. 1952, 42; Karis, "Joint Action and the Defiance Campaign," 2:418–21; Lodge, *Black Politics in South Africa*, 42–44; Borstelmann, *Apartheid's Reluctant Uncle*, 170–76; Fredrickson, *Black Liberation*, 246–47.

34. M. D. Cartwright, "Africa in Our Schools," *New York Amsterdam News*, 10 Jan. 1953, 14; "Black Africa: Primitive Society Holds Out South of the Sahara," *Life*, 4 May 1953, 91.

35. "African Chief Eats Brother," *Pittsburgh Courier*, 10 Mar. 1951, 15. On the other hand, see Hunton, *Resistance Against Fascist Enslavement in South Africa*, 48–62. See also Von Eschen, *Race against Empire*, 145–46.

36. "Colored Americans in Paris Resent Being 'Tagged' as African Natives," *Baltimore Afro-American*, 4 Oct. 1952, 7.

37. E. B. Thompson, *Africa, Land of My Fathers*, 16–17.

38. Marjorie McKenzie, "Pursuit of Democracy," *Pittsburgh Courier*, 28 Feb. 1953, 7.

39. Cayton, *Long Old Road*; Drake and Cayton, *Black Metropolis*.

40. Cayton, *Long Old Road*, 371.

41. Horace Cayton, "Cayton," *Pittsburgh Courier*, 20 June 1953, 7. For examples of African Americans putting democratic ideals to the fore, see "S. Africa Arrests Gandhi," Editorial, *New York Amsterdam News*, 13 Dec. 1952, 16; "Africa IS Important," Editorial, *New York Amsterdam News*, 9 May 1953, 18. See also Plummer, *Rising Wind*, 255.

42. Bayard Rustin, "Africa Looks to Colored America," *Baltimore Afro-American*, 29 Nov. 1952, *Afro Magazine*, 6; Anderson, *Bayard Rustin*, 143–45.

43. "Many of Our Race Leaders Cautious, Fear 'Red' Brand," *Pittsburgh Courier*, 14 June 1952, 20; "Readers Say Red 'Threat' Aids Race Progress in the U.S.," *Pittsburgh Courier*, 16 Aug. 1952, 2.

44. See, for example, "Enemies of America," Editorial, *Baltimore Afro-American*, 2 Aug. 1952, 4.

45. International President, Brotherhood of Sleeping Car Porters (Randolph) to President Eisenhower, 17 June 1953, *FRUS*, 1952–54, 11:46.

46. To help publicize the cruelties of apartheid, White also attempted to convince the U.S. delegation to support the opportunity for Africans to give oral testimony as part of UN investigations into apartheid. Walter White to "Dear Friends," 13 Nov. 1952, *NAACP Papers* 14, 5/233; Secretary's Report Fragment, n.d. [Nov. 1952], ibid., 5/251; NAACP Press Release, 13 Nov. 1952, ibid., 5/172; Draft Letter to the United States Delegation to the United Nations, 28 Oct. 1952, ibid., 5/228–32; Letter to the United States Delegation to the United Nations, 5 Dec. 1952, ibid., 5/254–59; NAACP Press Release, 5 Dec, 1952, ibid., 5/260–61. "Group Urges U.S. To Support Aspirations of Africans," *Atlanta Daily World*, 11 Dec. 1952, 2; "Africa — Continent in Turmoil," *New York Amsterdam News*, 20 Dec. 1952, 8; "Urge UN Action on South Africa," Editorial, *Baltimore Afro-American*, 22 Nov. 1952, 5.

47. "Another Gandhi Begins Fast," Editorial, *Chicago Defender*, 22 Mar. 1952, 10. See also "Malan Cracks the Whip," Editorial, *Chicago Defender*, 9 Feb. 1952, 10; "The Case of Seretse Khama," Editorial, *Chicago Defender*, 5 Apr. 1952, 10; "How To Win Friends," Editorial *Baltimore Afro-American*, 5 Apr. 1952, 4; William Gordon, "Reviewing the News," *Atlanta Daily World*, 28 Dec. 1952, 4.

48. Secretary of State to the Embassy at Pretoria, 19 Sept. 1952, *FRUS*, 1952–54, 11:934–35. See also Memorandum by Assistant Secretary of State for European Affairs (Perkins) to Acting Assistant Secretary of State for Near Eastern, South Asian, and African Affairs (Berry), 10 Apr. 1952, ibid., 11:907–8; Secretary of State to Embassy at Pretoria, 21 Apr. 1953, ibid., 11:995–96; Ambassador in Union of South Africa (Gallman) to Department of State, 27 Apr. 1953, ibid., 11:997–98.

49. "UN Strong, US Weak," Editorial, *New York Amsterdam News*, 29 Nov. 1952, 14. See also "UN Votes vs. Freedom," Editorial, *Baltimore Afro-American*, 23 May

1953, 4. For more on U.S. officials' determination to stay the course with South Africa during these years, see Borstelmann, *Apartheid's Reluctant Uncle*, 166–94.

50. "Uranium and S. Africa," Editorial, *New York Amsterdam News*, 30 May 1953, 14. For more on the importance of uranium to U.S. policymakers and relations with South Africa, see Borstelmann, *Apartheid's Reluctant Uncle*, 91–98, 162–65, 185–86, 198–99.

51. "The Single Issue," Editorial, *Crisis*, June–July 1952, 344. In the end, the *Baltimore Afro-American*, *Chicago Defender*, and *New York Amsterdam News* endorsed Adlai Stevenson; the *Atlanta Daily World* and the *Pittsburgh Courier* endorsed Dwight Eisenhower.

52. Anderson, *Bayard Rustin*, 140–42; Houser, *No One Can Stop the Rain*, 12; Manilal Gandhi to Bayard Rustin, 18 Apr. 1951, *Bayard Rustin Papers* (microfilm), 2/48; Gandhi to Rustin, 30 Apr. 1955, *Bayard Rustin Papers*, 2/50. Anderson is mistaken, however, to identify AFSAR as "the first organized effort in the United States on behalf of any African freedom movement." Certainly the CAA's efforts predate AFSAR.

53. Charles Trigg and Donald Harrington to Walter White, 6 Oct. 1952, *NAACP Papers* 14, 4/795–96; George Houser to Anonymous, 26 June 1953, ibid., 10/848; Houser, "Thoughts on Organization for Effective Work on Africa," n.d. [1953], ibid., 10/855–58; "Plan Protest Against S. African Race Laws," *New York Amsterdam News*, 22 Mar. 1952, box 1, folder 16, Hunton Papers. For a list of members of AFSAR in April 1953, see "Support the Nonviolent Campaign Against Unjust Laws in South Africa," *Schomburg CCF*, 004,657-2.

54. Alphaeus Hunton to Rev. Donald Harrington, 21 Mar. 1952, and George Houser to Alphaeus Hunton, 28 Mar. 1952, both in box 1, folder 16, Hunton Papers.

55. Arthur Spingarn to Walter White, 6 Aug. 1953, *NAACP Papers* 14, 11/184; Roy Wilkins to White, 7 Aug. 1953, ibid., 11/187. See also Shepherd, *Anti-Apartheid*, 30–65.

56. "Urges Silent Campaigns to Aid S. Africa," *New York Amsterdam News*, 22 Mar. 1952, 2; "African Riots Loom; Harlemites Protest," *New York Amsterdam News*, 5 Apr. 1952, 1; "Harlemites to Picket For So. Africa's Freedom," *Atlanta Daily World*, 8 Apr. 1952, 4; Walter White to James Moroka, 8 Apr. 1952, *NAACP Papers* 14, 4/696.

57. Alphaeus Hunton to W. E. B. Du Bois, 2 Apr. 1952, *Du Bois Papers*, 68/187; "African Riots Loom; Harlemites Protest," *New York Amsterdam News*, 5 Apr. 1952, 1; "Harlemites To Picket for So. Africa's Freedom," *Atlanta Daily World*, 8 Apr. 1952, 4; "Harlem Speaks for South African Freedom" and "30 Hours of Picketing," *Spotlight on Africa*, 14 Apr. 1952, 1; "Picket S. African Embassy in D.C.," *Pittsburgh Courier*, 19 Apr. 1952, 1.

58. "An Important Message from Paul Robeson," *Spotlight on Africa*, 25 Feb. 1952, 1.

59. Benjamin Mays, "Mays," *Pittsburgh Courier*, 19 Apr. 1952, 7; Mary McLeod Bethune, "Mary McLeod Bethune," *Chicago Defender*, 19 July 1952, 10; Mary

McLeod Bethune, "Mary McLeod Bethune," *Chicago Defender*, 26 July 1952, 10 (quote).

60. "Another Gandhi Begins Fast," Editorial, *Chicago Defender*, 22 Mar. 1952, 10; "Our Business, Too," Editorial, *New York Amsterdam News*, 12 Apr. 1952, 16; "Look Who's Talking," Editorial, *Baltimore Afro-American*, 24 May 1952, 4.

61. "Protest in South Africa," Editorial, *New York Amsterdam News*, 5 July 1952, 15; "They Cannot Lose," Editorial, *Baltimore Afro-American*, 5 July 1952, 4.

62. Circular from W. E. B. Du Bois et al., 12 Mar. 1952, *Du Bois Papers*, 68/395; "Petition to the President of the United States and the United States Delegation to the United Nations," n.d. [Mar. 1952], ibid., 68/395–97; Du Bois to Harry S. Truman, 27 June 1952, ibid., 68/399; Du Bois Press Release, 29 June 1952, ibid., 68/402–4; Lillian Hyman for Du Bois to Petition Sponsors, 3 July 1952, ibid., 68/401; "Plan Drive in Behalf of Africa," *New York Amsterdam News*, 5 July 1952, 5.

63. Circular from Alphaeus Hunton et al., 14 July 1952, *Du Bois Papers*, 68/197; Hunton to Du Bois, 17 July 1952, ibid., 68/197; Hunton to Du Bois, 25 July 1952, ibid., 68/198; CAA News Release, 25 July 1952, ibid., 68/198; Hunton to Du Bois, 17 Sept. 1952, ibid., 68/199; "Contributions of $900 Sent to Aid Freedom Struggle in South Africa as Petition Drive Continues to Oct. 15," *Spotlight on Africa*, 18 Sept. 1952, 1; "Campaign of the CAA in Aid of Arrested Volunteers and Their Families, Statement of Income and Disbursements, July 24 to Dec. 31, 1952," box 1, folder 18, Hunton Papers; "Lend Support to S. Africans," *New York Amsterdam News*, 10 Jan. 1953, 20; "Z. K. Matthews' Son Among Convicted S. Africans," *New York Amsterdam News*, 11 Apr. 1953, 36; Walter Sisulu, "Message to the Negro People of the United States of America," n.d. [Sept. 1952], box 1, folder 16, Hunton Papers; Lynch, *Black American Radicals and the Liberation of Africa*, 44–45.

64. For example, the *Daily World* remained absolutely silent on events in South Africa, while the *Courier*, which had been a militant voice in the 1930s and 1940s, offered only one three-sentence editorial concerning South Africa throughout 1952, "Drama in South Africa," Editorial, *Pittsburgh Courier*, 16 Aug. 1952, 6.

65. William Clarke, New York, to the Editor, *Pittsburgh Courier*, 24 May 1952, 11; Cliff Mackay, "Election of Ike '52's Biggest Story," *Baltimore Afro-American*, 10 Jan. 1953, 14; Charles Terrell to the Editor, *Baltimore Afro-American*, 17 Jan. 1953, 4.

66. Evangeline Johnson, New York City, to the Editor, *Pittsburgh Courier*, 6 Sept. 1952, 11.

67. Jaime Suarez, New York City, to the Editor, *Pittsburgh Courier*, 22 Nov. 1952, 11.

68. Lester Granger, "Manhattan and Beyond," *New York Amsterdam News*, 9 May 1953, 18; Evangeline Washington, New York City, to the Editor, *Pittsburgh Courier*, 21 Feb. 1953, 11.

69. Walter White to Eugene Black, 1 Feb. 1951, *NAACP Papers* 14, 5/3; Black to White, 6 Feb. 1951, ibid., 5/5; White to Black, 8 Feb. 1951, ibid., 5/4; White to Black, 16 Feb. 1951, ibid., 5/7; Black to White, 28 Feb. 1951, ibid., 5/6.

70. Roy Garvin to Walter White, 9 May 1952, *NAACP Papers* 14, 5/13; White to Garvin, 19 May 1952, ibid., 5/12; White to Jonas Reiner, 19 May 1952, ibid., 5/11; White to Ralph Bunche, 31 Oct. 1952, ibid., 5/14; White to Bunche, Spingarn, Tobias and Mitchell, 21 Nov. 1952, ibid., 5/15; White to Eugene Black, 21 July 1953, ibid., 5/17; Black to White, 30 July 1953, ibid., 5/16; White to Prof. Z. K. Matthews, 3 Aug. 1953, ibid., 5/19–20.

71. 1950 Annual Convention Resolution, *NAACP Papers* 1, 12/947; 1952 Annual Convention Resolution, *NAACP Papers* 1, 1951–55 suppl., 5/179–80.

72. 1952 Annual Conference Resolutions, June 1952, *NAACP Papers* 1, 1951–55 suppl., 5/182.

73. Board of Directors Minutes, 9 Sept. and 13 Oct. 1952, *NAACP Papers* 14, 5/373; Walter White to Benjamin Mays, 4 Nov. 1952, ibid., 4/788.

74. "Statement on Violence in New Brighton, Port Elizabeth on October 18," 20 Oct. 1952, in Karis and Carter, *From Protest to Challenge*, 2:484–85; Borstelmann, *Apartheid's Reluctant Uncle*, 173–74.

75. Thomas Karis, "1953: Inside and Outside the Political Arena," in Karis and Carter, *From Protest to Challenge*, 3:6.

76. Karis, "Joint Action and the Defiance Campaign," 2:425–28; Borstelmann, *Apartheid's Reluctant Uncle*, 175–76; Kuper, "African Nationalism in South Africa," 462–63; Kuper, *Passive Resistance*, 144–5; Roux, *Time Longer than Rope*, 393–94; Houser, *No One Can Stop the Rain*, 18–19; Fredrickson, *Black Liberation*, 247–49.

77. "Let's Look at Africa," Editorial, *Chicago Defender*, 29 Nov. 1952, 10; "Africa in Turmoil," Editorial, *Pittsburgh Courier*, 30 May 1953, 6. Haynes, who wrote the book *Africa: Continent of the Future* based on his 1947 trip, began his series in June 1952, while the Cayton series started in November 1952, and the Jack series in January 1953.

78. Lawrence Jenkins, Mount Vernon, N.Y., *Pittsburgh Courier*, 6 June 1953, 17. See also William A. Clarke, New York City, *Pittsburgh Courier*, 24 May 1952, 11; Evangeline Johnson, New York City, *Pittsburgh Courier*, 6 Sept. 1952, 11; D. W. Blakeslee, Pittsburgh, *Pittsburgh Courier*, 15 Nov. 1952, 11; Elmo Dinkins, Victorville, Calif., *Pittsburgh Courier*, 31 Jan. 1953, 11; June Bohannon, *Pittsburgh Courier*, Newark, N.J., 18 July 1953, 17. For editorials discussing these issues, see "Africa in Turmoil," Editorial, *Pittsburgh Courier*, 30 May 1953, 6; "Africa IS Important," Editorial, *New York Amsterdam News*, 9 May 1953, 18.

79. Matthew Holden, in the Albert Barnett column, *Chicago Defender*, 15 Mar. 1952, 11.

80. Randolph to Eisenhower, 17 June 1953, *FRUS*, 1952–54, 11:43–46; Director, Office of African Affairs (Utter) to Chief of Protocol (Simmons), "Recommendations for White House Reply to Mr. A. Philip Randolph," 4 Sept. 1953, ibid., 11:51–52.

81. "Africa: Next Goal of Communists," *U.S. News & World Report*, 1 May 1953, 52–63. Walter White article, 7 May 1953, *NAACP Papers* 14, 3/771–72; Board of Directors Minutes, June 1953, *NAACP Papers* 1, 1951–55 suppl., 1/714; Lester Granger, "Manhattan and Beyond," *New York Amsterdam News*, 23 May 1953, 18;

Beatrice Davoen, Brooklyn, to the Editor, *New York Amsterdam News*, 18 July 1953, 18; Willard Townsend, "Labor in the News," *Pittsburgh Courier*, 4 July 1953, 6.

82. "Leaders Change Tactics," Editorial, *Chicago Defender*, 3 Mar. 1951, 6.

83. "Germ Warfare in Deep South," Editorial, *Pittsburgh Courier*, 26 July 1952, 6; "A Different Procedure," Editorial, *Atlanta Daily World*, 19 Apr. 1950, 6.

84. Marjorie McKenzie, "Civil Disobedience Is Undesirable in America," *Pittsburgh Courier*, 12 July 1952, 7.

85. Horace Cayton, "Cayton," *Pittsburgh Courier*, 19 Apr. 1952, 6; "South Africa and World Opinion," Editorial, *Chicago Defender*, 23 Aug. 1952, 10. In portraying the Defiance Campaign and the U.S. civil rights movement as largely disconnected, George Fredrickson understates the long-term influence of the Defiance Campaign. See Fredrickson, *Black Liberation*, 252–53.

86. A. L. Foster to the Editor, *Baltimore Afro-American*, 12 July 1952, 4.

Chapter Four

1. Lonsdale, "Mau Maus of the Mind," 398. Bruce Berman cites slightly different figures: 1,920 "loyal" Africans killed, of whom 1,819 were civilians; 95 Europeans killed, of whom 35 were civilians. Berman, *Control and Crisis in Colonial Kenya*, 352.

2. Edgerton, *Mau Mau*, 1–41.

3. Maloba, *Mau Mau and Kenya*, 24–44; Throup, *Economic and Social Origins of Mau Mau*, 3–11; Edgerton, *Mau Mau*, 1–41.

4. Lonsdale, "Mau Maus of the Mind," 399. Some estimates claim that as many as 90 percent of the Kikuyu took a version of the oath. Edgerton, *Mau Mau*, 49–61.

5. Maloba, *Mau Mau and Kenya*, 40–59; Throup, *Economic and Social Origins of Mau Mau*, 3–11; Ogot and Zeleza, "Kenya: The Road to Independence and After," 404; Kershaw, *Mau Mau from Below*. The Mau Mau left no written manifesto or list of objectives, and knowledge about the movement remains murky. Indeed, even the origin, meaning, and use of the name "Mau Mau" generates mystery and debate. Disagreement also arises over its exact nature, whether it was atavistic or progressive, tribalist or nationalist, successful or not. However, an analysis of the specific origins and characteristics of Mau Mau are of less concern here than the context within which contemporary African Americans viewed the Mau Mau. For more on Mau Mau, see Lonsdale, "Mau Maus of the Mind"; Berman, *Control and Crisis in Colonial Africa*; Edgerton, *Mau Mau*; Furedi, *The Mau Mau War in Perspective*; Buijtenhuijs, *Essays on Mau Mau*.

6. Edgerton, *Mau Mau*, 41–68, 85–87; Maloba, *Mau Mau and Kenya*, 70–77; Throup, *Economic and Social Origins of Mau Mau*, 11–12.

7. Borstelmann, *Apartheid's Reluctant Uncle*, 195.

8. "Political and Economic Problems in Africa," n.d., *FRUS*, 1950, 5:1504; Memorandum by Assistant Secretary of State for Near Eastern, South Asian and African

Affairs (McGhee) to the Secretary of State (Acheson) and to Under Secretary of State (Webb), 12 Apr. 1950, ibid., 5:1515; McGhee, *Envoy to the Middle World*, 114.

9. "Political and Economic Problems in Africa," *FRUS*, 1950, 5:1503–9; Memorandum by Assistant Secretary of State for Near Eastern, South Asian and African Affairs (McGhee) to Secretary of State and to the Deputy Under Secretary of State (Rusk), 17 Feb. 1950, ibid., 5:1510. See also McGhee, *Envoy to the Middle World*, 115–17.

10. McGhee to Acheson and Webb, 12 Apr. 1950, *FRUS*, 1950, 5:1514–23, quote on 1519. McGhee himself would later admit about the meeting that "there was no hint of boldness with respect to the promotion of decolonization" and that at best there were "vague references to African — as distinguished from metropolitan — opinion." McGhee, *Envoy to the Middle World*, 123–25.

11. "United States Policy Toward Dependent Territories," 26 Apr. 1950, *FRUS*, 1952–54, 3:1077–1102; "Regional Policy Statement on Africa South of the Sahara," 29 Dec. 1950, *FRUS*, 1950, 5:1588, 1590.

12. "Regional Policy Statement on Africa South of the Sahara," 29 Dec. 1950, *FRUS*, 1950, 5:1590.

13. George McGhee, "Africa's Role in the Free World Today," *State Department Bulletin* 25 (16 July 1951): 101.

14. Some scholars have concluded that U.S. officials did not show interest in Africa until at least the time of Ghana's independence in 1957, or even until the Congo turmoil in 1960. Henry Jackson, for instance, argues that U.S. policymakers began to examine Africa only when African nations arose as new and independent in the 1960s. H. F. Jackson, *From the Congo to Soweto*, 18. Yet, although Africa held no high priority, the State Department did try to coordinate policy toward dependent areas, including Africa, during the late 1940s and throughout the 1950s. Further, Borstelmann's *Apartheid's Reluctant Uncle* and Noer's *Cold War and Black Liberation* plainly show that South Africa held particular concern for the Truman administration.

15. Memorandum by Acting Deputy Director of the Office of Western European Affairs (Knight), 21 Apr. 1952, *FRUS*, 1952–54, 3:1103–4. Knight further argued that U.S. assistance to the evolution of all peoples toward political autonomy should be part of a long-term project only. He believed that a strong alliance with the European allies would help contain the Soviets and circumvent the danger of communists taking control of independent and weak colonial areas. "[W]here self-government is attained prematurely, these problems are magnified. . . . Premature independence, even with non-Communist governments in control at the start will usually lead to mass dissatisfactions and disillusionments which can be skillfully exploited by the Communists and which can lead within a relatively short period of time to a Communist seizure of power" (1106–7).

16. Draft Memorandum Prepared in the Office of Dependent Area Affairs and the Office of United Nations Political and Security Affairs, 8 May 1952, *FRUS*, 1952–54, 3:1111–15; quote on 1114.

17. Ibid., 3:1114; Memorandum by Assistant Secretary of State for European Affairs (Perkins) to Deputy Under Secretary of State (Freeman Matthews), 4 June 1952, *FRUS*, 1952–54, 3:1118. See also Noer, *Cold War and Black Liberation*, 1–2.

18. Plummer, *Rising Wind*, 255; Noer, *Cold War and Black Liberation*, 34.

19. "Address before the World Affairs Council of Northern California," 31 Oct. 1953, *FRUS*, 1952–54, 11:54–65.

20. "Semi-Monthly Politico-Economic Summary—British East Africa," RG 59, DF, 1950–54, British Africa-East, 745P.00/11-951; "Mau Mau Activity," Angus Ward, Consul General, Nairobi, ibid., 745R.00/2-1852; "Semi-Monthly Politico-Economic Summary—British East Africa," ibid., 745P.00/5-2652.

21. "Fortnightly Survey, British East Africa, November 13–26, 1952" RG 59, DF, 1950–54, British Africa-East, 745P.00/11-2652; "Fortnightly Survey, British East Africa, November 27–December 10, 1952," ibid., 745P.00/12-1052; "Weekly Review, Kenya, December 25–31, 1952," ibid., British Africa—Kenya Colony, 745R.00/12-3152; "The Mau Mau Movement," Edmund Dorsz, 2 Jan. 1953, ibid., 745R.00/1-253.

22. "Turmoil and Progress," Editorial, *Pittsburgh Courier*, 18 Apr. 1953, 6.

23. Lonsdale, "Mau Maus of the Mind," 398. For more on British and Mau Mau actions during the war, see Maloba, *Mau Mau and Kenya*, 81–133.

24. "Kenyatta Sentence Reversed," Editorial, *Pittsburgh Courier*, 25 July 1953, 6; "Tougher Policy in Kenya," Editorial, *Pittsburgh Courier*, 20 June 1953, 6; Joel Rogers, "Rogers Says," *Pittsburgh Courier*, 8 Nov. 1952, 7; "Looking & Listening," *Crisis*, Dec. 1952, 651, and Feb. 1953, 106; George Shepherd, "Mau Mau and Agricultural Development," *Crisis*, Jan. 1954, 13–18; George Padmore, "British Parliamentary Delegation Reports on Kenya," *Crisis*, May 1954, 273–77, 314. See also "New Hope for Kenya," Editorial, *Chicago Defender*, 16 May 1953, 11.

25. "The Mau Mau Grows," Editorial, *Baltimore Afro-American*, 18 Apr. 1953, 4; "New Hope For Kenya," Editorial, *Chicago Defender*, 16 May 1953, 11; Joel Rogers, "Murder in Kenya!" *Pittsburgh Courier*, 30 May 1953, 1. See also "The Truth About Kenya," Editorial, *Baltimore Afro-American*, 20 Dec. 1952, 4; "Two Reports on Mau Mau," Editorial, *New York Amsterdam News*, 7 May 1955, 16.

26. "The Truth about Kenya," Editorial, *Baltimore Afro-American*, 20 Dec. 1952, 4; "Red Puppet or Black Patriot?" Editorial, *New York Amsterdam News*, 11 July 1953, 14.

27. Ruark, *Something of Value*, foreword; Furedi, *Mau Mau War in Perspective*, 4. This section is informed by the insightful analysis in Foreman, "Mau Mau's American Career."

28. "Africans in Bloody Revolt against Whites," *Chicago Defender*, 1 Nov. 1952, 2; "Peace Can Come Now to Africa with More Reason," *Chicago Defender*, 20 Dec. 1952, 3; "British Send Brigade to Fight Mau Mau," and "Experts See Climax of Cult Terror," *Chicago Defender*, 11 Apr. 1953, 2 and 6; "Fear Grips African Colony in Wake of Mau Mau Group's Mass Murders," *Baltimore Afro-American*, 18 Oct. 1952, 5; "British Arrest More Africans," *Baltimore Afro-American*, 22 Nov. 1952,

22; "Police in Kenya Seize 300 More Natives in Purge," *Baltimore Afro-American*, 20 Dec. 1952, 3.

29. Malcolm Johnson, "Turmoil in Africa," *Chicago Defender*, 17 Jan. 1953, 1, and 24 Jan. 1953, 15, and following weeks; "Turmoil in Africa," Editorial, *Chicago Defender*, 24 Jan. 1953, 10. The *Atlanta Daily World* ran the series starting 5 Feb. 1953.

30. "All Africa Is Aflame," *Baltimore Afro-American*, 22 Nov. 1952, *Afro Magazine*, 5; "Hottest Spot in the World," *Baltimore Afro-American*, 20 Dec. 1952, 9.

31. "Mau Maus Slay Hundreds," *Atlanta Daily World*, 28 Mar. 1953, 1; "New Reign of Terror Launched by Mau Maus," *Pittsburgh Courier*, 4 Apr. 1953, 1; "200 Africans Killed by Mau Mau Raiders," *Chicago Defender*, 4 Apr. 1953, 6; Edgerton, *Mau Mau*, 78–80.

32. Rayford Logan, "The American Negro's View of Africa," 225. On African American reluctance to associate with the Mau Mau rebellion, see Plummer, *Rising Wind*, 240–44.

33. For more on Schuyler's conservatism, see Schuyler, *Black and Conservative*; O. Williams, "Making of a Black Conservative." On Yergan, see Anthony, "Max Yergan and South Africa."

34. "Africa: Next Goal of the Communists — Interview with Dr. Max Yergan," *U.S. News & World Report*, 1 May 1953, 54–56.

35. George Schuyler, "World Today," *Pittsburgh Courier*, 6 June 1953, 7. For more examples of Schuyler's comments regarding Mau Mau, see his column, "World Today," in the *Pittsburgh Courier*: 27 Sept. 1952, 1; 18 Oct. 1952, 4; 28 Feb. 1953, 5; 11 Apr. 1953, 1; 18 Apr. 1953, 4.

36. "A Call from the Heroic People of Africa to Negro and White Americans," 24 Apr. 1954, *Du Bois Papers*, 70/536–38.

37. W. E. B. Du Bois, "Africa and Afro-America," 24 Apr. 1954, *Du Bois Papers*, 81/840–42.

38. W. E. B. Du Bois, "Africa and Afro-America," *Du Bois Papers*, 81/840; Alphaeus Hunton to W. E. B. Du Bois, 1 Apr. 1954, ibid., 70/532; "A Call from the Heroic People of Africa to Negro and White Americans," 24 Apr. 1954, ibid., 70/536–38; "Declaration in Support of African Liberation," 24 Apr. 1954, *NAACP Papers* 14, 11/392; "Proposals for a Kenya Aid Program," 24 Apr. 1954, *NAACP Papers* 14, 11/391; "Conference Pledges Aid to Kenya Africans," *Spotlight on Africa*, 18 May 1954, 1.

39. Check from Council on African Affairs to Kenya African Union, 20 Mar. 1953, photocopy, box 1, folder 16, Hunton Papers; F. L. Tonge, Secretary/Treasurer Kenyatta Defence Fund, to W. A. Hunton, 22 Sept. 1954, ibid; "For the Defense of Kenya's Heroes," *Spotlight on Africa*, 15 Sept. 1954, 1; Lynch, *Black American Radicals and the Liberation of Africa*, 45. See also Von Eschen, *Race against Empire*, 141, 166; Gerald Horne, *Black and Red*, 189–90.

40. "Tougher Policy in Kenya," Editorial, *Pittsburgh Courier*, 20 June 1953, 6; "The Wrong Way," Editorial, *Baltimore Afro-American*, 4 Apr. 1953, 4; "Too Little, Too Late," Editorial, *Baltimore Afro-American*, 13 Mar. 1954, 4.

41. "Powell Asks Cut in Aid to Kenya," *Baltimore Afro-American*, 11 July 1953, 3; "Mass Meeting to Protest Africa Racism," *New York Amsterdam News*, 27 June 1953, 1; Sidney Williams to "My Effective and Purposeful Friends," 9 Jan. 1955, *NAACP Papers* 14, 2/645–46.

42. "Mass Meeting to Protest Africa Racism," *New York Amsterdam News*, 27 June 1953, 1; Resolution Submitted by BSCP Delegates to the AFL Convention, Sept. 1953, box 123, folder "Resolutions 1940–1953," BSCP Records.

43. Resolution Submitted by the BSCP Delegates to the AFL Convention, Dec. 1955, box 124, folder "Resolutions 1954–56," BSCP Records.

44. "Resolutions," *NAACP Papers* 1, 1951–55 suppl., 8/233, 12/239–40.

45. International President, Brotherhood of Sleeping Car Porters (Randolph) to President Eisenhower, 17 June 1953, *FRUS*, 1952–54, 11:43–46.

46. Lester Granger, "Manhattan and Beyond," *New York Amsterdam News*, 16 Apr. 1955, 16, and 28 May 1955, 18; Walter White, "A Major Report on Africa Today," *New York Herald Tribune Book Review*, 26 Sept. 1954, sec. 6, 11. Some leading papers of the day, including the *Amsterdam News* and the *Defender*, also voiced their disagreement with using violence to bring about social change. "Let's Look at Africa," Editorial, *Chicago Defender*, 29 Nov. 1952, 10; "Red Puppet or Black Patriot?" Editorial, *New York Amsterdam News*, 11 July 1953, 14.

47. "A Black Harlemite" to the Editor, *New York Amsterdam News*, 15 May 1954, 16; "What Can We Do about Kenya?" Editorial, *New York Amsterdam News*, 15 May 1954, 16.

48. Gordon Hancock, "What Would Actually Happen," *Chicago Defender*, 3 Jan. 1953, 10; Horace Cayton, "Cayton," *Pittsburgh Courier*, 1 Nov. 1952, 7, and 6 Dec. 1952, 7.

49. Joel Rogers, "Rogers Says," *Pittsburgh Courier*, 8 Nov. 1952, 7, and 9 May 1953, 7; "Late UNIA Leader the Patron Saint of Restless Africa," *Chicago Defender*, 6 June 1953, 1; B. D. Davis to the Editor, *Baltimore Afro-American*, 27 Mar. 1954, 4.

50. Untitled paper, n.d., MG 309, box 49, folder 8 "ANLCA," Drake Papers.

51. William Clarke to the Editor, *Pittsburgh Courier*, 7 Mar. 1953, 17; Rev. Ivan Harrison, Sneads, Fla., to the Editor, *New York Amsterdam News*, 24 Jan. 1953, 4; A Constant Reader to the Editor, *New York Amsterdam News*, 1 Nov. 1952, 20.

52. "British Concede Mau Mau Victory, Try To Save Face," *Chicago Defender*, 16 May 1953, 1; "New Hope for Kenya," Editorial, *Chicago Defender*, 16 May 1953, 11; Horace Cayton, "Cayton," *Pittsburgh Courier*, 3 Apr. 1954, 7, and 8 Aug. 1953, 7; "Tougher Policy in Kenya," Editorial, *Pittsburgh Courier*, 20 June 1953, 6; "Red Puppet or Black Patriot?" Editorial, *New York Amsterdam News*, 11 July 1953, 14; George Schuyler, "The World Today," *Pittsburgh Courier*, 20 Mar. 1954, 1, and 1 May 1954, 4.

53. "Africa Teeters Near Brink of Revolution; Violence Continuing," *Pittsburgh Courier*, 22 Nov. 1952, 1; "Racial Fires Flare as Africans Stiffen," *New York Amsterdam News*, 25 Oct. 1952, 1; Horace Cayton, "Africa Series," 22 Nov. 1952 and

following weeks, *Pittsburgh Courier*, 1; "Africa Awakes," Editorial, *Crisis*, Nov. 1952, 578.

54. For more on Tom Mboya, see Goldsworthy, *Tom Mboya*. For Mboya and his links to the ACOA, see Houser, *No One Can Stop the Rain*, esp. 81–90. On Mboya, the U.S. government, and his 1959 trip, see RG 59, Lot and Office Files, Bureau of African Affairs, Office of Eastern and Southern African Affairs, Country Files, 1951–65, box 1, folder 22.6, 250/63/18/4–5.

55. Harry Belafonte, Jackie Robinson, Sidney Poitier to Roy Wilkins, 17 Dec. 1959, GOF, 1956–65, ser. A, box 34, folder "Africa, General, 1956–59"; Rampersad, *Jackie Robinson*, 346–48.

56. On Granger's efforts, see part II, ser. 1, box 83, folder "Africans," NUL Records. On Prattis's efforts, see box 144–49, folders 14 and 15, "Correspondence: Mboya, Tom and Kenyatta Students, 1957–1959," Prattis Papers, Moorland-Spingarn Research Center, Howard University, Washington, D.C. On King's efforts, see Tom Mboya to Martin Luther King, 16 June 1959, box 26A, folder 33b, MLK/BU; King to Mboya, 8 July 1959, box 26A, folder 33b, MLK/BU; King to William Scheinman, 18 Aug. 1959, box 32, folder 20, MLK/BU. King's support for African education extended beyond his efforts to secure institutional funding for African students. A bill from Tuskegee noted that for Rabala's expenses in the second semester of the school year, the SCLC contributed $200, the Dexter Avenue Baptist Church $100, and King himself the balance of $127.30. Tuskegee Financial Statement, June 1960, box 35, folder 42, MLK/BU.

57. Martin Luther King to Julius G. Kiano, 19 Aug. 1959, box 26A, folder 33b, MLK/BU; King to Kiano, 30 Nov. 1959, box 29, folder 9, ibid.

58. Mboya invited Marshall to participate in the Lancaster House constitutional talks held in early 1960. For information on Marshall and these talks, see Goldsworthy, *Tom Mboya*, 133–34.

59. Tyson, "Robert F. Williams, 'Black Power,' and the Roots of the African American Freedom Struggle," Medgar Evers on 546; Tyson, *Radio Free Dixie*. See also Plummer, *Rising Wind*, 295–96.

60. Gambino, "Transgression of a Laborer: Malcolm X in the Wilderness of America," 23.

61. Breitman, *Malcolm X Speaks*, 106–7.

Chapter Five

1. Sherwood, *Kwame Nkrumah*, 27–70.

2. Ibid., 84–91. Sherwood notes that Nkrumah and Du Bois met at the NAACP conference, although Du Bois later appears to have forgotten this when he wrote that "the Fifth Pan-African Congress in England in 1945 [was where] I first saw Nkrumah," 86.

3. Nkrumah, *Autobiography*, 111–12.

4. Hargreaves, "Toward the Transfer of Power in British West Africa," 135–38; Low, "End of the British Empire in Africa," 39; Austin, *Politics in Ghana*, 49–152; George Padmore, "A Review of the Gold Coast — Final Stage to Independence," *Crisis* 62 (Jan. 1955): 11–16, 59.

5. "African Leader in Jail, Followers Sweep Election," *Pittsburgh Courier*, 24 Feb. 1951, 3; "Lincoln Graduate's Party Sweeps African Election," *Baltimore Afro-American*, 24 Feb. 1951, 13, and "Lincoln Grad Elected to African Parliament," *Baltimore Afro-American*, 10 Mar. 1951, 15; "Africans Move for Self-Rule," *New York Amsterdam News*, 3 Mar. 1951, 3; "A Great People's Victory for Gold Coast Africans," *New Africa*, Mar. 1951, 5.

6. Horace Mann Bond to Dean Acheson, 30 Mar. 1951, RG 59, DF, 1950–54, British Africa, 611.45K/3-3051; Bourgerie to George McGhee, 3 Apr. 1951, Bourgerie to Horace Mann Bond, 20 Apr. 1951, and Guest List for the Luncheon in Honor of Kwame Nkrumah and Kojo Botsio, all in RG 59, Lot and Office Files, Bureau of African Affairs, Office of West African Affairs, Country Files, 1951–63, box 1, folder 22.7, 250/63/10/2–3; "Gold Coast Official Returns from U.S.," 14 July 1951, RG 59, DF, 1950–54, British Africa, 745K.00/7-1451.

7. "Africa's First Black Premier," *Pittsburgh Courier*, 15 Mar. 1952, 6; Walter White, "Africa and Its People Are Far from Being as Primitive as Some People Think," *Chicago Defender*, 4 Apr. 1953, 10; Mary McLeod Bethune, *Chicago Defender*, 4 Apr. 1953, 10; Bayard Rustin, "Africa Gets Its First Black Prime Minister," *Baltimore Afro-American*, 18 Oct. 1952, *Afro Magazine*, 5.

8. NAACP Board of Directors Minutes, May 1953, *NAACP Papers* 1, 1951–55 suppl., 1/702; Kwame Nkrumah to Walter White, 4 May 1953, *NAACP Papers* 14, 2/310; Walter White to George Padmore, 27 May 1954, *NAACP Papers* 14, 2/478–79; Utter to Byroade, 17 Apr. 1953, RG 59, Lot File 58D627, General Records of the Office of Southern African Affairs, 1950–56, Correspondence — Asst. Secretary and Deputy Asst. Secretary; Kwame Nkrumah to Walter White, 9 June 1953, *NAACP Papers* 14, 2/321; "Annual Convention Resolutions," *Crisis* 60 (Aug.–Sept. 1953): 443.

9. "Progress in Africa," Editorial, *Chicago Defender*, 3 July 1954, 11. It is worth noting that not all black Americans were so positive about prospects for independence throughout Africa. Channing Tobias, chairman of the board of the NAACP and an elder statesman among African American leaders, wrote at the start of 1955, "Africans will continue to agitate for self-rule, whether they are ready for it or not." The *Daily World* likewise declared that it did not believe all colonial areas should be given immediate freedom, although colonial powers should make definitive progress in that direction. Rayford Logan worried that African countries were moving too rapidly toward independence. Channing Tobias, "Notable Civil Rights Gains Seen in 1955," *Baltimore Afro-American*, 8 Jan. 1955, 9; "The UN and Colonial Peoples," Editorial, *Atlanta Daily World*, 5 Jan. 1955, 6; Von Eschen, *Race against Empire*, 149.

10. Kwame Nkrumah to Richard Wright, 16 Apr. 1953, ser. II, box 102, folder

1504, Richard Wright Papers, Beinecke Library, Yale University, New Haven, Conn.; Kwame Nkrumah to Richard Wright, 4 May 1953, ibid.

11. Richard Wright to George Padmore, 16 July 1953, box 103, folder 1522, Wright Papers, Beinecke Library, Yale University. Nkrumah may have been well advised to keep Wright at a distance. Before departing the Gold Coast, Wright gave the U.S. consulate a detailed assessment of left-wing politics in the nation. Describing the CPP as "a Communist minded political party, borrowing Marxist concepts and applying them with a great deal of flexibility to local African social and economic conditions," Wright shared what he knew of the CPP's inner workings. This included revealing the shifting membership of the "Secret Circle," the behind-the-scenes group that charted CPP (and thus government) policy. The Secret Circle had six members in Accra and one, George Padmore, in London. Wright even revealed what he knew of the secret communications channel for correspondence between Nkrumah and Padmore. "Transmitting Memorandum on Left-Wing Politics in the Gold Coast," RG 59, DF, 1950–54, British Africa (microfilm), Gold Coast, 745K.00/9-1553.

12. Wright, *Black Power*, 4.

13. Ibid., 57, 113, 136–37. For a sharp critique of Wright's assumptions and attitudes, see Appiah, "A Long Way from Home," 173–90.

14. Wright, *Black Power*, 147, 348–49; Reilly, "Self-Creation of the Intellectual," 225.

15. Wright, *Black Power*, 342; see also 77.

16. Fabre, *Unfinished Quest of Richard Wright*, 401–2.

17. White, "Major Report on Africa Today," 1.

18. Previously, there were only three self-ruling countries in Africa south of the Sahara: Liberia, Ethiopia, and white-ruled South Africa. Sudan gained independence in 1956, but few African Americans at the time strongly connected this to "black Africa."

19. "Jail, Fines for Truman Aides," *Chicago Defender*, 6 Mar. 1957, 1. Lead headlines from other newspapers that made few connections with Africa following Ghanaian independence include "Golden State Fires 120 Agents," *California Eagle*, 7 Mar. 1957, 1; "Dixie White Youths Would Abide by Law," *Norfolk Journal & Guide*, 9 Mar. 1957, 1; "Push Plans to March on D.C.," *New York Age*, 9 Mar. 1957, 1.

20. Garrow, *Bearing the Cross*, 91; "King Gets a Hearing," Editorial, *Chicago Defender*, 14 Mar. 1957, 9.

21. Lester Granger, "Battleaxe and Bread," *California Eagle*, 21 Mar. 1957, 6.

22. "The World At Large," *Pittsburgh Courier*, 13 July 1957, 10; " 'We'll Show the World' — Nkrumah," *Baltimore Afro-American*, 9 Mar. 1957, 1.

23. "Dominion of Ghana," Editorial, *Chicago Defender*, 6 Mar. 1957, 9.

24. "The Rebirth of the Republic of Ghana, the Second African Independent Nation," Editorial, *Atlanta Daily World*, 3 Mar. 1957, 5; "A Nation is Born," Editorial, *California Eagle*, 28 Mar. 1957, 4; "The Negro and World Diplomacy," Editorial, *New York Age*, 2 Mar. 1957, 13.

25. "Powell's Trip to Ghana Stirs Political Pot," *Baltimore Afro-American*, 16 Mar.

1957, 11. Powell himself would have to go as a private citizen, for Speaker of the House Sam Rayburn worked to prevent Powell from attending the independence ceremonies as a member of the U.S. delegation. See Hamilton, *Adam Clayton Powell Jr.*, 280–81.

26. "Ghana Sets High Goals as Independence Nears," *Chicago Defender*, 28 Feb. 1957, 3; "Lincoln, Morgan Fete Ghana," *Baltimore Afro-American*, 9 Mar. 1957, 11. The church leaders represented all the large African American denominations, with memberships totaling over 8 million. "The Negro Church in America Has Been a Powerful Voice for Good," *Pittsburgh Courier*, 9 Mar. 1957, Ghana Suppl., 26.

27. Ralph Bunche, "Remarks" at the Accra Municipal Council Civic Luncheon, 5 Mar. 1957, box 140, folder 13, Bunche Papers, Young Research Library, University of California, Los Angeles; "Can Ghana Make It?," *New York Amsterdam News*, 30 Mar. 1957, 1; Claude Barnett to Kwame Nkrumah, 30 Mar. 1957, box 178, folder 3, Barnett Papers, Chicago Historical Society. Langston Hughes later wrote to Nkrumah, "On March 7, 1957, pride rose within me and within many other of your fellow Lincolnites that you had been chosen to carve the path of African independence." Langston Hughes to Kwame Nkrumah, 28 Feb. 1958, box 114, folder "Nkrumah, Kwame," Langston Hughes Papers, Beinecke Library, Yale University, New Haven, Conn.

28. Independence Day Celebrations in Chicago, 1957, MG309, box 70, Drake Papers; "Senator at Town Hall Ghana Rally," *New York Amsterdam News*, 9 Mar. 1957, 16; "Lincoln University Observes Ghana Independence Day," *Atlanta Daily World*, 27 Feb. 1957, 2; J. Hamilton Johnson to the Editor, *Chicago Defender*, 25 Feb. 1957, 9; "Ghana Anthem Publication Delayed," *New York Amsterdam News* 30 Mar. 1957, 4.

29. "Ghana Called Big Boost to Negro Morale," Newspaper Clipping dated 8 Mar. 1957, *Schomburg CCF*, 001,923-1 (Williams quote); Anonymous Letter to the Editor, *Chicago Defender*, 11 Mar. 1957, 9 ("Negro leadership"); Isaacs, *New World of Negro Americans*, 292 ("I am happy").

30. The *Courier* proclaimed, "It is a far cry from the hand-picked legislature of 1888 to the all-Negro government of today. In between there have been stirring events which have shown the political genius of the people and their determination to order their own affairs." "From Dependence to Independence," *Pittsburgh Courier*, 9 Mar. 1957, 8. The *Afro-American* provided similar messages, noting, "Ghana has redeemed her lost freedom. . . . Let's all acknowledge what's true; Britain took Ghana's freedom and gave it back only when forced to do so." "Let's Keep the Record Straight," Editorial, *Baltimore Afro-American*, 16 Mar. 1957, 4.

31. "The *Courier* Salutes Ghana," Editorial, *Pittsburgh Courier*, 9 Mar. 1957, Ghana Suppl., 1.

32. "Independence . . . Here," Editorial, *Pittsburgh Courier*, 16 Mar. 1957, 9. See also P. L. Prattis, "Ghana and Us," *Pittsburgh Courier*, 23 Mar. 1957, 8.

33. "Hail Ghana!" Editorial, *New York Amsterdam News*, 9 Mar. 1957, 6.

34. "Proudly We Can Be Africans," Editorial, *Baltimore Afro-American*, 6 Apr. 1957, 4.

35. David Licorish, "Salute to Ghana — Day of Deliverance," 3 Mar. 1957, *Schomburg CCF*, 001,918-1; "Ghana, Rebirth of Old Nation, Minister Says," *New York Age*, 16 Mar. 1957, 12.

36. Interview of Martin Luther King Jr. by Etta Moten Barnett in Accra, Mar. 1957, Sound Recordings Division, Schomburg Center for Research in Black Culture, SC Audio C-567 (side 1, no. 3, counter no. 35); Coretta Scott King, *My Life with Martin Luther King Jr.*, 154–57, quote on 155; Homer Jack, "Conversation in Ghana," *Christian Century*, 10 Apr. 1957, 447.

37. Reddick, *Crusader without Violence*, 183 ("inspired"); Interview of Martin Luther King Jr. by Etta Moten Barnett in Accra, Mar. 1957 ("give impetus"). For more on King's visit to Ghana, see Oates, *Let the Trumpet Sound*, 117–18; Branch, *Parting the Waters*, 214–16.

38. Martin Luther King Jr., "The Birth of a New Nation," Apr. 1957, in *Papers*, 4:155–67, quotes on 161–64.

39. "Nixon on Africa," Editorial, *Baltimore Afro-American*, 20 Apr. 1957, 4.

40. Nielsen, *The Great Powers and Africa*, 191.

41. "Conditions and Trends in Tropical Africa," 22 Dec. 1953, *FRUS*, 1952–54, 11:72–73.

42. "Conditions and Trends in Tropical Africa," 14 Aug. 1956, *FRUS*, 1955–57, 18:45–47.

43. Nielsen, *The Great Powers and Africa*, 263–65; Noer, *Cold War and Black Liberation*, 48.

44. Richard Nixon, "The Emergence of Africa: Report to President Eisenhower," *State Department Bulletin* 36 (22 Apr. 1957): 636–37.

45. Plummer, *Rising Wind*, 296; Schlesinger, *A Thousand Days*, 554; Noer, *Cold War and Black Liberation*, 50–52; Nielsen, *The Great Powers and Africa*, 265.

46. Memorandum from Assistant Secretary of State for Congressional Relations (Hill) to Vice President, "Communist Bloc Activities in West Africa," 18 Feb. 1957, *FRUS*, 1955–57, 18:373 n.

47. "Report to the President on the Vice President's Visit to Africa," 5 Apr. 1957, *FRUS*, 1955–57, 18:60, 65–66; Memorandum of Discussion at the 335th Meeting of the National Security Council, Washington, 22 Aug. 1957, ibid., 18:72.

48. Nixon, "The Emergence of Africa," 635 and 638.

49. "Statement of U.S. Policy toward Africa South of the Sahara Prior to Calendar Year 1960," NSC 5719/1, 23 Aug. 1957, *FRUS*, 1955–57, 18:76–87, quote on 79–80; "Statement of U.S. Policy toward Africa South of the Sahara Prior to Calendar Year 1960," NSC 5818, 26 Aug. 1958, *FRUS*, 1958–60, 14:24–37.

50. Memorandum of Discussion at the 432d Meeting of the National Security Council, 14 Jan. 1960, *FRUS*, 1958–60, 14:74–77. For more on the racial views of high U.S. officials, see Hunt, *Ideology and U.S. Foreign Policy*, esp. 162–66 regarding Africa.

51. "South Africa, the Gold Coast, and the $64 Question," *Spotlight on Africa*, 21 Apr. 1954, 4. See also "Testing Time for Nkrumah," *Spotlight on Africa*, 21 Jan. 1954, 3; "The Man, the Myth, and the Machine Won," *Spotlight on Africa*, 20 July 1954, 4. At the very same time, pan-Africanist George Padmore attacked the radical black left in America, again bringing into question the degree of unity achieved among these elements. In May 1954, Padmore wrote to Richard Wright, "My publisher Dobson showed me a letter from a man called Dr. W. A. Hunton and two other Harlem C.P. Negroes objecting to the publication of a biography on Robeson." According to Padmore, the proofs of the biography, written by Briton Marie Seaton, had been approved by Robeson, but now Hunton and company had sent a letter to Dobson "vetoing the book," for they feared that it would "discredit him as a leader of his people." Dobson had written to Robeson, who said the matter was "up to the Negro party leaders to decide." Padmore gave Dobson the address of Du Bois so that he could appeal to "get the book released from the Red Inquisition in Harlem." Padmore concluded, "Boy, boy! It was a lucky day when we got out of this." George Padmore to Richard Wright, 24 May 1954, box 103, folder 1522, Wright Papers, Beinecke Library, Yale University.

52. For more on the final destruction of the CAA, see box 1, folder 17 "Administrative, 1944–55" and folder 19 "Legal, 1949–55," Hunton Papers; Lynch, *Black American Radicals*, 50–52; Von Eschen, *Race against Empire*, 134–44.

53. Prospectus of the American Committee on Africa, Nov. 1953, box 49, folder 6, Drake Papers; "Aims and Purposes of the American Committee on Africa," Dec. 1954, *NAACP Papers* 14, 10/884.

54. Prospectus of the American Committee on Africa, Nov. 1953, Drake Papers; Donald Harrington to St. Clair Drake, 22 Sept. 1955, and George Houser to St. Clair Drake, 22 Oct. 1956, box 49, folder 6, Drake Papers. For more on George Houser and the ACOA, see Houser, *No One Can Stop the Rain*.

55. Kilson, "African Americans and Africa," 363–65. For more on Richard Wright and his connections to the Society of African Culture and AMSAC, see Fabre, *World of Richard Wright*, 192–213; Fabre, *Unfinished Quest of Richard Wright*, 435–38.

56. Davis, "Influence of Africans on American Culture," 82.

57. Davis, "Black Americans and United States Policy toward Africa," 240–41.

58. AMSAC would command even less influence in the mid-1960s, especially after it was revealed in 1967 that it had received clandestine funding from the CIA. See Schechter, Ansara, and Kolodney, "CIA as Equal Opportunity Employer."

59. For example, George Fredrickson's generally outstanding study of liberation struggles in South Africa and the United States downgrades too much the nonstructural influence that Nkrumah, and particularly his 1958 visit, exerted on black America. See Fredrickson, *Black Liberation*, 278.

60. "Nkrumah Visiting U.S., Given Big Welcome," *Pittsburgh Courier*, 26 July 1958, 3; "Department of State Program for the Visit of Kwame Nkrumah from 23 July to 2 August 1958," 15 July 1958, box 128-10, folder 10, Dabu Gizenga

Collection on Kwame Nkrumah, Moorland-Spingarn Research Center, Howard University, Washington, D.C.; "Premier Nkrumah's Itinerary," *Baltimore Afro-American*, 26 July 1958, 2; "Nkrumah Hailed in Washington," *Baltimore Afro-American*, 2 Aug. 1958, 2; Joint Statement by Prime Minister Nkrumah and President Eisenhower, 26 July 1958, RG 59, DF, 1955–59, British Africa, 611.45J/7-2558; Embassy in Ghana to Department of State, 13 Aug. 1958, *FRUS*, 1958–60, 14:652; "Welcome, Dr. Nkrumah," Editorial, *Baltimore Afro-American*, 2 Aug. 1958, 5; Du Bois, *Autobiography*, 401. See also "Ghana's Prime Minister OK's Summit Conference," *Pittsburgh Courier*, 2 Aug. 1958, 4; "Diplomats Greet Guest," *Baltimore Afro-American*, 2 Aug. 1958, 2; "Nkrumah Gets Plush Welcome to Capital," *Atlanta Daily World*, 25 July 1958, 1.

61. "100,000 Harlemites Welcome Nkrumah," *Baltimore Afro-American*, 2 Aug. 1958, 2; Claude Barnett to Hon. Richard Jones, Ambassador to Liberia, 10 July 1958, ser. 2, box 178, folder 4 "Ghana, July 1957–December 1958," Barnett Papers, Chicago Historical Society; "Nkrumah in Chicago," box 70, Drake Papers; "Nkrumah Here, Gets Welcome," *Chicago Defender*, 31 July 1958, 3; "Kwame Nkrumah Returns," Editorial, *Pittsburgh Courier*, 2 Aug. 1958, 12.

62. Hope Stevens and Elmer Carter to Roy Wilkins, 27 June 1958, GOF, 1956–65, ser. A, box 34, folder "Africa, Ghana, 1957–1963"; "Program for the Harlem Lawyers Association and the Harlem Citizens' Committee Reception in Honor of Kwame Nkrumah," 28 July 1958, box 128-7, folder 143, Gizenga Collection on Kwame Nkrumah, Moorland-Spingarn Research Center, Howard University; "Nkrumah Visiting U.S., Given Big Welcome," *Pittsburgh Courier*, 26 July 1958, 3; " 'We're Brothers' — Nkrumah," *New York Amsterdam News*, 2 Aug. 1958, 1.

63. Ralph Bunche, "Introduction of Kwame Nkrumah," box 52, folder "Committee of 100, Harlem Citizens' Reception honoring Dr. K. Nkrumah," Bunche Papers, Young Research Library, University of California, Los Angeles; emphasis in original.

64. For more on Bunche, see Henry, *Ralph J. Bunche: Selected Speeches and Writings*; and Henry, *Ralph Bunche: Model Negro or American Other?*

65. Report by Raymond F. Talbert, attached to letter from P. L. Prattis to Kwame Nkrumah, 12 Aug. 1958, box 144-10, folder 17, Prattis Papers, Moorland-Spingarn Research Center, Howard University.

66. "Seating Arrangement for Dinner Honoring Dr. Kwame Nkrumah," 29 July 1958, *Schomburg CCF*, 001,918-3; "1,000 at Nkrumah Dinner," *Pittsburgh Courier*, 9 Aug. 1958, 4; Lester Granger, "Welcoming Remarks," 29 July 1958, Part I, ser. 1, box 39, folder "1958 Nkrumah Dinner," NUL Records; "Prime Minister of Ghana Honored," *Crisis*, Aug.–Sept. 1958, 411.

67. Plummer, *Rising Wind*, 282.

68. Robeson, *Here I Stand*, 64.

69. Du Bois made a concerted effort to attend the independence celebrations, writing on 22 February 1957 to Secretary of State John Foster Dulles and to congressmen Charles C. Diggs, William Dawson, and Adam Clayton Powell, asking them for

help in securing a passport. He said that he had applied long before and had heard nothing. He then wrote to Mohammed Assad, chairman of the UN Subcommission on Prevention of Discrimination and Protection of Minorities. His efforts went for naught, as the State Department officially denied him permission on 27 February. Du Bois to Charles C. Diggs, 22 Feb. 1957, *Du Bois Papers*, 72/512; Du Bois to John Foster Dulles, 22 Feb. 1957, ibid., 72/1045; Du Bois to William Dawson, 22 Feb. 1957, ibid., 72/1046; Du Bois to Adam Clayton Powell, 22 Feb. 1957, ibid., 72/1047; Du Bois to Mohammed Amad, 27 Feb. 1957, ibid., 72/1042–43. Also, "Nkrumah Intervened in Vain for Dr. Du Bois," *Baltimore Afro-American*, 23 Mar. 1957, 2; "Horizon," *Pittsburgh Courier*, 9 Mar. 1957, 8.

70. Sitkoff, *Struggle for Black Equality*, 23.

71. Maria Garden to the Editor, *Chicago Defender*, 6 Aug. 1958, 11; Mary Gause-Bey, *Chicago Defender*, 4 Aug. 1958, 10.

72. Morris Williams to the Editor, *Pittsburgh Courier*, 23 Aug. 1958, 4; Minnie Cartwright to the Editor, *Chicago Defender*, 30 July 1958, 11; "You and the NAACP," *New York Amsterdam News*, 2 Aug. 1958, 8; "Africa and World Outlook," Editorial, *Chicago Defender*, 5 Aug. 1958, 11. See also "Welcome! Prime Minister Nkrumah," Editorial, *Chicago Defender*, 30 July 1958, 11; "Kwame Nkrumah Returns," Editorial, *Pittsburgh Courier*, 2 Aug. 1958, 12; "Welcome, Dr. Nkrumah," Editorial, *Baltimore Afro-American*, 2 Aug. 1958, 5.

73. "Africa and World Outlook," Editorial, *Chicago Defender*, 5 Aug. 1958, 11.

74. Quoted in Isaacs, *New World of Negro Americans*, 276.

75. Interestingly, in an interview on the eve of Ghana's independence Du Bois was asked whether he ever "had the urge to remain abroad and just not return" from his travels. He responded that he had never entertained for a moment permanently staying out of the land of his birth. "At 89, Dr. Du Bois is — Most Controversial American," *Baltimore Afro-American*, 23 Feb. 1957, *Afro Magazine*, 4. For more on Du Bois's move to Ghana, see Horne, *Black and Red*, 338–53.

76. Angelou, *All God's Children*, 23.

77. For Kwame Nkrumah on pan-Africanism, see Nkrumah, *I Speak of Freedom*, x–xii, 186–91. He dedicated the book to "all those who are engaged in the struggle for the political unification of Africa." Nkrumah and Sekou Toure of Guinea linked their countries in a federation in 1958, and in 1960 Mali briefly joined them. However, the federation never integrated these countries economically or politically and did not last long.

78. Angelou, *All God's Children*, 19, 40.

79. Angelou, *All God's Children*, 20, 208. The following include some of the other records left by African American expatriates who went to live, not just visit or spend a sabbatical, in Ghana: Lacy, *Rise and Fall of a Proper Negro*; Feelings, *Black Pilgrimage*; W. G. Smith, *Return to Black America*; E. Smith, *Where To, Black Man?*; interviews with Tom Feelings, Priscilla Stevens Kruize, and Dr. Robert E. Lee, in Dunbar, *Black Expatriates*, 39–87. An article that explores the issue from a slightly

different vantage point is Zimmerman, "Beyond Double Consciousness: Black Peace Corps Volunteers in Africa."

80. Lacy, *Rise and Fall of a Proper Negro*, 213; Drake, "Diaspora Studies and Pan-Africanism," 362–63.

Chapter Six

1. Thomas Karis, "The Freedom Charter and the ANC," in Karis and Carter, *From Protest to Challenge*, 3:57–58, 63; Gail Gerhart, "Origins of the Africanist Movement," in ibid., 3:16–17; "Freedom Charter," adopted 26 June 1955, in ibid., 3:205–8.

2. Gerhart, "Origins of the Africanist Movement," 3:16–19; Gail Gerhart, "Formation of the Pan Africanist Congress, 1958–1959," in Karis and Carter, *From Protest to Challenge*, 3:307–25, Lutuli quote on 310.

3. Gerhart, "Formation of the Pan Africanist Congress," 3:318–19; Lodge, *Black Politics in South Africa*, 80–86. For a critique of Sobukwe and the PAC, see Fredrickson, *Black Liberation*, 280–86.

4. Gail Gerhart, "The Eve of Sharpeville and Afterwards," in Karis and Carter, *From Protest to Challenge*, 3:327–29; Lodge, *Black Politics in South Africa*, 86, 203–4.

5. Mangaliso R. Sobukwe to Major-General Rademeyer, 16 Mar. 1960, in Karis and Carter, *From Protest to Challenge*, 3:565–66; Gerhart, "Eve of Sharpeville," in ibid., 3:331–32; Lodge, *Black Politics in South Africa*, 201–4. The street flyers announced four demands: that pass laws be abolished, that a minimum wage of £35 per month be instituted, that a guarantee be given that no worker would be dismissed as a result of the campaign, and that campaign leaders not be victimized by the government as a result of the people's actions. The flyers also declared that no one could call off the campaign except for Sobukwe, who would have to do so at a public meeting. At the same time, the PAC suggested that the campaign would not ultimately confine itself to the four stated issues. The PAC regional secretary for the Western Cape, Philip Kgosane, declared to listeners the day before the start of the campaign: "[The PAC has] drawn up an unfolding programme—which starts tomorrow and ends up in 1963 with the realization of the United States of Africa. We start with the Pass Laws, then the next thing and the next, etc.—up to 1963." "Calling the Nation! No Bail! No Defence! No Fine!!!," (PAC flyer), n.d., in Karis and Carter, *From Protest to Challenge*, 3:564–65; Philip Kgosane, "Launching Address" [quoting text of R. M. Sobukwe's final instructions], in Karis and Carter, *From Protest to Challenge*, 3:567–72.

6. Gerhart, "Eve of Sharpeville," 3:332–34; Lodge, *Black Politics in South Africa*, 205–10.

7. Gerhart, "Eve of Sharpeville," 3:334; Lodge, *Black Politics in South Africa*, 214–17.

8. Gerhart, "Eve of Sharpeville," 3:336–37; Lodge, *Black Politics in South Africa*, 220.

9. "Troops, Police 'Club' Natives, Apply Bullwhips," *Atlanta Daily World*, 5 Apr. 1960, 1; "Beat Scores of South Africans," *Chicago Defender*, 5 Apr. 1960, 3; Gerhart, "Eve of Sharpeville," 3:337–39, 343; Lodge, *Black Politics in South Africa*, 220–24.

10. Gerhart, "Eve of Sharpeville," 3:335.

11. Memorandum from Representative at the Trusteeship Council (Sears) to Secretary of State, 15 Feb. 1956, *FRUS*, 1955–57, 18:37–38; Editorial Note, ibid., 18:39–40; RG 59, Lot File No. 62D417 "Subject Files Relating to the Union of South Africa, 1946–1959."

12. "Embassy Staff Study on the South African Race Problem I," 11 Apr. 1957, *FRUS*, 1955–57, 18:807–15; "Embassy Staff Study on the South African Race Problem II: Diplomatic Policy Recommendation," 11 Apr. 1957, ibid., 18:816–22, quote on 821.

13. Memorandum of Discussion at the 443d Meeting of the National Security Council, 5 May 1960, Editorial Note, *FRUS*, 1958–60, 14:274; Eisenhower, *Waging Peace*, 572.

14. Noer, *Cold War and Black Liberation*, 52–53.

15. Statement by Lincoln White, Director of the Office of News, 22 Mar. 1960, in *State Department Bulletin* 42 (11 Apr. 1960): 551.

16. Editorial Note, *FRUS*, 1958–60, 14:741–42; Telegram from the Embassy in South Africa to the Department of State, 25 Mar. 1960, ibid., 14:743–44.

17. Editorial Note, *FRUS*, 1958–60, 14:749; Memorandum of Conversation among A. B. Burger, Counselor of the South African Embassy, and C. Vaughan Ferguson, Director of AFS [Office of South African Affairs], William Wight, Deputy Director of AFS, and Robert Schneider of AFS, 21 Apr. 1960, RG 59, DF, 745A.00/4-2160; Gerhart, "Eve of Sharpeville," 3:336.

18. Walter Sisulu to W. E. B. Du Bois, 23 Mar. 1953, and Du Bois to Sisulu, 9 Apr. 1953, *Du Bois Papers*, 69/438–39; Von Eschen, *Race against Empire*, 139–40.

19. Walter White to Ralph Bunche, 9 Sept. 1954, *NAACP Papers* 14, 4/896.

20. In addition to soliciting donations, ACOA urged supporters to write letters of protest to U.S. officials and to South Africa's ambassador to the United States. ACOA also helped sponsor Erwin Griswold, dean of Harvard Law School, to attend the trial as an observer. American Committee on Africa, "Special Bulletin on South African Arrests," 11 Dec. 1956, *Schomburg CCF*, 004,655-10; American Committee on Africa, "Who Speaks for Africa? A Report on the Activities of the ACOA," June 1959, ibid., 000,242-2; Houser, *No One Can Stop the Rain*, 119–23.

21. John Gunther to "Dear Friend," 11 Oct. 1957, and the "Declaration of Conscience: An Appeal to South Africa," n.d., *Schomburg CCF*, 000,242-1; "Looking & Listening," *Crisis*, Dec. 1957, 622–23; Houser, *No One Can Stop the Rain*, 123–24; L. V. Baldwin, *Toward the Beloved Community*, 1–24.

22. Martin Luther King to Homer Jack, 31 Aug. 1959, box 19, folder 6, MLK/BU; Martin Luther King to "Dear Friend," 12 Nov. 1959, *Schomburg CCF*, 000,242-2;

Hope Stevens, Chairman of Africa Freedom Day 1960, to "Dear Friend," Apr. 1960, *Schomburg CCF*, 000,242-2. For more on King's involvement with ACOA, see L. V. Baldwin, *Toward the Beloved Community*, 13–57.

23. Martin Luther King to Enoch Dumas, 11 Jan. 1960, box 25, folder 32, MLK/ BU. In the years following Sharpeville, King would continue to advocate stronger efforts to end apartheid. For example, he worked jointly with South African chief Albert Lutuli to promote the Appeal for Action Against Apartheid, timed to coincide with Human Rights Day 1962. King and Lutuli called on people to take actions against apartheid ranging from holding meetings and demonstrations, to not buying South African products and not trading or investing in South Africa, to urging governments to support economic sanctions against South Africa and isolate the country internationally. In December 1964, while stopping in Britain en route to Norway to accept his Nobel Peace Prize, King spoke at length about South Africa and issued another appeal for an economic boycott of that country. King and Lutuli, "Appeal for Action Against Apartheid," 9; Fredrickson, *Black Liberation*, 274–75; Garrow, *Bearing the Cross*, 364. For more on King's relationship with South Africa, see L. V. Baldwin, *Toward the Beloved Community*; Shepherd, "Who Killed Martin Luther King's Dream?," 2.

24. Roy Wilkins to Christian Herter, 22 Mar. 1960, GOF, 1956–65, ser. A, box 35, folder "Africa, South Africa, 1956–65." See also "Urge U.S. to Break with South Africa" and "Wilkins Hits Massacre in South Africa," *Baltimore Afro-American*, 2 Apr. 1960, 9.

25. "South Africa Will Face a Day of Reckoning," Editorial, *Atlanta Daily World*, 31 Mar. 1960, 6; "Our Ally," Editorial, *New York Amsterdam News*, 26 Mar. 1960, 10; "Massacre in South Africa," Editorial, *Chicago Defender*, 24 Mar. 1960, 12. See also "Thunder in Africa," Editorial, *Baltimore Afro-American*, 2 Apr. 1960, 5; "America Is Officially Outraged," Editorial, *Pittsburgh Courier*, 2 Apr. 1960, 12.

26. "Avert This Impending Race War in South Africa," Editorial, *Atlanta Daily World*, 25 Mar. 1960, 4; "Hendrik Verwoerd, The Monster," Editorial, *Chicago Defender*, 12 Apr. 1960, 10; "The High Price of Freedom," Editorial, *Baltimore Afro-American*, 2 Apr. 1960, 4.

27. "America Is Officially Outraged," Editorial, *Pittsburgh Courier*, 2 Apr. 1960, 12; "South Africa and Dixie," Editorial, *Chicago Defender*, 28 Mar. 1960, 10; "Johannesburg, U.S.A.," Editorial, *Baltimore Afro-American*, 23 Apr. 1960, 4. See also "A Suggestion," Editorial, *New York Amsterdam News*, 9 Apr. 1960, 10.

28. "Negro Labor Group Pickets South African Consulate," *Pittsburgh Courier*, 9 Apr. 1960, 10; "AME's Picket South African Consulate," *New York Amsterdam News*, 9 Apr. 1960, 1; "Ministers Can't See South African Consul," *New York Amsterdam News*, 23 Apr. 1960, 34. The AME Church took particular interest in South Africa due at least in part to its historic ties to the nation. See Campbell, *Songs of Zion*.

29. "AME Bishops Council Asks African Aid," *Atlanta Daily World*, 15 Apr. 1960, 1; "Bishops Support Students, Blast South Africa," *Baltimore Afro-American*, 23 Apr.

1960, 9; "Powell Seeks Boycott of S. African Goods," *New York Amsterdam News*, 16 Apr. 1960, 20; "Powell Urges Halt of Credit to S. Africa," *Baltimore Afro-American*, 23 Apr. 1960, 8; "ICFTU Sets Boycott of S. African Goods," *Baltimore Afro-American*, 30 Apr. 1960, 14; Roy Wilkins to the Grocery Manufacturers of America, the National Association of Food Chains, the U.S. Wholesale Grocers Association, the Association of Food Distributors, the Eastern Frozen Foods Association, and the South African Rock Lobster Association, 14 Apr. 1960, GOF, 1956–65, ser. A, box 35, folder "Africa, South Africa, 1956–65."

30. Roy Wilkins to Oliver Tambo, 13 May 1960, GOF, 1956–65, ser. A, box 35, folder "Africa, South Africa, 1956–65"; "1960 Annual Convention Resolution," *NAACP Papers* 1, 1956–60 suppl., 12/454.

31. Quoted in Fierce, "Selected Black American Leaders and Organizations and South Africa," 317. Political efforts became more integral to AMSAC in the 1960s, with its 1963 conference, "Southern Africa in Transition," marking the movement to an avowedly political interest in Africa. While never establishing a strong mass following or lobbying apparatus itself, AMSAC would support organized African American political counterparts to its more cultural and intellectual mission. Davis, "Black Americans and United States Policy Toward Africa," 240–41; Davis and Baker, *Southern Africa in Transition*; Kilson, "African Americans and Africa," 363–65; H. F. Jackson, "U.S. Foreign Policy and African Americans," 9–10; Kornegay, "Black America and U.S.–Southern African Relations," 146–47.

32. George Houser to President Eisenhower, 22 Mar. 1960, RG 59, DF, 1960–63, 745A.00/3-2260; George Houser to President Eisenhower, 5 Apr. 1960, RG 59, DF, 1960–63, 745A.00/4-560; Letterhead of the Africa Defense and Aid Fund, May 1960, *Schomburg CCF*, 004,657-3; American Committee on Africa, "Action Against Apartheid," 1960, *Schomburg CCF*, 004,657-3. By May 1961, the total reached $19,000. "Annual Report of the American Committee on Africa," 1 June 1960 to 31 May 1961, *Schomburg CCF*, 000,242-2.

33. A. Philip Randolph and Donald Harrington to "Dear Friend," 19 May 1960, *Schomburg CCF*, 000,242-2; American Committee on Africa, "Action Against Apartheid," 1960, ibid., 004,657-3.

34. American Committee on Africa, "Action Against Apartheid," 1960, *Schomburg CCF*, 004,657-3.

35. "How Long? How Long?" Editorial, *New York Amsterdam News*, 9 Apr. 1960, 10; "Time To Act," Editorial, *New York Amsterdam News*, 16 Apr. 1960, 10. See also "Thunder in Africa," Editorial, *Baltimore Afro-American*, 2 Apr. 1960, 5.

36. Horace Cayton, "World At Large," *Pittsburgh Courier*, 16 Apr. 1960, 14; "African Slaughter and U.N.," Editorial, *Chicago Defender*, 29 Mar. 1960, 12; "Our Ally," Editorial, *New York Amsterdam News*, 26 Mar. 1960, 10; "Keep Walking?" Editorial, *New York Amsterdam News*, 2 Apr. 1960, 10; "Avert This Impending Race War in South Africa," Editorial, *Atlanta Daily World*, 25 Mar. 1960, 4; "Ministers Protest African Lynchings," *New York Amsterdam News*, 26 Mar. 1960, 1.

37. "Time To Act," Editorial, *New York Amsterdam News*, 16 Apr. 1960, 10;

"What Can We Do about Kenya?" Editorial, *New York Amsterdam News*, 15 May 1954, 16.

38. Chafe, *Civilities and Civil Rights*, 71.

39. "America Is Officially Outraged," Editorial, *Pittsburgh Courier*, 2 Apr. 1960, 12.

40. A. Philip Randolph, "Upsurge of Warfare by Negroes in U.S., Africa Against Color and Caste Systems," *Pittsburgh Courier*, 16 Apr. 1960, 4.

41. "Rising Tide of Color," Editorial, *Crisis*, May 1960, 306–7.

42. Lester Granger, "Manhattan and Beyond," *New York Amsterdam News*, 23 Apr. 1960, 10.

43. "South Africa and Dixie," Editorial, *Chicago Defender*, 28 Mar. 1960, 10; "They Can't Win," Editorial, *New York Amsterdam News*, 9 Apr. 1960, 10; "Easter 1960," *New York Amsterdam News*, 16 Apr. 1960, 10; "Avert This Impending Race War in South Africa," Editorial, *Atlanta Daily World*, 25 Mar. 1960, 4.

44. "African Slaughter 'Shame of History,'" *Baltimore Afro-American*, 23 Apr. 1960, 8.

45. "Hendrik Verwoerd, The Monster," Editorial, *Chicago Defender*, 12 Apr. 1960, 10; "South Africa's Labor Policy," Editorial, *Chicago Defender*, 21 Apr. 1960, 12; "The John Brown of South Africa," Editorial, *Baltimore Afro-American*, 23 Apr. 1960, 4; L. V. Baldwin, *Toward the Beloved Community*, 35.

46. "The High Price of Freedom," Editorial, *Baltimore Afro-American*, 2 Apr. 1960, 4.

47. Mali and Senegal initially formed a federation in June; two months later this dissolved, and they became separate independent countries.

48. "Day of Reckoning," Editorial, *Chicago Defender*, 27 Aug. 1960, 10.

49. United Nations, *Official Records of the General Assembly*, Sess. 15, Part 1 (Sept. 1960–Apr. 1961), 1:45–50; "The Dawn of a New Day," Editorial, *Chicago Defender*, 26 Sept. 1960, 10.

50. "The Dawn of a New Day," Editorial, *Chicago Defender*, 26 Sept. 1960, 10; William Fowlkes, "Seeing and Saying," *Atlanta Daily World*, 25 Sept. 1960, 4.

51. Variations in coverage of course existed. Given its locale, the *New York Amsterdam News* showed an extensive interest in Castro and those who came to visit him. The conservative, sharply anticommunist *Atlanta Daily World* gave more coverage, extremely negative, to Castro and Krushchev. For more on Castro in Harlem, see Plummer, *Rising Wind*, 289–97.

52. United Nations, *Official Records of the General Assembly*, Sess. 15, Part 1 (Sept.–Apr. 1960–61), 1:61–68.

53. "Herter Denounces Nkrumah as 'Red,'" *California Eagle*, 29 Sept. 1960, 1; "Did Herter 'Cut A Hog' on Kwame?" *Pittsburgh Courier*, 8 Oct. 1960, 2.

54. "Nkrumah Speaks Out," Editorial, *Baltimore Afro-American*, 8 Oct. 1960, 4; "A Mistake," Editorial, *New York Amsterdam News*, 1 Oct. 1960, 10; "Herter Knows Better," Editorial, *Chicago Defender*, 6 Oct. 1960, 10; "Who Speaks for Africa?" Editorial, *California Eagle*, 29 Sept. 1960, 4.

55. "'World Must Hear Africa'—Nkrumah," *Pittsburgh Courier*, 1 Oct. 1960, 2.

56. "Africa's Impact on the White World Shown before UN," *Pittsburgh Courier*, 1 Oct. 1960, 3.

57. "Nkrumah Makes Visit to Harlem," *New York Amsterdam News*, 8 Oct. 1960, 1; "'Ghana Welcomes Negro Technicians'—Nkrumah," *Pittsburgh Courier*, 15 Oct. 1960, 2; "Ghana's Nkrumah Extends Welcome," *Baltimore Afro-American*, 15 Oct. 1960, 3.

58. Malcolm X, *Autobiography*, 356. In another case Eldridge Cleaver, jailed in San Quentin, published an article focusing on the need for African Americans to accept African, not Caucasian, standards of beauty. He chose to use Nkrumah to make his concluding point. "When a black president, Kwame Nkrumah of Ghana, arrayed majestically in colorful tribal robes, can stride in towering dignity and pride onto the highest rostrum of the United Nations General Assembly, and deliver a rousing, epoch-making speech—without first pausing to either 'straighten' his hair or 'bleach' his skin, the unspoken message to his brethren is unmistakable: Black is Coming Back!" Cleaver, "As Crinkly as Yours," 132.

59. "Herter Knows Better," Editorial, *Chicago Defender*, 6 Oct. 1960, 10.

60. Quoted in Isaacs, *New World of Negro Americans*, 292–93.

61. M. L. King, "The Time for Freedom Has Come," 118; Cone, "Martin Luther King, Jr., and the Third World," 200. See also Klarman, "How *Brown* Changed Race Relations," 91; Skinner, "The Dialectic between Diasporas and Homelands," 38.

62. Farmer, "An American Leader's View of African Unity," 72. See also Houser, "Freedom's Struggle Crosses Oceans and Mountains," 176–79; Challenor, "Influence of Black Americans on U.S. Foreign Policy toward Africa," 159–60; M. D. Morris, "Black Americans and the Foreign Policy Process," 451; Weisbord, *Ebony Kinship*, 184–88; Chick, "American Negroes' Changing Attitude Toward Africa," 534; Isaacs, *New World of Negro Americans*, 276, 287, 288–93. Rupert Emerson and Martin Kilson go so far as to assert that "like emancipation from slavery," the break from colonialism was indispensable to the struggle for equality. Emerson and Kilson, "The American Dilemma in a Changing World," 1066.

63. Walton, "The Walking City: A History of the Montgomery Bus Boycott," *Negro History Bulletin*, Apr. 1957, in Garrow, *Walking City*, 49. See also Isaacs, *New World of Negro Americans*, 50–54; Sitkoff, *Struggle for Black Equality*, 16; Shepherd, *Anti-Apartheid*, 54.

64. Marable, *Race, Reform, and Rebellion*, 54; M. L. King, *Why We Can't Wait*, 83. See also Carson, *In Struggle*, 16; A. Morris, "A Man Prepared for the Times," 54–55; Moss, "Civil Rights Movement and American Foreign Policy," 86; Emerson, *Africa and U.S. Policy*, 25, 55–57.

65. While various scholars have made note of Africa's influence on the black American civil rights struggle, few have done more than mention it in passing. Manning Marable is illustrative: even as he refers to the influence, he does so relatively briefly and without documentary support. Marable, *Race, Reform, Rebellion*, 52–54.

66. "Gentle Imperialism for Africa," Editorial, *New York Age*, 11 July 1959, 8.

67. Kilson, "African Americans and Africa," 363.

68. James Farmer and E. J. Odom to Roy Wilkins, 23 Nov. 1960, GOF, 1956–65, ser. A, box 34, folder "Africa, General, 1960–65."

69. A. Philip Randolph to George McCray, 10 July 1958, *Randolph Papers*, 2/90–92. Both the *Papers of A. Philip Randolph* and the BSCP Records contain much material on the efforts of Randolph to promote African labor. Representative cites for these projects include Randolph to Arthur A. Ochwada, Assistant General Secretary of the Kenya Federation of Labour, 15 Aug. 1957, box 95, folder "Africa," BSCP Records; Randolph to Tom Mboya, 25 Aug. 1958, box 18, folder "Mboya, Tom," BSCP Records; Randolph to Sascha Voliman, Institute of International Labor Research, 29 Apr. 1958, box 95, folder "Africa," BSCP Records; Mary-Louise Hooper, West Coast Representative of the South Africa Defense Fund, to Randolph, 27 Jan. 1959, box 95, folder "Africa," BSCP Records; Randolph to George McCray, 2 Mar. 1959, box 95, folder "Africa," BSCP Records.

70. George Houser to A. Philip Randolph, 17 Dec. 1954, *Randolph Papers*, 3/504; Randolph to Houser, 23 Dec. 1954, ibid., 3/507; "Address to the Africa Freedom Day Celebration," 15 Apr. 1959, box 95, folder "Africa," BSCP Records; A. Philip Randolph, Reinhold Niebuhr, and Walter Reuther to the Editor, *Crisis*, June/July 1960, 385–86. For more on Randolph and his 1960s work with ACOA, see box 1, folder "American Committee on Africa." BSCP Records.

71. A. Philip Randolph to George McCray, 10 July 1958, *Randolph Papers*, 2/90–92; McCray to Randolph, 3 July 1958, ibid., 2/89; Randolph to McCray, 5 Feb. 1959, box 95, folder "Africa," BSCP Records.

72. James Farmer to Roy Wilkins, John Morsell, Henry Lee Moon, and Gloster Current, 28 Dec. 1959, GOF, 1956–65, ser. A, box 34, folder "Africa, General, 1956–59"; A. Philip Randolph to Maida Springer, 19 Aug. 1960, box 95, folder "Africa," BSCP Records; Davis, "Influence of Africans on American Culture," 82; George Houser to St. Clair Drake, 7 June 1961, box 49, folder 6, Drake Papers.

73. The following people formed themselves into a planning committee: John A. Davis, AMSAC; James Farmer, CORE; George Houser, ACOA; Clarence Jones, Gandhi Society; David Jones, ACOA; Frank Montero, African-American Students Foundation; John Morsell, NAACP; Guichard Parris, National Urban League (NUL); A. Philip Randolph, BSCP; and Hope Stevens, ACOA. Sponsoring Letter for the American Negro Leadership Conference on Africa (hereafter ANLCA), 21 Aug. 1962, GOF, 1956–65, ser. A, box 198, folder "ANLCA, 1962." The printed resolutions following the conference include the additional names of attorney Samuel R. Pierce and Rev. James Robinson, Operation Crossroads Africa.

74. The Call Letter for the ANLCA, n.d. [Aug. 1962], part 2, ser. 1, box 2, folder "ANLCA 1962," NUL Records.

75. Theodore Brown to the Call and Planning Committees, 1 Nov. 1962, part 2, ser. 1, box 2, folder "ANLCA, 1962," NUL Records; Program for the Arden House Conference, Nov. 1962, GOF, 1956–65, ser. A, box 198, folder "ANLCA, 1962."

76. Organizers made a concerted effort to ensure attendance by a widely repre-

sentative slice of African American organizations and interests. Their efforts bore fruit, as can be seen in a sampling of participants by category: *academic*—Rayford Logan and James Nabrit, Howard University; *African-oriented*—E. Frederic Morrow, African-American Institute; David Jones, Frank Montero, and Hope Stevens, ACOA; James K. Baker and John A. Davis, AMSAC; Leo Sam, Operation Crossroads Africa; *black nationalist*—Daniel Watts, Liberation Committee for Africa; *business*—Arnold Johnson, Small Business Chamber of Commerce, New York City; *civil rights*—James Farmer, CORE; Robert Carter, Gloster Current, Clarence Mitchell, John Morsell, and Roy Wilkins, NAACP; Martin Luther King Jr., Lawrence Reddick, and Wyatt Tee Walker, SCLC; Ella Baker, SNCC; George Butler, Isobel Clark, Guichard Parris, and Whitney Young, NUL; *fraternal*—Margery Parker, Alpha Kappa Alpha Sorority; Aaron Brown and William Hale, Alpha Phi Alpha Fraternity; Wilma Ray, Delta Sigma Theta Sorority; *labor*—A. Philip Randolph, BSCP; William Miller, Refuse and Salvage Drivers and Helpers Union; William Oliver, United Auto Workers, AFL-CIO; Charles Hayes and Russell Lasley, United Packing House Workers, AFL-CIO; Boyd Wilson, United Steelworkers, AFL-CIO; *philanthropic*—R. O'Hara Lanier, Phelps-Stokes Fund; *professional*—Edward Mazique, National Medical Association; Washington Rhodes, National Newspaper Publishers Association; *religious*—James Clark and Smallwood Williams, Bible Way Churches World Wide; Maurice Dawkins, Western Christian Leadership Conference; *social*—Hobson Reynolds, Independent Benevolent Protective Order, Elks; *women*—Dorothy Ferebee, Minnie Gaston, and Dorothy Height, NCNW; Regina Andrews, National Council of Women of the United States. Participant List for ANLCA, n.d., part 2, ser. 1, box 2, folder "ANLCA, 1962," NUL Records.

77. Participant List, NUL Records.

78. Call Letter for the ANLCA, n.d. [Aug. 1962], part 2, ser.1, box 2, folder "ANLCA 1962," NUL Records.

Chapter Seven

1. Reader, *Africa*, 543–47.

2. The abuses George Washington Williams saw led him to write "An Open Letter to His Serene Majesty Leopold II," which detailed twelve specific charges against the administration and called for an international commission of inquiry. For more on the efforts of Williams, see Franklin, *George Washington Williams*, 195–221. See also Morel, *Red Rubber*. Roger Casement quoted in Reader, *Africa*, 547.

3. Reader, *Africa*, 547.

4. Kabongo, "Catastrophe of Belgian Decolonization," 384; Stengers, "Precipitous Decolonization," 321–23; Kalb, *Congo Cables*, xxi–xxiii. The *Conscience Africaine* manifesto and a counter-manifesto released by Abako calling for immediate independence can be found in Merriam, *Congo*, 321–36.

5. Stengers, "Precipitous Decolonization," 307–11; H. F. Jackson, *From the Congo to Soweto*, 26.

6. Kabongo, "Catastrophe of Belgian Independence," 384; Stengers, "Precipitous Decolonization," 326–31.

7. "Congo Freedom," Editorial, *Baltimore Afro-American*, 13 Feb. 1960, 4. See also "Independence for the Congo," Editorial, *Chicago Defender*, 3 Feb. 1960, 10.

8. "Dinner to Commemorate Congo independence," *New York Amsterdam News*, 25 June 1960, 6; "Kongo Unit Slates Fete for July 1," *Baltimore Afro-American*, 25 June 1960, 18; "Group Here Hails Congo Independence," *New York Amsterdam News*, 16 July 1960, 8.

9. Weissman, *American Foreign Policy in the Congo*, 17–19.

10. For Lumumba's speech, see Merriam, *Congo*, 352–54; Ralph J. Bunche, "Diary Notes," box 178, folder "Congo, June–July 1960," Bunche Papers, Young Research Library, University of California, Los Angeles.

11. Telegram from U.S. Mission to the United Nations to Secretary of State, 9 July 1960, RG 59, DF, 755A.00/7-960; Urquhart, *Ralph Bunche*, 307–10, quote on 308. Urquhart's account clearly sympathizes with Bunche's Congo efforts and portrays Lumumba as an obstacle in the effort to find a peaceful resolution. See also Kalb, *Congo Cables*, 4–5.

12. Kalb, *Congo Cables*, 6–7; Weissman, *American Foreign Policy in the Congo*, 55–58.

13. Department of State to the Mission at the United Nations, 11 July 1960, *FRUS*, 1958–60, 14:1292–93; Kalb, *Congo Cables*, 6–15; Weissman, *American Foreign Policy in the Congo*, 55–63.

14. Weissman, *American Foreign Policy in the Congo*, 24–38.

15. Telegram from Department of State to Consulate General in Leopoldville, 23 June 1960, *FRUS*, 1958–60, 14:277–78; Memorandum of Discussion at the 452nd National Security Council Meeting, 21 July 1960, ibid., 14:338–42; Circular Telegram from Department of State to Certain Diplomatic Missions, 21 July 1960, ibid.,14:344–45. See also Kalb, *Congo Cables*, 31–32; Weissman, *American Foreign Policy in the Congo*, 66–84; J. Helmreich, *U.S. Relations with Belgium and the Congo*, 216–21.

16. Telegram from the Embassy in Belgium to the Department of State, 1 May 1960, *FRUS*, 1958–60, 14:272–74; Memorandum of Discussion at the 452nd Meeting of the National Security Council, 21 July 1960, ibid., 338–42, quote on 338. See also Kalb, *Congo Cables*, xxvii; H. F. Jackson, *From the Congo to Soweto*, 30–33.

17. "Intelligence Note on Communist Influence in the Congo," Hugh S. Cumming, Director of Intelligence and Research, to Secretary of State, 25 July 1960, RG 59, DF, 755A.00/7-2560. See also "Comments on the Congo Growing Out of My Recent Trip to Africa," Richard H. Sanger to Hugh S. Cumming, 22 Aug. 1960, RG 59, Lot and Office Files, Bureau of African Affairs, Office of Central African Affairs, Country Files, 1955–63, box 7, folder 14.4, 250/63/10/4.

18. Kalb, *Congo Cables*, 17–18; Urquhart, *Ralph Bunche*, 310–13.

19. Kalb, *Congo Cables*, 25–28, quote on 27. For Ralph Bunche's views on Lu-

mumba and his expectations concerning UN personnel, see "The UN Operation in the Congo," in Henry, *Ralph J. Bunche*, 189–204, especially 193–96.

20. Kalb, *Congo Cables*, 42–70; Urquhart, *Ralph Bunche*, 320–29.

21. Kevin Whitelaw, "A Killing in Congo," *U.S. News & World Report*, 24 July/31 July 2000, 63; Witte, *L'assassinat de Lumumba*; J. Helmreich, *U.S. Relations with Belgium and the Congo*, 231. Kalb and Weissman, on the other hand, indicate that at this point the CIA had not yet attempted to assassinate Lumumba, but that Washington sought to remove him from political power. Kalb, *Congo Cables*, 51–55, 63–66, 101–3, 129–33, 149–52; Weissman, *American Foreign Policy in the Congo*, 79–84.

22. Kalb, *Congo Cables*, 71–75, 85; Weissman, *American Foreign Policy in the Congo*, 88–95.

23. Kalb, *Congo Cables*, 89–97; Weissman, *American Foreign Policy in the Congo*, 95–99. The UN never backed down in protecting Lumumba from arrest. It did not believe Mobutu or Kasavubu had the legal authority to arrest Lumumba and did not want to seem to be complicit in the Mobutu coup. Further, Hammarskjöld needed the support of the African states to ward off Krushchev's attacks and his proposals for a troika for the office of UN secretary-general. Kalb, *Congo Cables*, 133–39.

24. Transcript of "Africa: Revolution in Haste," program 6 in series *Mrs. Eleanor Roosevelt: Prospects of Mankind*, National Educational Television, 6 Mar. 1960, box 2, Henry Morgenthau III Papers, Franklin D. Roosevelt Library, Hyde Park, N.Y.

25. "The New Congo Republic," Editorial, *Chicago Defender*, 30 June 1960, 12.

26. Emmett Marshall to the Editor, *Baltimore Afro-American*, 30 July 1960, 4; "Free to Riot," Editorial, *New York Amsterdam News*, 16 July, 10. In a similarly stinging rebuke, Gordon Hancock, writing for the Associated Negro Press, declared, "This 'not ready' argument is a hoary-headed argument for perpetuating colonial imperialism and its concomitant slavery." Hancock, "Whose Fault Is It?" *Atlanta Daily World*, 15 July 1960, 4. See also "And So a New Nation Is Born," Editorial, *Baltimore Afro-American*, 9 July 1960, 4; "Chinese Puzzle for the West," Editorial, *Chicago Defender*, 16 Aug. 1960, 10.

27. "Congo's Freedom Trials," Editorial, *California Eagle*, 14 July 1960, 4; Joel Rogers, "History Shows," *Pittsburgh Courier*, 13 Aug. 1960, 13; P. L. Prattis, "Horizon," *Pittsburgh Courier*, 30 July 1960, 13; "Real Culprit in the Congo," Editorial, *Baltimore Afro-American*, 23 July 1960, 4; "And So a New Nation Is Born," Editorial, *Baltimore Afro-American*, 9 July 1960, 4; "Is Belgium Responsible for the Congo Trouble?" Editorial, *Atlanta Daily World*, 19 July 1960, 6; "Congo — Struggle for Power," Editorial, *Chicago Defender*, 13 July 1960, 12.

28. Mrs. John Stewart to Roy Wilkins, 21 July 1960, GOF, 1956–65, ser. A, box 34, folder, "Africa, Congo, 1959–1965"; "Ask Negroes to Volunteer to Aid Congolese," *California Eagle*, 28 July 1960, 3; "Nationalists Seeking Volunteers for Congo," *New York Amsterdam News*, 27 Aug. 1960, 19; Amos Gilliam to Roy Wilkins, 22 July 1960, GOF, 1956–65, ser. A, box 34, folder, "Africa, Congo, 1959–1965"; Frances Walters to the Editor, *Baltimore Afro-American*, 12 Nov. 1960, 4. For

similar expressions, see Edward Lewis to the Editor, *Chicago Defender*, 16 Aug. 1960, 11; Pfc. John Morgan to the Editor, *Baltimore Afro-American*, 19 Nov. 1960, 4; S. Kollock, Vineland, N.J., to the Editor, *Baltimore Afro-American*, 26 Nov. 1960, 4.

29. "The New Congo Republic," Editorial, *Chicago Defender*, 30 June 1960, 12; "Colonial Benefits?" Editorial, *Baltimore Afro-American*, 18 June 1960, 4.

30. Earl Brown, "Fair Shake for Congo," *New York Amsterdam News*, 20 Aug. 1960, 11; Luvenia Cowles to the Editor, *Baltimore Afro-American*, 16 July 1960, 4; Joel Rogers, "History Shows," *Pittsburgh Courier*, 30 July 1960, 13. For further examples of Belgian colonial rule being blamed, see "Real Culprit in the Congo," Editorial, *Baltimore Afro-American*, 23 July 1960, 4; "What's with Congo?" Editorial, *Baltimore Afro-American*, 30 July 1960, 5; "Slap in the Face," Editorial, *New York Amsterdam News*, 23 July 1960, 10; "The Way It Is," Editorial, *New York Amsterdam News*, 30 July 1960, 10; Horace Cayton, "World At Large," *Pittsburgh Courier*, 23 July 1960, 14.

31. Jackie Robinson, "Jackie Robinson," *Chicago Defender*, 4 Aug. 1960, 18 Aug. 1960, and 22 Aug. 1960, all on 13; "Some Congo History," Editorial, *Crisis*, Oct. 1960, 536–37; "Congo's Freedom Trials," Editorial, *California Eagle*, 14 July 1960, 4; "Congo Freedom Came Too Suddenly?" *Baltimore Afro-American*, 13 Aug. 1960, 5; "Man on the Street," *Chicago Defender*, 21 Sept. 1960, 4.

32. "Congo: Monstrous Hangover," *Time*, 18 July 1960, 17; "Mutiny in the Congo — More Troubles Coming," *U.S. News & World Report*, 18 July 1960, 51; "Savagery in the Congo," *Newsweek*, 18 July 1960, 49.

33. "Eyewitness Report: Savagery in the Jungle," *U.S. News & World Report*, 12 Sept. 1960, 48–50.

34. "Press Plot against Congo Exposed," *Baltimore Afro-American*, 17 Sept. 1960, 1. Regarding wire service reports, the United Press International (UPI) correspondent in the Congo, George Sibera, sent dispatches such as the following: "Belgian paratroopers attacked rebel Congolese army troops besieging two Congo towns Sunday and saved thousands of whites from slaughter"; and "The newly independent Congo, already beset in its first eleven days of freedom by a rampage of rape, riot and murder by mutinous soldiers, was rocked again Monday." "Belgian Paratroopers Attack Congo Troops," *Chicago Defender*, 11 July 1960, 2; "Katanga Province Secedes from the Congo," *Chicago Defender*, 12 July 1960, 2.

35. "Slap in the Face," Editorial, *New York Amsterdam News*, 23 July 1960, 10; Joseph Watkins to the Editor, *Pittsburgh Courier*, 8 Oct. 1960, magazine section, 3.

36. "Real Culprit in the Congo?" Editorial, *Baltimore Afro-American*, 23 July 1960, 4.

37. "Look Who's Crying Rape," Editorial, *Baltimore Afro-American*, 13 Aug. 1960, 4.

38. Jackie Robinson, "Jackie Robinson," *Chicago Defender*, 18 Aug. 1960, 13. Even Secretary of State Dean Rusk later commented, "In cynical moments I always suspect that some Belgians decided to turn the Congo loose so precipitously, hoping

that in the ensuing chaos mineral-rich Katanga Province would secede, becoming an independent state, and grant favorable concessions to Western mining interests." Rusk, *As I Saw It*, 276.

39. Henry Langdon, Montreal, to the Editor, *Baltimore Afro-American*, 27 Aug. 1960, 4; "Abe Had Solution," Editorial, *Baltimore Afro-American*, 30 July 1960, 4; "They Can't Afford to Be Polite," Editorial, *Baltimore Afro-American*, 27 Aug. 1960, 4; "Nigeria's New Status," Editorial, *Chicago Defender*, 4 Oct. 1960, 10. For additional condemnation of Tshombe and Belgium, see "Big Time Uncle Tom," Editorial, *California Eagle*, 11 Aug. 1960, 4; P. L. Prattis, "Horizon," *Pittsburgh Courier*, 3 Sept. 1960, 13; Earl Brown, "Fair Shake for Congo," *New York Amsterdam News*, 20 Aug. 1960, 11; "Some Congo History," Editorial, *Crisis*, Oct. 1960, 536–37.

40. "Real Culprit in the Congo," Editorial, *Baltimore Afro-American*, 23 July 1960, 4. See also "Is Belgium Responsible for the Congo Trouble?" Editorial, *Atlanta Daily World*, 19 July 1960, 6; "Peace Outlook in Congo," Editorial, *Chicago Defender*, 27 July 1960, 12.

41. "They Can't Afford to Be Polite," Editorial, *Baltimore Afro-American*, 27 Aug. 1960, 4; "They Hate Lumumba," Editorial, *Baltimore Afro-American*, 17 Sept. 1960, 4; "A Sickening Business," Editorial, *Baltimore Afro-American*, 19 Nov. 1960, 4.

42. "The Dawn of a New Day," Editorial, *Chicago Defender*, 26 Sept. 1960, 10.

43. "Dr. Bunche — Congo Casualty," Editorial, *Chicago Defender*, 24 Aug. 1960, 10; "A Good Proposal," Editorial, *Chicago Defender*, 10 Oct. 1960, 10; "Congo's Continuing Crisis," Editorial, *Chicago Defender*, 13 Oct. 1960, 14; Alphaeus Hunton to Friends, 1 Dec. 1960, Additions, folder 1, Hunton Papers.

44. The NAACP board of directors never made more than passing reference to the Congo throughout 1960–61. The 1961 Annual Convention passed a resolution regarding the Congo that essentially reaffirmed support for the UN and commended its efforts to bring peace and order to the nation. GOF, 1956–65, ser. A, box 13, folder "Annual Convention File, 1961 Resolutions." ACOA also supported an expansive UN role. George Houser argued, "The United Nations must be given the power effectively to fill the vacuum which exists in the Congo." He urged the United States to take the lead in enabling the UN to do so, for instance, by allowing the UN the power to take over government functions in the Congo for a limited period. "A Proposal for a New U.S. Policy on the Congo," George Houser, Dec. 1960, MSS 61, box 2, folder 2 "Africa File, Central Africa — Congo (Zaire), 1960," American Society of African Culture Papers, Schomburg Center for Research in Black Culture, New York.

45. John Morsell [for Roy Wilkins] to Amos Gilliam, 29 July 1960, GOF, 1956–65, ser. A, box 34, folder "Africa, Congo, 1959–1965." For similar responses, see other letters in the same folder: Morsell to Mrs. John T. Stewart, 29 July 1960; Morsell to Mr. E. Ellens, 7 Sept. 1960; Morsell to Mr. Irvin Green, 7 Sept. 1960.

46. "'Mama — Look at Boo-Boo!'," Editorial, *New York Amsterdam News*, 17 Sept. 1960, 10.

47. Benjamin Mays, "My View," *Pittsburgh Courier*, 3 Sept. 1960, 13; Lester

Granger, "Battleaxe and Bread," *California Eagle*, 22 Sept. 1960, 4. In an extreme case, George Schuyler even accused the black press of purposefully omitting and distorting historical facts in order to miseducate the public about the situation in the Congo. Schuyler argued that Leopold's administration was "an improvement over the anarchy that prevailed before it took over" and praised the rule of the Belgian government. According to Schuyler, "It is a fact that there have been no atrocities in the Congo for over 50 years — until it got a black government." George Schuyler, "Views and Reviews," *Pittsburgh Courier*, 13 Aug. 1960, 12. Unsurprisingly, Schuyler supported Moise Tshombe. "The Reminiscences of George Schuyler (1960)," 340–42, in the Oral History Collection of Columbia University, New York.

48. "What's with Congo?" Editorial, *Baltimore Afro-American*, 30 July 1960, 5; "Question for Herter," Editorial, *Baltimore Afro-American*, 15 Oct. 1960, 4; "A Sickening Business," Editorial, *Baltimore Afro-American*, 19 Nov. 1960, 4.

49. Kalb, *Congo Cables*, 152–55; Weissman, *American Foreign Policy in the Congo*, 106–7.

50. Kalb, *Congo Cables*, 158–61.

51. Memorandum Prepared in the Central Intelligence Agency, "Death of Patrice Lumumba," n.d. [Mar. 1961], FRUS, 1961–63, 20:93–94; Editorial Note, ibid., 20:16–18; Kalb, *Congo Cables*, 184–86; Weissman, *American Foreign Policy in the Congo*, 137–38.

52. "Petition Backing Patrice Lumumba Signed by 1,500," *Pittsburgh Courier*, 18 Feb. 1961, sec. 2, 7; Welton Cephas to the Editor, *Baltimore Afro-American*, 11 Feb 1961, 4; Kalb, *Congo Cables*, 224–25.

53. "Lumumba's Savage Slaying," Editorial, *Chicago Defender*, 16 Feb. 1961, 14.

54. "Blood on Their Hands," Editorial, *Baltimore Afro-American*, 25 Feb. 1961, 4; "Chicagoans Blast Tshombe as an 'Uncle Tom,'" *Chicago Defender*, 14 Feb. 1961, 3. While the CIA had sent an assassin in September to kill Lumumba, it appears the CIA did not engineer Lumumba's transfer to Katanga. Instead, the Belgians apparently masterminded the transfer and execution. Still, the CIA likely knew of the plan, had encouraged the slaying of Lumumba, and the United States certainly did nothing to warn against the transfer or to protect Lumumba's life after the flight to Katanga. Whitelaw, "A Killing in Congo," 63; Witte, *L'assassinat de Lumumba*; J. Helmreich, *U.S. Relations with Belgium and the Congo*, 231; Kalb, *Congo Cables*, 189–96.

55. "Murder in the Congo," Editorial, *California Eagle*, 23 Feb. 1961, 4; James Hicks, "Patrice Lumumba," *New York Amsterdam News*, 18 Feb. 1961, 8; Emmett Marshall to the Editor, *Baltimore Afro-American*, 25 Feb. 1961, 4; "For Lumumba's Death, Who Is Responsible?" *Baltimore Afro-American*, 25 Feb. 1961, 5.

56. F. L. Shuttlesworth, "A Southerner Speaks . . . ," *Pittsburgh Courier*, 25 Feb. 1961, sec. 2, 8; Bishop Smallwood Williams to the Editor, *Pittsburgh Courier*, 18 Mar. 1961, sec. 2, 26.

57. Mary Phillips to the Editor, *Chicago Defender*, 27 Feb. 1961, 10; Eugene Johnson to the Editor, *New York Amsterdam News*, 18 Mar. 1961, 10; Eduardo

Sprinkle to the Editor, *New York Amsterdam News*, 18 Mar. 1961, 10. See also "Lumumba's Savage Slaying," Editorial, *Chicago Defender*, 16 Feb. 1961, 14; "The Tragedy of Lumumba," Editorial, *Atlanta Daily World*, 15 Feb. 1961, 6.

58. "Testimonials to a Patriot," Editorial, *Chicago Defender*, 20 Feb. 1961, 10. See also "Angry African Students Storm Embassies," *Chicago Defender*, 15 Feb. 1961, 12; "Lumumba Riots Rake London," *Chicago Defender*, 20 Feb. 1961, 3; "Rioting Over Patrice Eases," *Chicago Defender*, 21 Feb. 1961, 8; "Belgium and United States Key Targets in Protests of Lumumba's Slaying in Congo," *Atlanta Daily World*, 15 Feb. 1961, 1; Kalb, *Congo Cables*, 227–30.

59. "Russia Accused of 'Virtual' War Declaration on U.N.; Lumumba's Death Protested in 'Near Riot,'" *Atlanta Daily World*, 16 Feb. 1961, 1; "U.S. Blames Reds for Negroes' Act," *Chicago Defender*, 16 Feb. 1961, 3; "Can the U.N. Survive?" *Newsweek*, 27 Feb. 1961, 17–22; "Riot in Gallery Halts U.N. Debate" *New York Times*, 16 Feb. 1961, 1. *Life* magazine published photographs with captions describing "extremist U.S. Negroes" who intended the riot to "foment black anger against the white race." "Lumumba's Legacy: Troubles All Over," *Life*, 24 Feb. 1961, 18.

60. Davis, "American Ethnic Minorities and the New Nations," 134–36; "U.N. Rioting Laid to Pro-Africans," *New York Times*, 16 Feb. 1961, 11; Plummer, *Rising Wind*, 302–3.

61. "'The Hoodlums'," Editorial, *New York Times*, 16 Feb. 1961, 30; "We're Not Alarmed," Editorial, *Baltimore Afro-American*, 25 Mar. 1961, 4.

62. "The Disgraceful Spectacle at the U.N.," Editorial, *Atlanta Daily World*, 17 Feb. 1961, 4; John Henry to the Editor, *New York Amsterdam News*, 18 Mar. 1961, 10. A series of editorials help define the continuing conservative and accommodationist nature of the *Daily World*. It spoke out against the sit-ins, against communism, for the Republican Party, and in support of being loyal Americans. See the following editorials: "Are Repeated Demonstrations Necessary?" 26 June 1960, 4; "The Students Should Make Bond," 16 Feb. 1961, 6; "A Film to Remember," 17 Feb. 1961, 4; "More Power to Nixon," 14 Sept. 1960, 6; "The Nixon-Lodge Team Best Qualified to Lead Nation," 7 Oct. 1960, 1; "We Need Loyal Americans," 24 July 1960, 4.

63. NAACP Press Release, 16 Feb. 1961, GOF, 1956–65, ser. A, box 34, folder "Africa, Congo, 1959–1965."

64. "Bunche Deplores Riot by Negroes in Council," *New York Times*, 18 Feb. 1961, 3; Urquhart, *Ralph Bunche*, 339; P. L. Prattis, "Horizon," *Pittsburgh Courier*, 4 Mar. 1961, sec. 2, 9.

65. Jimmy McDonald to Roy Wilkins, 9 Mar. 1961, GOF, 1956–65, ser. A, box 34, folder "Africa, General, 1960–65."

66. James Hicks, "The Apologists," *New York Amsterdam News*, 25 Feb. 1961, 8. See the following letters to the *Amsterdam News*, all written in support of Hicks: Leroy Woods, 11 Mar. 1961, 10; Ben Davis, 11 Mar. 1961, 10; Eduardo Sprinkle, 18 Mar. 1961, 10; Warren Hall, 25 Mar. 1961, 11; B. Paul Sims, 25 Mar. 1961, 11; Ella Sample, 25 Mar. 1961, 12; Mrs. Grace Johnson, 1 Apr. 1961, 8; Rowena Montgomery, 1 Apr. 1961, 8; D. Parker, 1 Apr. 1961, 8.

67. Venia M. Stampers to Ralph Bunche, 20 Feb. 1961, and R. Weston to Ralph Bunche, 17 Feb. 1961, box 125, folder 4, Bunche Papers, Young Research Library, University of California, Los Angeles.

68. M. L. King, "'The Time for Freedom Has Come,'" 118.

69. "U.S. Negroes: The New Pride," *Newsweek*, 6 Mar. 1961, 32.

70. J. Baldwin, "A Negro Assays the Negro Mood," 25, 104.

Epilogue

1. Consulate General at Lagos to the Department of State, 5 Sept. 1960, *FRUS*, 1958–60, 14:220.

2. Boahen, "Ghana Since Independence," 208–24; Esedebe, *Pan-Africanism*, 207–11, 224–26; W. S. Thompson, *Ghana's Foreign Policy 1957–1966*, 145–61, 198–262; D. Williams, "English-Speaking West Africa," 345–46, 358–60.

3. Secretary's Report, 8 Dec. 1958, GOF, 1956–65, ser. A, box 31, folder "Secretary's Reports, 1958"; Martin Luther King Jr. to Editorial Committee of *Dissent*, 1 June 1959, box 25, folder 32, MLK/BU.

SELECTED BIBLIOGRAPHY

Manuscript Collections

Boston, Mass.
  Mugar Memorial Library, Boston University
    Martin Luther King Jr. Papers
Chicago, Ill.
  Chicago Historical Society
    Claude A. Barnett Papers
Hyde Park, N.Y.
  Franklin D. Roosevelt Library
    Papers of Henry Morgenthau III
Los Angeles, Calif.
  Young Research Library, University of California, Los Angeles
    Ralph J. Bunche Papers
New Haven, Conn.
  Beinecke Rare Book and Manuscript Library, Yale University
    James Weldon Johnson Collection
      Langston Hughes Papers
      Walter White and Poppy Cannon White Correspondence
    Yale Collection of American Literature
      Richard Wright Papers
New York City, N.Y.
  Columbia University Oral History Collection
    Lester Granger Memoir
    William Jay Schieffelin Memoir
    George Schuyler Memoir
  Schomburg Center for Research in Black Culture
    Manuscripts, Archives, and Rare Books Division
      American Society of African Culture Papers
      St. Clair Drake Papers
      William Alphaeus Hunton Papers
    Photographs and Prints Division
      Kwame Nkrumah Portrait Collection
    Moving Images and Recorded Sound Division

Interview of Martin Luther King Jr. by Etta Moten Barnett

Washington, D.C.

  Library of Congress

    Papers of Arthur B. Spingarn

    Papers of Roy Wilkins

    Papers of the National Association for the Advancement of Colored People

    Records of the Brotherhood of Sleeping Car Porters

    Records of the National Urban League

  Moorland-Spingarn Research Center, Howard University

    Dabu Gizenga Collection on Kwame Nkrumah

    Percival L. Prattis Papers

  National Archives

    U.S. Department of State Records, RG 59

      Central Files, Decimal File, 1930–1963

      Lot and Office Files

        Bureau of African Affairs

          General Records of the Office of Southern African Affairs, 1950–1956

          Office of Central African Affairs, Country Files, 1955–1963

          Office of Eastern and Southern African Affairs, Country Files, 1951–1965

          Office of West African Affairs, Country Files, 1951–1963

Newspapers and Periodicals

Africa News

African World

Atlanta Daily World

Baltimore Afro-American

California Eagle

Chicago Defender

The Crisis

Life

New Africa

New York Age

New York Amsterdam News

New York Herald Tribune

New York Times

Newsweek

Norfolk Journal & Guide

Pittsburgh Courier

Spotlight on Africa

Time

U.S. News & World Report

Published Archives, Documents, and Microform Collections

[Council on African Affairs.] *Proceedings of the Conference on Africa—New Perspectives.* New York: Council on African Affairs, 1944.

Du Bois, W. E. B. *Papers of W. E. B. Du Bois.* Sanford, N.C.: Microfilming Corporation of America, 1980. Microfilm.

National Association for the Advancement of Colored People (NAACP). *Papers of the National Association for the Advancement of Colored People.* Bethesda, Md.: University Publications of America, 1981–1995. Microfilm.

> Part 1: "Meetings of the Board of Directors, Records of Annual Conferences, Major Speeches, and Special Reports, 1909–1950," edited by Mark Fox, editorial advisor August Meier (1981); Supplements to Part 1, 1951–1955 and 1956–60, edited by August Meier and John H. Bracey Jr., associate editor Randolph Boehm (1991)
>
> Part 11: "Special Subject Files, 1912–1939," edited by John H. Bracey Jr. and August Meier (1991)
>
> Part 14: "Race Relations in the International Arena, 1940–1955," edited by John H. Bracey Jr. and August Meier (1993)

Public Papers of the Presidents of the United States: Harry S. Truman. Washington D.C.: U.S. Government Printing Office, 1961–66.

Randolph, A. Philip. *Papers of A. Philip Randolph.* Bethesda, Md.: University Publications of America, 1990. Microfilm.

Rosenman, Samuel I., comp. *Public Papers and Addresses of Franklin D. Roosevelt.* 13 vols. New York: Macmillan, 1938–50.

Rustin, Bayard. *Bayard Rustin Papers.* Frederick, Md.: University Publications of America, 1988. Microfilm.

Schomburg Center for Research in Black Culture. *Schomburg Center Clipping File* (microfiche). New York: Schomburg Center for Research in Black Culture, New York City Public Library.

United Nations. *Official Records of the General Assembly,* Fifteenth Session, Part I: Plenary Meetings, Vol. 1: 20 September–17 October 1960. New York: United Nations.

U.S. Department of State. *Department of State Bulletin.* Washington, D.C.: U.S. Government Printing Office, 1945–1963.

———. *Foreign Relations of the United States,* 1934–1961/63. Washington, D.C.: U.S. Government Printing Office, 1951–1994.

Books

Acheson, Dean. *Present at the Creation: My Years in the State Department.* New York: W. W. Norton, 1969.

Albert, Peter J., and Ronald Hoffmann, eds. *We Shall Overcome: Martin Luther King, Jr., and the Black Freedom Struggle.* New York: Pantheon, 1990.

Anderson, Jervis. *Bayard Rustin: Troubles I've Seen: A Biography*. New York: HarperCollins, 1997.

Angell, Stephen Ward. *Bishop Henry McNeal Turner and African-American Religion in the South*. Knoxville: University of Tennessee Press, 1992.

Angelou, Maya. *All God's Children Need Traveling Shoes*. New York: Vintage, 1986.

Austin, Dennis. *Politics in Ghana, 1946–1960*. London: Oxford University Press, 1964.

Baldwin, James. *The Fire Next Time*. New York: Dial, 1963.

Baldwin, Lewis V. *Toward the Beloved Community: Martin Luther King Jr. and South Africa*. Cleveland, Ohio: Pilgrim, 1995.

Berman, Bruce. *Control and Crisis in Colonial Kenya: The Dialectic of Domination*. London: James Currey, 1990.

Boley, G. E. Saigbe. *Liberia: The Rise and Fall of the First Republic*. London: Macmillan, 1983.

Borstelmann, Thomas. *Apartheid's Reluctant Uncle: The United States and Southern Africa in the Early Cold War*. New York: Oxford University Press, 1993.

Branch, Taylor. *Parting the Waters: America in the King Years, 1954–63*. New York: Simon and Schuster, 1988.

Breitman, George, ed. *Malcolm X Speaks: Selected Speeches and Statements*. New York: Grove Weidenfeld, 1990.

Brooks, Maxwell R. *The Negro Press Re-examined: Political Content of Leading Negro Newspapers*. Boston: Christopher Publishing House, 1959.

Buijtenhuijs, Rob. *Essays on Mau Mau: Contributions to Mau Mau Historiography*. Leiden, the Netherlands: African Studies Centre, 1982.

Buni, Andrew. *Robert L. Vann of the Pittsburgh Courier: Politics and Black Journalism*. Pittsburgh: University of Pittsburgh Press, 1974.

Campbell, James T. *Songs of Zion: The African Methodist Episcopal Church in the United States and South Africa*. Oxford: Oxford University Press, 1995.

Carson, Clayborne. *In Struggle: SNCC and the Black Awakening of the 1960s*. Cambridge, Mass.: Harvard University Press, 1981.

Cayton, Horace. *Long Old Road: An Autobiography*. Seattle: University of Washington Press, 1963.

Chafe, William. *Civilities and Civil Rights: Greensboro, North Carolina, and the Black Struggle for Freedom*. Oxford: Oxford University Press, 1980.

Clarke, John Henrik, ed. *Marcus Garvey and the Vision of Africa*. New York: Vintage, 1974.

Coffey, Thomas M. *Lion by the Tail: The Story of the Italian-Ethiopian War*. New York: Viking, 1974.

Collum, Danny Duncan, ed. *African Americans in the Spanish Civil War: "This Ain't Ethiopia, But It'll Do."* New York: G. K. Hall, 1992.

Cromwell, Adelaide, ed. *Dynamics of the African/Afro-American Connection: From Dependency to Self-Reliance*. Washington, D.C.: Howard University Press, 1987.

Dallek, Robert. *Franklin D. Roosevelt and American Foreign Policy, 1932–1945.*
Oxford: Oxford University Press, 1979.

Davis, John A., ed. *Africa Seen By American Negroes.* Paris: Presence Africaine,
1958.

Davis, John A., and James K. Baker, eds. *Southern Africa in Transition.* New York:
Published for the American Society of African Culture by F. A. Praeger, 1966.

DeConde, Alexander. *Ethnicity, Race, and American Foreign Policy: A History.*
Boston: Northeastern University Press, 1992.

Degler, Carl. *In Search of Human Nature: The Decline and Revival of Darwinism in
American Social Thought.* Oxford: Oxford University Press, 1991.

Dickson, David A. *United States Foreign Policy towards Sub-Saharan Africa.*
Lanham, Md.: University Press of America, 1985.

Drake, St. Clair, and Horace Cayton. *Black Metropolis: A Study of Negro Life in a
Northern City.* 1945. Reprint, New York: Harper & Row, 1962.

Du Bois, W. E. B. *The Autobiography of W. E. B. Du Bois: A Soliloquy on Viewing
My Life from the Last Decade of Its First Century.* U.S.A.: International
Publishers, 1968.

———. *Darkwater: Voices from Within the Veil.* 1920. Reprint, New York:
Schocken, 1969.

———. *The World and Africa.* New York: Viking, 1946.

Duberman, Martin. *Paul Robeson.* New York: Alfred Knopf, 1988.

Duignan, Peter, and L. H. Gann. *The United States and Africa: A History.*
Cambridge: Cambridge University Press, 1984.

Dunbar, Ernest. *The Black Expatriates: A Study of American Negroes in Exile.*
London: Victor Gollancz, 1968.

Edgerton, Robert. *Mau Mau: An African Crucible.* New York: Free Press, 1989.

Eisenhower, Dwight D. *Waging Peace, 1956–1961.* Garden City, N.Y.: Doubleday,
1965.

Emerson, Rupert. *Africa and United States Policy.* Englewood Cliffs, N.J.: Prentice-
Hall, 1967.

Esedebe, P. Olisanwuche. *Pan-Africanism: The Idea and Movement, 1776–1963.*
Washington, D.C.: Howard University Press, 1982.

Fabre, Michel. *The Unfinished Quest of Richard Wright.* New York: William
Morrow, 1973.

———. *The World of Richard Wright.* Jackson: University Press of Mississippi, 1985.

Fairclough, Adam. *Race and Democracy: The Civil Rights Struggle in Louisiana,
1915–1972.* Athens: University of Georgia Press, 1995.

Feelings, Tom. *Black Pilgrimage.* New York: Lothrop, Lee & Shepard, 1972.

Fierce, Milfred C. *The Pan-African Idea in the United States, 1900–1919: African-
American Interest in Africa and Interaction with West Africa.* New York:
Garland, 1993.

Foner, Philip S., ed. *W. E. B. Du Bois Speaks: Speeches and Addresses, 1890–1919.*
New York: Pathfinder, 1970.

Forman, James. *High Tide of Black Resistance and Other Literary & Political Writings*. 1967. Reprint, Seattle: Open Hand, 1994.

Franklin, John Hope. *George Washington Williams: A Biography*. Chicago: University of Chicago Press, 1985.

Franklin, John Hope, and Alfred A. Moss Jr. *From Slavery to Freedom*. 6th ed. New York: McGraw-Hill, 1988.

Fredrickson, George. *Black Liberation: A Comparative History of Black Ideologies in the United States and South Africa*. Oxford: Oxford University Press, 1995.

———. *White Supremacy: A Comparative Study in American & South African History*. Oxford: Oxford University Press, 1981.

Fried, Richard M. *Nightmare in Red: The McCarthy Era in Perspective*. New York: Oxford University Press, 1990.

Furedi, Frank. *The Mau Mau War in Perspective*. London: James Currey, 1989.

Gaddis, John Lewis. *The United States and the Origins of the Cold War, 1941–1947*. New York: Columbia University Press, 1972.

Garrow, David J. *Bearing the Cross: Martin Luther King, Jr., and the Southern Christian Leadership Conference*. New York: William Morrow, 1986.

———, ed. *The Walking City: The Montgomery Bus Boycott, 1955–1956*. Brooklyn: Carlson, 1989.

Geiss, Imanuel. *The Pan-African Movement: A History of Pan-Africanism in America, Europe, and Africa*. New York: Africana, 1974.

Gifford, Prosser, and Wm. Roger Louis, eds. *Decolonization and African Independence: The Transfers of Power, 1960–1980*. New Haven: Yale University Press, 1988.

———. *The Transfer of Power in Africa: Decolonization 1940–1960*. New Haven: Yale University Press, 1982.

Goldsworthy, David. *Tom Mboya: The Man Kenya Wanted to Forget*. London: Heinemann Educational Books, 1982.

Gruesser, John Cullen. *White on Black: Contemporary Literature about Africa*. Urbana: University of Illinois Press, 1992.

Hamilton, Charles V. *Adam Clayton Powell, Jr.: The Political Biography of an American Dilemma*. New York: Atheneum, 1991.

Harris, Joseph E. *African-American Reactions to War in Ethiopia, 1936–41*. Baton Rouge: Louisiana State University Press, 1994.

———, ed. *Global Dimensions of the African Diaspora*. Washington, D.C.: Howard University Press, 1982.

Haynes, George E. *Africa: Continent of the Future*. New York: Association Press, 1950.

Heale, M. J. *American Anticommunism: Combating the Enemy Within, 1830–1970*. Baltimore: Johns Hopkins University Press, 1990.

Helmreich, Jonathan. *United States Relations with Belgium and the Congo, 1940–1960*. Newark: University of Delaware Press, 1998.

Helmreich, William B. *Afro-Americans and Africa: Black Nationalism at the Crossroads.* Westport, Conn.: Greenwood, 1977.

Henry, Charles P. *Ralph Bunche: Model Negro or American Other?* New York: New York University Press, 1999.

———, ed. *Ralph J. Bunche: Selected Speeches and Writings.* Ann Arbor: University of Michigan Press, 1995.

Hickey, Dennis, and Kenneth C. Wylie. *An Enchanting Darkness: The American Vision of Africa in the Twentieth Century.* East Lansing: Michigan State University Press, 1993.

Hill, Adelaide C., and Martin Kilson, eds. *Apropos of Africa: Sentiments of Negro American Leaders on Africa from the 1800s to the 1950s.* London: Frank Cass, 1969.

Hill, Robert A., ed. *The FBI's RACON: Racial Conditions in America during World War II.* Boston: Northeastern University Press, 1995.

———. *Pan-African Biography.* Los Angeles: UCLA African Studies Center and Crossroads Press, 1987.

Hill, Robert, ed., and Barbara Bair. *Marcus Garvey: Life and Lessons.* Berkeley: University of California Press, 1987.

Hogan, Lawrence D. *A Black National News Service: The Associated Negro Press and Claude Barnett, 1919–1945.* London: Associated University Presses, 1984.

Hooker, James R. *Black Revolutionary: George Padmore's Path from Communism to Pan-Africanism.* New York: Praeger, 1967.

Horne, Gerald. *Black and Red: W. E. B. Du Bois and the Afro-American Response to the Cold War, 1944–1963.* Albany: State University of New York Press, 1986.

———. *Communist Front?: The Civil Rights Congress, 1946–1956.* London: Associated University Presses, 1988.

Houser, George. *No One Can Stop the Rain: Glimpses of Africa's Liberation Struggle.* New York: Pilgrim, 1989.

Hull, Cordell. *The Memoirs of Cordell Hull.* 2 vols. New York: Macmillan, 1948.

Hunt, Michael. *Ideology and U.S. Foreign Policy.* New Haven: Yale University Press, 1977.

Hunton, Alphaeus. *Africa Fights for Freedom.* New York: Century, 1950.

———. *Resistance against Fascist Enslavement in South Africa.* New York: Council on African Affairs, 1953.

Isaacs, Harold. *The New World of Negro Americans.* New York: Viking, 1963.

Jackson, Henry F. *From the Congo to Soweto: U.S. Foreign Policy toward Africa since 1960.* New York: William Morrow, 1982.

Jackson, Walter A. *Gunnar Myrdal and America's Conscience: Social Engineering and Racial Liberalism, 1938–1987.* Chapel Hill: University of North Carolina Press, 1990.

Jacobs, Sylvia. *The African Nexus: Black American Perspectives on the European Partitioning of Africa, 1880–1920.* Westport, Conn.: Greenwood, 1981.

Kalb, Madeleine G. *The Congo Cables: The Cold War in Africa — From Eisenhower to Kennedy*. New York: Macmillan, 1982.

Kapur, Sudarshan. *Raising Up a Prophet: The African-American Encounter with Gandhi*. Boston: Beacon, 1992.

Karis, Thomas, and Gwendolyn M. Carter, eds. *From Protest to Challenge: A Documentary History of African Politics in South Africa, 1882–1964*. 4 vols. Stanford, Calif.: Hoover Institution Press, 1972–77.

Kelley, Robin D. G. *Hammer and Hoe: Alabama Communists during the Great Depression*. Chapel Hill: University of North Carolina Press, 1990.

Kershaw, Greet. *Mau Mau from Below*. Oxford: James Currey, 1997.

King, Coretta Scott. *My Life with Martin Luther King, Jr*. New York: Holt, Rinehart, and Winston, 1969.

King, Martin Luther, Jr. *The Papers of Martin Luther King, Jr*. Vol. 4: *Symbol of the Movement, January 1957–December 1958*. Edited by Clayborne Carson et al. Berkeley: University of California Press, 2000.

——. *Why We Can't Wait*. New York: Harper & Row, 1963.

Kuper, Leo. *Passive Resistance in South Africa*. New Haven: Yale University Press, 1957.

Lacy, Leslie. *The Rise and Fall of a Proper Negro: An Autobiography*. New York: Macmillan, 1970.

LaFeber, Walter. *America, Russia, and the Cold War, 1945–1984*. New York: Alfred A. Knopf, 1985.

Lauren, Paul G. *Power and Prejudice: The Politics and Diplomacy of Racial Discrimination*. Boulder, Colo.: Westview, 1988.

Lawson, Steven. *Running for Freedom: Civil Rights and Black Politics in America since 1941*. Philadelphia: Temple University Press, 1991.

Leffler, Melvyn. *A Preponderance of Power: National Security, the Truman Administration, and the Cold War*. Stanford: Stanford University Press, 1992.

Leffler, Melvyn P., and David S. Painter, eds. *Origins of the Cold War: An International History*. London: Routledge, 1994.

Lewis, David Levering. *W. E. B. Du Bois: Biography of a Race, 1868–1919*. New York: Henry Holt, 1993.

Lodge, Tom. *Black Politics in South Africa since 1945*. New York: Longman, 1983.

Logan, Rayford. *What the Negro Wants*. 1944. Reprint, New York: Agathon, 1969.

Lynch, Hollis. *Black American Radicals and the Liberation of Africa: The Council on African Affairs, 1937–1955*. Ithaca, N.Y.: Cornell University Africana Studies and Research Center, 1978.

——. *Edward Wilmot Blyden: Pan-Negro Patriot, 1832–1912*. New York: Oxford University Press, 1967.

McCarthy, Michael. *Dark Continent: Africa as Seen by Americans*. Westport, Conn.: Greenwood, 1983.

McGhee, George. *Envoy to the Middle World: Adventures in Diplomacy*. New York: Harper & Row, 1983.

Maloba, Wunyabari O. *Mau Mau and Kenya: An Analysis of a Peasant Revolt.* Bloomington: Indiana University Press, 1993.

Marable, Manning. *Race, Reform, and Rebellion: The Second Reconstruction in Black America, 1945–1982.* Jackson: University Press of Mississippi, 1984.

———. *W. E. B. Du Bois: Black Radical Democrat.* Boston: Twayne, 1986.

Meredith, Martin. *In the Name of Apartheid: South Africa in the Postwar Period.* London: Hamish Hamilton, 1988.

Merriam, Alan P. *Congo: Background of Conflict.* Chicago: Northwestern University Press, 1961.

Morel, E. D. *Red Rubber: The Story of the Rubber Slave Trade Flourishing on the Congo in the Year of Grace 1906.* 1906. Reprint, New York: Negro Universities Press, 1969.

Moses, Wilson J. *Afrotopia: The Roots of African American Popular History.* Cambridge: Cambridge University Press, 1998.

———. *Alexander Crummell: A Study of Civilization and Discontent.* New York: Oxford University Press, 1989.

———. *The Golden Age of Black Nationalism, 1850–1925.* Hamden, Conn.: Archon, 1978.

———. *The Wings of Ethiopia: Studies in African-American Life and Letters.* Ames: Iowa State University Press, 1990.

Mullen, Bill. *Popular Fronts: Chicago and African-American Cultural Politics, 1935–1946.* Urbana: University of Illinois Press, 1999.

Myrdal, Gunnar. *An American Dilemma.* New York: Harper & Row, 1944.

Naison, Mark. *Communists in Harlem during the Depression.* Urbana: University of Illinois Press, 1983.

Nielsen, Waldemar. *The Great Powers and Africa.* New York: Praeger, 1969.

Nkrumah, Kwame. *Autobiography of Kwame Nkrumah.* Edinburgh: Thomas Nelson and Sons, 1957.

———. *I Speak of Freedom.* London: Panaf, 1961.

Noer, Thomas J. *Cold War and Black Liberation: The United States and White Rule in Africa, 1948–1968.* Columbia: University of Missouri Press, 1985.

Oates, Stephen. *Let the Trumpet Sound: The Life of Martin Luther King, Jr.* New York: Harper & Row, 1982.

Ottley, Roi. *"New World A-Coming": Inside Black America.* Cambridge, Mass.: Riverside, 1943.

Padmore, George. *Pan-Africanism or Communism?: The Coming Struggle for Africa.* London: D. Dobson, 1956.

Plummer, Brenda Gayle. *Rising Wind: Black Americans and U.S. Foreign Affairs, 1935–1960.* Chapel Hill: University of North Carolina Press, 1996.

Raboteau, Albert J. *A Fire in the Bones: Reflections on African-American Religious History.* Boston: Beacon, 1995.

Rampersad, Arnold. *Jackie Robinson: A Biography.* New York: Alfred A. Knopf, 1997.

Reader, John. *Africa: Biography of a Continent.* New York: Alfred A. Knopf, 1999.

Reddick, Lawrence D. *Crusader without Violence: A Biography of Martin Luther King, Jr.* New York: Harper & Brothers, 1959.

Redkey, Edwin. *Black Exodus: Black Nationalist and Back-to-Africa Movements, 1890–1910.* New Haven: Yale University Press, 1969.

Rivlin, Benjamin. *The United Nations and the Italian Colonies.* New York: Carnegie Endowment for International Peace, 1950.

Robinson, Armstead, and Patricia Sullivan, eds. *New Directions in Civil Rights Studies.* Charlottesville: University of Virginia Press, 1991.

Robeson, Paul. *Here I Stand.* New York: Othello Associates, 1958.

Rogers, Joel A. *100 Amazing Facts about the Negro.* 23d rev. ed. New York: H. M. Rogers, 1957.

———. *World's Great Men of Color.* 2 vols. New York: J. A. Rogers, 1947.

Roosevelt, Theodore. *African Game Trails: An Account of the African Wanderings of an American Hunter-Naturalist.* New York: Charles Scribner's Sons, 1909–1910.

Roux, Edward. *Time Longer than Rope.* Madison: University of Wisconsin Press, 1964.

Ruark, Robert. *Something of Value.* Garden City, N.Y.: Doubleday, 1955.

Rusk, Dean. *As I Saw It.* New York: W. W. Norton, 1990.

Said, Abdul Aziz, ed. *Ethnicity and U.S. Foreign Policy.* New York: Praeger, 1981.

Schild, Georg. *Bretton Woods and Dumbarton Oaks: American Economic and Political Postwar Planning in the Summer of 1944.* New York: St. Martin's, 1995.

Schlesinger, Arthur. *A Thousand Days: John F. Kennedy in the White House.* Boston: Houghton Mifflin, 1965.

Schraeder, Peter J. *United States Foreign Policy toward Africa: Incrementalism, Crisis, and Change.* Cambridge: Cambridge University Press, 1994.

Schuyler, George S. *Black and Conservative: The Autobiography of George S. Schuyler.* New Rochelle, N.Y.: Arlington House, 1966.

———. *Slaves Today: A Story of Liberia.* New York: Brewer, Warren, and Putnam, 1931.

Scott, William R. *The Sons of Sheba's Race: African-Americans and the Italo-Ethiopian War, 1935–1941.* Bloomington: Indiana University Press, 1993.

Shepherd, George. *Anti-Apartheid: Transnational Conflict and Western Policy in the Liberation of South Africa.* Westport, Conn.: Greenwood, 1977.

———, ed. *Racial Influences in American Foreign Policy.* New York: Basic, 1970.

Sherwood, Marika. *Kwame Nkrumah: The Years Abroad, 1935–1947.* Legon, Ghana: Freedom Publications, 1996.

Sitkoff, Harvard. *The Struggle for Black Equality, 1954–1980.* New York: Hill and Wang, 1981.

Skinner, Elliott. *African Americans and U.S. Policy toward Africa, 1859–1924.* Washington, D.C.: Howard University Press, 1992.

Smethurst, James E. *The New Red Negro: The Literary Left and African American Poetry, 1930–1946.* New York: Oxford University Press, 1999.

Smith, Ed. *Where To, Black Man?* Chicago: Quadrangle, 1967.

Smith, William Gardner. *Return to Black America*. Englewood Cliffs, N.J.: Prentice-Hall, 1970.

Sosna, Morton. *In Search of the Silent South: Southern Liberals and the Race Issue*. New York: Columbia University Press, 1977.

Staniland, Martin. *American Intellectuals and African Nationalists, 1955–70*. New Haven: Yale University Press, 1991.

Stuckey, Sterling. *Slave Culture: Nationalist Theory and the Foundations of Black America*. Oxford: Oxford University Press, 1987.

[Study Commission on U.S. Policy toward Southern Africa.] *South Africa: Time Running Out*. Berkeley: University of California Press, 1981.

Teller, Judd L., and Nahum Guttman. *The Free World and the New Nations*. New York: A. S. Barnes, 1964.

Thompson, Era Belle. *Africa, Land of My Fathers*. Garden City, N.Y.: Doubleday, 1954.

Thompson, W. Scott. *Ghana's Foreign Policy 1957–1966: Diplomacy, Ideology, and the New State*. Princeton, N.J.: Princeton University Press, 1969.

Throup, David. *Economic and Social Origins of Mau Mau, 1945–1953*. Athens: Ohio University Press, 1987.

Tyson, Timothy B. *Radio Free Dixie: Robert F. Williams and the Roots of Black Power*. Chapel Hill: University of North Carolina Press, 1999.

Urquhart, Brian. *Ralph Bunche: An American Life*. New York: W. W. Norton, 1993.

Von Eschen, Penny. *Race against Empire: Black Americans and Anticolonialism, 1937–1957*. Ithaca, N.Y.: Cornell University Press, 1997.

Weisbord, Robert. *Ebony Kinship: Africa, Africans, and Afro-Americans*. Westport, Conn.: Greenwood, 1973.

Weissman, Stephen R. *American Foreign Policy in the Congo, 1960–1964*. Ithaca, N.Y.: Cornell University Press, 1974.

White, Walter. *A Rising Wind*. New York: Doubleday, Doran, 1945.

Williams, Walter L. *Black Americans and the Evangelization of Africa, 1877–1900*. Madison: University of Wisconsin Press, 1982.

Witte, Ludo de. *L'assassinat de Lumumba*. Paris: Karthala, 2000.

Wolseley, Roland E. *The Black Press, U.S.A.* Ames: Iowa State University Press, 1971.

Wright, Richard. *Black Power: A Record of Reactions in a Land of Pathos*. 1954. Reprint, Westport, Conn.: Greenwood, 1974.

Wynn, Neil. *The Afro-American and the Second World War*. New York: Holmes and Meier, 1975.

X, Malcolm. *The Autobiography of Malcolm X*. New York: Ballantine, 1964.

Articles, Essays, and Dissertations

Anosike, Benji. "Africa and Afro-Americans: The Bases for Greater Understanding and Solidarity." *Journal of Negro Education* 51 (1982): 434–49.

Anthony, David. "Max Yergan and South Africa: A Transatlantic Interaction." In *Imagining Home: Class, Culture, and Nationalism in the African Diaspora*, edited by Sidney J. Lemelle and Robin D. G. Kelley, 185–206. London: Verso, 1994.

Appiah, Kwame Anthony. "A Long Way from Home: Wright in the Gold Coast." In *Richard Wright*, edited by Harold Bloom, 173–90. New York: Chelsea House, 1987.

Asante, S. K. B. "The Afro-American and the Italo-Ethiopian Crisis, 1934–36." *Race* 15 (1973): 167–84.

Baldwin, James. "A Negro Assays the Negro Mood." *New York Times Magazine* (12 March 1961): 25, 103–4.

Boahen, Adu. "Ghana since Independence." In *Decolonization and African Independence: The Transfers of Power, 1960–1980*, edited by Prosser Gifford and Wm. Roger Louis, 199–224. New Haven: Yale University Press, 1988.

Challenor, Herschelle. "The Influence of Black Americans on United States Foreign Policy toward Africa." In *Ethnicity and U.S. Foreign Policy*, edited by Abdul Aziz Said, 143–75. New York: Praeger, 1981.

Chick, C. A., Sr. "The American Negroes' Changing Attitude toward Africa." *Journal of Negro Education* 31, no. 4 (Fall 1962): 531–35.

Clarke, John Henrik. "The New Afro-American Nationalism." *Freedomways* 1, no. 3 (Fall 1961): 285–95.

Cleaver, L. Eldridge. "As Crinkly as Yours." *Negro History Bulletin* 25 (March 1962): 127–32.

Cone, James H. "Martin Luther King, Jr., and the Third World." In *We Shall Overcome: Martin Luther King, Jr., and the Black Freedom Struggle*, edited by Peter Albert and Ronald Hoffman, 197–221. New York: Pantheon, 1990.

Davis, John A. "Black Americans and United States Policy toward Africa." *Journal of International Affairs* 23 (1969): 236–49.

——. "The Influence of Africans on American Culture." *Annals of the American Academy of Political and Social Science* 354 (July 1964): 75–83.

——. "American Ethnic Minorities and the New Nations." In *The Free World and the New Nations*, edited by Judd Teller and Nahum Guttman, 119–38. New York: A. S. Barnes, 1964.

Drake, St. Clair. "Diaspora Studies and Pan-Africanism." In *Global Dimensions of the African Diaspora*, edited by Joseph Harris, 341–402. Washington, D.C.: Howard University Press, 1982.

Du Bois, W. E. B. "Inter-Racial Implications of the Ethiopian Crisis: A Negro View." *Foreign Affairs* 14 (October 1935): 83–92.

——. "My Evolving Program for Negro Freedom." In *What the Negro Wants*, edited by Rayford Logan, 31–70. 1944. Reprint, New York: Agathon, 1969.

Dudziak, Mary. "Desegregation as a Cold War Imperative." *Stanford Law Review* 41 (November 1988): 61–120.

——. "Josephine Baker, Racial Protest, and the Cold War." *Journal of American History* 81 (September 1994): 543–70.

Emerson, Rupert. "Race in Africa: United States Foreign Policy." In *Racial Influences in American Foreign Policy*, edited by George Shepherd. New York: Basic, 1970.

Emerson, Rupert, and Martin Kilson. "The American Dilemma in a Changing World: The Rise of Africa and the Negro American." *Daedalus* 94 (Fall 1965): 1055–84.

Farmer, James. "An American Leader's View of African Unity." *African Forum* 1 (Summer 1965): 69–89.

Fierce, Milfred. "Selected Black American Leaders and Organizations and South Africa, 1900–1977: Some Notes." *Journal of Black Studies* 17 (March 1987): 305–26.

Finkle, Lee. "The Conservative Aims of Militant Rhetoric: Black Protest during World War II." *Journal of American History* 60 (December 1973): 692–713.

Foreman, Joel. "Mau Mau's American Career, 1952–1957." In *The Other Fifties: Interrogating Midcentury American Icons*, edited by Joel Foreman, 78–100. Urbana: University of Illinois Press, 1997.

Gaines, Kevin. "Black Americans' Racial Uplift Ideology as 'Civilizing Mission.'" In *Cultures of United States Imperialism*, edited by Amy Kaplan and Donald Pease, 433–55. Durham, N.C.: Duke University Press, 1993.

Gambino, Ferruccio. "The Transgression of a Laborer: Malcolm X in the Wilderness of America." *Radical History Review* 55 (1993): 7–31.

Gbadegesin, Segun. "Kinship of the Dispossessed: Du Bois, Nkrumah, and the Foundations of Pan-Africanism." In *W. E. B. Du Bois on Race and Culture*, edited by Bernard Bell, Emily Grosholz, and James Stewart, 219–242. New York: Routledge, 1996.

Hargreaves, John. "Toward the Transfer of Power in British West Africa." In *The Transfer of Power in Africa: Decolonization, 1940–1960*, edited by Prosser Gifford and Wm. Roger Louis, 117–40. New Haven: Yale University Press, 1982.

Harris, Robert. "Racial Equality and the United Nations Charter." In *New Directions in Civil Rights Studies*, edited by Armstead Robinson and Patricia Sullivan, 126–48. Charlottesville: University of Virginia Press, 1991.

Hill, Robert A. "Before Garvey: Chief Alfred Sam and the African Movement, 1912–1916." In *Pan-African Biography*, edited by Robert A. Hill, 57–77. Los Angeles: UCLA African Studies Center and Crossroads Press, 1987.

Holt, Thomas C. "Afro-Americans." In *Harvard Encyclopedia of American Ethnic Groups*, edited by Stephen Thernstrom, 5–23. Cambridge: Harvard University Press, 1980.

Hooker, James R. "The Impact of African History on Afro-Americans, 1930–1945." *Black Academy Review* 3 (Spring–Summer 1972): 39–62.

———. "The Negro American Press and Africa in the 1930s." *Canadian Journal of African Studies* 1 (March 1967): 43–50.

Houser, George. "Freedom's Struggle Crosses Oceans and Mountains: Martin Luther King, Jr., and the Liberation Struggles in Africa and America." In *We Shall*

Overcome: Martin Luther King, Jr., and the Black Freedom Struggle, edited by Peter Albert and Ronald Hoffman, 169–96. New York: Pantheon, 1990.

Ivy, James. "Traditional NAACP Interest in Africa (as reflected in the pages of *The Crisis*)." In *Africa as Seen by American Negroes*, edited by John A. Davis, 229–46. Paris: Presence Africaine, 1958.

Jack, Homer. "Conversation in Ghana." *Christian Century* (10 April 1957): 446–48.

Jackson, Henry F. "U.S. Foreign Policy and African Americans." *UCLA Center for Afro-American Studies Report* (Spring/Fall 1990): 6–9, 40–46.

Kabongo, Ilunga. "The Catastrophe of Belgian Decolonization." In *Decolonization and African Independence: The Transfers of Power, 1960–1980*, edited by Prosser Gifford and Wm. Roger Louis, 381–400. New Haven: Yale University Press, 1988.

Karis, Thomas. "Joint Action and the Defiance Campaign, 1950–1952." In *From Protest to Challenge: A Documentary History of African Politics in South Africa, 1882–1964*, edited by Thomas Karis and Gwendolyn M. Carter, 2:403–40. Stanford, Calif.: Hoover Institution Press, 1973.

Kelley, Robin D. G. " 'But a Local Phase of a World Problem': Black History's Global Vision, 1883–1950." *Journal of American History* 86 (December 1999): 1045–77.

———. "This Ain't Ethiopia, But It'll Do." In *African Americans in the Spanish Civil War: "This Ain't Ethiopia, But It'll Do,"* edited by Danny Duncan Collum, 5–57. New York: G. K. Hall, 1992.

Kent, John. "British Policy and the Origins of the Cold War." In *Origins of the Cold War: An International History*, edited by Melvyn P. Leffler and David S. Painter, 139–53. London: Routledge, 1994.

Kilson, Martin. "African Americans and Africa: A Critical Nexus." *Dissent* (Summer 1992): 361–69.

King, Martin Luther, Jr. " 'The Time for Freedom Has Come.' " *New York Times Magazine* (10 September 1961): 25, 118–19.

King, Martin Luther, Jr., and Chief Albert Lutuli. "Appeal for Action Against Apartheid." 1962. Reprinted in *Appeal for an International Boycott of South Africa*. New York: United Nations, 1982.

Klarman, Michael. "How *Brown* Changed Race Relations: The Backlash Thesis." *Journal of American History* 81 (June 1994): 81–118.

Kornegay, Francis A. "Black America and U.S.–Southern African Relations: An Essay Bibliographical Survey of Developments during the 1950s, 1960s, and Early 1970s." In *American–Southern African Relations: Bibliographic Essays*, edited by Mohamed A. El-Khawas and Francis A. Kornegay, 138–87. Westport, Conn.: Greenwood, 1975.

Kuper, Leo. "African Nationalism in South Africa, 1910–1964." In *The Oxford History of South Africa, II: South Africa 1870–1966*, edited by Monica Wilson and Leonard Thompson, 424–76. New York: Oxford University Press, 1971.

Lawson, Steven F. "Freedom Then, Freedom Now: The Historiography of the Civil Rights Movement." *American Historical Review* 96 (April 1991): 456–71.

Lee, Wallace. "Does the Negro Press Speak for Most Negroes?" *Negro Digest* 14 (February 1943): 54.

Lemann, Nicholas. "Black Nationalism on Campus." *The Atlantic* 271 (January 1993): 31–34, 43–47.

Logan, Rayford. "The American Negro's View of Africa." In *Africa as Seen by American Negroes*, edited by John A. Davis, 217–27. Paris: Presence Africaine, 1958.

Lonsdale, John. "Mau Maus of the Mind: Making Mau Mau and Remaking Kenya." *Journal of African History* 31 (1990): 393–421.

Louis, Wm. Roger. "Libyan Independence, 1951: The Creation of a Client State." In *Decolonization and African Independence: The Transfers of Power, 1960–1980*, edited by Prosser Gifford and Wm. Roger Louis, 159–84. New Haven: Yale University Press, 1988.

Louis, Wm. Roger, and Ronald Robinson. "The United States and the Liquidation of the British Empire in Tropical Africa, 1941–1951." In *The Transfer of Power in Africa: Decolonization, 1940–1960*, edited by Prosser Gifford and Wm. Roger Louis, 31–56. New Haven: Yale University Press, 1982.

Low, Anthony. "The End of the British Empire in Africa." In *Decolonization and African Independence: The Transfers of Power, 1960–1980*, edited by Prosser Gifford and Wm. Roger Louis, 33–72. New Haven: Yale University Press, 1988.

Lynch, Hollis. "Pan-African Responses in the United States to British Colonial Rule in Africa in the 1940s." In *The Transfer of Power in Africa: Decolonization, 1940–1960*, edited by Prosser Gifford and Wm. Roger Louis, 57–86. New Haven: Yale University Press, 1982.

Maier, Charles S. "Hegemony and Autonomy within the Western Alliance." In *Origins of the Cold War: An International History*, edited by Melvyn P. Leffler and David S. Painter, 154–74. London: Routledge, 1994.

Marable, Manning. "The Pan-Africanism of W. E. B. Du Bois." In *W. E. B. Du Bois on Race and Culture*, edited by Bernard Bell, Emily Grosholz, and James Stewart, 193–218. New York: Routledge, 1996.

Meier, August. "Epilogue: Toward a Synthesis of Civil Rights History." In *New Directions in Civil Rights Studies*, edited by Armstead Robinson and Patricia Sullivan, 211–24. Charlottesville: University of Virginia Press, 1991.

Moore, Richard B. "Africa Conscious Harlem." *Freedomways* 3 (Summer 1963): 315–34.

Morris, Aldon. "A Man Prepared for the Times: A Sociological Analysis of the Leadership of Martin Luther King, Jr." In *We Shall Overcome: Martin Luther King, Jr., and the Black Freedom Struggle*, edited by Peter Albert and Ronald Hoffman, 35–58. New York: Pantheon, 1990.

Morris, Milton D. "Black Americans and the Foreign Policy Process: The Case of Africa." *Western Political Quarterly* 25 (September 1972): 451–63.

Moss, James A. "The Civil Rights Movement and American Foreign Policy." In *Racial Influences in American Foreign Policy*, edited by George Shepherd, 79–99. New York: Basic, 1970.

Ndibe, Okey. "Can African Americans Save Africa?" *African World* 1, no. 1 (November–December 1993): 4–9.

Noer, Thomas J. "Truman, Eisenhower, and South Africa: The 'Middle Road' and Apartheid." *Journal of Ethnic Studies* 11 (Spring 1983): 75–104.

Norrell, Robert J. "One Thing We Did Right: Reflections on the Movement." In *New Directions in Civil Rights Studies*, edited by Armstead Robinson and Patricia Sullivan, 65–80. Charlottesville: University of Virginia Press, 1991.

Ogot, Bethwell A., and Tiyamba Zeleza. "Kenya: The Road to Independence and After." In *Decolonization and African Independence: The Transfers of Power, 1960–1980*, edited by Prosser Gifford and Wm. Roger Louis, 401–26. New Haven: Yale University Press, 1988.

Redkey, Edwin S. "The Meaning of Africa to Afro-Americans, 1890–1914." Paper presented at the Council on International Studies conference "The Meaning of Africa to Afro-Americans," SUNY Buffalo, Buffalo, N.Y., 1969.

Reilly, John M. "The Self-Creation of the Intellectual: American Hunger and Black Power." In *Critical Essays on Richard Wright*, edited by Yoshinobu Hakutani, 213–27. Boston: G. K. Hall, 1982.

Roark, James. "American Black Leaders: The Response to Colonialism and the Cold War, 1943–53." *African Historical Studies* 4, no. 2 (1971): 253–70.

Robinson, Cedric J. "The African Diaspora and the Italo-Ethiopian Crisis." *Race & Class* 27 (Autumn 1985): 51–65.

Ross, Rodney. "Black Americans and Haiti, Liberia, the Virgin Islands, and Ethiopia, 1929–1936." Ph.D. diss., University of Chicago, 1975.

Schechter, Dan, Michael Ansara, and David Kolodney. "The CIA as Equal Opportunity Employer." *Ramparts* 7, no. 13 (June 1969): 25–33.

Shepherd, George W. "Who Killed Martin Luther King's Dream?: An Afro-American Tragedy." *Africa Today* 15, no. 2 (April–May 1968): 2.

Shepperson, George. "Notes on Negro American Influences on the Emergence of African Nationalism." *Journal of African History* 1, no. 2 (1960): 299–312.

Sitkoff, Harvard. "African American Militancy in the World War II South." In *Remaking Dixie: The Impact of World War II on the American South*, edited by Neil McMillen, 70–92. Jackson: University Press of Mississippi, 1997.

———. "Harry Truman and the Election of 1948: The Coming of Age of Civil Rights in American Politics." *Journal of Southern History* 37 (November 1971): 597–616.

Skinner, Elliott. "Afro-Americans in Search of Africa: The Scholars' Dilemma." In *Transformation and Resiliency in Africa: As Seen by Afro-Americans*, edited by Pearl T. Robinson and Elliott Skinner, 3–26. Washington, D.C.: Howard University Press, 1983.

———. "Black Leaders as Foreign Policymakers." *Urban League Review* 9 (Summer 1985): 112–22.

———. "The Dialectic between Diasporas and Homelands." In *Global Dimensions of the African Diaspora*, edited by Joseph E. Harris, 17–45. Washington, D.C.: Howard University Press, 1982.

Solomon, Mark. "Black Critics of Colonialism and the Cold War." In *Cold War Critics: Alternatives to American Foreign Policy in the Truman Years*, edited by Thomas G. Paterson, 205–39. New York: Quadrangle, 1971.

Stengers, Jean. "Precipitous Decolonization: The Case of the Belgian Congo." In *The Transfer of Power in Africa: Decolonization, 1940–1960*, edited by Prosser Gifford and Wm. Roger Louis 305–55. New Haven: Yale University Press, 1982.

Sullivan, Patricia. "Southern Reformers, the New Deal, and the Movement's Foundation." In *New Directions in Civil Rights Studies*, edited by Armstead Robinson and Patricia Sullivan, 81–104. Charlottesville: University of Virginia Press, 1991

Theoharis, Athan. "The Threat to Civil Liberties." In *Cold War Critics: Alternatives to American Foreign Policy in the Truman Years*, edited by Thomas G. Paterson, 266–98. New York: Quadrangle, 1971.

Tyson, Timothy B. "Robert F. Williams, 'Black Power,' and the Roots of the African American Freedom Struggle." *Journal of American History* 85, no. 2 (September 1998): 540–70.

Von Eschen, Penny. "African Americans and Anti-Colonialism, 1937–1957: The Rise and Fall of the Politics of the African Diaspora." Ph.D. diss., Columbia University, 1994.

White, Walter. "A Major Report on Africa Today." *New York Herald Tribune Book Review* (26 September 1954), sec. 6, pp. 1, 11.

Whitelaw, Kevin. "A Killing in Congo." *U.S. News & World Report* (24–31 July 2000): 63.

Williams, David. "English-Speaking West Africa." In *The Cambridge History of Africa: From c. 1940 to c. 1971*, edited by Michael Crowder, 331–82. Cambridge: Cambridge University Press, 1984.

Williams, Oscar. "The Making of a Black Conservative: George S. Schuyler." Ph.D. diss., Ohio State University, 1997.

Wood, Robert E. "From the Marshall Plan to the Third World." In *Origins of the Cold War: An International History*, edited by Melvyn P. Leffler and David S. Painter, 201–14. London: Routledge, 1994.

Zimmerman, Jonathan. "Beyond Double Consciousness: Black Peace Corps Volunteers in Africa, 1961–1971." *Journal of American History* 82, no. 3 (December 1995): 999–1028.

INDEX

Wilkins, Roy, 37, 78, 89, 112, 171, 242; and 1945 conferences, 63, 66–67; on Congo crisis and UN demonstrations, 227, 236; on institutional links with Africa, 203, 205; and Nkrumah, 173–75, 176; and South Africa, 189, 191
Williams, George Washington, 210
Williams, Henry Sylvester, 20
Williams, Robert F., 148
Williams, Sidney, 140, 161
Williams, Smallwood, 206, 232

Woodson, Carter, 19, 37
World War II, 3, 57, 59–60, 91
Wright, Louis, 66
Wright, Richard, 155–56, 171, 178

Yergan, Max, 59, 61, 80, 120–21, 137–38
Young, Coleman, 114
Young, P. B., 37
Young, Whitney, 205

Zaphiro, Lij Tasfaye, 49, 50